INSTITUTION OF CIVIL ENGINEERS

Coastlines, structures and breakwaters

Proceedings of the international conference organized by the Institution of Civil Engineers and held in London, UK, on 19–20 March 1998

Edited by N.W.H. Allsop

Thomas Telford

Organizing Committee:
N.W.H. Allsop, *HR Wallingford, University of Sheffield*, Chairman
P.C. Barber, *Shoreline Management Partnership*
K.A. Burgess, *Sir William Halcrow & Partners*
G. Heald, *Environment Agency*
J.F. O'Hara, *Consultant*
A.C. Polson, *Ministry of Agriculture, Fisheries and Food*

International Scientific Advisory Committee:
Dr K. Bodge, *USA, Olsen Associates Inc.*
Professor Y. Goda, *Japan, Yokahama National University*
Professor N. Kobayashi, *USA, University of Delaware*
Professor H. Ligteringen, *The Netherlands, De Weger Consultants and Technical University, Delft*
Professor A. Noli, *Italy, University of Rome / Modimar Consultants*
Professor H. Oumeraci, *Germany, University of Braunschweig*

Co-sponsors
American Society of Civil Engineers, *USA*
Association of Technical Officers, *UK*
Environment Agency, *UK*
Japan Society of Civil Engineers, *Japan*
Ministry of Agriculture, Fisheries and Food, *UK*
Permanent International Association of Navigation Congresses, *UK Section*

Distributors for Thomas Telford books are
USA: ASCE Press, 1801 Alexander Bell Drive, Reston, VA 20191-4400, USA.
Japan: Maruzen Co. Ltd, Book Department, 3–10 Nihonbashi 2-chome, Chuo-ku, Tokyo 103
Australia: DA Books and Journals, 648 Whitehorse Road, Mitcham 3132, Victoria

A catalogue record for this book is available from the British Library

Availability: Unrestricted
Content: Collected papers
Status: Refereed
User: Civil engineers, coastal and harbour engineers

ISBN 0 7277 2668 4

Printed and bound in Great Britain by Redwood Books, Trowbridge, Witlshire

Editor's preface

This volume presents 22 papers and discussion from the latest of the ICE breakwaters conferences, the 6th in a series of international events run in 1983, 85, 88, 91 and 95. Taken together, the papers and the discussions arising from these meetings describe important advances in the field of coastal and harbour engineering and comment, sometimes trenchantly, on the wisdom, usefulness, and/or cost-effectiveness of the schemes or techniques being advanced by the authors.

Important points of focus for this conference were "solutions and sustainability." The conference committee tried to encourage contributions with a strong emphasis on practical solutions developed from analysis of experience as well as from the results of formal research studies. I am sure you will agree they succeeded. The proceedings reflect a substantially greater proportion of papers based on practical construction experience than in most other coastal/harbour conferences. Research papers in particular have been required to demonstrate application in practical coastal engineering.

The papers cover issues relating to coastal defence and management; from assessment of risks faced by coastal areas, through design and analysis of breakwaters and other structures, to construction and management of coastal defence systems. The authors offer positive guidance to engineers on options available in areas of problem definition, development and selection of solutions, construction of solutions and post-project performance. New perspectives are presented on the implications of developing coastal or harbour structures with particular reference to marine life.

In this volume, attention has been paid to field monitoring of the response of coastlines to protection schemes, and to the performance of breakwaters under storm attack. Case studies from around the world (UK, Italy, Spain, USA, Iceland) are used to show innovative methods of design and construction, and to present experience gained in service or during construction, repair or reconstruction of breakwaters. Strategic approaches to coastal defence and beach management techniques and alternative methods of coast protection are presented.

In considering and using these papers to advance knowledge and understanding, readers should note any supplementary data or conclusions added by the authors, and indeed should also note any contrary or qualifying arguments, information and conclusions drawn by the attendees.

Lastly, as Conference Chairman, I wish to thank the Thomas Telford Conferences for assisting to organize the event; the authors and contributors for the papers and discussions, without which this volume could not be published; and the helpful and tolerant team at Thomas Telford who helped do so. I wish to record my particular thanks to the members of my Organizing Committee, to whom much of the success of the event is due, and to my predecessors Paul Lacey and John Clifford who nurtured this conference to its present strength.

N.W.H. Allsop
Editor and Chairman of the Organizing Committee

Contents

Evaluating project risks / optimization

Experiences in breakwater construction

Repair / reconstruction of breakwaters

Strategic approaches to coast defence

Application of beach management

Alternatives in coast protection

Discusson

Closing remarks

Keynote address : Six conferences later...
A progress report on the achievements made in research and their influence on the design of breakwaters

PROFESSOR H LIGTERINGEN
De Weger Consultants and Technical University, Delft, the Netherlands

The sudden intensification of research on rubble mound breakwaters in the 1980s was triggered by severe damage to a series of relatively new breakwaters. Starting with Sines West Breakwater in Portugal in February 1978, followed by San Ciprian North and South Breakwaters in early 1980, Arzew Main Breakwater in December 1980 and Tripoli New Breakwater in January 1981, each of these caused years of despair for the owners of these expensive structures and years of excitement for researchers. Damage to rubble mound breakwaters is however common, and there had been some interesting cases before 1978, like Crescent City Breakwater in California. But the above mentioned cases were exceptional. As in Japan, where a substantial number of damage cases led to review of existing design formulae and the development of the Goda formula, it was evident that there were fundamental problems with our methods of designing rubble mound breakwaters.

With the increased research activity there was the need for professional interaction and it was for this reason that the Institution of Civil Engineers held in 1983 the conference *Breakwaters; design and construction*. It was a great success, not only because there was enough to present in terms of questions and preliminary answers, but especially due to the ample time for discussion. In his keynote speech, the late Ian Stickland listed all the questions and concerns of that moment, such as

- is the Hudson formula valid?
- what is the effect of wave grouping on stability?
- how important is the concrete strength issue?
- what is the contribution of geotechnical instability to the failures?

Since then we have seen much research activity by institutes all over the world. In Europe the EU MAST programme has brought together the efforts of individual institutes, initially on rubble mound design and later on vertical breakwaters as well. So it is appropriate to look back and to evaluate the progress. This is based on 'engineering judgement' as I am neither directly, nor indirectly involved in any of the ongoing programmes. But through a period of time the design practice is a good sieve of what is valuable and what not.

RUBBLE MOUND BREAKWATERS
The first questions to be addressed are: do we understand the reasons for the past damage to rubble mound breakwaters and can we avoid this now? The answer to both is positive. The excessive damage was in most cases caused by breakage of concrete armour units, although

Coastlines, structures and breakwaters. Thomas Telford, London, 1998

other factors played a (secondary) role. We have now a much better understanding of rocking behaviour of armour units and the high impact forces incurred. We are also able to design an armour layer in such way that the breakage is nil or sufficiently low. Sophisticated methods have been developed to quantify rocking impacts and related tensile stresses in the concrete, and to determine the tensile strength for given units and concrete mix designs. But the practical approach, which is followed in most new projects, is to avoid rocking and breakage by applying mass-type units and a lower K_D value. And with that approach the application of Hudson formula for preliminary design and 2-D / 3-D model tests for the detailed design is considered to be acceptable engineering practice, as if nothing has happened in the past 20 years.

Of course we have a much better understanding of the influence of wave steepness as represented in Van der Meer's formulae.

Of course we know now, that for steep slopes in deep water the geotechnical stability must be checked.

And it is also true that more reliable formulae are available for the stability of rock in toe structures and in low-crested or submerged breakwaters.

But it is interesting to see that the basic approach of the 1970s for hydraulic stability of primary armour has not changed. The progress has been made in the definition of wave conditions (hindcast techniques), in the recognition of armour unit breakage and geotechnical instability as failure modes, and in the adoption of safety considerations in the definition of design criteria.

In parallel progress has been made in the development and acceptance of alternative designs. In this respect the berm breakwater should be mentioned, which is very attractive under certain conditions. The concept is old, but the turmoil in breakwaterland and the uncertainty about concrete armour units were inducive to carry out the systematic research needed to develop it into an accepted alternative. In this respect I would also like to mention the Accropode unit, which was conceived prior to the major damage cases. It was introduced at the worst possible moment, when there was a general trend against new experimentation in primary amour units. But meanwhile it has demonstrated its robustness on many breakwaters of increasing sizes.

In the US the continuing research on dolosse strength led to the development of the Core-Loc unit. Like the Accropode, it is applied in a single layer. With new additions to the list of armour unit types, it has been demonstrated that the ingenuity of coastal engineers is unabated by the previous failure cases.

VERTICAL WALL BREAKWATERS
An important side effect of the concerns regarding rubble mound breakwaters was the interest for vertical breakwaters, also in the 'rubble mound part of the world'. The fervent plea of Professor Lundgren in his keynote speech to one of the earlier breakwater conferences was not to deaf ears. Notwithstanding the increased attention that vertical wall breakwaters receive internationally, the actual experience remains limited mostly to those countries where they were applied before: Japan and other countries in east Asia, Italy, Spain and France. The

progress assessment is therefore mostly based on the progress within the MAST programme, and less on actual design or construction projects.

The research projects within the MAST programme have shown that the Goda formula for wave pressures is reliable for spilling breakwaters in deep water. For waves breaking on a foundation berm, the somewhat higher pressures are correctly predicted by applying the impact coefficient in the extended Goda formula. With respect to wave loads the remaining gap in the knowledge of pressures due to impulsive breaking waves (or slamming wave fronts) has been described by the 'church roof model.' However, no conclusive translation of model results to full scale values has been achieved so far. The peak pressures remain very high and, although of short duration, the best approach is still to avoid a vertical wall solution in circumstances where these wave conditions will occur.

Much progress has been made in the modelling of the dynamic response of a caisson breakwater to wave impacts and in the understanding of the soil parameters in the numerical model. It has been shown however that in most cases the impact forces should be considered as quasi-static in the design of the structure.

The ongoing MAST-3 project is now in its final year and it is surprising that only one paper in this conference is dealing with its results, I am told however that this should not be interpreted as a restrictive policy. We simply have to keep our patience for another year. The same can be said about the report of the PIANC Working Group on Vertical Breakwaters: it is almost finished, but will require some more time before being printed and distributed.

CONCLUSION

The above evaluation may easily give the impression that we know enough and that no further research is needed. It could even lead to the conclusion that this conference might as well be the last 'breakwaters' conference. This is not correct. The main conclusion is that the available tools, including model tests, are adequate to design rubble mound or vertical breakwaters properly, i.e. in accordance with the required safety. But there are still areas where analytical formulae are inadequate or missing and hydraulic models are the only resource. An important component for which this holds is the roundhead. The design formulae for roundheads are merely extensions of those for the trunk design.

The complex hydraulic phenomena at the roundhead are very difficult to catch in a simple formula, but further research in this area is warranted. The same holds for scour at roundheads, especially for vertical breakwaters and taking into account the effects of currents.

The subjects presented in this conference are also good examples of my statement that progress on different aspects of design continues to be made and feedback from prototypes will be needed as much as ever before. But I do not need to convince you: there is sufficient need for research and there will be scope for another breakwater conference in the future.

After having taken away this threat of it being the very last, it is a great pleasure for me to declare this conference opened and to wish you all a very productive and pleasant conference.

A code for dike height design and examination

Dr J.W. VAN DER MEER, Infram, PO Box 688, 7500 AR, Enschede, The Netherlands. Formerly Delft Hydraulics. Email: infram.j.vanderMeer@wxs.nl, P. TÖNJES, Public Works Department, Road and Hydraulics Division, Delft, and J.P. DE WAAL, Public Works Department, Institute for Inland Water Management and Waste Water Treatment, Lelystad

INTRODUCTION

Dikes protect the hinterland from flooding by storm surges from the sea or by high river discharges. Both situations are well known in low-laying countries and the safety in The Netherlands relies heavily on good and strong dikes. Design of dikes and other structures differs from examination of existing structures, but in both situations the same knowledge on hydraulic loads and resistance of the structure can be used. Geometrical parameters such as heights and slopes can be chosen and optimised in a design procedure, where they have to be determined for existing structures and examined against given criteria. The result of an examination may be a qualification ranging from good to unsafe; the latter result has to lead to design of a modified and safe structure.

The new law in The Netherlands on water defences (Staatsblad, 1996) states that existing water defences have to be examined every five years and a first round of examination is now underway. A code on examination of safety has been developed in the recent years. The examination can be divided into two main criteria: the height and the geotechnical stability of the water defence structure. This paper will deal only with the determination of the required height of dikes.

Dikes usually have a rather mild slope, mostly of the order of 1:2 or milder. A dike consists of a toe construction, an outer slope, often with a berm, a crest of a certain height and an inner slope, see Figure 1. The outer slope may consist of various materials such as asphalt, a revetment of concrete blocks, or grass on a clay cover layer. Combinations of these are also possible.

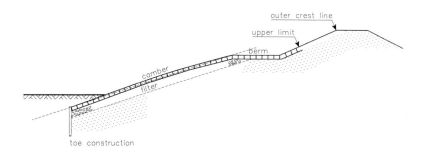

Figure 1. Cross-section of a dike: outer slope

Coastlines, structures and breakwaters. Thomas Telford, London, 1998

Slopes are not always straight; the upper and lower parts do not always have a similar gradient if a berm has been applied. The crest height does not wholly depend on run-up or overtopping when designing or examining a dike. Design guidelines may account for a design water level, for an increase in this water level caused by sea level rise, both local wind set-up and squalls/oscillations (resulting in the adjusted water level) and settlement. In the following the adjusted water level at the toe of the structure will be used.

CRITERIA FOR DIKE HEIGHTS

It is obvious that too low dikes will lead to flooding: either by direct overflow (rivers), or by breaching of the dike by too much wave overtopping. A safe approach is if no significant overtopping is allowed. In general this means that the crest height should not be lower than the 2%-wave run-up level. Another criterion for dike height design and examination is the admissible wave overtopping rate. This admissible overtopping rate depends on various conditions:

- how passable, practicable or trafficable the dike crest and inner berms must be in view of emergency measures under extreme conditions.

    Large scale tests in Delft Hydraulics' Deltaflume showed that, with a significant wave height of 1.5 m and an overtopping discharge of 25 l/s per m, a man on the crest of the dike (attached to a life line) could not resist the overtopping water and was swept away. From these experiments it was concluded that if people should be present on the crest of the dike the overtopping discharge should be less than 10 l/s per m.

- the admissible total volume of overtopping water with regard to storage or drain off.

    Storage or drain off problems behind the dike may have an effect on safety. If so, the overtopping should be limited.

- the resistance against erosion and local sliding of crest and inner slope due to overtopping water.

    The Dutch Guideline on river dykes (TAW, 1986) quotes "Which criterion applies depends of course also on the design of the dike and the possible presence of buildings. In certain cases, such as a covered crest and inner slopes, sometimes 10 l/s per m can be tolerated". In Dutch Guidelines it is assumed that the following average overtopping rates are allowable for the inner slope:
    - 0.1 l/s per m for sandy soil with a poor turf
    - 1 l/s per m for clayey soil with relatively good grass
    - 10 l/s per m with a clay protective layer and grass according to the standards for an outer slope or with a revetment construction

For examination of the dike height also the governing height has to be defined and determined. The dike has an outer slope, a certain crest width and an inner slope. Heights have to be measured at the *outer crest line*, see Figure 1, at least every 20 m of a dike section, and the lowest value is then taken as the governing dike height. A dike section is determined by similar characteristics within its length.

WAVE RUN-UP AND OVERTOPPING

Wave run-up and overtopping on sloping and vertical structures has been a major research topic in the recent years in Europe, mainly due to European collaboration in MAST-programmes which are financed by the European Union, national funds and own research funds of companies. Related papers are: Owen (1980), Franco et al. (1994), De Waal and Van der Meer (1992) and Van der Meer and Janssen (1995). All research related to wave run-up and overtopping on sloping dikes has been summarised in a second edition of a practical Dutch guideline which can be used for design and examination of dike heights. An English version of this early guideline is

given by the work of Van der Meer and Janssen (1995). In the new edition this has been extended with respect to:
- a better description of the influence of a berm
- application (multiple berms, very long and high berms, very shallow water)
- varying roughness on slopes and berms, based on extensive Polish research (Szmytkiewicz et al. (1994))
- (almost) vertical walls on dikes
- overtopping formulae in accordance with run-up formulae

The new formulae and the main modifications and improvements have been described in this paper.

General formula on wave run-up

Wave run-up is often indicated by $R_{u2\%}$. This is the run-up level, vertically measured with respect to the (adjusted) still water level (SWL), which is exceeded by two per cent of the incoming waves. Note that the number of exceedance is here related to the number of incoming waves and not to the number of run-up levels.

The relative run-up is given by $R_{u2\%}/H_s$, with H_s the significant wave height, being the average value of the highest 1/3 part of the wave heights, or the wave height based on energy: $4\sqrt{m_0}$, with m_0 the zeroth moment of the energy density spectrum. This H_s is the significant wave height at the toe of the structure. The relative run-up is usually given as a function of the surf similarity parameter or breaker parameter which is defined as

$$\xi_{op} = \tan\alpha / \sqrt{s_{op}} \tag{1}$$

where: ξ_{op} = the breaker parameter, α = the average slope angle and s_{op} = the wave steepness. The wave steepness is a fictitious or computation quantity, especially meant to describe the influence of a wave period. This quantity is fictitious as the wave height at the location of the toe is related to the wave length in deep water ($gT_p^2 / 2\pi$).

With $\xi_{op} < 2 - 2.5$ the waves will tend to break on the dike or seawall slope. This is mostly the case with slopes of 1:3 or milder. For larger values of ξ_{op} the waves do not break on the slope any longer. In that case the slopes are often steeper than 1:3 and/or the waves are characterised by a smaller wave steepness (for example swell).

The general design formula that can be applied for wave run-up on dikes is given by:

$$R_{u2\%}/H_s = 1.6\,\gamma_b\,\gamma_f\,\gamma_\beta\,\xi_{op} \qquad \text{with a maximum of } 3.2\,\gamma_f\,\gamma_\beta \tag{2}$$

with : γ_b = reduction factor for a berm, γ_f = reduction factor for slope roughness and γ_β = reduction factor for oblique wave attack.

The formula is valid for the range $0.5 < \gamma_b\xi_{op} < 4$ or 5. The relative wave run-up $R_{u2\%}/H_s$ depends on the breaker parameter ξ_{op} and on three reduction factors, namely: for berms, roughness on the slope and for oblique wave attack. The question of how the reduction factors should be computed is given further on in the paper.

Equation 2 is shown in Figure 2 where the relative run-up $R_{u2\%}/(\gamma_f\gamma_\beta H_s)$ is set out against the breaker parameter $\gamma_b\xi_{op}$. The relative run-up increases till $\gamma_b\xi_{op} = 2$ and remains constant for larger values. The latter is the case for relatively steep slopes and/or low wave steepnesses. The theoretical limit for a vertical structure ($\xi_{op} = \infty$) is $R_{u2\%}/H_s = 1.4$ in Equation 2 or Figure 2, but this is far outside the application range considered here.

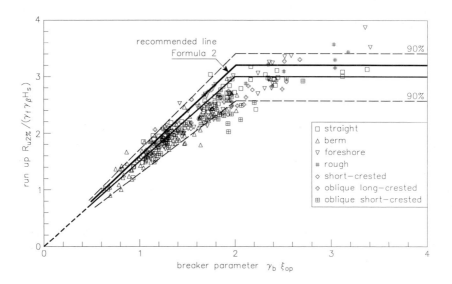

Figure 2. Wave run-up as a function of the breaker parameter, including data with possible influences

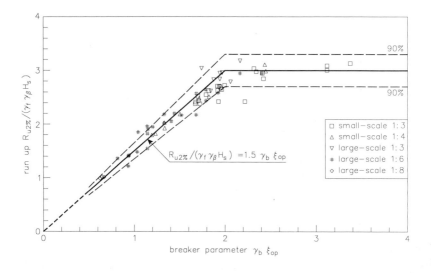

Figure 3. Wave run-up for a smooth slope with measured data

In manuals or guidelines it is advisable that one should not deal with a general trend in design formulae. Instead, it is recommended that a more conservative approach should be used. In many international standards a safety margin of one standard deviation is applied. This value is also incorporated in Equation 2. Figure 2 gives all the available data points pertaining to wave run-up. Equation 2 is only based on smooth and straight slopes under perpendicular wave attack. Those data points are only from the small-scale tests of De Waal and Van der Meer (1992), and from results of available large-scale tests which can be considered reliable. Amongst these large scale tests are the tests of Führböter et al. (1989). These data are shown in Figure 3.

The *average* value of the wave run-up can be described by:

$$R_{u2\%}/H_s = 1.5\ \gamma_b\gamma_f\gamma_\beta\ \xi_{op} \text{ with a maximum of } 3.0\ \gamma_f\gamma_\beta \tag{3}$$

The scatter around equation 3 can be described by interpreting the coefficient 1.5 as a normally distributed stochastic variable with a mean value of 1.5 and a variation coefficient (standard deviation divided by the mean value) of $V = \sigma/\mu = 0.085$. Figure 2 shows all available data points pertaining to slopes with berms or roughness and obliquely incoming, short-crested waves. When all the influences are incorporated into one figure the scatter becomes larger than for only smooth, straight slopes, see Figure 3.

However, equation 3 should not be used for the wave run-up when deterministically designing dikes: for that purpose one should use equation 2. For probabilistic designs equation 3 should be taken with the above variation coefficient.

In TAW (1974) a formula is given for mild (milder than 1:2.5), smooth, straight slopes. After rearrangement, this formula has the form:

$$R_{u2\%}/H_s = 1.61\ \xi_{op} \tag{4}$$

The formula is virtually identical to equation 2 except for the reduction factors and the limit for steeper slopes, which has here the value of 3.2. In other words, the run-up formula used for twenty years will be maintained and complemented on specific points.

General formula on wave overtopping
With wave overtopping the crest height is lower than the run-up levels of the highest waves. The parameter to be considered here is the crest freeboard R_c. This is the difference between SWL and the governing dike height. Wave overtopping is mostly given as an average discharge q per unit width, for example in m³/s per m or in l/s per m. The Dutch Guideline on river dykes (TAW, 1989) indicates that for relatively heavy seas and with wave heights of up to a few meters the 2%-wave run-up criterion yields an overtopping discharge of the order of 1 l/s per m. It becomes 0.1 l/s per m with lower waves such as those occurring in rivers. An acceptable overtopping of 1 l/s per m in the river area, instead of the 2%-wave run-up, can then lead to a reduction of the freeboard of the dike.

The former formulae on wave overtopping, see Van der Meer and Janssen (1995), made a distinction between breaking (plunging) and non-breaking (surging) waves on the slope. The new set of formulae relates to breaking waves and is valid up to a maximum which is in fact the non-breaking region. This procedure is in accordance with wave run-up on a slope. The new (rewritten) formula for wave overtopping on dikes is as follows:

$$\frac{q}{\sqrt{gH_s^3}} = \frac{0.06}{\sqrt{\tan\alpha}} \gamma_b \xi_{op} \exp\left(-4.7 \frac{R_c}{H_s} \frac{1}{\xi_{op} \gamma_b \gamma_f \gamma_\beta \gamma_v}\right) \tag{5}$$

with as maximum:

$$\frac{q}{\sqrt{gH_s^3}} = 0.2 \exp\left(-2.3 \frac{R_c}{H_s} \frac{1}{\gamma_f \gamma_\beta}\right) \tag{6}$$

where: q = average overtopping rate (m³/s per m width); R_c = crest freeboard (m); and
    γ_v = reduction factor due to a vertical wall on a slope (-).

Figure 4 gives prediction curves as a function of the breaker parameter, similar to Figures 2 and 3, but now with the dimensionless wave overtopping on the vertical axis instead of the wave run-up and with various curves in relation to the crest height. Figure 4 yields for a straight, smooth slope of 1:3 and different curves are given for relative freeboards of R_c/H_s = 1, 2 and 3. Around ξ_{op} = 2 the wave overtopping reaches its maximum just as for wave run-up.

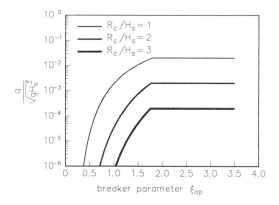

Figure 4. Dimensionless wave overtopping on a straight, smooth 1:3 slope as a function of the breaker parameter and for various relative crest heights

Figure 5 gives an overall view of available information on breaking waves. It shows the results of many tests and gives a good idea of the scatter. In this figure the important parameters are given along the axes, all existing data points are given with a mean and 95% confidence bands and typical applications are indicated along the vertical axis. Besides data of Delft Hydraulics also data for smooth slopes from Owen (1980) and Führböter et al. (1989) are included. The dimensionless overtopping discharge is given on the ordinate and the dimensionless crest height on the abscissa. The overtopping discharge is given on a logarithmic scale, assuming a kind of exponential function. Owen (1980) was the first who gave explicitly the exponential relationship between dimensionless overtopping discharge and relative crest height. Most of other researchers have used this kind of relationship to describe their overtopping data. The differences then are mainly the treatment of the influence of the wave period or steepness and the slope angle. In fact equation 5 includes the original equation of Owen (1980) and also his data.

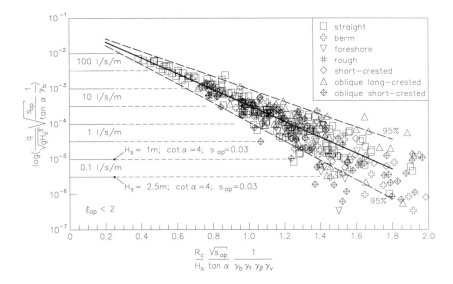

Figure 5. Wave overtopping data for breaking waves with mean, confidence bands and with an indication of typical applications

The average of all the observations in Figure 5 is not described by equation 5, but by a similar equation where the coefficient 4.7 has been changed to 5.2. The reliability of the formula is given by taking the coefficient 5.2 as a normally distributed stochastic variable with an average of 5.2 and a standard deviation $\sigma = 0.55$. By means of this standard deviation also confidence bands ($\mu \pm x\sigma$) can be drawn with for x times the standard deviation (1.64 for the 90% and 1.96 for the 95% confidence limit). The average for all data at the maximum, described by equation 6 is given by a coefficient 2.6 instead of 2.3. The reliability of this formula can be given by taking the coefficient 2.6 as a normally distributed stochastic variable having a standard deviation of $\sigma = 0.35$. As is the case with wave run-up, a somewhat more conservative formula should be applied for design and examination purposes than the average value. An extra safety of about one standard deviation is taken into account in equations 5 and 6. Figure 6 shows the recommended equation 5, the mean and the 95% confidence limits. Also in this Figure 6 the formula from TAW (1974) is drawn and is practically the same as the recommended line.

Also, in Figure 5 several overtopping discharges are illustrated, namely, 0.1, 1, 10 and 100 l/s per m. The discharges apply for a 1:4 slope and a wave steepness of $s_{op} = 0.03$. The upper line of the interval applies to a significant wave height of 1.0 m (for example river dikes) and the lower one for a wave height of 2.5 m (for example for sea dikes).

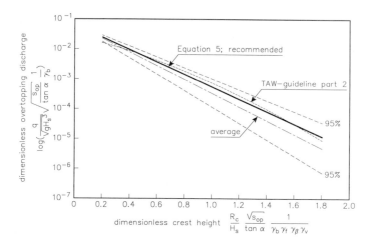

Figure 6. Wave overtopping with confidence limits

REDUCTION FACTORS ON WAVE RUN-UP AND WAVE OVERTOPPING

Above equations, described as general formulae on wave run-up and wave overtopping, include the effects of a berm, friction on the slope, oblique wave attack and a wall on the slope. These effects will be described now.

Definition of the average slope angle

Research is very often performed with nice straight slopes and the definition of $\tan\alpha$ is then obvious. In practice, however, a dike slope may consist of various more or less straight parts and the definition of the slope angle needs to be more precisely defined. The slope angle becomes an average slope angle. Figure 7 gives the definition that is used in this paper.

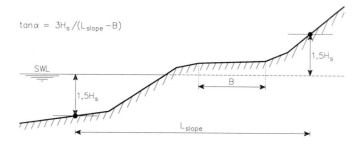

Figure 7. Determination of the average slope angle

The wave action is concentrated on a certain part of the slope around the water level. Examination of many tests showed that the part 1.5 H_s above and below the water line is the governing part. As berms are treated separately the berm width should be omitted from the definition of the average slope. The average slope is then defined as:

$$\tan\alpha = 3H_s/(L_{slope} - B) \tag{7}$$

Where L_{slope} = the horizontal length between the two points on the slope 1.5 H_s above and below the water line, and B = the berm width.

Reduction factor γ_b for a berm

A berm is defined as a flat part in a slope profile with a slope not steeper than 1:15. The berm itself is described by its berm width, B (see Figure 7), and by its location with respect to the still water level, d_h. This depth parameter is the vertical distance between the still water level and *the middle of the berm*. A berm at the still water level gives $d_h = 0$.

The influence of a berm on wave run-up and wave overtopping is graphically given in Figure 8. The horizontal axis gives the relative depth d_h/H_s of the berm below (positive) or above (negative) the still water level. The vertical axis shows the reduction factor γ_b to be used in equations 2, 3 and 5. The reduction is limited to a value of 0.6 and reaches its minimum value (maximum influence) if the berm is *at* the still water level: $d_h/H_s = 0$. No influence of a berm is found if the berm is higher than the 2%-runup level on the down slope. The influence vanishes if the berm is more than two wave heights below the still water level. Various curves show the influence of the relative berm width B/H_s. A larger berm width gives a larger influence.

The influence of the *berm width* can be described by taking into account the change in slope angle with and without the berm. Now the influence is described with respect to *the middle of the berm* (and not with respect to the water level), see Figure 9. The ratio B/L_{berm} describes this influence, where L_{berm} is the horizontal length of the total slope (including the berm) between the points 1.0 H_s above and below the *middle of the berm*.

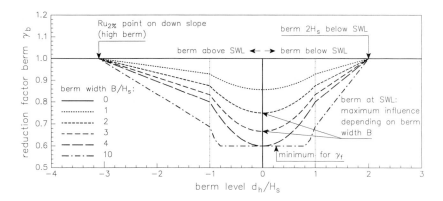

Figure 8. The reduction factor γ_b for a bermed slope

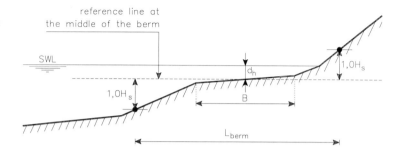

Figure 9. Definition of L_{berm}

Figure 8 can be described by the following equation:

$$\gamma_b = 1 - \frac{B}{L_{berm}}\left(1 - 0.5\left(\frac{d_h}{H_s}\right)^2\right) \qquad (8)$$

with $0.6 \le \gamma_b \le 1.0$ and $-1.0 \le d_h/H_s \le 1.0$

Between $d_h = 1\ H_s$ and $d_h = 2\ H_s$ the reduction factor γ_b increases linearly to $\gamma_b = 1$ (the influence of the berm reduces linearly to zero). See Figure 8. With a high berm the influence also decreases linearly from $\gamma_b = 1 - 0.5B/L_{berm}$ at $d_h/H_s = -1\ H_s$ to $\gamma_b = 1$ if $R_{u2\%}$ is reached on the down slope.

The berm is most effective when lying at the still water level, or around it if upper and lower slopes are different. An optimum berm width will be obtained if the reduction factor reaches the value of 0.6. In principle, this optimum berm width can be determined with equation 8 for every berm geometry (with *one* berm). For a berm at the still water level the optimum berm width becomes:

$$B = 0.4\ L_{berm} \qquad (9)$$

It might be possible that a dike profile includes more than one berm. Then the reduction factors have to be determined separately for each berm. The total reduction factor is the product of the separate reduction factors, of course with a minimum of 0.6. The ratio B/L_{berm} in equation 8 should then be modified a little:

$$B/L_{berm} = B_i / (L_{berm,i} - \Sigma L_{other\ berms}), \qquad (10)$$

with "i" for the berm considered.

Reduction factor γ_f for roughness on the slope
The influence of a kind of roughness on the slope is given by the reduction factor γ_f. Reduction factors for various types of revetments have been published earlier. The origin of these factors dates back to Russian investigations performed in the 1950's with regular waves. A table on

these factors was further developed in TAW (1974) and published in several international manuals. New studies, often large-scale, and conducted with random waves have led to a new table (Table 1) of reduction factors for rough slopes.

Type of slope	Reduction factor γ_f	Old reduction factors
Smooth, concrete, asphalt	1.0	1.0
Closed, smooth, block revetment	1.0	0.9
Grass (3 cm)	0.95	0.85-0.90
Block revetment (basalt, basalton)	0.90	0.85-0.90
1 rubble layer ($H_s/D = 1.5$-3)	0.60	0.80
¼ of placed block revetment ($0.5*0.5$ m^2) 9 cm above slope	0.75	

Table 1. Reduction factors γ_f for a rough slope

The reduction factors in Table 1 apply for $\gamma_b\xi_{op} < 3$. Above $\gamma_b\xi_{op} = 3$, the reduction factor increases linearly to 1 at $\gamma_b\xi_{op} = 5$. The reduction factors in Table 1 apply if the part between $0.25\ R_{u2\%,\ smooth}$ below and $0.5\ R_{u2\%,\ smooth}$ above the still water level is covered with roughness. The extension "smooth" means the wave run-up on a smooth slope. If the coverage is less, the reduction factor has to be reduced, see further.

Research on roughness units on a slope, such as blocks and ribs, has also been performed by Szmytkiewitcz et al. (1994). Their results have been re-analysed by the authors. The width of a block or rib is defined by f_b, the height by f_h and the rib distance by f_L. The optimal rib distance is $f_L/f_b = 7$, with an area of application of $f_L/f_b = 5$-8. If the total area is covered with blocks or ribs and if the height is at least $f_h/H_s = 0.15$, the following (minimal) reduction factors are found:

Block, covered area 1/25th of total	$\gamma_f = 0.80$
Block, covered area 1/9th of total	$\gamma_f = 0.70$
Ribs, rib distance $f_L/f_b = 5$-8	$\gamma_f = 0.65$

A larger block or rib height dan $f_h/H_s = 0.15$ has no further reducing effect. If the height is smaller one can interpolate linearly to $\gamma_f = 1$ for $f_h/H_s = 0$. Just like for the reduction factors in Table 1, the application of the reduction factors is limited by $\gamma_b\xi_{op} < 3$ and increase linearly to 1 for $\gamma_b\xi_{op} = 5$.

Run-up formulae for rock slopes with a double layer of rock have been given by Van der Meer and Stam (1992). After some modification from mean period to peak period the equations become:

$$R_{u2\%}/H_s = 0.88\ \xi_{op} \qquad \text{for } \xi_{op} < 1.5 \text{ and}$$

$$R_{u2\%}/H_s = 1.1\ \xi_{op}^{0.46} \qquad \text{for } \xi_{op} > 1.5$$

(11)

One can use these formulae to calculate wave-runup for rock slopes. For wave overtopping one still has to use the reduction factor γ_f. This reduction factor is found by calculating the $R_{u2\%}$ both for the rock slope and for a smooth slope for the same ξ_{op} and by determining the ratio of these figures.

It is possible that roughness is only present on a small part of the slope. First of all, tests showed that roughness solely below the still water level (and a smooth slope above) does not have any influence. If also roughness above the still water level is present an average weighing can be done over the area 0.25 $R_{u2\%, \text{smooth}}$ below and 0.5 $R_{u2\%, \text{smooth}}$ above the water level. The part to be taken into account below SWL may never exceed the part above SWL. Suppose that within the given area three different slope sections exist with lengths of respectively l_1, l_2 and l_3 and reduction factors of $\gamma_{f,1}$, $\gamma_{f,2}$ and $\gamma_{f,3}$. The average reduction factor for roughness becomes then:

$$\gamma_f = \frac{\gamma_{f,1} l_1 + \gamma_{f,2} l_2 + \gamma_{f,3} l_3}{l_1 + l_2 + l_3} \tag{12}$$

As artificial roughness works in a fairly small area, the entire reduction can be reached by just placing the roughness in this area. Costs for this artificial roughness may be much smaller than if a total slope is covered by artificial roughness.

Reduction factor γ_β for the angle of wave attack
The angle of the wave attack ß is defined as the angle of the propagation direction with respect to the normal of the alignment axis of the dike. Perpendicular wave attack is therefore given by ß = 0°. The reduction factor for the angle of wave attack is given by γ_β. Until recently few investigations were carried out with obliquely incoming waves but these investigations had been performed with long-crested waves. "Long-crested" means that the length of the wave crest is in principle assumed to be infinite. In investigations with long-crested waves the wave crest is as long as the wave board and the wave crests propagate parallel to one another.

In nature, waves are short-crested. This implies that the wave crests have a certain length and the waves a certain main direction. The individual waves have a direction around this main direction. The extent to which they vary around the main direction (directional spreading) can be described by a spreading value. Only long swell, for example coming from the ocean, has such long crests that it may virtually be called "long-crested". A wave field with strong wind is short-crested.

In Van der Meer and Janssen (1995) results of an investigation were described into wave run-up and overtopping where the influence of obliquely incoming waves and directional spreading was studied. Figure 10 summarises these results. The reduction factor γ_β has been set out against the angle of wave attack ß.

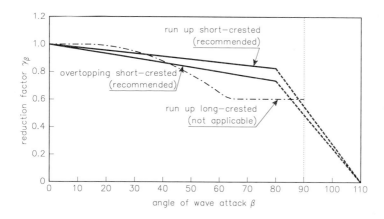

Figure 10. The reduction factor for oblique wave attack γ_β

Long-crested waves with $0° < ß < 30°$ cause virtually the same wave run-up as with perpendicular attack. Outside of this range, the reduction factor decreases fairly quickly to about 0.6 at $ß = 60°$. With short-crested waves the angle of wave attack has apparently less influence. This is mainly caused by the fact that within the wave field the individual waves deviate from the main direction $ß$. For both run-up and overtopping with short-crested waves the reduction factor decreases linearly to a certain value at $ß = 80°$. This is around $\gamma_\beta = 0.8$ for the 2% run-up and around 0.7 for overtopping. So, for wind waves the reduction factor has a minimum of 0.7 - 0.8 and not 0.6, as was found for long-crested waves. Since a wave field under storm conditions can be considered to be short-crested, it is recommended that the lines in Figure 10 be used for short-crested waves.

For oblique waves, different reduction factors apply to run-up levels or to overtopping discharges. The cause for this is that here the incoming wave energy per unit length of structure is less than that for perpendicular wave attack. The wave overtopping is defined as a volume per unit length, while the run-up does not depend on the structure length. The use of the lines given in Figure 10 for short-crested waves is recommended and can be described by the following formulae:

For the 2%-wave run-up with short-crested waves:

$$\gamma_\beta = 1 - 0.0022\beta \quad (ß \text{ in degrees}) \tag{13}$$

For wave overtopping with short-crested waves:

$$\gamma_\beta = 1 - 0.0033\beta \quad (ß \text{ in degrees}) \tag{14}$$

For wave angles with $\beta > 80°$ the reduction factor will of course rapidly diminish. As at $\beta = 90°$ still some wave run-up can be expected, certainly for short-crested waves, it is fairly arbitrary stated that between $\beta = 80°$ and $110°$ the reduction factor linearly decreases to zero.

Reduction factor γ_v for a (vertical) wall on a slope

In some situations it may occur that a vertical wall or a very steep slope at the top of a slope has been designed to reduce wave overtopping. These walls are relatively small and not comparable with vertical structures like caissons or quay walls. Due to limited research the application of a reduction factor γ_v is restricted by the following area:

- slopes from 1:2.5 to 1:3.5, possibly with a berm with dimensions $B/H_s = 2$-3 or $B/L_{op} = 0.05$-0.08
- the toe of the wall should lie between 1.2 H_s above and below the still water level
- the minimum height of the wall (with a high toe level) is about 0.5 H_s and the maximum height (with a low toe level) is about 3 H_s.

An average slope has been defined in Figure 7. With a vertical wall this procedure will very soon lead to a large value of the breaker parameter ξ_{op}, which means that waves do not break in such situations. In fact the wall is situated at the top of the slope and waves will possibly break on the slope before they reach the wall. In order to keep the relationship between the type of breaking and the breaker parameter, *the vertical wall has to be schematised as a 1:1 slope*, starting at the toe of the wall. Then the procedure of Figure 7 and equation 7 can be applied.

The reduction factor for a vertical wall on top of a slope is $\gamma_v = 0.65$. Data with a vertical wall and with the application of the reduction factor are shown in Figure 11. The lines in the graph are similar to Figure 6. Wave overtopping will increase again if the wall is not completely vertical, but a little sloping. With a steep slope of 1:1 the reduction factor becomes $\gamma_v = 1$. For a steeper slope, between 1:1 and vertical, one may interpolate linearly:

$$\gamma_v = 1.35 - 0.0078\alpha_{slope} \tag{16}$$

with α_{slope} = the angle of the steep wall (between 45° at 1:1 and 90° for a vertical wall).

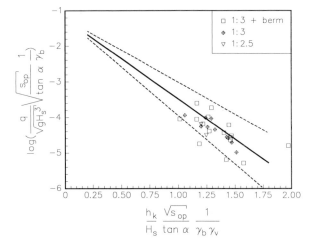

Figure 11. Data with a vertical wall on top of a (bermed) slope with $\gamma_v = 0.65$

CONCLUSIONS
Formulae have been given for conceptual design on wave run-up and wave overtopping of dikes and sloping structures. Influences of structure geometry and wave boundary conditions have been included in a practical way by the use of reduction factors. Formulae were given for deterministic design, including some safety, but also for probabilistic design, giving the average trend and the reliability by a variation coefficient.

ACKNOWLEDGEMENTS
The Rijkswaterstaat, Dutch Public Works Department and the TAW, the Technical Advisory Committee on Water Defences in The Netherlands are gratefully acknowledged for their financial and technical support.

REFERENCES
De Waal, J.P. and J.W. van der Meer (1992). *Wave runup and overtopping on coastal dikes.* ASCE, Proc. ICCE, Ch. 134, p. 1758-1771,Venice, Italy.

Franco, L., M. de Gerloni and J.W. van der Meer (1994).*Wave overtopping on vertical and composite breakwaters.* ASCE, Proc. ICCE, Kobe, Japan.

Führböter, A., Sparboom, U. and Witte, H.H., 1989. *Großer Wellenkanal Hannover: Versuchsergebnisse über den Wellenauflauf auf glatten und rauhen Deichböschungen met der Neigung 1:6.* Die Küβte. Archive for Research and Technology on the North Sea and Baltic Coast. In German.

Owen, M.W. (1980). *Design of seawalls allowing for wave overtopping.* Hydraulics Research, Wallingford, Report No. EX 924, UK.

Staatsblad, 1996. *Wet op de waterkering.* Staatsblad van het Koninkrijk der Nederlanden, 1996 8. Sdu publishers, The Hague, The Netherlands.

Szmytkiewicz, M., J. Kolodko and R.B. Zeidler (1994). *Irregular wave run-up on various slopes and optimization guidelines.* Report Polish Academy of Sciences, Institute of Hydro-engineering, Polen.

TAW, 1974. *Wave run-up and overtopping.* Technical Advisory Committee on Water Defences in The Netherlands. Government publishing office, The Hague, The Netherlands.

TAW, 1986. *Leidraad voor het ontwerpen van rivierdijken. Deel 1 - boven-rivierengebied.* "Guideline for the design of river dikes. Part 1 - Upper river area". In Dutch.

Van der Meer, J.W. and C.J.M. Stam (1992). *Wave run-up on smooth and rock slopes.* ASCE, Journal of WPC and OE, Vol. 188, No.5, p. 534-550. Also Delft Hydraulics Publication No. 454 (1991).

Van der Meer, J.W. and J.P.F.M. Janssen (1995). *Wave run-up and wave overtopping at dikes.* In: Wave Forces on Inclined and Vertical Wall Structures. ASCE. Ed. N. Kobayashi and Z. Demirbilek. Ch. 1, p. 1-27.

Establishing Coastal Flood Risks From Single Storms and the Distribution of the Risk of Structural Failure

DR. R. J. MADDRELL & DR. D. E. REEVE,
Sir William Halcrow & Partners Ltd, Burderop Park, Swindon, Wiltshire, SN4 0QD, UK

C. R. HEATON,
UK Meteorological Office, Johnson House, London Road, Bracknell, RG12 2SY, UK

INTRODUCTION

Land areas potentially at risk from coastal flooding represent only about 3% of the area of England and Wales, but they have been extensively developed and the value of their insured assets is high. Two major storms events in October 1987 and January 1990, which caused wind rather than flood damage, sharpened the insurance and reinsurance companies concern about their exposure to weather and coastal flooding risks. Consequently, in 1992 the Association of British Insurers (ABI) asked Sir William Halcrow & Partners Ltd, (Halcrow), to categorise the flood risks from coastal storm events for the benefit of their members.

The Halcrow study examined those areas in England and Wales that were protected by some 1300km of coastal flood defence, containing approximately 2000 structures, the defences of only four main estuaries, namely, Tees, Humber, Thames (Upper and Lower) and Severn, but none of the other estuaries and channels. This analysis included the increase in risk resulting from 50 years increase in mean sea level as a result of isostatic and eustatic changes at each defence. The pilot study in 1993 examined a detailed design-based approach and one using the more generalised structural data contained in the Sea Defence Survey (SDS) data. As the results in terms of flood risk were similar, the latter was chosen as it had the shortest completion time and was the most cost effective.

The first main study report, published in 1994, was subsequently updated in 1995 to include new defences and improvements to existing defences constructed since 1990. The assessment from the first study provided flood areas defined in 1km squares falling in Risk Bands 1, 2 and 3 corresponding to return periods of 50, 100 and 200 years respectively. In addition, disks giving the post codes in each square, their risk classification and flood depth were provided to ABI members, Maddrell et al (1996). Additional subsequent studies included the prediction of flood risk from individual storms, examining defence lengths at greatest risk and the flood risks to London from combined tidal and high fresh water flows.

In this paper we describe how the structural and flood risk assessment methods developed for the earlier studies maybe applied to determine the geographical extent of flood risk for single severe

Coastlines, structures and breakwaters. Thomas Telford, London, 1998

storm events. These results were linked with data on structural characteristics, integrity, land use and assets to assist in focussing future management resources and investment more effectively.

BACKGROUND

Previous studies have provided a measure of the risk posed by extreme storm conditions experienced at individual defences, Maddrell et al (1995, 1997). The risk classification represented the risk summed over all storm types, but did not provide information about the spatial extent of the flood risk associated with individual storms.

In 1995 the ABI commissioned Halcrow, in conjunction with the UK Meteorological Office, to establish a classification of storm types experienced by the UK. A detailed statistical treatment, such as proposed by Coles & Tawn (1990), was not considered a viable option when assessing a large number of defences and thus the approach adopted was based on the methods developed in the earlier studies. The study defined the impact of single storm events of each type for each of the defence structures around England and Wales, (numbering approximately 2000). Each structure was assessed for its potential failure risk due to overtopping, overflow and toe failure, and for this study, the coasts of England and Wales were divided into three areas: West, South and East. Meteorological records dating back to the last century were analysed to determine generic storm types affecting one or more of the areas. These storms included hypothetical storms which were constructed by changing the relative timing of the passage of the generic storms so that storm surges coincided more closely with, say, the time of high waters, thus providing 'worst case' storms. The flood risk at each defence during each storm was assessed on the ability of the flood defences to withstand the wave and water level conditions throughout the duration of the storm.

For this study it should be noted that:
* the impact of successive tides or storms has not been taken into account, nor the likely time for breach repair;
* no account has been taken of fresh water floods for the estuaries studies, which would influence local water levels and waves;
* flood risk has also been determined for generic storm types. These are meteorologically feasible storms based upon, and similar to, storms that have occurred in the past.

Flood risk areas are normally protected by more than one defence length and thus the flood risk for the area is related to the risk of failure of the weakest defence protecting it. In the context of the studies and this paper it should be noted that the word 'failure' does not imply that total functional failure of the defence will definitely occur under the extreme event. Rather, 'failure' is the exceedance of particular threshold levels at which overflow or damage to the defences might be expected to commence. Therefore, the 'failure' of a defence indicates that it is potentially at risk and vulnerable under particular conditions. Likewise, the risk of flooding to any area relates to its potential for flooding. It does not follow that such flooding will definitely occur throughout the whole area should a particular storm occur.

STRUCTURAL RISK ASSESSMENT
Coastal flood defences and modes of failure
Coastal flood defences provide protection to low-lying areas against flooding by the sea.

Defences vary considerably in form and comprise both man-made structures such as embankments and natural features such as dunes. A higher standard of protection and regular maintenance will usually be afforded to defending an urban area rather than a rural area and relate to the 'standards of service' for those defences.

The classification of defences and analysis of modes of failure follows that described by Reeve & Burgess (1993), a brief synopsis of which is given here. The defences are classified into four main categories based upon their shape: narrow or wide structures and sloped or vertically faced. Within these four categories, subdivision is made according to the protection offered to different components of the defence. A flood defence will typically comprise a front face (the base of which is the toe), a crest (the top of the structure) and a backface. Some structures also have a crest wall. The area in front of the structure is the beach or foreshore, the level and slope of which can have a significant influence on the performance of the defence. Information on the structures and foreshore for all defences around England and Wales was obtained from sources available in the public domain such as local authorities and agencies. This data reflected, as far as was practicable, the status of sea defences at the end of 1994. Approximately 2000 structures were identified from these sources. Three primary modes of failure were defined by:

overflow	-	when the water level exceeds the crest level of the defence
overtopping	-	when waves run up and over or break over the top of the defence crest
toe failure	-	undermining of the toe of the structure leading to a loss of structural integrity

Table 1 below summarises the key data requirements for examining each mode of failure. The list is not intended to be exhaustive but indicates the range of data required.

TABLE 1: Outline data requirements for risk asessment by failure mode

Data \ Failure Mode	Overflow	Overtopping	Toe Failure
Peak water level	✔	✔	
Wave conditions		✔	
Seawall condition	✔	✔	✔
Crest level	✔	✔	
Seawall composition		✔	✔
Seawall slope		✔	✔
Toe level			✔
Beach slope		✔	
Beach level at toe		✔	✔
Beach variability		✔	✔

A key input to the risk assessment is the cross-sectional profile of the defence. This is especially so for overtopping. With the exception of engineering drawings data on structures is seldom compiled in the format of profiles. More typically, records might describe the longshore extent, composition and conditions of particular elements of a flood defence, such as a wave return wall on the crest of the main part of the structure. Considerable effort was required to synthesise records of this form into cross-sectional profiles for use in the analysis.

The ability of a defence to withstand the environmental conditions will depend on its condition, construction material and exposure to non-tidal water level variations (such as those due to atmospheric pressure variations, wave set-up and wind set-up). The temporal development from an incipient failure to full failure and the estimated integrity of the structures are a major source of uncertainty. This uncertainty was addressed in two ways. Firstly, failure by overtopping was considered to occur when the peak overtopping rate exceeded the threshold for structural damage by an order of magnitude. Secondly, an effective level for each defence was defined by reducing the crest level, by between 0.0m and 1.0m, to account for the condition, type and exposure of the structure based on past experience and engineering judgement.

Risk assessment method
For each of the eleven storms considered, wave and water level conditions were defined at twenty four offshore points around England and Wales, (see Figure 1). The offshore wave conditions were transformed inshore using a spectral refraction model to provide a time series of wave and water level conditions at each location over the duration of each storm. The ability of each defence to withstand the conditions throughout the storm was assessed by checking whether or not the imposed loads exceeded the 'strength' of the structures. That is:
- for overflow total water levels were compared against effective crest levels;
- for overtopping peak overtopping rates were compared against ten times the thresholds for initiation of damage presented in Owen (1980);
- and for toe failure, where the data allowed, both probabilistic and qualitative assessments were made of the ability of the structure to withstand lowering of the beach level at the base of the defence, (see Burgess & Reeve (1994)).

The assessment was automated using specifically developed software for flood risk analysis and classification (FRANC). This software runs in Windows on a PC and accesses structural and environmental information in a database in order to perform the necessary calculations, and outputs results in a format suitable for use in mapping with geographical information systems, Reeve (1996). Figure 2 illustrates the steps in the assessment. In relation to standard reliability theory, (see eg Thoft-Christensen & Baker 1982), the procedure is probably most appropriately classified as a Level II or First-order risk method.

The study used previously defined flood protection zones, which are those areas considered to be vulnerable to flooding in the absence of flood defences for events exceeding the 1 in 200 year level. In practical terms the landward boundary of the protection zones correspond closely with the +5m contour. In this study the flood protcetion zones are considered to be 'self-contained' in that flooding may occur in one of two neighbouring zones without necessarily affecting the other. If one or more of the defence lengths protecting a flood protection zone did not withstand the specified storm conditions, the whole of the zone was considered to have the risk associated with the weakest defence along its open coast length. The flood protection zones were overlaid with a matrix of one kilometre grid squares aligned to the National Grid. A grid square was marked as being 'at risk' if it overlapped with any part of a flood protection zone also considered 'at risk'. Where a grid square was established as being 'at risk', the postal sector(s) which lie within that square were identified. Other methods of mapping flood risk have been proposed by Meadowcroft et al. (1996) but these require a detailed topographic survey of the hinterland.

SINGLE STORM ANALYSIS

The object of the meteorological study was to identify and examine storms that may have given the worst reported coastal flooding in the present climatic regime. Storms were primarily selected on the basis of meteorological factors, but where possible supporting information on the extent of coastal flooding associated with the storm was also considered. Given the restrictions imposed by the available data, it was necessary to balance the need to identify the worst case storm with the capacity to produce usable numerical data for use in the flood risk assessment.

For each coast, records of storms that had the potential to produce major coastal flooding were examined for the period January 1900 to August 1995 by the UK Meteorological Office. From the search, it was possible to establish two critical storms per coast which had caused large surges. For each storm selected, wave, water level and surge data were compiled for a set of twenty four data points around the coastline as can be seen in Figure 1. The data comprised a 3-hourly time series of wind direction, total water level, surge height, significant wave height and wave period for each location. Where appropriate, data from recent examples of each storm type were used since these provided the most comprehensive information. Each of the selected storms was also examined to see if flooding could have occurred on more than one coast.

TABLE 2: List of storm events

Storm dates	Coast	Characteristics	Additional aspects
21 Jan - 01 Feb 1953	East	Northerly storm, high spring tide coincident with surge	Effect of westbound surge on South Coast
11 Jan - 12 Jan 1978	East	Northeasterly storm, surge coincident with waves and spring tide	Modification to increase waves
13 Dec - 14 Dec 1981	West	Exceptionally high surge	
16 Dec - 17 Dec 1989	South	Eastbound surge, some waves	
05 Jan - 06 Jan 1991	West	Exceptionally high surge with waves	Modification to increase tidal level
03 Feb - 04 Feb 1994	South	Eastbound surge, some waves	Modification to maximise waves
08 Dec 1994	West and South	Eastbound surge plus high tide	

The selected storms were then examined to see if the surge conditions could have been worse had the storm development been different as regards track, timing and severity. For three of the storms (one per coast), differences were identified which could have produced more severe flooding. For each of these storms a modified time series of water level and wave data was produced. Table 2 shows the chronological list of storm events examined. Conditions for a total of eleven storms (actual and hypothetical) were compiled. In the period examined (1900 to 1995) the selected storms were all post-1953, with the most recent being in 1994. Clearly, the more recent events were better documented than the earlier events, but this did not unduly influence the choice of storms. The selection criteria were fulfilled by assessing whether the storms represented the worst case conditions by reference to documented evidence on actual flooding and to the severity of the storm itself. Further discussion and references of the particular storms selected can be found in Reeve et al. (1997).

The 1953 storm affected mainly the east coast of England. It caused widespread flooding and loss of life, and prompted the construction and refurbishment of many defences on the east coast, Cooling & Marsland (1953). The key aspects of this type of storm are the northerly winds and the track of the centre of the depression, which passes over the north of Scotland and moves southeastwards. The surface pressure chart for this storm is shown in Figure 3.

It was apparent from the search that the types of storms that have the potential to cause flooding are not necessarily rare or extreme events from a meteorological point of view and that they occur more frequently than the major coastal floods to which they are linked. This suggests that a finely-balanced combination of weather and tides is necessary for coastal flooding to occur.

FLOOD RISK AREAS

Results of the risk assessment were used determine the areas vulnerable to flooding as a result of all or part of their frontage being protected by defences which were shown to be at risk in the assessment. Where insufficient data was available to make an assessment of a structure its flood risk was designated as 'unclassified'. This only occurred where the structure passed one or two of the failure mode tests, but there was insufficient data to test the remaining modes. For example, if only the crest level of a structure was known then only the overflow test could be performed. If sufficient structural information was available, the overtopping and toe failure tests could also be performed. Thus, if there was only sufficient information to test one mode of failure on a particular structure, and the structure did not pass the test, then the structure was denoted as being at risk. The lack of data preventing other modes of failure to be analysed is of secondary importance in this case. However, if the the structure had passed the test there would still be uncertainty as to whether it would be vulnerable to the other, untested, modes of failure.

If two or more structures defended a protection zone then that zone was assigned the worst of the risks determined for the two structures. Thus, for the case of a zone protected by two defences, (labelled A and B): if A passed but B failed then the zone failed; if both A and B passed the zone passed; if A passed but B was unclassified then the zone had 'indeterminate' flood risk and if A failed and B was unclasified then the zone failed. This procedure avoided making optimistic assumptions in the absence of data. Figure 4 illustrates this process.

To be useful, a risk assessment methodology has to demonstrate its ability in identifying structures which merit closer inspection and survey. It is not the purpose of this paper to present detailed results of the study and some aspects of the work are still ongoing. However, a positive measure of the performance of the methodology can be gauged in general terms for specific storms. For example, the storm of 13-14 December 1981 was associated with a very high surge and affected the west coast of England and Wales. The method identified several areas in Somerset and Wales as being vulnerable to this type of storm. Local newspaper reports of the time mention localised flooding in the same areas. Similar observations can be made for the south and east coasts. Information on the damage inflicted by the 1989/90 winter storms is presented in ICE (1990) and includes the incidence and type of damage, and the costs.

The original study ranked 1232 out of a total of 1848 defences as being at either Band 1 or 2 risk. As described earlier, there are a number of possible reasons for the structure being classified as 'at risk'. A total of 332 defences were identified as being at risk of failure from overtopping. Of these, 213 were due to solely to the limited nature of the structure. Even though the remaining defences were at risk from overtopping, more detailed and accurate foreshore, water level and structure information would be required to determine the true degree of that risk. From a total of 316 defences that were at risk of toe failure, 91 could be classified as being at risk due to their structure. Thus, some 70% of the structures in this classification require additional, or improved data to enable an accurate assessment to be performed and thus establish the true level of risk of these defences.

The type of defence, the standard of protection it offers and the commitment to maintaining it will often depend on the nature of the area it is protecting. A higher standard of protection and regular maintenance will usually be afforded to defending an urban rather than a rural area. The area at risk behind the defence was defined by the flood protection zone. This is the potential flood area based on land levels and extreme open sea water levels; it does not necessarily represent the extent of flooding from a single event or subsequent tides. Information on the land use within each flood protection zone has been gathered. It includes estimates of quantities such as: area; principal land use; the number of domestic properties and commercial properties.

This information was assigned to all flood areas and Figure 5 shows some typical results. While it is not possible to draw general conclusions from this there are two points which are of interest:

- there are numerous cases where the length of the highest risk defence is a small proportion of the total length of defences. This highlights opportunities for selecting sites for maintenance and upgrading, which will have the greatest benefit for a given cost;

- many of the areas classified as high risk are low grade agricultural land with few or no properties and whose defences do not require a level of service of 1 in 50 years.

CONCLUSIONS
Historically, major flood events have rarely occurred during wind storms and pressure events of special severity, an observation supported by this study. The timing of storm surge and its coincidence with high tides and severe wave conditions can be as important, if not more important, as the severity of the storm. The study also showed that the '1953 type' East coast storm was the worst type of storm to have occurred in the past century with respect to flood risk.

While return periods can be assigned to individual aspects of storms, eg surge and wave heights, it is not straightforward to put return periods on the storms. This is because there are many variables associated with storms (eg pressure, storm track, wind speed) and to assign a return period to a storm would require an analysis of the joint probability of all these variables.

Flood zones are typically protected by more than one length of defences and thus the flood risk is related to the potentially weakest defence. This study, together with the earlier work already referenced, has not only provided insurers with an improved appreciation of the scale of their potential exposure due to a single event, but can also be used by funders to identify defences which may be at particular risk and relate that risk to the protected areas. This should allow capital and maintenance spending to be allocated to schemes which will have a large benefit in relation to their cost, as well as denying it to those whose 'level of service' makes such expenditure questionable.

The results of these studies indicate that there is a need for risk assessment in normal management practice. In particular, much still remains to be done in respect of incorporating qualitative uncertainties into assessment methodologies and in the presentation of uncertainty to 'end users'. Finally, it should be noted that risk assessments are, in essence, snap-shots of the situation at a particular time. In order to be an effective management tool, risk assessment must be a regular activity, linked to ongoing monitoring programmes. A key element of the risk assessment process is the effective transfer of data between surveys and analyses.

ACKNOWLEDGEMENTS
The work presented in this paper has been reproduced with the kind permission of the Association of British Insurers and the Environment Agency. The authors would like to thank Kevin Burgess and Rob Deakin (Sir William Halcrow & Partners Ltd) and Jack Hopkins (UK Meteorological Office) for their assistance with this paper.

REFERENCES
Burgess, K.A. and Reeve, D.E., 1994. The development of a method for the assessment of sea defences and risk of flooding. Proceedings of 29th MAFF Conference of River and Coastal Engineers, Loughborough, p5.3.1-5.3.12.

Coles, S.G. and Tawn, J.A., 1990. Statistics of coastal flood prevention, Phil. Trans. R. Soc. Lond. A332, p457-476.

Cooling, L.F. and Marsland, A., 1953. Soil mechanics of failures in the sea defence banks of Essex and Kent, Conference on the North Sea floods of 31 January - 1 February, 1953, Institution of Civil Engineers, December, p58-73.

The Institution of Civil Engineers, 1990. A statistical survey of storm damage to coastal defences, Winter 1989-1990, ICE Maritime Engineering Board, Coastal Engineering Research and Advisory Committee, November 1990.

Maddrell, R.J., Mounsey, C. and Burgess, K.A., 1996. Coastal flooding: Assessing the risk for the insurance industry, ICE Conference 1995, Brighton, UK.

Maddrell, R.J., Burgess, K.A., Deakin, R. & Mounsey, C., 1995. Identification of coastal flood areas in England and Wales for the insurance industry, Proceedings of 30th MAFF Conference of River and Coastal Engineers, Keele, p2.1.1-2.1.11.

Maddrell, R.J., Fleming, C.A. and Mounsey, C., 1997. Assessing coastal flood risks, 25th ICCE Conference, (1996), USA, *to appear*.

Meadowcroft, I.C., Reeve, D.E., Allsop, N.W.H., Diment, R.P. and Cross, J., 1996. Development of new risk assessment procedures for coastal structures', (including discussion), Advances in Coastal Structures and Breakwaters, Ed J.E.Clifford, Thomas Telford, p6-46.

Owen, M.W., 1980. Design of seawalls allowing for wave overtopping. Hydraulics Research Station Wallingford, Report EX 924.

Reeve, D.E., 1996. Climate change and assessment of coastal flood risk, Research Activities in Atmospheric and Oceanic Modelling, Report No23, WMO/TD - No734, p244-245.

Reeve, D.E. and Burgess, K.A., 1993. A method for the assessment of coastal flood risk. IMA J. of Mathematics Applied in Business & Industry, Vol. 5, p197-209.

Reeve, D.E., Maddrell, R.J. and Heaton, C.R., 1997. The extent of coastal flood risk in England and Wales due to individual storms, 2nd Edinburgh Conference on Risk Analysis, Assessment and Management, 14-16 Sept., University of Edinburgh., *to appear*.

Thoft-Christensen, P. And Baker, M.J., 1982. Structural reliability theory and its applications, Springer-Verlag, Berlin, p267.

Figure 1: Coastal data points for the single storm study and definition of coastal areas.

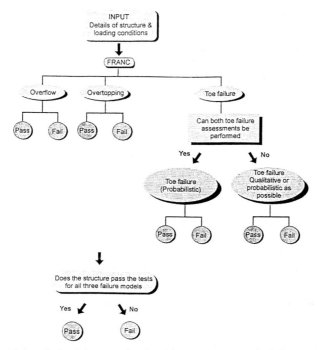

Figure 2: Decision tree for the risk assessment methodology.

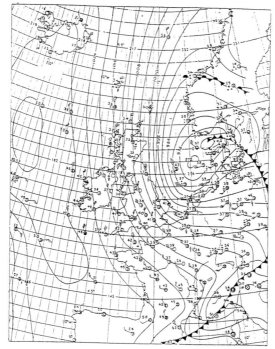

Figure 3: Surface pressure chart for 1800hours GMT January 31 1953.

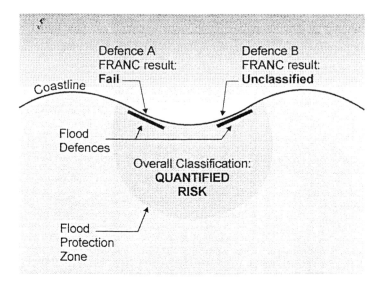

(a) *Storm Event 1*

In this example, a flood protection zone is defended by two sea defence lengths, one of which cannot be adequately classified by flood risk. In the first storm, Defence A is classified as having a risk of failure, and this risk is assigned to the flood protection zone.

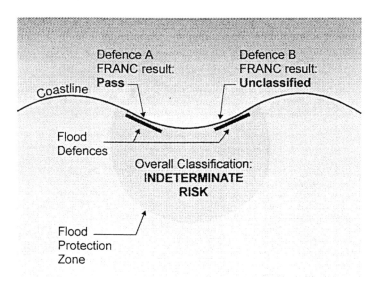

(b) *Storm Event 2*

In this example, Defence A passses the assessment tests, but the flood protection zone is now given an indeterminate flood risk due to the unknown performance of Defence B.

Figure 4:   Illustration of risk classification of flood protection zones

Area ID	Risk Band	Flood Area (sq km)	Total Defence Length (km)	Length of Highest Risk Defence (km)	% of Highest Risk Length to Total Length	Principal Land Type	No. of Domestic Properties	No. of Commercial Properties
203	3	2.23	3.47	3.47	-	Medium Agr/Conservation	Less than 10	None
204	1	0.23	5.24	1.76	34%	Medium Agr/Conservation	Less than 10	None
205	3	0.46	1.69	1.69	-	Medium Agr/Conservation	None	None
206	2	0.97	6.05	2.47	41%	Medium Agr/Conservation	None	Less than 5
207	1	2.79	6.62	1.21	18%	Medium Agr/Conservation	None	Less than 5
208	1	0.24	4.86	4.86	100%	Low Grade Agricultural	None	None
209	1	0.38	2.30	2.30	100%	Low Grade Agricultural	Less than 10	None
210	1	0.22	2.30	2.30	100%			
211	1	1.33	4.10	4.10	100%	Medium Agr/Conservation	None	None
212	3	0.23	1.32	1.32	-	Low Grade Agricultural	Less than 10	None
213	1	0.89	2.05	2.05	100%	High Grade Agricultural	None	Less than 5
214	3	0.78	2.60	2.60	-	Low Grade Agricultural	Less than 10	None
215	1	0.19	0.85	0.85	100%	High Grade Agricultural	None	Less than 5
216	1	0.90	5.85	0.49	8%	Low Grade Agricultural	None	None
217	1	0.30	0.72	0.09	13%	Dense Conurbations	10 to 100	5 to 10
218	1	3.78	3.37	2.00	59%	Dense Conurbations	10 to 100	More than 20
219	1	0.47	0.92	0.92	100%	High Grade Agricultural	Less than 10	Less than 5
220	3	0.37	0.80	0.80	-	Predominantly Urban	10 to 100	None
221	X	2.20	2.75	n/a	n/a			
222	1	0.08	5.30	2.55	48%	Medium Agr/Conservation	Less than 10	None
223	1	0.73	2.55	2.55	100%			
224	1	60.22	14.63	13.27	91%	Predominantly Urban	101 to 1000	5 to 10
225	1	3.46	1.09	1.09	100%	Low Grade Agricultural	None	None
226	1	2.03	3.50	3.50	100%	Low Grade Agricultural	None	Less than 5
227	1	1.79	3.19	0.80	25%	Medium Agr/Conservation	10 to 100	Less than 5
228	3	3.08	4.27	1.09	-	Low Grade Agricultural	Less than 10	None
229	1	0.34	6.52	4.91	75%	Low Grade Agricultural	None	None
230	3	0.94	1.36	1.36	100%	Low Grade Agricultural	Less than 10	None
231	1	11.87	1.07	1.07	100%	Dense Conurbations	101 to 1000	11 to 20
232	X	2.81	1.66	n/a	n/a			
233	3	0.81	2.36	2.36	-	Low Grade Agricultural	Less than 10	None
234	X	2.97	0.68	n/a	n/a			
235	3	0.26	0.50	0.50	-	Low Grade Agricultural	None	None
236	1	1.09	2.42	2.42	100%	Low Grade Agricultural	None	None
237	1	0.11	1.21	1.21	100%	Low Grade Agricultural	None	None
238	2	1.33	0.98	0.98	100%	Medium Agr/Conservation	None	None
239	X	4.86	2.49	n/a	n/a			
240	1	0.31	0.30	0.30	100%	Low Grade Agricultural	None	None
241	X	0.46	0.32	n/a	n/a			

Figure 5: Detailed results showing risk assessment and land use data from the SDS.

ADDENDUM

This note presents additional information not available for inclusion in the original paper, giving an example of a flood risk map and subsequent work that provides independent corroboration of the level of risks identified.

A map, Figure 6, shows the results of the analysis for a region covering the Bristol Channel, Wales and NW England for the case of the west coast storm of December 1981. Note that this shows the flood protection zones, as defined in the NSDS, for which at least one section of the defences protecting the zone was assessed as being at risk from the storm conditions. Flood protection zones for which the flood risk was indeterminate are coloured in a lighter shade. The storm conditions at most coastal locations were severe. Although it is not possible to define a return period for the storm as a whole, the water levels and waves associated with the storm can be compared to previously derived extremes. At most locations the conditions exceeded those for the 100-year event and at many exceeded the 1 in 200-year conditions.

A more detailed review of the results of the main study, commissioned by the ABI and the EA, is being undertaken to determine the primary reasons for potential failure at all of the defences around England and Wales which were identified as being at high or medium risk of failure. This involved a:
- comparison of extreme values of wave heights and water levels against values determined independently;
- more detailed structural review;
- review of the assumptions made in assessing different modes of failure;
- recalculation of the risks where additional data has become available.

The initial findings suggest that the original classification should remain unchanged for approximately 90% of the structures of which one quarter of the structures was attributable to poor, and potentially unreliable, data for the toe of the structure or the foreshore fronting it. For approximately 7% of the remaining 10% of structures, significant differences between extreme water levels from independent sources were found. For the remaining 3%, primarily composite defences with extremely complicated profiles, a requirement for a more sophisticated analysis of the risks has been identified.

The outcome of this detailed review indicates that the assessment methodology is robust and provides results which are, for all but the most complicated structures, in line with current engineering practices. This provides additional confidence in the validity of the results of the single storm study.

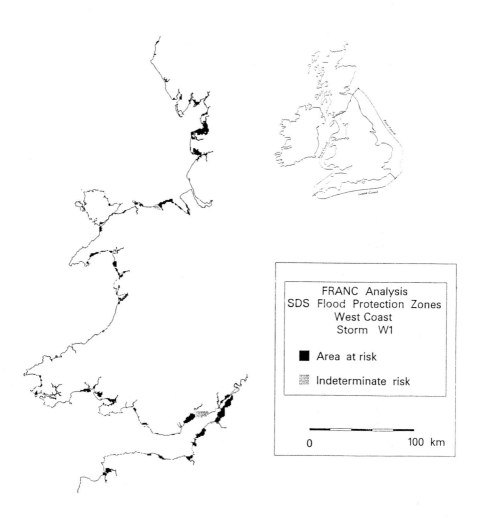

Figure 6 : Results for the 13-14 December 1981 storm affecting the West coast.

Influence of core permeability on Accropode armour layer stability

Prof., dr.techn. H.F. Burcharth, PhD student Morten Christensen, research ass. M.Sc.
Thomas Jensen and Associate Prof. Peter Frigaard
Aalborg University

INTRODUCTION

Hedar (1960 and 1986) and van der Meer (1988a) studied the influence of core permeability on the stability of two layer rock armour. In both cases a significant influence was found. However, it is to be expected that for single layer armour there will be an even larger influence of the core permeability. This is because the dissipation of wave energy in single layer armour will be smaller than in double layer armour, thus giving room for larger flow velocities in and over the armour layer. On this background a laboratory study of single layer Accropode®️ stability was undertaken at Aalborg University in 1995. The test results as well as a comparison with results of other researchers are presented in the paper. The expected sensitivity of Accropode armour stability to core permeability was confirmed.

Test set-up and test programme

Tests were performed in a 1.2 m wide and a 1.5 m deep wave flume. Two types of core material were used in the cross section shown in Fig. 1. The *fine* core material was sharp sand with gradation 2-3 mm, while the coarse material was crushed stones with gradation 5-8 mm. The Accropodes were 111 g having an equivalent cube length of $D_n = 0.036$ m and mass density $\rho_s = 2330$ kg/m^3.

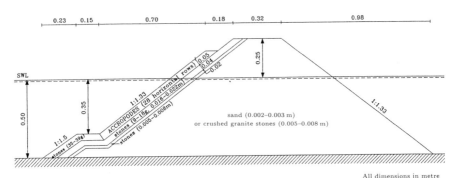

Fig. 1. Cross section of model.

The Accropode armour layer was built corresponding to the recommendation laid out by SOGREAH (1991) and guidelines given by M. Denechere, Manager of the Accropode Division at SOGREAH. Hence the armour layer consisted of a total of 504 armour units placed in 18 columns and 28 rows. As recommended by SOGREAH (1991) the distance between two horizontal rows was $0.6H_{B,Acc}$ and the horizontal mesh was $1.24H_{B,Acc}$, where $H_{B,Acc} = 0.052$m is the block height. See SOGREAH (1991) for further details.

Coastlines, structures and breakwaters. Thomas Telford, London, 1998

Irregular waves (JONSWAP-type) corresponding to Iribarren numbers $\xi_P = \frac{tan\alpha}{\sqrt{H_{mo}/L_p}} =$ 3.75 and 5.00, with increasing wave heights within the range $H_{mo} = 0.08$–0.20 m were used. Each seastate contained app. 1,000 waves. The target values for the applied sea states in one test are presented in Table 1. It is seen that one test is composed of seven seastates of increasing severity, so that the loading history on the test structure represents the build up of a natural storm. This test procedure also allows the armour layer to settle during the smaller wave heights ($H_{mo} = 0.08$ m and $H_{mo} = 0.10$ m) and thereby obtain its natural stability . The damage level D was defined as percentage of all units displaced a distance D_n or more, and was determined by photo overlay technique.

Table 1. *Target values for the applied sea states in each test.*

H_{mo} [m]*	0.08	0.10	0.12	0.14	0.16	0.18	0.20
fp [Hz] for $\xi_p = 3.75$	0.85	0.73	0.64	0.57	0.51	0.46	0.42
fp [Hz] for $\xi_p = 5.00$	0.57	0.47	0.40	0.35	0.31	0.28	0.26

* H_{mo} is the estimate on the significant wave height derived from the wave spectrum.

To prevent boundary effects along the sides of the flume, the damage analysis was carried out within a 0.75 m wide test section. This corresponds to 12 columns of Accropode units, i.e. the total number of Accropode units in the test section was 336.

After the end of each test (i.e., when the armour layer has failed) the test structure was totally rebuilt and prepared for the succeeding test.

Incident and reflected waves were separated by surface elevation analysis, Mansard and Funke (1980). Each test series was repeated minimum 5 times in order to evaluate the scatter.

A wave gauge was placed along the face of the armour layer in order to measure the run–up levels. The armour layer was extended to the top of the breakwater while recording run–up.

Surface Armouring of the fine core material

Little attention is in general paid to scaling of soil strength in hydraulic model tests with rubble mound breakwaters. This is mainly bacause soil mechanics failures in prototype structures are very rare and consequently not considered a problem. Moreover, correct scaling of soil strength is very difficult. In models with steep slopes and fine core materials the mound will be close to instability even without wave action. In the present case was used sharp sand with a narrow gradation, 2 mm $\leq d \leq 3$ mm, ($d_{50} = 2.8$ mm, $d_{15} = 2.3$ mm, $d_{85} = 3.1$ mm) in order to model the porous flow in a rather impermeable prototype structure. However, in the first test series a surprisingly low armour stability was observed. A closer investigation revealed that geotechnical sheet slip failure had occurred in the surface of the core material. Being very difficult to observe, especially in 3–dimensional models where cross section development cannot be studied through a glass wall, such failure can be misinterpreted as armour instability. To prevent further geotechnical problems it was chosen to reinforce the core with 90 steel wire spears placed in a mesh with a width of 15–16 cm. This method proved successful and it did not change the permeability of the core or caused bias of the stability of filter and armour layers.

Hydraulic stability of Accropode armour

Figs. 2, 3, and 4 show the test results given as the damage level D as function of the stability number $N_S = \frac{H_{mo}}{\Delta D_n}$, where $\Delta = \frac{\rho_s}{\rho_w} - 1 = 1.33$.

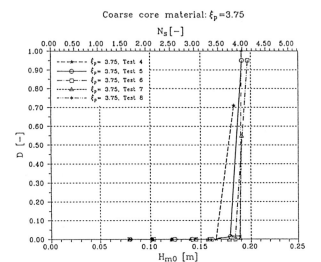

Fig. 2. Damage level (D) versus H_{mo} and N_S. Coarse core material and $\xi_p = 3.75$.

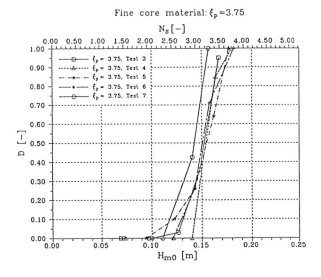

Fig. 3. Damage level (D) versus H_{mo} and N_S. Fine core material and $\xi_p = 3.75$.

Both fine and coarse core material: ξ_p=5.00

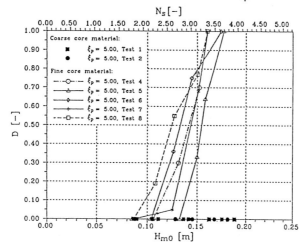

Fig. 4. Damage level (D) versus H_{mo} and N_S. Fine and coarse core materials and $\xi_p = 5.00$.

Figs. 5, 6, and 7 show the expected value μ and the 90% confidence levels of N_s based on the assumption of a Gaussian distribution for a certain damage level, i.e. $\mu \pm 1.64 \cdot \sigma$ where σ is the standard variation. The figures also show the coefficient of variation, $V = \sigma/\mu$.

Coarse core material: ξ_p=3.75

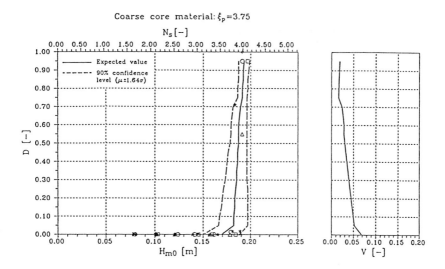

Fig. 5. Expected values and 90% confidence intervals of N_s. Coarse core material and $\xi_p = 3.75$.

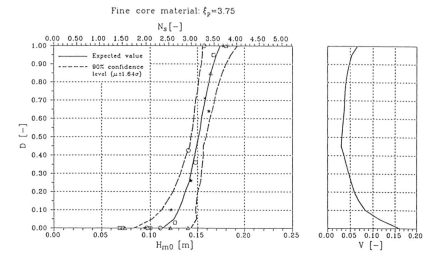

Fig. 6. *Expected values and 90% confidence intervals of* N_s. *Fine core material and* $\xi_p = 5.00$.

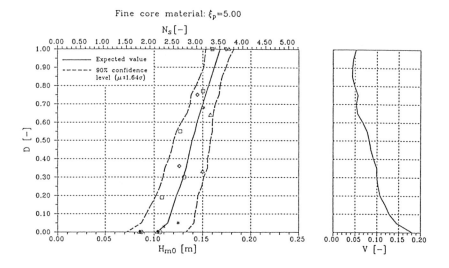

Fig. 7. *Expected values and 90% confidence intervals of* N_s. *Fine core material and* $\xi_p = 5.00$.

Tables 2 and 3 summarize the test results by giving the N_s-values corresponding to damage levels $D = 0\%$ and $D = 5\%$.

Table 2. Statistics of the stability number N_s corresponding to zero and 5% damage. Coarse core material.

	Coarse core material					
Iribarren number, ξ_p	3.75			5.00		
Statistical parameter	$\mu - 1.64\sigma$	μ	$\mu + 1.64\sigma$	$\mu - 1.64\sigma$	μ	$\mu + 1.64\sigma$
Stability number corresponding to zero damage, $N_{s,0\%}$	3.1	3.5	3.9	-	$> 3.9^*$	-
Stability number corresponding to 5% damage, $N_{s,5\%}$	3.5	3.8	4.1	-	-	-

* As it appears from Fig. 4 no damage occurred for the coarse core material and $\xi_p = 5.00$. Therefore the highest N_s-value obtained during the test is presented. The actual $N_{s,0\%}$ is of course larger than this value.

Table 3. Statistics of the stability number N_s corresponding to zero and 5% damage. Fine core material.

	Fine core material					
Iribarren number, ξ_p	3.75			5.00		
Statistical parameter	$\mu - 1.64\sigma$	μ	$\mu + 1.64\sigma$	$\mu - 1.64\sigma$	μ	$\mu + 1.64\sigma$
Stability number corresponding to zero damage, $N_{s,0\%}$	1.7	2.4	3.0	1.5	2.1	2.8
Stability number corresponding to 5% damage, $N_{s,5\%}$	2.1	2.6	3.1	1.8	2.4	2.9

Influence of core permeability on Accropode stability

For rather massive single layer armour like Accropode armour with relatively small pore volume it is expected that low porosity core material has a significant negative influence on the stability. The present test results confirm this.

Not only the magnitude of the stability number seems to be influenced by the permeability of the core, but also the evolution of the damage differs significantly in the two cases. The stability is significantly higher in the case of coarse core material. However, the structure fails very suddenly, almost as a collapse in the case of coarse core material, whereas the failure of the structure with fine core material develops less rapidly.

For the short waves ($\xi_p = 3.75$) the expected value of $N_{s,0\%}$ is 3.5 for the coarse core material and only 2.4 for the fine core material, i.e. almost a difference of 50%. For the long waves ($\xi_p = 5.00$) the significance of the core permeability is even larger, since the difference is in the order of 100%, still with the coarse core material yielding the highest stability numbers. This large difference in hydraulic stability is magnified by the apparently opposite influence of the Iribarren number for the coarse and the fine core material.

The reason for the generally smaller stability in the case of fine core material is, that because of the relatively impermeable core the water cannot percolate into the voids of the core, if no water is allowed to percolate into the voids of the structure, the long waves ($\xi_p = 5.00$) will be more damaging than the short waves, since each wave carry more water onto the structure than for short waves. On the other hand, in the case of coarse core material, the long waves have time enough to penetrate deep into the structure, and thereby reducing the flow in the very armour layer. The short waves have less time to penetrate into the core, and hence a larger amount of the flow is situated in the armour layer, and thereby reducing its stability. The tendencies described above supports the *reservoir effect* presented by Burcharth & Thompson (1982).

Comparison with results from other researchers

A few papers dealing with the hydraulic stability of Accropode armour have been published during the recent years. The most important are Kobayashi and Kaihatsu (1994), Holtzhausen and Zwamborn (1991) and van der Meer (1988b). The results found by these researchers are presented in Table 4 together with the results of the present study and a previous study at Aalborg University (1995).

Table 4. Results obtained by other researchers and results from the present and a previous study at Aalborg University.

Researchers	Reported Stability number for a slope 1 : 1.33		Reported (N_s, ξ_p)-relationship
Kobayashi and Kaihatsu (1994)	$N_{s,0\%} = 3.5 - 4.0$	$(\xi_p \approx 2.4 - 3.9)$	Decreasing N_s with increasing ξ_p for gravel filter layer. No influence of ξ_p for a filter layer of concrete blocks.
Holtzhausen and Zwamborn (1991)	$N_{s,1\%} = 3.0$	$(\xi_p \approx 4.3)$	Increasing N_s with increasing ξ_p (this was reported on basis of tests on other slopes than 1 : 1.33)
van der Meer (1988b)	$N_{s,0\%} = 3.7$	$(\xi_p \approx 2.6 - 4.5)$	No influence of ξ_p [**]
Aalborg University (1995) [*]	$N_{s,0\%} \approx 2.0 - 2.5$	$(\xi_p \approx 4)$	Nothing reported
Present study (Coarse core material)	$N_{s,0\%} = 3.5 \pm 0.4$ $N_{s,0\%} > 3.9$	$(\xi_p = 3.75)$ $(\xi_p = 5.00)$	Increasing N_s with increasing ξ_p
Present study (Fine core material)	$N_{s,0\%} = 2.4 \pm 0.6$ $N_{s,0\%} = 2.1 \pm 0.6$	$(\xi_p = 3.75)$ $(\xi_p = 5.00)$	Decreasing N_s with increasing ξ_p

[*]   Same structural layout as in the present study with fine core material.

[**] van der Meer tested two models, a high and a lower. For the higher model where no overtopping took place, increasing N_s with increasing ξ_p was recorded.

However, due to differences in the experimental set-up and especially in the test procedure it is difficult to perform a proper comparison to the results of the present study. For example the other researchers performed their tests with constant peak period, whereas the present tests were performed with constant Iribarren number. This means that the loading history varies in the different tests, making a proper comparison of the test results difficult. The significant influence of core permeability, which has been verified in the present study, is another perfect example on why different experimental set-ups yield different results. To enable a comparison of the permeability of the different structures, their cross sections have been sketched in Figure 8. From this it is also seen that the crest height relative to the Accropode size (D_n) differs significantly. This certainly influences the stability as larger overtopping increases the front armour stability. Moreover, the height of the armour layer (i.e. number of rows of Accropodes) varies considerably. This also influences the stability because prestressing due to the weight of the blocks is significant on steep slopes like the 1:1.33 slope.

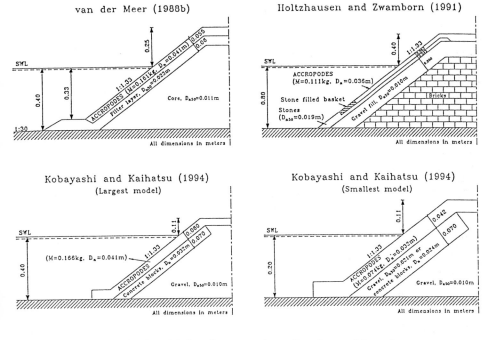

Fig. 8. *Cross sections of models by other researchers. Drawings not to scale.*

Run–up

Selected run-up data have been plotted in Figs. 9 and 10 for the case of coarse core material and fine core material, respectively. $R_{u,2\%}$ is the run-up level corresponding to an exceedence probability of 2% and $h=0.50$ m is the water depth in front of the structure.

Coarse core material

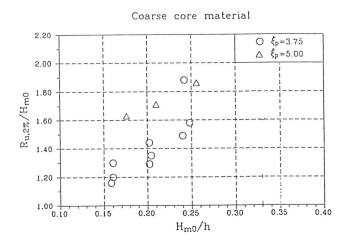

Fig. 9. *Run–up in the case of coarse core material.*

Fine core material

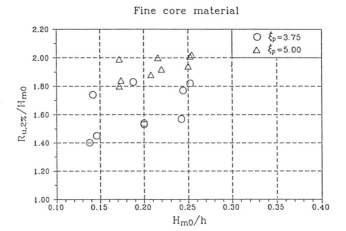

Fig. 10. Run–up in the case of fine core material.

It is seen that the relative run–up $R_{u,2\%}/H_{mo}$ increases with H_{mo} for constant ξ_p. Moreover, the relative run–up is 5–15% larger for $\xi_p = 5.00$ than for $\xi_p = 3.75$, and 10–15% larger for the fine core compared to the coarse core.

Prototype interpretation of model test results

The significant influence of the core permeability on the armour stability and the run–up makes it important to consider porous flow scale effects when designing a model of a prototype or, the other way around, when converting model test results to prototype conditions.

Generally, in order to avoid bias in the hydraulic response at the surface of the breakwater it is necessary to ensure similarity between the flow fields in the prototype and model cores. This again requires the hydraulic gradient I to be the same in geometrically similar points, i.e.

$$I_P = I_M \tag{1}$$

in which subindex P and M refer to prototype and model, respectively.

I can be estimated from the Forchheimer equation, for example the formulation for the one–dimensional, steady flow case, given by Burcharth et al. (1995)

$$I = \alpha \left(\frac{1-n}{n}\right)^2 \frac{\nu}{g\,d^2} \left(\frac{U}{n}\right) + \beta \frac{1-n}{n} \frac{1}{g\,d} \left(\frac{U}{n}\right)^2 \tag{2}$$

in which

$$
\begin{aligned}
n &= \text{porosity} \\
\nu &= \text{kinematic viscosity of water} \\
d &= \text{characteristic diameter of grains} \\
U &= \text{discharge velocity, } \tfrac{U}{n} = \text{pore velocity} \\
g &= \text{gravitational constant} \\
\alpha \text{ and } \beta &= \text{coefficients dependent on Reynolds' number } Re = \dfrac{U \cdot d}{\nu},
\end{aligned}
$$

and on grading and shape of the grain material.

For given length scale ratio $\dfrac{\ell_P}{\ell_M} = \lambda$ the velocity scale is $\dfrac{U_P}{U_M} = \sqrt{\lambda}$ in a Froude model. Given f.ex. the prototype values of n_P, ν_P, d_P, α_P, β_P and U_P and the model values of n_M, ν_M, α_M, β_M, $U_M = U_P/\sqrt{\lambda}$ it is possible by the use of eqs (1) and (2) to calculate d_M.

For the presented two cases of core material the characteristic pore velocities U under design conditions were estimated to be $\frac{1}{50}$ and $\frac{1}{200}$ of a characteristic surface velocity $U_W = \sqrt{g\,H_s}$, for the coarse and fine core materials, respectively. The following values of α and β estimated from information given in Burcharth et al. (1995) were applied, Table 5.

Table 5.

Gradation	Re	α	β
narrow	< 5	650	0
narrow	5–600	360	3.6
wide	> 600	13,000	3.6
very wide	> 600	13,000	4.0

The length scale in the present study was $\lambda = 54.6$.

The relationship between model and prototype core characteristics is as follows:

Coarse core. $N_s = 3.34$
Prototype $d_{50} = 0.200\,\text{m}$, $\dfrac{d_{85}}{d_{15}} = 3.3$
1:54.6 model $D_{50} = 0.0060\,\text{m}$, gradation 0.0050–0.0080 m

Fine core. $N_s = 2.50$
Prototype $d_{50} = 0.050\,\text{m}$, $\dfrac{d_{85}}{d_{15}} = 5.5$
1:54.6 model $D_{50} = 0.0028\,\text{m}$, $D_{50} = 0.0028\,\text{m}$, $D_{85}/D_{15} = 3.1/2.3 = 1.35$,
gradation 0.0020–0.0030 m

Comparison with core permeability influence on rock armour stability
van der Meer (1988a) investigated the sensitivity of conventional two–layer rock armour stability to core permeability. Generally the same trends, also with respect to influence of ξ, were observed. A quantitative comparison of the two sets of results can be made if it is assumed that van der Meer's stability formulae can be expanded to cover also a 1:1.33 slope.

The van der Meer formulae for rock reads:

$$N_s \cdot \sqrt{\xi_m} = 6.2 \cdot P^{0.18} \left(S/\sqrt{N} \right)^{0.2} \qquad \text{plunging waves} \qquad (3)$$

$$N_s = 1.0 \cdot P^{-0.13} \, \xi_m^P \left(S/\sqrt{N} \right)^{0.2} \sqrt{cot\alpha} \qquad \text{surging waves} \qquad (4)$$

The intersection between eqs (3) and (4) is given by

$$\xi_m = \left(6.2 \cdot P^{0.31} \sqrt{tan\alpha} \right)^{1/(P+0.5)} \qquad (5)$$

The Accropode test conditions correspond to:

$$N \;\; = \;\; 1,000 \;, \text{ number of waves}$$

$$\cot \alpha \;\; = \;\; 1.33$$

$$S \;\; = \;\; \begin{cases} 2 \quad \text{for} \quad D = 0\% \\ \simeq 8 \quad \text{for} \quad D = 5\% \end{cases} \qquad \text{damage level}$$

$$\xi_m \;\; = \;\; \begin{cases} 3.00 \quad \text{for} \quad \xi_P = 3.75 \\ 4.00 \quad \text{for} \quad \xi_P = 5.00 \end{cases}$$

$$P \;\; \simeq \;\; \begin{cases} 0.2 \quad \text{fine core material} \\ 0.4 \quad \text{coarse core material} \end{cases}$$

By the use of eqs (3)–(5) we get the following N_s–values for rock slopes, Table 6:

Table 6. Approximate values for rock armour on 1:1.33 slope.

	fine core		coarse core	
ξ_P	3.75	5.0	3.75	5.0
$N_{s, D=0\%}$	1.54	1.33	1.75	1.52
$N_{s, D=5\%}$	2.04	1.77	2.31	2.01

By comparing with the Accropode results given in Tables 2 and 3 it is seen that the sensitivity to core permeability is much higher for Accropode armour than for conventional rock armour. This conclusion also holds for rock armour on 1:2 slopes.

Conclusions

- Stability factors and related statistical uncertainties are given for Accropode®️ armour on 1:1.33 slope based on model tests with coarse and fine core materials.
- The large sensitivity of Accropode armour stability to core permeability is demonstrated.
- An example of scaling core material between model and prototype is given.
- Fine core material reduces the stability considerably. However, the failure develops more gradually than in case of coarse core material.
- The large sensitivity makes it very important to scale the core permeability in Accropode models correctly with respect to the porous flow.
- It is equally important to control the core permeability during construction of prototype structures.

References

Burcharth, H.F. and Thompson, A.C. (1982): *Stability of Armour Units in Oscillatory Flow.* Paper presented at Coastal Structures '83, Washington D.C., USA, March 1983. Aalborg University, November 1982.

Burcharth, H.F. and Andersen, O.H. (1995): *On the one-dimensional steady and unsteady porous flow equations.* Coastal Engineering, 24 (1995), pp 233-257.

Christensen, M. and Burcharth, H.F. (1995): *Hydraulic Stability of Single-Layer Dolos and Accropode Armour Layers.* Contract: MAS2-CT92-0042, Rubble Mound Breakwater Failure Modes. Department of Civil Engineering, Aalborg University, Denmark. December 1995.

Hedar, P.A. (1960): *Stability of rock–fill breakwaters.* Doctoral Thesis, Univ. of Göteborg, Sweden.

Hedar, P.Å. (1986): *Armour layer stability of rubble–mound breakwaters.* Proc. ASCE, Journal of WPC and OE, Vol. 112, No. 3.

Holtzhausen, A.H. and Zwamborn, J.A. (1991): *Stability of Accropode(R) and comparison with dolosse.* Coastal Engineering, 15 (1991), pp.59-86, Elsevier Science B.V., The Netherlands

Kobayashi, M. and Kaihatsu, S. (1994): *Hydraulic Characteristics and Field Experience of New Wave Dissipating Concrete Blocks - (ACCROPODE).* Proc. of the 24th International Conference on Coastal Engineering (ICCE), October 23-28, 1994, Kobe, Japan.

Mansard, E.P.D. and Funke, E. (1980): *The Measurement of Incident and Reflected Spectra Using a Least Squares Method.* Proc. 17th Int. Conf. on Coastal Engineering, Sydney, Australia.

SOGREAH (1991): *Accropode - Preliminary Study and Placing of Armourings.* SOGREAH Ingénierie, Grenoble, France.

van der Meer, J.W. (1988a): *Rock Slopes and Gravel Beaches under Wave Attack.* Doctoral Thesis approved by Delft University of Technology. Reprinted as Delft Hydraulics Publications, number 396. Delft Hydraulics, The Netherlands.

van der Meer, J.W. (1988b): *Stability of cubes, tetrapods and accropode.* Proc. Conf. Breakwaters '88. England. Design of Breakwaters. Thomas Telford Limited, London, 1988.

vertical   structures: new   prediction
ınt for shallow water conditions

NWH Allsop
llingford, Wallingford, OX10 8BA, UK

SYNOPSIS

One of the primary objectives of an engineer designing coastal sea defence structures is to limit overtopping discharge to acceptable levels. It is usual for engineers to establish limiting tolerable discharges for design wave conditions, and then use prediction methods and physical model studies to confirm that discharge limits are not exceeded.

This paper examines the influence of shallow water conditions on the overtopping performance of vertical wall structures. The results of model tests carried out at HR Wallingford are used to formulate equations to predict overtopping discharge. Measurements from a site in north Wales are used to validate the equations. In addition, a method is outlined for predicting the maximum single overtopping event in a sequence of waves. This information is of considerable importance in determining overtopping limits to minimise danger to users.

INTRODUCTION

A significant proportion of the United Kingdom coastline is protected from flooding by vertical sea walls. In deep water the response characteristics of vertical walls are relatively straight forward as energy is either reflected, or transmitted by overtopping. Most sea walls are commonly fronted by sand / shingle beaches or rock platforms and water depths are much less. Any bathymetry may have a significant effect in changing the form of the wave, and hence in modifying the overtopping performance. The form of waves breaking onto vertical walls depends critically on the local sea bed slope, the local water depth, and the incident wave conditions. These processes are complex, and cannot yet be reproduced by numerical models. Design methods therefore rely on the use of empirical prediction methods, supported where appropriate by generic or site specific physical model tests.

As the form of the wave reaching the structure is so important, a good estimation of wave conditions at the toe is essential. All the empirical formulae reported here are based on reliable wave measurements taken during physical model studies. This paper describes prediction methods and relationships between a number of overtopping parameters, which include the mean overtopping discharge, the number of waves overtopping, and the maximum volume overtopping per wave. New recommendations for tolerable discharges are made, based upon individual wave overtopping volumes rather than mean discharges.

PREDICTION METHODS BASED ON PHYSICAL MODEL STUDIES
Background

Previous work by Goda (1985) investigated approach slopes of 1:10 and 1:30 and offshore sea steepness of $s_{om} = 0.012$, 0.017 and 0.036. Many of the structures around the UK coast are, however, located behind beaches in relatively shallow water where the interaction of the incident wave with the bathymetry and the seawall become more important. The conditions used in the prediction method by Goda are therefore not representative of conditions around the UK coastline, where storm waves are generally steeper and approach bathymetries are generally shallower. Herbert (1993) extended the work of Goda (1985) to slopes of 1:100 and S_{om} of up to 0.06. Both methods are based on offshore wave conditions and assume a constant approach slope, so the form of the incident wave at the toe of the structure is not taken into account. Both methods are graphical and hence require interpolation.

Recently, Franco et al (1994) and Van der Meer and Janssen (1995) have used an exponential relationship to predict the mean overtopping discharge (q) at sea walls :-

$$Q\# = a \exp(-bR') \tag{1}$$

Where a and b are coefficients. $Q\#$ is the dimensionless discharge given by :-

$$Q\# = q/(gH_{si}^{3})^{0.5} \tag{2}$$

and R' is the dimensionless crest freeboard given by :-

$$R' = (R_c/H_{si})\,(1/\gamma_x) \tag{3}$$

R_c is the crest freeboard and H_{si} is the inshore significant wave height. γ_x is a reduction factor and is applicable to a wide range of structures, including simple vertical walls, wave screens and rubble mound protection. For deep water conditions the overtopping of a simple vertical wall may be predicted using coefficients proposed by Franco et al (1994) :-

$$Q\# = 0.2 \exp(-4.295\ R_c/H_{si}) \tag{4}$$

Equation 4 is valid within the range $0.9 < R_c/H_{si} < 2.2$.

Results from physical model tests at Wallingford (Allsop et al (1995)) and independent tests in the Netherlands by De Waal (1994) covered a wider range of relative freeboards $0.03 < R_c/H_{si} < 3.2$. These data sets are compared with Franco et al's (1994) prediction line in Figure 1. Franco et al's (1994) formula significantly under-estimates overtopping discharges at larger values of R_c/H_{si}. As the bathymetry and the crest of the model structure were fixed, high values of R_c/H_{si} corresponded to low values of h_s/H_{si} and therefore wave breaking onto the structure was more likely. Scatter of the data increases above $R_c/H_{si} = 1.5$, suggesting that the simple empirical formula does not take into account the effect of wave breaking onto the structure.

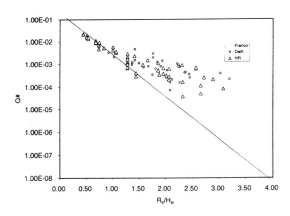

Figure 1   **Comparison of independent overtopping data**

Franco et al (1994) also showed that for relatively deep-water conditions the percentage of waves overtopping the structure, $N_{wo\%}$, may be related to R_c/H_{si} (equation 14). The result of equation 14 is plotted in figure 2 along with the data set from HRWallingford.

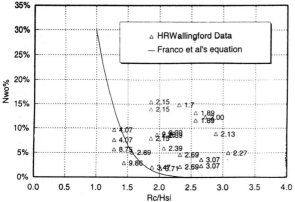

Figure 2   The relationship between the percentage of overtopping waves and R_c/H_{si}

Each data point is labelled with the ratio h_s/H_{si}, where h_s is the depth of water in front of the structure and H_{si} is the inshore wave height. The new data confirms the fit line of Franco et al (1994) for non-breaking waves, i.e, when $h_s/H_{si} > 3.0$. For breaking waves, however, ($h_s/H_{si} < 3.0$) the data are very scattered.   Figures 1 and 2 suggest that, for vertical walls subject to breaking waves, the mean discharge and the number of waves overtopping may be underestimated if the equations describing non-breaking waves (equations 1 and 14) are used. A new approach is required for situations in which breaking waves predominate. This is dealt with in the following sections.

Mean overtopping discharge of vertical structures

The influence of shallow water on overtopping discharges over vertical walls was examined by Allsop et al (1995). For simple vertical walls constructed on shallow sloping bathymetry a wave breaking parameter, h^*, was defined which dictates whether waves at the structure are dominated by impact (breaking) waves or by deflecting/pulsating (non-breaking) waves. h^* is defined by :-

$$h^* = (h_s/H_{si}) \, (2\pi h_s/gT_{mi}^2) \tag{5}$$

where T_{mi} is the inshore mean wave period

Deflecting waves dominate when $h^* > 0.3$. Impacting waves dominate when $h^* \leq 0.3$. The formulation of h^* reflects the fact that waves are more likely to break if the wavelength or the wave height is large compared to water depth.

Separating their data according to h^*, Allsop et al (1995) determined that, for $h^* > 0.3$, the mean overtopping discharge was accurately described by an equation similar to equation 1:-

$$Q\# = 0.05 \exp (-2.78 \, R_c/H_{si}), \text{ for } h^* > 0.3 \tag{6}$$

For $h^* \leq 0.3$, however, a different relationship was determined. To reflect the importance of wave breaking, new dimensionless discharge and freeboard parameters were defined thus :-

$$Q_h = q / (g \, h_s^3)^{0.5} / h^{*2} \tag{7}$$

$$R_h = (R_c/H_{si}) \, h^* \tag{8}$$

Examination of all the results for which h* ≤ 0.3 produced the following relationship :-

$$Q_h = 1.37 \times 10^{-4} \, R_h^{-3.24}, \text{ for } h^* \leq 0.3 \tag{9}$$

Equation 9 thus provides a prediction of the mean overtopping discharge of a vertical wall subject to breaking waves.

For composite vertical walls on submerged rubble mounds the wave breaking parameter is re-defined using the depth of water over the mound, d, instead of h_s as follows :-

$$d^* = (d/H_{si}) \, (2\pi h_s/g T_{mi}^{\,2}) \tag{10}$$

When $d^* > 0.3$ the mound has little effect on the incident wave. In this case the structure behaves as a plain vertical wall and, since $h^* > d^*$, deflected wave conditions apply. The overtopping discharge is then described by equation 6.

When $d^* \leq 0.3$, however, the mound is larger and begins to affect the incident wave. The dimensionless discharge and freeboard are then defined in a similar manner to those of vertical walls (equations 7 and 8) as follows :-

$$Q_d = q / (g d^3)^{0.5} / d^{*2} \tag{11}$$

$$R_d = (R_c/H_{si}) \, (d/H_{si}) \, d^* \tag{12}$$

The discharge can then be determined from :-

$$Q_d = 4.63 \times 10^{-4} \, R_d^{-2.79}, \text{ for } d^* \leq 0.3 \tag{13}$$

When $d^* \leq 0.3$ both deflected or impacting waves may occur. Equation 13 applies strictly only to impacting waves. However as the overtopping resulting from impacting waves is generally greater than that resulting from deflecting waves, equation 13 can be applied conservatively to the deflecting wave case.

Most design methods for composite vertical walls, whether the caisson is supported on a natural rock reef or on dredged fill, recommend that the foundations should not cause waves to break onto the structure. Allsop et al (1996) provided a decision chart to guide engineers away from designs likely to cause breaking onto vertical walls. Although the chart was intended to define wave loading, it is also relevant for wave overtopping. The method of Allsop et al (1996) will also be invaluable during the rehabilitation of deteriorating seawalls.

Number of Waves Overtopping
An intermediate step in the estimation of peak discharge is to estimate the number of waves that overtop the structure. Franco et al (1994) developed an equation based on tests in relatively deep water :-

$$N_{wo}/N_z = \exp \left(- (R_c/H_{si} / 0.91)^2\right) \tag{14}$$

where N_{wo} is the number of waves overtopping and N_z is the number of waves in the sample.

The number of waves overtopping the structure equates to the number of run-up events exceeding the crest level. As run-up level in deep water is dependent on wave height, the distribution of overtopping events is of Raleigh form.

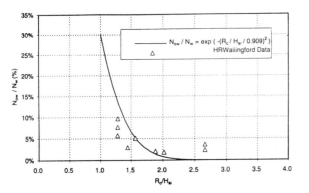

Results of the tests conducted by HRWallingford are shown in Figure 2 with equation 14. The data labels indicate values of h_s/H_{si}. Values of $h_s/H_{si} > 3.0$ indicate relatively deep water for which deflected waves predominate. It can be seen that equation 14 offers a reasonable approximation to the results for $h_s/H_{si}>3.0$. When water is shallow and breaking waves predominate, this equation under-predicts N_{wo}. It was clear that the results for breaking conditions must be distinguished from those for non-breaking conditions, and that they required a different method of analysis. The fit through the deflecting data results only is shown in Figure 3.

Figure 3   Number of waves overtopping (non-breaking wave conditions only)

$$N_{wo}/N_w = \exp\left(- (R_c/H_{si} / 0.909)^2\right) \qquad (15)$$

Although the data set is rather limited in size, it produces a very similar result to that of Franco et al (1994).

Where waves break in significant numbers the distribution of individual wave heights diverges from the Raleigh form. In addition the mechanism by which individual waves overtop the structure is altered, being no longer dominated by run-up.

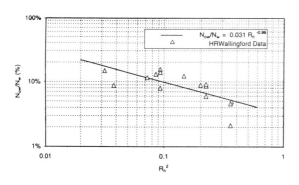

Allsop et al (1995) found that when $h^* > 0.3$, the overtopping discharge is well described by an equation relating it to R_c/H_{si}. When $h^* \leq 0.3$ however it was found that the overtopping discharge was better described by relating it to, R_h, defined in equation 8.

Figure 4   Number of waves overtopping (breaking wave conditions only)

The data of Allsop et al (1995) concerning the number of waves overtopping, N_{wo}, was re-examined. Values of N_{wo} are plotted against R_h for all results with $h^* \leq 0.3$ in Figure 4, and produce the following equation :-

$$N_{ow}/N_w = 0.031 \ R_h^{-0.99}$$ (16)

It is interesting to note that the proportion of waves overtopping is most over-predicted when $h* = 0.26$, close to the upper limit of $h* \leq 0.3$.

It is recommended that when $h* > 0.3$, the proportion of waves overtopping the structure should be estimated using equation 14. When $h* \leq 0.3$ equation 16 should be used.

Maximum Individual Overtopping Event
Given that the number of overtopping events N_{wo} and the mean discharge q can be predicted using the methods described above, it is now possible to estimate the magnitude of the largest individual overtopping event.

The volume of individual overtopping events, V, can be described by a Weibull distribution:-

$$P(V) = 1 - \exp(- ((V-C)/A)^B)$$ (17)

where $P(V) =$ probability of non-exceedance and A, B and C are empirical coefficients. The coefficient C represents the lower limit of the data, representing the minimum individual volume that the experimental method can distinguish.

The maximum expected individual overtopping volume, V_{max}, in a sequence of N_{wo} events is then given by :-

$$V_{max} = C + A \ (\ln(N_{wo}))^{1/B}$$ (18)

Franco et al (1994) determined values of A and B for overtopping of a vertical wall in relatively deep water giving an expression for A in terms of V_{bar} the average individual overtopping volume :-

$$A = 0.84V_{bar}, \text{ and } B = 0.75$$ (19)

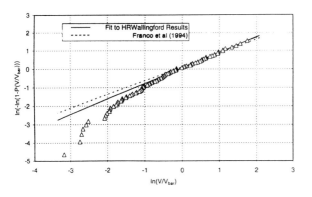

A two parameter Weibull distribution (assuming $C = 0$) was fitted to the results of the HRWallingford data. Sample probability plots of V/V_{bar} for impact and deflecting conditions are shown in Figures 5 and 6 respectively. The results correspond well with the Weibull distribution, except at low values of V/V_{bar}, where there is a divergence. Accurate prediction of discharges at low probabilities of non-exceedance is of little interest

Figure 5   Distribution of impacting overtopping events

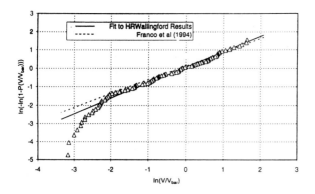

Figure 6   Distribution of deflecting overtopping events

to the present study. At high probabilities of non-exceedance, the inclusion of C makes little difference to the shape of the distribution as C is very small for all the data sets used. It was therefore decided that the Weibull distribution should be fitted to values of V > V_{bar} only, as this gives the most reliable estimate of V_{max}.

The average value of B for deflected waves (B = 0.754) was very similar to Franco et al's result of B=0.75. For impact dominated waves B was found to average 0.854.

Values of A can be determined from the relation:-

$$V_{bar} = C + A \, \Gamma \, (1 + 1/B) \qquad (20)$$

Where Γ is the Gamma function that can be found in mathematical tables. For deflecting waves A= 0.843 V_{bar} (compared with A = 0.84 V_{bar} from Franco et al (1994)), but for impacts, A=0.922 V_{bar}.

It is recommended that when deflected waves predominate (i.e., when h* > 0.3) the maximum individual overtopping volume, V_{max}, in a series of N_{wo} overtopping waves, is predicted by:-

$$V_{max} = 0.843 \ V_{bar} \ (\ln(N_{wo}))^{1/0.754} \qquad (21)$$

When impact waves predominate (i.e., when h* < 0.3) the maximum individual overtopping can be estimated using :-

$$V_{max} = 0.922 V_{bar} \ (\ln(N_{wo}))^{1/0.854} \qquad (22)$$

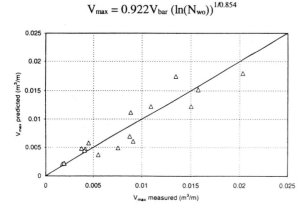

Values of V_{max} estimated from equations 21 and 22 are presented in Figure 7, plotted against measured values of V_{max}. A reasonable correlation is obtained.

Figure 7   Correlation between predicted and measured maximum individual overtopping volume

Relationship between Mean Discharge and Peak Events

Overtopping limits are generally defined in terms of the tolerable mean discharge, q. This approach is valid when considering the structures ability to withstand wave attack and to prevent damage. From the perspective of the safety of personnel and vehicles, however, peak events are probably much more significant. The analysis presented above may be used to develop relationships between mean discharge and peak events to be used in the setting of tolerable discharges.

Deflecting Waves

Deflected waves are those for which $h^* > 0.3$. The mean overtopping discharge, q can be estimated using equation 6, and the proportion of overtopping waves N_{wo} using equation 14. The average volume, V_{bar}, per overtopping wave can then be calculated. The volume of the largest overtopping event in a sequence of waves can then be estimated using equation 21.

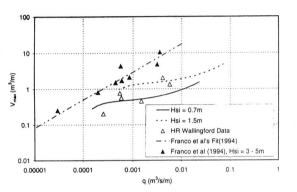

Measured values of V_{max} against q for the HRWallingford tests are plotted in Figure 8. Each data point represents a test having a length corresponding to 1177 wave periods. A nominal scale has been applied to present the data as prototype equivalent values. Incident wave height ranged H_{si} from 0.7m to1.5m.

Figure 8   **Relationship between mean overtopping discharge and the peak overtopping volume, deflecting waves**

Predictions using equations 6, 14 and 21 for $H_{si} = 0.7$m and 1.5m are also plotted in Figure 8. For a given value of q, the maximum individual overtopping volume increases with increasing H_{si}. This is in accordance with the findings of van der Meer & Janssen (1995) for overtopping of sloping dykes.

The results of Franco et al's (1994) tests using 1000 waves are also plotted in Figure 8. The wave heights were varied from 3m to 5m, considerably higher than those used in this study. The values of V_{max} measured are accordingly higher. The general trend, however, follows that of the HRWallingford results.

Impacting Waves

Impacting waves are those with $h^* \leq 0.3$. The mean overtopping discharge, q can be estimated using equation 9, and the proportion of overtopping waves using the new equation 16. The average volume, V_{bar}, per overtopping wave can then be calculated. The volume of the largest overtopping event in a sequence of waves can then be estimated using equation 22.

The results of the impacting waves using HRWallingford data are shown in Figure 9. The incident wave conditions ranges from H_{si} = 0.16m to 0.2m, T_m = 1.59s to 2.5s, and h_s from 0.34m to 0.43m. The h^* parameter, which governs the "breaking performance" of the waves, varies from 0.1 to 0.26. Also plotted on Figure 9 is a prediction line valid between h^*=0.1 to 0.26. The predicted value of V_{max} is fairly insensitive to changes in h^*.

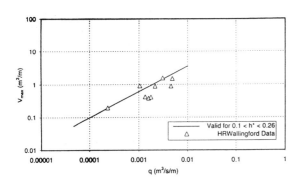

Figure 9 **Relationship between mean overtopping discharge and the peak overtopping, volume. impacting waves**

used to estimate the peak flow if required.

Model tests suggest the time over which the peak individual volume is discharged is approximately 40% of the mean wave period. This relation can be

COMPARISON OF PREDICTION METHODS WITH PROTOTYPE DATA
Field study
A vertical wall at Colwyn Bay in North Wales frequently suffers significant overtopping during storms from the north and north-east (Herbert 1996). The structure affords protection to a promenade and roadway immediately behind its crest. The coastline is characterised by a sandy

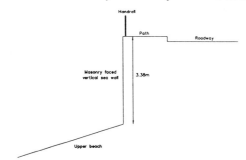

Figure 10 **Vertical stone faced seawall at Old Colwyn**

lower beach with some patches of cobbles and an upper shingle beach, the width of which varies along the frontage. A vertical stone-faced sea wall, approximately 3m high is sited at the rear of the beach, a typical cross section is illustrated in Figure 10. Overtopping measurements were undertaken in a series of short-term deployments during storm events in late January 1994. Storm events were predicted by identifying spring tidal dates and monitoring the Meteorological Office Weathercall forecasting system during periods of storm activity.

A wave/tide recorder was used to measure the inshore wave conditions and water levels. A large calibrated tank captured overtopping water. Each series of overtopping measurements was completed over about three hours during periods of high tides.

The data from the wave/tide recorder was filtered using high and low pass filters to separate

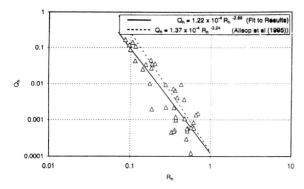

Figure 11 legend text:
$Q_h = 1.22 \times 10^{-4} R_h^{-2.88}$ (Fit to Results)
$Q_h = 1.37 \times 10^{-4} R_h^{-3.24}$ (Allsop et al (1995))

Figure 11   Comparison of prototype overtopping discharge and prediction values

the wave component (high frequency) from the water level record (low frequency). The wave record was analysed using spectral method to give the inshore significant wave height, H_{si}, and mean and peak wave periods, T_{mi} and T_{pi}. At the shoreline the direction of wave energy was perpendicular to the axis of the sea wall within $\pm$ 10°. Analysis of the wave conditions at the site indicated a mean wave period of approximately 5-6 seconds so an averaging interval of 10 minutes was equivalent to about 100 waves.

Prediction curve validation

The methods described previously to predict mean overtopping discharge were used to test prediction against measurements from the field. Equation 5 assessed the form of the wave reaching the structure, and it was found that $h^* < 3.0$ for all but one of the analysis intervals, which suggested that impacting waves dominate. For impacting waves the non-dimensional overtopping discharge Q_h is given by equation 9. The field data and the trend line by equation 9 are compared in Figure 11, with relatively good agreement. A best fit line is also shown.

Tolerable discharges

Presently accepted international guidelines (from Fukuda (1974)) summarised in Simm (1991) suggest the following admissible overtopping discharges for vehicles and pedestrians:-

Vehicles
Safe at all speeds	< 0.001 l/s/m
Unsafe at high speed	0.001 - 0.02 l/s/m
Unsafe at any speed	> 0.02 l/s/m

Pedestrians
Wet, but not uncomfortable	< 0.004 l/s/m
Uncomfortable but not dangerous	0.004 - 0.03 l/s/m
Dangerous	> 0.03 l/s/m

These limits have always been defined in terms of mean discharge. The analysis presented above demonstrates that, for a given level of q, the volume of the largest overtopping event will vary with wave conditions, thus changing the peak discharge / individual volume to be resisted. It is probable that tolerable discharges configured in terms of peak discharges or maximum individual volumes may give more reliable estimates of safety.

Franco et al (1994) conducted experiments that investigated safe overtopping limits for pedestrians on or behind the crests of vertical walls. It was demonstrated using model tests that the probability of a pedestrian falling over could be related to individual overtopping volume. An individual volume was considered as "safe" if it created a less than 10% chance of the pedestrian falling over. The upper "safe" limit thus determined was $0.1 \text{m}^3/\text{m}$. For Franco's tests shown in Figure 9, this corresponds to a mean discharge of approximately 0.02 l/s/m. This is very close to the lower limit to the "dangerous" zone suggested by Fukuda (1974) and still used today in international guidelines. Franco also defines a "very dangerous" overtopping volume of $2.0\text{m}^3/\text{m}$ causing a greater than 90% chance of a pedestrian falling over. This corresponded to a mean discharge of 0.2 l/s/m.

Franco also noted that an individual could be unbalanced when struck by an individual volume of only $0.05\text{m}^3/\text{m}$. This figure resulted from a test conducted on a person rather than on a model and can thus be considered to be more realistic.

Although not a direct objective of the Colwyn Bay fieldwork deployment, some consideration was given to the likely dangers posed by overtopping of the sea wall. Over one of the measurement periods, the maximum mean discharge at the crest was 16 l/s/m.

Work at the crest of the sea wall was able to proceed safely at discharges up to 0.1 l/s/m. For discharges in excess of this personnel could not safely be permanently positioned at the crest of the structure. It was estimated, using the methods outlined in the preceding sections of this paper, that the maximum individual overtopping volume, V_{max}, occurring over the critical period was $0.04\text{m}^3/\text{m}$. This accords with Franco's observation that a person can be unbalanced by an individual overtopping volume of $0.05\text{m}^3/\text{m}$. It should be noted, however, that these figures are applicable to adults who are expecting to get wet and are dressed in protective clothing. A more stringent criterion may apply to children and less mobile adults.

From observations made during the deployment it was considered that discharges in excess of 0.2 l/s/m might result in the loss of control of a vehicle driven at slow speed. It was estimated that this represented a V_{max} of $0.06\text{m}^3/\text{m}$.

Although the safety of personnel and control of cars at the crest of a seawall is very subjective, the present study confirms that of Franco (1994). It is proposed that the tolerable discharges concerning safety of individuals and vehicles be specified in terms of maximum individual overtopping volumes rather than mean discharges.

CONCLUSIONS

This paper discusses the importance of taking shallow water wave conditions into account when designing structure for overtopping performance. If wave breaking in shallow water is not taken into account, prediction methods developed specifically for deep water will significantly underestimate overtopping discharges. A method of assessing the inshore waveform and new shallow water overtopping prediction equations are provided. These equations are validated with overtopping data from field measurements.

Methods available to calculate mean overtopping discharges for non-breaking waves in deep water have been validated using three sets of independent physical model data.

It is often useful, especially at an existing site, to be able to predict the overtopping discharge. A formula based on the number of waves overtopping is advantageous because this parameter can be counted on site with no requirement for expensive measurement devices. Prediction methods to calculate the maximum volume overtopping in a sequence of waves is also discussed.

Model and field measurements suggest that overtopping limits for the safety of personnel or vehicles adjacent to the crest should be specified in terms of maximum individual volume rather than mean discharge. It is proposed that these limits should be 0.04m^3/m for pedestrians and 0.06m^3/m for vehicles.

ACKNOWLEDGEMENTS

The work described in this paper is based on work completed by members of the Coastal Group. The authors are grateful for the interest and funding provided by a number of bodies. The physical model test were carried out for the UK Department of Environment under research contracts PECD 7/6/263 and 7/6/312, further testing has been supported by the European Community MAST programme under the MCS project, MAS2-CT92-0047. The Ministry of Agriculture, Fisheries and Food (MAFF) funded the fieldwork, under Commission FD0201 and the present work is being supported by the Environment Agency (EA) under Commission W5B/006.

The authors would also like to thank colleagues and visiting researchers who have assisted in these tests and the analysis.

REFERENCES

Allsop, N.W.H., Besley, P., & Madurini, L.,(1995). "Overtopping Performance of Vertical and Composite Breakwaters, Seawalls and Low Reflection Alternatives". Paper 4.6 in Final proceedings of MCS Project, published by University of Hanover.

Allsop N W H, McKenna J E, Vicinanza D. & Whittaker T T J (1996) "New design methods for wave impact loadings on vertical Breakwaters and seawalls. Proc 25th ICCE, Orlando, published ASCE, New York.

Endoh, K., & Takahashi, S., (1994). Numerically Modelling Personnel Danger on a Promenade Breakwater due to Overtopping Waves, Proc 24th ICCE, Kobe, published ASCE, New York.

Franco L, de Gerloni M, van der Meer JW. (1994) 'Wave overtopping on vertical and composite breakwaters'. Proc 24th ICCE, Kobe, published ASCE, New York.

Fukuda N, Uno T & Irie I (1974). Field observations of wave overtopping of wave absorbing revetments, Coastal Engineering in Japan Vol 17, 1974, pp117-128.

Goda Y (1971). Expected rate of irregular wave overtopping of seawalls, Coastal Engineering in Japan, Vol 14, 1971. pp 45-51.

Goda Y (1985). Random seas and design of Maritime structures. University of Tokyo Press.

Herbert D M (1993). Wave overtopping of vertical walls. HR Wallingford, Report SR 316, 1993.

Herbert, D.M.,(1996) The overtopping of Seawalls, a comparison between prototype and physical model data. Report TR22, HR Wallingford.

Simm JD Editor (1991)Manual on the use of rock in coastal and shoreline engineering. CIRIA special publication 83, CUR report 154.

Smith, G.M., Klein Bretler, M., Seijiffert, J.W.W., & van der Meer, J.W.,(1994) Erosion and Overtopping of a Grass Dyke : 1:1 Scale Model Tests, Proc 24th ICCE, Kobe, published ASCE, New York.

van der Meer, J.W., & Janssen, J.P.F.M (1995), "Wave Run-up and Wave Overtopping at Dikes", Chapter 1, Wave Forces on Inclined and Vertical Wall Structures, ASCE, New York.

Low Reflection Walls for Harbours: Development of New Structures and Application in Hong Kong

K.J. MCCONNELL[1], D.M. ETHELSTON[2] & N.W.H. ALLSOP[3]
[1]Engineer, Coastal Structures, HR Wallingford, Howbery Park, Wallingford, UK
[2]Technical Director, Babtie BMT Harris & Sutherland, Hong Kong
[3]Manager Coastal Structures, HR Wallingford, Howbery Park, Wallingford, UK

ABSTRACT

This paper describes the development of a new type of seawall structure for Central Reclamation Phase III in Victoria Harbour, Hong Kong and potentially for use in other locations within the harbour. These seawall structures must retain and protect reclamation material, but are also designed to reduce reflected wave action in the harbour. The paper draws together information from background research used for the theoretical / empirical basis for the initial design. Details are given on new model tests to optimise the design of the structure for reflection performance. The paper discusses the implications of the results of the model tests and identifies the main practical constraints in the application of these results to the final structure design.

1. INTRODUCTION

Around many harbours, particularly Victoria Harbour, reclamations have often been retained / protected by solid vertical walls. Vertical walls provide easy access for berthing, and are very space-efficient, but they reflect close to 100% of the wave energy incident on them, significantly increasing local wave disturbance. This may cause increased problems for navigation, particularly where many walls reflect waves back out into the harbour.

In recent years, Victoria Harbour in Hong Kong has increasingly experienced such problems. Extensive development in and close to the harbour has included many reclamations retained by seawalls. Each new reclamation has reduced the size of the harbour, and vertical walls have been preferred for their low cost and reduced space requirements compared with sloping and piled deck seawalls. Vessel traffic within the harbour has increased in recent years, and the combination of this and the high reflections caused by vertical seawalls has produced severe wave conditions within the harbour, making navigation difficult and hazardous, particularly for the many smaller vessels that use Victoria Harbour.

In 1995, the Hong Kong government responded to these problems by directing that new structures within Victoria Harbour should reflect less than 50% of the incident wave energy. The design of a seawall for the new Central Reclamation Phase III (CRIII) shown in Figure 1 had to comply with this directive. Atkins China, the consulting engineer for CRIII, involved Babtie BMT (Hong Kong) as maritime consultant supported by HR Wallingford to review different types of low reflection structures for the reclamation. This review drew upon recent European and UK research which had studied innovative structures to limit wave reflections whilst maintaining the advantages of vertical walled structures.

Coastlines, structures and breakwaters. Thomas Telford, London, 1998

A perforated caisson was selected as the most appropriate design for the seawall structure for CRIII. Comprehensive hydraulic model studies were completed by HR Wallingford with Babtie BMT to optimise the design of the structure, to improve hydraulic performance, and to refine design details to improve ease of construction, and durability.

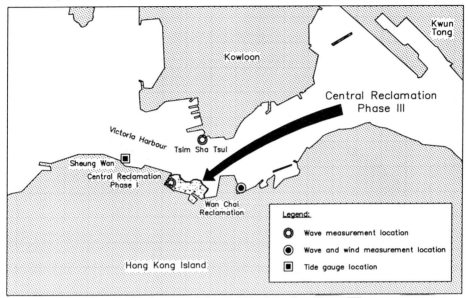

Figure 1   Victoria Harbour and Central Reclamation Phase III

This paper describes briefly model tests presented previously by McConnell et al (1996), and draws on the study description by McConnell (1997). This paper provides more information on the overall context and design aspects, and discusses more fully some of the test results.

2. CENTRAL RECLAMATION PHASE III

A review of possible types of vertical seawall was completed as part of the preliminary design for CRIII. Structure types which were considered were:
- Concrete gravity blockwork seawall;
- Piled deck seawall;
- Anti-reflection gravity seawall;
- Porous precast concrete units;
- Perforated vertical caisson seawall; and
- Staggered column seawall.

All structure options were required to fulfill the basic requirements of reclamation protection and load carrying. The various options were ranked using a points system based on:
- Energy dissipation in accordance with the Hong Kong government directive;
- Construction and maintenance costs;
- Constructability by local contractors using locally available plant and materials, this particularly suggested pre-casting methods rather than in-situ. ;
- Access for periodic inspection, cleaning, and maintenance;
- Compatibility with other services and structures along the waterfront, in particular Cooling Water Pumping Station (CWPS) units for air conditioning systems.

This evaluation indicated the perforated caisson as the preferred solution. This structure would use a concrete caisson with two main chambers, the first open to waves through a perforated front face. The second chamber would be filled with selected ballast material to provide self-weight to resist sliding. This was particularly important during the construction phase, when the seawall would be required to act as a breakwater around the reclamation area. The perforated front face and the hollow chamber behind it act to reduce reflections by destructive interference between incoming and reflected waves, described by Allsop (1995).

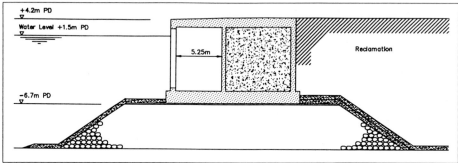

Figure 2   Cross-section of initial design for seawall

The initial design developed from the review was a composite structure with the perforated caisson sitting on a rubble mound founded at approximately –10mPD (Port Datum), Figure 2. The crest of the mound was at –6.7mPD, with a berm width of 5m and front slope of 1 in 1.5. The crest of the caisson was at +4.2mPD. Typical caissons were 20m long. Each caisson will consist of 6 chambers each 6m in length: 3 hollow at the seaward side for energy dissipation and three at the landward side filled with ballast material for stability. The front screen had two 1m slots per chamber giving an area porosity of 30%. The chamber width from the perforated face to the back wall of the hollow chamber, B_w, was 5.25 m.

It is important to note that the size of the rubble mound in this design is relatively large, particularly in relation to those (idealised) structures that had been studied in the background research, where most structures differed little over their full height. It was later found in the hydraulic model tests that this aspect of the structure geometry had an unexpected, but beneficial, effect on the reflection characteristics of the final structure.

3. PREVIOUS RESEARCH

A number of research studies have addressed the design and performance of low reflection structures. In studies in the UK on the design of harbour entrances, McBride et al (1993) and later Allsop (1995) considered the use of low reflection structures as an amelioration measure to assist safe passage of vessels in and out of harbours. A review of model and field investigations of wave screens and perforated screen caissons identified a number of alternative forms, but revealed relatively little reliable data on their hydraulic performance.

The reflection performance of a structure may be most simply defined in terms of the reflection coefficient, C_r, calculated as the ratio of reflected and incident wave heights, H_{sr} / H_{si}. Most design information is empirical, derived from model tests, many unfortunately using only regular waves. It is therefore very difficult to apply these results to realistic design situations, particularly with relatively wide wave energy spectra.

A numerical model described by Bennett (1992) can also be used to calculate the reflection coefficient, C_r, for idealised wave screens or perforated caissons, of given porosity and chamber depth, B_w. Allsop (1995) presented results from this model, shown in Figure 3. These indicate minimum reflections at a relative chamber width, B_w/L equal to 0.25 and 0.75, when the reflected wave is out of phase with the incident wave, causing destructive interference. Maximum reflections occur for B_w/L equal to 0.5 and 1.0. This indicates that the optimum B_w for the hollow caisson would be 0.25L or 0.75L. In practice there will be limits on the caisson size for economic and construction reasons, so the optimum dimension for such a structure would be $B_w = 0.25L$. These results also indicate that porosities of 19-28% more effectively reduce reflections than the lower porosity of 14% for $B_w/L = 0.25$.

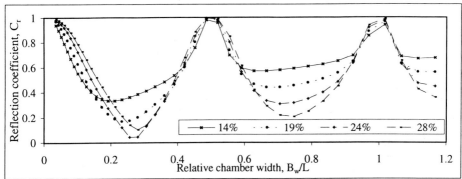

Figure 3   Reflections from single chamber system predicted by numerical model, after Allsop (1995)

McBride et al (1995) discuss a series of wave flume tests which consider the reflection performance of a range of combinations of full depth perforated wave screens. Results are presented in Figure 4 as reflection coefficient function $C_r(f)$, for each frequency band of the wave spectrum. Minimum values of $C_r(f)$ for these tests were found to occur at $B_w/L = 0.2$-0.25, confirming the findings from the numerical model.

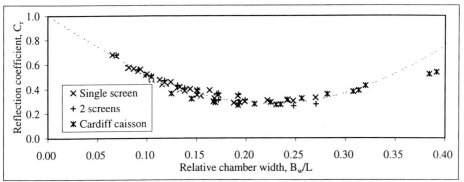

Figure 4 $C_r(f)$ against B_w/L for single and double chambers, after McBride et al (1995)

McBride et al (1995) and Allsop (1995) had previously considered simple full depth vertical structures with no mound and with homogeneous porosity on the front face. The initial design of the structure for CRIII was a composite structure with a rubble mound which would affect the incoming waves. The porosity of the front screen was also not homogeneous, changing with depth. Internal louvres to assist in energy dissipation had also been proposed, and their contribution to reflection performance was not known. These complexities of the design meant that the results of previous studies could not be readily applied in the design without further investigation. A physical model study was therefore carried out to study the complex hydrodynamics, assess reflection performance and optimise the structure design.

4. MODEL TESTS
4.1 Design & Construction
Model tests of the selected scheme were completed in a 1 : 20 scale model, constructed in the 2-d absorbing wave flume at Wallingford. The wave generator in this flume has two probes on the face of the paddle which measure the water level, and the paddle control then adjusts the signal to the paddle to counteract un-wanted re-reflections.

A 30m length of the caisson was constructed from marine plywood. The model was designed such that the lid and internal walls could be easily removed to allow the hollow chambers to be modified. Stability of the structure was not being tested so the caisson was attached directly to the floor of the flume. In the prototype, the rubble mound which extends seaward of the caisson was to be armoured by tightly fitting rock paving. The hydraulic effects of this type of armouring were reproduced by closely-placed concrete blocks.

4.2 Wave conditions
The wave conditions of most interest in assessing the reflection performance were those that occur frequently in the harbour, as they most influence safe navigation in the harbour on a daily basis. Analysis of a representative daily wave spectrum (RDWS) for Victoria Harbour indicated peaks at wave periods of 3, 4 and 6 seconds, Figure 5. The optimisation tests were therefore completed for three different JONSWAP spectra with T_p=3, 4 and 6 seconds. The mean period of the RDWS was T_m=3.7s, so it was deemed most important to have the best reflection performance for the 3 and 4 second wave conditions. A wave height of H_s=0.5m was chosen as this was towards the upper limit of wave heights experienced under normal conditions. These conditions were tested at a water level of +1.5mPD.

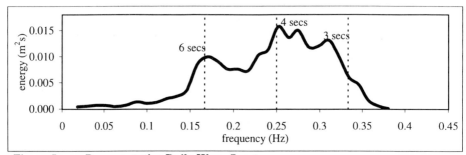

Figure 5   **Representative Daily Wave Spectrum**

An annual wave condition and an extreme wave condition were also used in the model tests. The annual condition, Typhoon No.3 (H_s = 0.8m, T_p = 3.2s) was tested at a water level of +1.5mPD. The extreme event had a 1 in 100 year return period (H_s = 1.96m, T_p = 4.6s) and was tested at a water level of +3.2mPD, which has a return period of 1 in 20 years.

4.3 Reflection performance tests
Wave reflections were measured in the conventional manner discussed by Gilbert & Thompson (1978), using an array of 3 twin wire wave probes located approximately 2 wavelengths from the structure.

Reflection measurements were initially presented as reflection coefficient function $C_r(f)$ against B_w/L over the frequency bands for the generated spectra. The overall reflection coefficient, C_r, was then calculated by weighting the reflection coefficient for each frequency band by the amount of energy that band contributed to the whole spectra. Only frequencies for wave periods between 3 and 6 seconds were considered (approx. 0.2 – 0.35 Hz).

The first Test Series, 1a, gave high reflections, C_r = 0.76. The minimum value of $C_r(f)$ occurred at B_w/L = 0.15, Figure 6, significantly lower than that indicated by the previous research which had suggested that the minimum would occur at B_w/L = 0.2 to 0.25. This indicated that the more complex geometry of the structure had changed the reflection performance from that predicted for idealised structures.

The caisson was modified to try to reduce reflections. Two parameters were known to influence the reflection performance of the structure: the chamber width, B_w, and the front screen configuration. The screen with the 1m slots still had significant areas of vertical wall between the slots which would cause reflections. The width of the slots was reduced and their number increased, while maintaining the same porosity. The new screen had 4 slots per chamber, 3 of 500mm and 1 of 600mm to allow for access to the chambers for maintenance.

As the majority of the wave energy occurred around the 4s period, the chamber width was reduced, to 4m, bearing in mind the finding from Test Series 1a that the minimum reflections occurred for B_w/L = 0.15. Reflections were improved with the modified structure, giving C_r = 0.55, but this still did not meet the requirements of the Client.

Test Series 2a and 2b addressed the use of internal louvres in the chambers to assist in energy dissipation. These tests are discussed in McConnell (1996). It was found that the louvres did not significantly improve the reflection performance of the structure.

Further improvements on the results obtained in Series 1b were sought by again modifying the chamber width. The width, B_w, was reduced to 3m in Series 3a. This improved reflection performance, with a value of C_r = 0.49, Figure 6, thus meeting the client's requirements, and possibly reducing overall construction costs by reducing the width of the seawall.

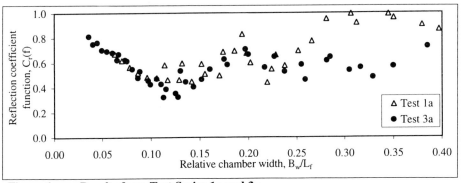

Figure 6   Results from Test Series 1a and 3a

It is well-known that wave impacts can cause high local pressures. It is also almost impossible to predict with reliability wave uplift pressures on the underside of decks within a confined caisson. Careful observation during testing showed that wave action inside the caisson would indeed lead to wave impacts at the junction of the rear wall and upper deck.

The addition of a curved fillet at this junction redirected these impacts and substantially reduced local stress concentrations.

Wave impacts are however often of short duration and it is expected that local wave impacts will not therefore cause excessive uplift forces if averaged over the full deck. In situations where air could be trapped between an uprising wave and the lid, however, any enclosed air pocket will damp the intensity of the uplift force, but significantly extend its duration. This may therefore extend a short duration impact to a longer duration (but less intense) uplift force which may be more dangerous. It is therefore not necessarily advantageous to trap this air pocket at the top of the wave absorption chamber. As it was clear that the upper deck would require beams running fore and aft, the front face was modified to ensure that any trapped air could escape back out seawards. Any severe waves inside the caisson would therefore tend to either hit the recurve at the back of the caisson, flowing forward and falling back into the chamber or, if very large, force trapped air back out seawards.

A protruding crest wall was also included on the front face to assist in reducing overtopping under more severe wave conditions. This had another benefit of preventing accidental vessel impact damage to the wave screen by larger vessels.

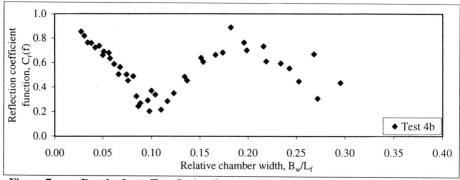

Figure 7   Results from Test Series 4b

The performance of the structure with the above modifications was assessed with a number of chamber widths. Chamber widths of 3m, 2.3m, 3.2m and 3.7m were tested in Test Series 4a to 4d, respectively. The width of the slots of the front screen was reduced to 185mm, with 8 per chamber. Porosity was slightly reduced to 22%.

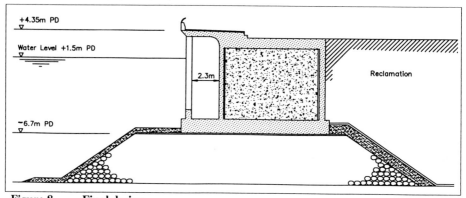

Figure 8   Final design

Test Series 4a to 4d gave reflections of C_r = 0.44, 0.4, 0.45 and 0.5 respectively. The screen with 185mm slots and chamber width, B_w=2.3m gave optimum reflection performance with minimum reflections at B_w/L= 0.11, Figure 7. This was adopted as the final design, Figure 8.

4.4 Further model tests
Other model tests were completed as part of the study to assess other aspects of the performance of the structure. These addressed overtopping, the possibility of blockage of the perforated screen and in-service performance following wear and tear on the screen elements which may reduce reflection performance.

Overtopping
Overtopping did not occur for the frequently occurring conditions. Overtopping was measured for the 1 in 100 year event, H_s = 1.96m, T_p = 4.6s, SWL = +3.2mPD. An overtopping rate of 9 l/s.m was recorded. The CIRIA/CUR guidelines indicate that this degree of overtopping may cause some minor structural damage and that access by pedestrians or vehicles would be unsafe during such extreme events. The crest wall assists in limiting the volume of water overtopping the structure. Without this modification to the structure significantly higher overtopping rates would be experienced.

Blockage of perforated screen
There is a high quantity of floating debris in Victoria Harbour. During design, there was concern that this could block the perforated screen, resulting in deterioration in performance. Tests were completed using scaled floating and neutrally buoyant material for frequently occurring and Typhoon No.3 conditions. Dye tracing allowed complex flow patterns at the structure to be studied. These tests indicated that although some material entered the chamber, this usually flowed back out again so little or no nett build-up of material resulted. Maintenance to ensure the chambers are clear of debris would probably not be excessive.

In-service tests
The final design for the perforated screen had sharp edges to the slots. It was likely that general wear and tear and possible accidental vessel impacts could result in damage to the sharp edges. Tests were completed to assess whether slots with worn edges would cause greater reflections. These tests indicated a slight deterioration in reflection performance, but the results were still well within the limits of the Client's requirements.

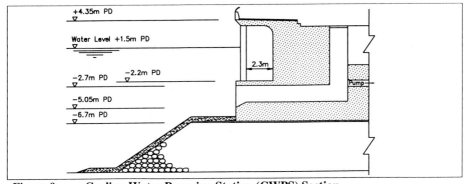

Figure 9   Cooling Water Pumping Station (CWPS) Section

Cooling Water Pumping Station (CWPS) tests

Parts of the seawall will have to incorporate intakes and outlets for cooling water for buildings on the reclamation. These caisson sections have additional hollow chambers at the bottom of the caisson leading to open chambers behind the caisson where the water can oscillate freely, Figure 9. Tests were conducted to see if this modified section would have a detrimental effect on reflection performance. Results indicated a very slight improvement in reflection performance when compared to the standard structure.

5. CONSTRUCTION ASPECTS

Policy regarding development within Victoria Harbour is presently under review, since the design of the structure has been completed. If construction is to proceed, it is likely that it will have to be completed under strict environmental constraints.

Simple blockwork seawalls which have been commonly adopted in Hong Kong are usually fabricated in mass concrete and are thus very robust and not susceptible to corrosion. These types of structures therefore achieve long operating lives and are virtually maintenance free. The requirement for seawalls with low wave reflectance however entails the use of more complex structural forms which necessitate the use of reinforced concrete. These types of structures are consequently more vulnerable to corrosion and due allowance was made in detailed design and specifications for corrosion protection and maintenance provisions.

The proposed caisson structures will be constructed, either wholly or in part, in the dry and then sealed, launched and towed into place for sinking. In the floating phase, the caisson holes will be temporary closed by steel plates, which are then removed after sinking. Precasting the units outside a marine environment has obvious advantages over in-situ work in the marine environment. The most important of these is that it allows the concrete to be placed and cured in more favourable conditions than would otherwise be possible. In designing the units, account has been taken of the associated problems of damage during the transport and placement of the units. For example, connections between units have been carefully detailed to ensure that they are not only structurally adequate but that they can accommodate the necessary tolerances required for the marine construction and placement.

In order to facilitate maintenance or replacement of any of the panel elements of the perforated screen, the concept of pre-cast panels was investigated. This has the advantage that it will allow the maintenance agent to employ a system whereby any damaged panels(s) can be removed and either replaced directly with a new element, or be repaired without having to use any in-situ underwater techniques. Disadvantages of such a configuration are:

- Reinforcement from the front panels cannot be carried through into the promenade deck slab, to assist in resisting the upward forces generated on the underside of the wave absorbing deck during the extreme events;

- Panels need to be firmly held in place so that no movement can occur which would result in damage to the actual nibs or the base slab the panels are seated on;

- This configuration reduces the height of the "vertical slot" between each panel which extends from -4.2 mPD up to +3.43 mPD (the underside of the promenade) by 1 metre. During the physical model tests, the length of the "gap" was increased to +3.43 mPD to improve the wave reflection characteristics and to reduce the forces under the promenade deck caused by trapped air during the extreme storm events;

- Cooling Water Pumping Stations (CWPS) require guide channels for their trash screens. Observations of guide channels in use at Central Reclamation Phase I have indicated that these channels can be readily damaged. For CRIII the CWPS guide channels are to be located and attached to the caisson structure within the wave absorbing seawall chambers. The guide channels require a rigid fixing, hence pre-cast panels would not be ideal.

Assessment of these factors, and aspects of constructability, suggested that casting of complete units would be preferred to the use of separate screen panels. The most likely construction sequence for the vertical seawall caisson structures is that described above: the walls would be cast to a level of + 2.3 mPD, and the gaps between the front panels sealed during the flotation stage, with the panels constructed as part of the caisson structure. If however the panels are to be precast units, then the Contractor would be posed with the problem of floating the caisson to its final location, either with precast panels attached at the base, or without the panels, which could create flotation and stability problems.

A caisson length of 20 metres provided the optimum size for the caissons considering the seawall configuration as shown in Figure 1, resulting in savings in construction time and material quantities. The optimisation also considered the practical aspects of construction, launching, towing, grounding and minimising damage to the units during their placement.

Concerns were expressed regarding likely maintenance problems associated with the wave absorbing seawalls. These concerns were allied to the safety of personnel working inside the chambers and difficulties in repairing any underwater structural damage.

Maintenance can be divided between the periodic removal of floating debris trapped within the wave absorbing seawall chamber, and the physical repair to damaged concrete sections. It is recognised that access must be provided to allow trained personnel to enter the wave absorbing chamber should any floating debris become trapped within the wave absorbing chamber. This material would be removed in a controlled manner, following standard procedures for working in Confined Spaces, with the appropriate safety back-up and equipment such as harnesses, life jackets etc.

Initial design of the perforated screen had allowed access through the 1m slots for maintenance in the chambers. The final design has slots of 185mm, too small for access through the front screen. In order to allow access to the chambers, every caisson structure has a watertight manhole cover to resist a minimum upward pressure of 5 metres head.

In order to reduce the general maintenance requirements the panels and walls creating the wave absorbing chamber will be designed with fibre-reinforced concrete to protect the edges from dynamic loads and any likely wear from abrasive objects in the sea water. Reinforcing the concrete with polypropylene fibres will give rise to the following improvements:

- Increased impact resistance;
- Significant reduction of plastic shrinkage cracking: and
- Increased impermeability and improved chemical resistance.

The concrete mix will be enhanced by the addition of a corrosion inhibitor Hydrophobic Poreblocking Ingredient. This will significantly reduce the absorption and permeability of concrete, which will provide corrosion protection over the long term, of importance for reinforced concrete in the marine environment.

6. CONCLUSIONS

The 'low reflection' solution adopted for CRIII uses an interference chamber formed as a concrete caisson on a rubble mound. This system offers relatively low reflections with a vertical face, but is quite strongly frequency dependent. An interesting and economically attractive feature of the seawall for CRIII is the reduced width needed for low reflections compared to that predicted by previous research for idealised structures.

The main differences in the reflection performance of the CRIII seawall tested in Series 4, and the idealised structures considered by Allsop (1995) and McBride et al (1995) are:
   a) Smearing of the reflection coefficient $C_r(f)$ against relative wave length B_w/L_f;
   b) Reduction of minimum reflection point from B_w/L_f=0.20-0.25, down to B_w/L_f=0.10-0.12, which gives the reflection characteristics of an effective chamber 2x larger.
The main differences in the structures tested in Series 4, and the idealised structures considered by Allsop (1995) and others are that the idealised structures were all of full-depth construction, placed on no rubble mound, and with no projecting berm at the toe. The wave screens/ perforated caissons were generally of the same configuration throughout depth.

Of the differences in reflection performance, the reduction of the minimum reflection point down to $B_w/L_f \approx 0.11$ is less easy to explain. It is probable that the apparent increase in effective chamber width, which gives the effect of an interference chamber of twice the width, arises from effects both of the mound itself, and the berm width at the top of the slope. The height of the mound, h_b, for the CRIII seawall is relatively large with $h_b/h_s = 0.4$, where h_s is the water depth at the toe of the mound. This suggests that there is a second interference process between the portion of the wave reflected by the mound and that reflected by the caisson. The relative wave height to depth over the mound at the seawall toe $H_{si}/d = 0.06$ is quite low but linear wave theory indicates that there are still significant orbital velocities at the berm elevation for the longer period waves, up to 60% of the orbital velocities at the surface for the 6s waves. These findings were confirmed by observations made during dye tracing tests.

Comparison of these results suggest the following to future designers:
   a) Reflections from full-depth structures are probably well predicted by the simple methods presented by previous authors;
   b) The addition of a mound will tend to give an apparent increase in effective width of the interference chamber B_w, probably increasing with both relative mound height, h_b/h_s, and/or with the mound berm width / caisson set-back distance;
   c) Minimum reflections will probably not be as low for composite structures as for simple full-depth screens, but moderate reflections may be given over a wider range of incident wavelengths;
   d) Empirical or computational design methods are not yet available to predict reflections accurately from composite walls. These studies have demonstrated that the response can be altered in unexpected ways and hydraulic model testing will continue to be necessary.

It is important to bear in mind that these caissons are optimised for a single wave condition, and as such will only be effective in dissipating wave energy within a very narrow band. Accurate descriptions of all important incident wave conditions will therefore be vital to ensure that the structure is optimised for the correct conditions.

ACKNOWLEDGEMENTS
The Central Reclamation Phase III project was completed by a team led by Atkins Haswell, and including Babtie BMT and HWR Asia in Hong Kong and HR Wallingford in the United Kingdom. The client for the study was the Territory Development Department (TDD) of the Hong Kong government.

The authors are grateful to TDD and their partners for permission to describe results from these studies. They also gratefully acknowledge assistance from their colleagues in UK and Hong Kong during the conduct of the studies, and in the compilation of this paper.

HR Wallingford are grateful for the support of the EU MAST program in the research projects MCS and PROVERBS (contracts MAS2 CT92-0047 and MAS3 – CT95-0041) and of the Department of the Environment Construction Division, in Research Contract PECD 7/6/263, all of which contributed background material to this project.

REFERENCES
Allsop N.W.H. (1995) "Vertical walls and breakwaters: optimization to improve vessel safety and wave disturbance by reducing wave reflections" Chapter 10 in Wave Forces on Inclined and Vertical Wall Structures, ed. Kobayashi N. & Demirbilek Z., ASCE, New York.

Bennett G.S., McIver P. & Smallman J.V. (1992) "A mathematical model of a slotted wave screen breakwater" Coastal engineering, Volume 18, Elsevier Science 1992. pp.231-249.

Gilbert G. & Thompson D.M. (1978) "Reflections in random waves: the frequency response function method" Report IT 173, Hydraulics Research Station, Wallingford.

McBride M.W., Allsop NW.H., Besley P., Colombo D. & Madurini L. (1995) "Vertical walls and low reflection alternatives: results of wave flume tests" Report IT 417, HR Wallingford.

McBride M.W., Hamer B.A., Besley P., Smallman J.V. & Allsop N.W.H. (1993) "The hydraulic design of harbour entrances: a pilot study" Report SR 388, HR Wallingford.

McConnell K.J. (1997) "Hong Kong Central Reclamation Phase III – the design of a low-reflection seawall" PIANC Bulletin, PIANC, Brussels.

McConnell K.J., Allsop N.W.H. & Ethelston D.M. (1996) "Wave reflections from coastal structures: development and application of new approaches" Proceedings of 10th Congress of the Asia and Pacific Division of IAHR, Langkawi Island, Malaysia, August 1996

Ecological implications of developing coastal protection structures

A. C. Jensen[1], B. A. Hamer[2], & J. F. Wickins[3]
[1] Department of Oceanography, University of Southampton, Southampton Oceanography Centre, European Way, Southampton, SO14 3ZH, UK.
[2] Sir William Halcrow & Partners Ltd, Burderop Park, Swindon, SN4 0QD.
[3] CEFAS Fisheries Laboratory, Benarth Road, Conwy, LL32 8UB

ABSTRACT
This paper seeks to give initial guidance to the engineer on some ecological implications of design, construction, and maintenance of coastal protection structures such as breakwaters, sea walls, revetments and submerged reefs. The paper includes suggestions for the future assessment, design and construction of such structures, to reduce undesirable ecological impacts and enhance benefits.

Keywords: coastal protection, ecology, artificial reefs

INTRODUCTION
Background
Coastal structures such as breakwaters, sea walls or submerged reefs may be constructed for a range of reasons, principally as follows :

i)   sea defence – to reduce the risk and/or severity of flooding from the sea:
ii)   coast protection – to reduce risk and/or severity of erosion of land by waves or tidal flow;
iii) protect an area of water for ship loading / unloading, mooring or manoeuvring
iv)   reclaim new land areas from the sea;
v)   increase environmental and socio-economic benefits.

The greatest proportion of active construction of breakwaters, sea walls and revetments is for purposes i) to iv), but recent developments in some areas suggest that there will be more use of artificial structures in the future for purpose v).

This paper identifies and discusses the ecological implications of constructing a range of maritime structures, chiefly breakwaters and submerged reefs. The paper draws on information currently being assembled under a Ministry of Agriculture, Fisheries and Food (MAFF) project (OCS978K), and a wider range of information and techniques developed under the EU funded European Artificial Reef Research Network (EARRN).

MAFF research project
In the current study, engineers and marine scientists are working together to assess the benefits that may be derived from an inter-disciplinary approach. The scope of published

Coastlines, structures and breakwaters. Thomas Telford, London, 1998

research in the areas of coastal structure design, fisheries enhancement using artificial structures, and areas where the two topics have overlapped is being examined. A database of structures in United Kingdom waters, likely to be of interest with regard to marine habitat enhancement, has been developed, and indicates that a range of suitable structures for further study exists. These structures include offshore reefs/breakwaters, such as those at Happisberg, (Gardner *et al.*, 1997), rock groynes, and harbour breakwaters.

The final output from the study will take the form of design guidance, to summarise best practice in engineering design for marine environmental enhancement. Such a document will allow bodies promoting maritime structures to fulfil their obligations under the EC Habitats Directives, whereby they must seek positive enhancements to the environment wherever possible.

EARRN

The European Artificial Reef Research Network (EARRN) was formed in May 1995, with funding from the European Commission (EC) Agriculture and Fisheries (AIR) programme. The formal network consists of 51 scientists plus 50 associates from 36 laboratories within the European Union (EU), who are active in artificial reef research. EARRN was formed to provide advice on the direction of future EU research into artificial reefs for the EC. This advice has been presented as formal conference proceedings and reports from four workshops, taking specific themes from the conference. It is anticipated that the advice given will be reflected within future EC-funded work programmes.

Marine scientists throughout Europe who belong to EARRN have identified the need to improve communication and develop collaboration between marine scientists and coastal engineers, to facilitate inclusion of worthwhile ecological features in coastal marine structures. The latter may include the provision of designs that can provide habitat for commercial and other ecologically important species in coastal waters, as well as options for the amelioration of specific anthropogenic activities affecting coastal zones.

FLORA & FAUNA
Background
The research activities described above will influence the future, but what can be said now to make coastal structures more environmentally friendly in terms of nature conservation, biodiversity and fisheries? There has been much previous work undertaken in the study of physical design guidance to improve the engineering aspects of coastal defence. There is also a wealth of literature on research into the use of artificial structures to develop the potential for fisheries enhancement and biodiversity (e.g. Sprague and Seaman, 1991; Various authors, 1994; Jensen, 1997). There is however very little work which draws both these aspects together.

Plant & animal life.
Increasing the environmental friendliness of coastal structures in the tidal zone needs some knowledge of the specific environmental objectives, and the needs of the target plants (i.e seaweeds, such as kelp; attached micro-algae) and animals (anemones, oysters, worms, crabs, fish etc.). These needs are not always fully understood, if at all, so the habitat design process can either be based on the intuitive "scientific" judgement of coastal ecologists or, preferably, on quantitative research into the critical features of habitat design.

The best natural model for coastal structures are rocky shores. Many of these are natural coastal protection structures. By mimicking a shore with a mixture of rock sizes, irregular outlines and variety of crevice sizes, marine life that requires hard surfaces can be encouraged to develop. Plants, such as seaweeds, need a surface for attachment and light for photosynthesis. The plants will naturally distribute themselves according to their ability to survive at various levels of dryness (normally linked to height above low water) or light penetration when under water. If the structure has elements that are at, or below, low water level, it may well be colonised by kelp and its associated fauna. Kelp and, indeed most seaweeds, often have a wide range of animal communities sheltering or feeding on or near them. Marine animals need to be kept wet or damp, to have a source of food (the smaller forms often exist on plankton and micro-detritus filtered from the current), and to find shelter. To achieve this, surfaces need to provide a variety of orientations for settlement of sessile animals (for example bryozoans, hydroids, and sponges), which can attach to the new hard surfaces, with a variety of nooks and crannies for small mobile species (for example fish, blennies, gobies, shrimps and prawns), as well as larger animals (such as anemones, urchins, crabs, lobsters and congers). After the initial colonisation period, a marine structure will develop a diverse and dynamic ecosystem in which all species play an interactive part essential to the balance and sustainability of the total community.

Habitat preference
Apart from the form of the structure, marine colonisation is dependent on other environmental factors acting at the structure. A significant drawback to colonisation by marine life is that, by their nature, many coastal structures are subject to extremes of wave energy that can severely limit the life forms able to settle or exist on the defences. However, animals and plants that live naturally on the shore are physiologically tough and have evolved the ability to cope with a variety of environmental conditions. Many are able to withstand wave action, rapid changes in salinity and temperature, and dessication. Their survival abilities `zone' them out down the shore: as the period of submersion by the tide increases, the number of species (i.e. biodiversity) also increases.

For lower shore animals to colonise the upper shore, they need refuges such as the underside of rocks, rock pools, or deep crevices, where they can avoid drying out. Shore dwelling animals are `pre-adapted' to colonise coastal structures and will take advantage of what habitat they can. Some use very efficient attachment devices (limpets and mussels), others with short life-spans re-colonise when conditions allow.

A species-friendly habitat design will expand the number of micro-habitats available, so increasing biodiversity. If the structure is in the littoral zone, layers of variable sized rock will produce additional habitat and biodiversity beyond that of the rock surface community. The provision of hollows and crevices to form rock pools, projections to create overhangs and placing of rocks in isolation from the main works to produce scour pools, can mimic many of the features of a rocky shore and will attract typical animals and plants. Fish and crustaceans can use the crevices between rocks and concrete blocks to hide from predators, lay eggs, or feed on the organisms growing on the structure. At mid-beach levels, the fuccoid seaweeds like bladder wrack may be widespread. If the structure is submerged, then shelters for edible crab (crevices on the outside of the structure) and lobsters (galleries within the structure), and shelter for fish species such as wrasse, lumpsuckers and conger eels can all be incorporated. Many marine organisms produce large numbers of planktonic larvae that are spread by water currents, so there is rarely a problem with supply of young animals and plants to a new habitat in coastal waters.

TYPES OF STRUCTURES
Coastal protection structures
The basic principles of giving due consideration to environmental enhancement should be applied to most maritime structures. For many of these structures, however, environmental enhancement will be of minor consequence when developing the design of expensive structures with a specific engineering purpose.

In some cases, and particularly in the EU, the promoters of coastal schemes have a duty under the EU Habitats Directive and, in the United Kingdom, under the Planning Policy Guidance Note 9, to actively seek environmental enhancements associated with new structures and schemes. Structures that fall under this Directive, which are of most potential interest for study by marine scientists, include coastal defence schemes. It is for this reason that the authors have, to date, focused on nearshore breakwaters, groynes and, to a lesser extent, harbour structures.

The potential for the development of multi-purpose structures is set to increase, with increased economic benefits, and hence more robust project justification, both for scheme promoters and for commercial fisheries interests. The scale of some potential economic benefits of environmental enhancement are discussed briefly later.

Artificial reefs
Artificial reefs have been used in a variety of coastal management functions throughout the world. Japan is the world leader in coastal management schemes which focus on increasing the yield of seafood. There is a national artificial reef development plan with each prefecture having responsibility for artificial reef development. The national government provides 50% funding for artificial reefs conforming to approved designs in steel and cement (Fig. 1.)(Grove *et al.*, 1994). The present programme (1994-2000) has a 6 billion Yen budget (Simard, 1997). It is not clear if the designs have a biological basis but they appear to provide a focus for fishing effort and good yields.

In the USA there is a national plan but no national funding (Seaman and Sprague, 1991). States run their own programmes of reef deployment and there is an emphasis on using "materials of opportunity" with a dominant aim of improving recreational angling catches. Probaly the most well known are the "rigs to reefs" programmes off the Gulf states of Texas and Louisiana (e.g. Wilson and Van Sickle, 1989). Purpose built structures have also been developed in the USA and commercial companies, such as Reef Ball Development Group Ltd (makers of an alveolar spherical module) (http://www.reefball.org/index.html) export their technology worldwide (125 projects, 20,000 reefballs).

European artificial reefs have developed within nation states, there was little communication between the scientists involved before the creation of the European Artificial Reef Research Network. Reef deployment is varied but tends to be dominated by Spain (Fig. 2) (Gomez-Buckley and Haroun, 1994), Italy and France and is primarily to protect shallow water (< 50 m) seagrass (*Posidonia oceanica*) and corraline algae habitats from damage by illegal trawling (Bombace *et al.*, 1993). These deployments have provided research opportunities in fishery enhancement (finfish and lobsters), nature conservation, resource management and aquaculture.

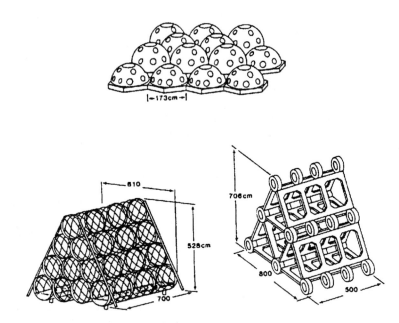

Fig. 1. Artificial reef structures used in Japan

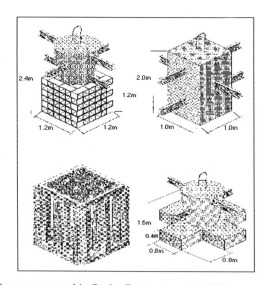

Fig. 2. Artificial reef structures used in Spain (Revenga *et al.*, 1997).

Materials

Most coastal structures are constructed from concrete or quarried rock. Under normal conditions, surfaces are rapidly colonised by naturally occurring micro-organisms that consume many of the dissolved and suspended substances in sea water. Settlement of larger organisms, such as barnacles and mussels, which can directly filter suspended matter for their food, also occurs on some parts of a reef. Grazing and browsing organisms living on the reef devour many of the plants and animals living sedentary lives on the hard surfaces, creating scope for continued colonisation.

There are also a variety of re-cycled materials, which have been or could be considered for intertidal structures or submerged artificial reefs (Collins and Jensen, 1997): tyres (Israel:Spanier, 1994: Global review: Collins *et al.*, 1995), cement-stabilised coal ash (Long Island, USA:Woodhead *et al.*, 1982; Poole Bay, UK: Jensen and Collins, 1995;Collins and Jensen, 1995; Liguria, Italy: Sampaolo and Relini, 1994; Relini *et al.*, 1995; Haifa, Israel: Spanier Pers. Com.), steel structures (e.g. Louisiana Gulf, USA: Wilson and Van Sickle,1989; Japan: Sonu and Grove,1985) and stabilised quarry fines (Sayer and Wilding, Pers. Com.). Apart from the engineering concerns over the physical stability of the material, the chemical stability should be considered as release of compounds may inhibit biological growth. Beware, natural does not always mean clean. Some quarried rocks may be potentially more toxic than others depending, for example, on their heavy metal content. The colonising organisms may bio-accumulate these substances providing a potential route to the human food chain. Although most existing coastal protection and artificial reefs are of quarried rock or conventional concrete blocks the use of re-cycled material, when found to be acceptable environmentally, will save on natural resources such as rock and so, in some cases, serve to reduce environmental impact in areas remote from the coastal zone.

Whilst the engineering requirements are paramount in exposed parts of a structure, other sections may be quite sheltered. Putting a variety of natural rock into a structure, or mixing wooden groynes with rock strong points may improve its overall aesthetic appearance, as well as encouraging different biota. It is also possible to actively promote biological colonisation on relatively conventional materials for use in new structures. In Japan, for example, concrete blocks have been manufactured with pellets of iron sulphate on the outer surface to promote the growth of seaweeds.

ECOLOGICAL IMPACTS OF COASTAL STRUCTURES

Ecological Potential

When a structure is placed on the seabed there is inevitably a loss of habitat and with it, associated species. Sandy or muddy seabed is not lifeless. It contains a multitude of organisms (worms, crabs, molluscs etc) many of which are important in the food chains of commercially fished species and birds (particularly in the inter-tidal zone).

Construction work can have significant negative environmental impacts as can the defence structure itself. The compensation for damage to and/or the loss of existing seabed habitat is the potential enhancement of the site with new, different substrata (the structure) and a more stable sedimentary environment which, together, may increase the biodiversity by creating diverse habitat.

Marine species are well adapted to take advantage of whatever opportunities come their way. Whether the habitat is colonised by a particular species depends on the needs of that species.

Some existing structures already do an outstanding job. Harbour construction provides opportunities for extensive habitat creation, beyond that of simple groynes. The construction of the Portland Harbour breakwaters in Dorset created a large body of sheltered, quiet water which led to an accumulation of muddy sediment within the harbour. This has created a seabed of fine mud, reminiscent of a Scottish sea loch, colonised by seapens (*Virgularia* sp.) not found anywhere else on the south coast of England. Thus, a very special marine habitat has been produced that would not exist except for the harbour engineers. Whilst the fauna in Portland Harbour is exceptional, that on the outside of the breakwaters that form the harbour is not. The breakwaters were constructed from huge boulders which provide little in the way of niches for animals, and the exposed surfaces are topped with concrete to facilitate human activities.

Provision of new habitat in the littoral (i.e. visible) zone can serve nature conservation interests, increase the tourism possibilities (most children and many adults like exploring rock pools) and provide the ultimate way of blending coastal defence structures into the environment. However, the sub-littoral zone is where habitat engineering can really become creative. Designer habitats for target species become a much more realistic option. The physiological challenges of life on a beach are reduced below low water spring tide and the diversity of life increases. Here, hard substratum is an extremely limited commodity in the marine environment and will, physical and chemical conditions allowing, be rapidly colonised by animals and plants. The further the structure extends into the sub-littoral zone the more likely it is that marine life will be able to make use of it as wave energy ceases to be a limiting factor. The level of benefit will depend on the species, its requirements and the location of the structure. There may even be opportunity for environmental remediation (Laihonen, 1996; Miyaoka, 1995).

Coastal structures and fisheries

The most important species, in terms of UK commercial fishing, that may benefit from coastal structures are lobsters and crabs, but the benefits could extend to other static gear fisheries. Naturally, this is where there is considerable interest in a merging of engineering and marine science to facilitate habitat creation for these valuable animals (e.g. Jensen and Collins, 1997; Jensen *et al.*, in press).

As a first step the authors are assessing the engineering feasibility of including lobster habitat in realistic structure designs. Issues such as stability, cost, and practicability are of paramount importance. Laboratory experiments to determine preferred shelter sizes for given size ranges of lobsters are being conducted, and are providing data that will be used to extend computational model techniques developed in earlier work, to estimate gallery configuration and chamber size in rock structures. This approach arises because in most natural rocky reefs, there are far more small crevices than large ones, and a lobster normally encounters fewer, appropriately-sized shelters as it gets bigger (Caddy, 1986). Some members of a population will, as they grow, a) be obliged to move to a different locality to gain shelter or, b) suffer stress and reduced growth through increased competion for shelters.

To maximise lobster numbers, therefore, it would be more useful to design a structure which provided adequate habitat for all sizes of lobsters, but especially the larger ones close to the 85 mm carapace length minimum landing size (Wickins, 1995). To do this, models are being used to study design features for reefs that contain an appropriate number of crevices for lobsters of selected size groups, based on mapping theoretical perforated surfaces (Caddy and

Stamatopoulos, 1990) or modelling specific mixtures of particular sizes of simulated rocks (Barry and Wickins, 1992). Models are also being developed to provide quantitative estimates of both the external and internal structure of reefs (Wickins and Barker, 1997) since occupation by lobsters is influenced by the sizes and inter-connectivity of internal galleries and chambers.

Whilst a computer modelling approach can help to estimate how many lobsters could occupy a reef, it is realised that actual occupancy of a crevice will depend on many factors including its entrance position, shape and local food availability. Obviously, water depth plays a vital role in determining habitability. For a structure to have any role in fisheries, it must be submerged for at least part of the tidal cycle and the more useful section will be that which is permanently immersed i.e. below low water springs.

Monitoring
Much of the research available to date has been carried out in laboratories, and at relatively small-scale artificial reef sites. Through the work of EARRN and the MAFF-funded research project, the authors are seeking to increase the understanding of marine life preferences on real, large-scale structures.

The authors are keen to see growth in the monitoring of structure's biological colonisation, changes in the neighbouring animal and plant communities, free-swimming fish populations and commercially fished species. Through a focused monitoring effort an increased level of understanding will develop, reducing the risk of expensive mitigation measures.

Scale of Impacts
Whilst a new breakwater can have demonstrable tourist benefits (most obviously, sport anglers, although surfers (Anderson, 1996) have been seen using the reefs constructed in Norfolk (Weight, Pers. Com.)) and nature conservation value, the commercial fishery value of most coastal defence and harbour structures is likely to be small. For example, a typical coastal lobster fishery along 10 to 20 miles of coastline involves 10 to 20 lobstermen, each probably landing approximately 4,500 lobsters per annum. To construct and stock a reef to provide an annual catch of 45,000 lobsters would mean a very substantial and long term undertaking. It may be more realistic to think in terms of adding, say, 10% to the annual yield of a local fishery (Anon., 1995). A typical UK coastal defence structure is unlikely to provide enough catch to support one full-time fisherman, never mind a fleet, but it is believed that structures can have a positive effect on habitat provision for crabs and lobsters, the degree of benefit depending on design, location and scale. It is important to note, however, that if the animals inhabiting the structures are breeding, then it is likely that their offspring will contribute to the overall fishable population.

CONCLUSIONS
Formal ecological engineering enhancement is a relatively new field in Europe, still requiring research. In the UK, apart from experimental artificial reefs such as the Poole Bay reef, there has been little or no development of this technology. However, there is considerable investment in coastal defence structures, breakwaters and harbours which could enhance fishing opportunity and nature conservation by providing new hard habitat for fish to forage around and upon which other organisms can settle, shelter, feed and reproduce. As a starting point for ecological enhancement, these following points are believed to be worthy of consideration when planning a coastal protection structure.

(1) Location. Think about the apperance of rocky habitat and mimic it where you plan to build the defence structure. If you are building below the low tide level your opportunities for fishery habitat enhancement increase with water depth.

(2) Maximise the diversity of crevices created. The greater the heterogeneity of the habitat the more diverse the final biological community is likely to be.

(3) Consider using a mix of materials - does everything have to be made from Scandanavian granite?

(4) Get creative, use the CAD package for the structural part but does the surface realy have to be smooth neat and symetrical? When did you ever see a rocky shore like that?

(5) Build in animal friendly features, intertidal rockpools, isolated boulders for scour pools, projections to create underhangs...

(6) Talk with the local residents and users. Wildlife Trusts, local authority ecologists, university academics, English Nature and Sea Fishery Committees are professionals too and will be delighted that nature conservation and or fishery provision is being considered.

(7) Use the fact that you are taking extra care to promote your approach to coastal structure construction, a defence scheme that blends in will be more popular than one that "jars" the eye.

(8) Be realistic. No single scheme will do everything. Take a long term view and over time the benefits will mount up.

(9) To assess these benefits be prepared to monitor. Quantification of benefits may require professional surveys, especially sub-tidally, but descriptive evaluation allows local enthusiasts to get involved. Encourage local schools & colleges and/or Marine Conservation Society groups to adopt your structure as a study site (shore ecology is a favourite theme for field trips). You will be able to use their data and images to follow the biological community development over time.

ACKNOWLEDGEMENTS
This paper was prepared with the assistance of K.J. Collins and I.P. Smith (Southampton Oceanography Centre) who are involved in the activities of EARRN and specifically in research into reef materials and ecology and the guidance of D.E. Reeve (Research and Development Manager for the Maritime Department at Sir William Halcrow and Partners). Acknowledgement is also given to G. C. Barker, of the Institute of Food Research, Colney, Norwich, for his work on computational modeling of reef structures.

REFERENCES
Anderson, I. (1996). Let's go surfin'. New Scientist, (2040) 26-27.

Anon. (1995). Lobster stocking: progress and potential. Significant results from the UK restocking studies 1982 to 1995. MAFF Direct. Fish. Res. Lowestoft, (mimeo) 12 pp.

Barry, J. and Wickins, J.F. (1992). A model for the number and sizes of crevices that can be seen on the exposed surface of submerged rock reefs. Environmetrics **3** (1) 55-69.

Bombace, G., Fabi, G. and Fiorentini, L. (1993). Census results on artificial reefs in the Mediterranean Sea. Bollettino di Oceanologia teoretica ed applicata. Vol. XI, N.3-4:257-263.

Caddy, J.F. (1986). Modelling stock-recruitment processes in Crustacea: some practical and theoretical perspectives. Can. J. Fish. Aquat. Sci. **43**: 2330-2344.

Caddy, J.F. and Stamatopoulos, C. (1990). Mapping growth and mortality rates of crevice-dwelling organisms onto a perforated surface: the relevance of 'cover' to the carrying capacity of natural and artificial habitats. Estuarine, Coastal and Shelf Science **31**: 87-106.

Collins, K.J. and Jensen A.C. (1997). Acceptable use of waste materials. In Jensen, A.C. (ed). *European Artificial Reef Research.* pp 377-390. Proceedings of the first EARRN conference, March 1996 Ancona, Italy. Pub Southampton Oceanography Centre, 449p.

Collins, K.J. and Jensen A.C. (1995). Stabilised coal ash reef studies. Chemistry & Ecology, **10**, 193-203.

Collins, K.J., Jensen A.C. and Albert, S. (1995). A review of waste tyre utilisation in the marine environment. Chemistry & Ecology, **10**, 205-216.

Gardner, J., Hamer, B. and Runcie, R. (1997). Physical protection of the seabed and coasts by artificial reefs. In Jensen, A.C. (ed). *European Artificial Reef Research.* pp 17-36. Proceedings of the first EARRN conference, March 1996 Ancona, Italy. Pub Southampton Oceanography Centre, 449p.

Gomez-Buckley, M.C. and Haroun, R.J. (1994). Artificial reefs in the Spanish coastal zone. Bulletin of Marine Science **55** (2&3):1021-1028.

Grove, R.S., Nakamura, M., Kakimoto, H. and Sonu, C.J. (1994). Aquatic habitat technology innovation in Japan. Bulletin of Marine Science **55**(2&3):276-294.

Jensen, A.C. (1997). *European Artificial Reef Research.* Proceedings of the first EARRN conference, March 1996 Ancona, Italy. Pub Southampton Oceanography Centre, 449p.

Jensen, A.C. and Collins, K.J. (1997) The use of artificial reefs in crustacean fisheries enhancement. In Jensen, A.C. (ed). *European Artificial Reef Research.* pp 115-122. Proceedings of the first EARRN conference, March 1996 Ancona, Italy. Pub Southampton Oceanography Centre, 449p.

Jensen, A.C. and Collins, K.J.(1995). The Poole Bay artificial reef project 1989 to 1994. Biol. Mar.Medit. **2**(1): 111-122.

Jensen, A.C., Collins K.J. and Smith I.P. (In press). Artificial reefs in lobster enhancement programmes. Workshop on lobster stock enhancement (Magdalen Islands, Quebec, Canada). Canadian Industry Report of Fisheries and Aquatic Science. Pub Canadian Department of Fisheries and Oceans

Laihonen, P., Hänninen, J., Chojnacki, J.C. and Vuorinen, I. (1997). The prospects of nutrient
removal with artificial reefs. In Jensen, A.C. (ed). *European Artificial Reef Research*. pp 85-96. Proceedings of the first EARRN conference, March 1996 Ancona, Italy. Pub Southampton Oceanography Centre, 449p.

Miyaoka, S., Tsuji, H., Fujii, S., Kita, D., Ishigaki, M. and Kobayashi, M. (1995). Development of an ecological seawater purification system with a rubble mound. Proc. int. conf. on Ecological System Enhancement Technology for Aquatic Environments, Tokyo , Japan, 30 Oct - 2 Nov. 1995. v.II pp. 905-910.

Relini, G., Relini, M. and Torchia, G. (1995). La barrieria artificiale di Loano. Biologia Marina Mediterranea **2**(1):21-64.

Revenga, S., Fernandez, F., Gonzalez, J.L. and Santaella, E. (1997). Artificial reefs in Spain: the regulatory framework. In Jensen, A.C. (ed). *European Artificial Reef Research*. pp 161-174. Proceedings of the first EARRN conference, March 1996 Ancona, Italy. Pub Southampton Oceanography Centre, 449p.

Sampaolo, A. and Relini, G. (1994). Coal ash for artificial habitats in Italy. Bulletin of Marine Science **55** (2):1279-1296.

Seaman, W. (1997). Does the level of design influence success of an artificial reef? In Jensen, A.C. (ed). *European Artificial Reef Research*. pp 359-376. Proceedings of the first EARRN conference, March 1996 Ancona, Italy. Pub Southampton Oceanography Centre, 449p.

Seaman, W. and Sprague, L.M. (1991). *Artificial habitats for marine and freshwater fisheries*. Academic Press Inc. 285p.

Simard, F. (1997). Socio-economic aspects of artificial reefs in Japan. In Jensen, A.C. (ed). *European Artificial Reef Research*. pp 233-240. Proceedings of the first EARRN conference, March 1996 Ancona, Italy. Pub Southampton Oceanography Centre, 449p.

Sonu, C.J. and Grove, R.S. (1985). Typical Japanese reef modules. Bulletin of Marine Science **37**(1):348-355.

Spanier, E. (1994). What are the characteristics of a good artificial reef for lobsters? Crustaceana, **67**: 173- 86.

Various authors (1994). Fifth International Conference on Aquatic Habitat Enhancement, 3-7 November 1991, Long Beach Ca. USA. Bulletin of Marine Science 2&3 (combined) 265 - 1359.

Wickins, J.F. (1995). Experimental studies of lobster habitat requirements in reef structures. In Ecoset '95. International Conference on Ecological System Enhancement Technology for Aquatic Environments. The Sixth International Conference on Aquatic Habitat Enhancement. 29th Oct. - 2nd Nov. 1995, Tokyo, Japan. **2**: 652-657.

Wickins, J.F. and Barker, G.C. (1997). Quantifying complexity in rock reefs. In Jensen, A.C.(ed.) (1997). *European Artificial Reef Research.* pp 423-430.Proceedings of the first EARRN conference, March 1996 Ancona, Italy. Pub Southampton Oceanography Centre, 449p.

Wilson, C.A. and Van Sickle, V.R. (1989). Development of the Louisianna artificial reef program. In, Fourth International Conference on artificial habitats for fisheries. Bulletin of Marine Science **44**(2): 1071-1072.

Woodhead, P.M.J., Jacobsen, M.E., Parker, J.H. and Duedall, I.W. (1982). The coal waste artificial reef program (C-WARP): investigations of an important new resource potential for fishing reef construction. Marine Fish. Rev. **44**(6/7):16-23

Beach fill stabilization with tuned structures: Experience in the southeastern U.S.A. and Caribbean

DR. KEVIN R. BODGE, P.E.
Olsen Associates, Inc., 4438 Herschel Street, Jacksonville, FL 32210 USA

ABSTRACT. A design protocol for structurally-stabilized shore protection projects prescribes that the structures' geometry and orientation be"tuned" to the incident wave field and the computed alongshore transport potential, and suggests that the structure-induced shoreline can be approximately predicted by a simple "one-third rule". Numerous projects constructed since 1990 in the southeastern U.S. and the Caribbean have thus far performed per the predictions upon which the design protocol is based.

INTRODUCTION

Use of coastal structures to stabilize beach restoration projects has recently re-emerged in the United States and the Caribbean. In the early 1990's, the author's firm was among the first to successfully introduce such structures after a 10 to 20 year informal "ban" of their use in much of the U.S. The present paper describes the design methodology and performance of beach restoration projects that include structures which partly or completely stabilize the beach fill. Such "shoreline stabilization structures" are specifically intended to develop or extend the practical life of the beach fill. They typically include headlands, groins, and/or nearshore breakwaters.

PROJECT CONDITIONS THAT MAY WARRANT STRUCTURES

In the author's design experience to-date, the incorporation of coastal structures to beach fill projects has been warranted in a variety of circumstances. These include instances where

(1) erosion stress is sufficiently severe to preclude an economically- or physically-practical beach fill life;

(2) the proximity of environmentally sensitive natural resources or marine structures preclude construction of a wide beach fill; and/or

(3) the desired beach amenity is advanced far seaward of the adjacent shoreline, or is located upon an otherwise non-littoral coastline.

The first instance includes project sites that feature accelerating (erosive) longshore transport gradients or sediment deprivation, including sites where the littoral drift has been interrupted or where there are alongshore losses to littoral sinks (such as inlets). In these cases, the rate at which the beach fill erodes may be so high that excessively frequent renourishment is required to maintain the project shoreline. Attempts to extend the renourishment interval by increasing the "advance nourishment" fill volume increases the project's width, and therefore increases its perturbative effect to the shoreline. This, in turn, increases the fill's loss rate (primarily via end-effects) so that, the increased fill volume yields little net decrease of the requisite renourishment frequency.

The second instance includes cases where an otherwise wide beach fill would bury nearshore natural resources such as reefs or seagrasses beds; or, encroach upon (shoal) marine facilities such as docks, outfalls or water intakes. A related instance includes cases where the nearshore seabed

Coastlines, structures and breakwaters. Thomas Telford, London, 1998

slope is steep or abruptly drops. Each of these cases physically limit the size of the allowable beach fill; and, as such, restrict the project's life and/or its likelihood of success.

The third instance includes sites that do not naturally (or no longer) feature sandy beaches. This includes coastlines that are naturally rocky or irregular, or where a historically sandy beach has mostly vanished due to sediment starvation, mining, etc. This also includes sites where an "artificial" beach is to be constructed at a new location within a lagoon or along a finite section of a lakefront park, etc. In each of these cases, the desired beach represents a perturbation to the existing coastline that is inherently unstable, primarily due to severe end-losses of the beach fill.

AVOIDING IMPACTS TO ADJACENT SHORELINES

It is well known that "hard" coastal structures (groins, breakwaters, etc.) placed amidst a sedimentary coastline with obliquely incident waves can induce erosion of the adjacent (downdrift) shoreline. This effect can occur via impoundment of the ambient littoral drift against the structure, and via offshore losses induced by rip-currents created by the structure. This adverse effect may be avoided or minimized in the following circumstances.

1. Most simplistically, project sites that are located at the terminus of a littoral cell inherently avoid adverse downdrift impacts (since there is no downdrift beach). Practically, such sites include the ends of an island or the terminus of the strand along an otherwise rocky coastline.

2. Structural fields that are pre-filled with sand (imported from outside of the littoral system) are theoretically "transparent" to the ambient littoral drift. The purpose of this "advance nourishment" is to mitigate the structures' tendency to impound sand by "saturating" the field to (or beyond) its design beach capacity during or immediately after its construction.

3. Structures that include spurs or perpendicular heads at their seaward ends appear less prone to create rip-currents, and are therefore less likely to promote offshore losses. While the author knows of no definitive test results of this specific assertion, field experience suggests that T-head groins lend particular stability to the beach cells between the groins -- even in storms with high cross-shore transport potential. Likewise, rough-surfaced (dissipative) structures appear less likely to create rips than smooth-surfaced structures.

4. Structural fields that terminate within a *decelerating* longshore transport gradient are less likely to promote erosion downdrift of the field. In contrast, fields that terminate within a *stable* gradient are marginally resistant to downdrift erosion effects (so long as the structural field remains filled and "transparent" to the ambient littoral drift). Fields that terminate within an *accelerating* transport gradient are more-or-less inherently *prone* to downdrift erosion -- as the last structure(s) in the field preclude beach fill material from being transported into the zone where the erosion stress increases.

DESIGN METHODOLOGY

In general, our design protocol of a structurally-stabilized beach fill involves the following steps:

1. Computation of the average and extreme wave angle orientation -- and the alongshore gradients in net and gross longshore sediment transport potential -- along the project site;

2. Prediction of the nominal shoreline location that will result from the principal and extreme wave angles in response to the width and orientation of the gap between adjacent structures;

3. Translation of the predicted nominal shoreline location to the upper (berm) shoreline location, and identification of the minimum "target" shoreline location to be maintained;

4.   Determination of the approximate number and size of the structures and beach "cells" needed to create the target shoreline;

5.   Orientation of the structures' ends such that the openings between structures are aligned in desired accordance with the principal, local wave angle; and

6.   Lay-out of the structural field and prediction of the resultant beach contours for principal and extreme wave angles; and, iterative re-design to optimize the lay-out as a function of construction quantities, risk of shoreline stability, architectural considerations, etc.

Each of these design elements are specifically described below.

1.   Wave Angle & Longshore Transport Potential

Computation of the principal (and extreme) wave angle and the alongshore variation in the longshore transport potential are central to designing the limits and orientation of the structure -- and to predicting the resultant beach fill response within and adjacent to the structural field. Toward this end, we typically employ a grid-based, numerical wave refraction model with alongshore grid spacing not greater than the anticipated distance between structures. Offshore wave conditions are input from hindcast or measured data -- but more often (and more simply) are input in 15° to 25° arc-increments with assumed periods and heights for sea and for swell.

For each input wave condition, and at each alongshore grid column, the wave angle α_b and height H_b at the point of *incipient* breaking are estimated by reference to the shoreward-most *non*-broken wave angle α_1 and height H_1 at each column of the refraction grid. (The latter are identified as the shoreward-most occurrence of a wave height that is less than κd, where κ is the breaker index (usually about 0.8) and d is the local grid depth). Assuming regular depth contours between the shoreward-most non-breaking wave and incipient breaking, and assuming shallow water waves,

$$H_b = A_1 / [1 - (A_1 A_2) / 5] \tag{1}$$

$$\alpha_b = \sin^{-1} [(\sin \alpha_1)(g H_b / \kappa)^{1/2} / C_1] \tag{2}$$

where g is gravitational acceleration, C_1 is the wave celerity at the reference wave location, and

$$A_1 = (\kappa/g)^{1/5} H_1^{4/5} (C_{g1} \cos \alpha_1)^{2/5} \tag{3}$$

$$A_2 = (g \sin^2 \alpha_1) / C_1^2 \tag{4}$$

after Bodge et al. (1996), where C_{g1} is the group celerity at the reference wave location and α_1 is expressed relative to the grid column's local shoreline orientation. The magnitude of the corresponding longshore transport potential is estimated from the "CERC formula" as

$$Q_L = K H_b^{5/2} \sin(2\alpha_b) \tag{5}$$

where K is taken as an arbitrary coefficient of value 1.0 and units are neglected. (Herein, alongshore *variations* in transport potential are of interest moreso than absolute magnitudes.) The *average* breaking wave angle α_b and longshore transport potential Q_L are computed as the weighted average of each input wave case's angle and transport values at each grid column; i.e.,

$$\alpha_b = \Sigma_i (p_i \, \alpha_{bi}) \quad \text{and} \quad Q_L = \Sigma_i (p_i \, Q_L) \tag{6}$$

where p_i is the average annual occurrence of wave case i. The occurrence data are taken from hindcasts or measurements, if available. Where such data are not available, the occurrence probabilities are simply assumed from local knowledge and/or examination of wind and fetch data. The latter point is particularly important where few data are available and time or budget preclude detailed study. In most cases, the average wave angle and transport gradient that characterize a project site are fairly insensitive to the assumed occurrences of input wave conditions -- relative to the uncertainty and annual variability that typically characterize measured or hindcast wave data. This is especially true where irregular nearshore bathymetry acts as a strong refractive "filter" that results in similar breaking conditions regardless of the offshore wave incidence. Such sites are very often those that warrant structural stabilization in the first place; i.e., sites of irregular coastline morphology or bathymetry. Accordingly, prior to undertaking complicated study of a project site's wave conditions, it can be fruitful to examine the breaking conditions' sensitivity (or lack thereof) to reasonable variations in *assumed* offshore conditions.

Once computed or estimated, the average wave crests and longshore transport gradient are plotted along the project area. The former are used to orient the structures; the latter are used to help identify limits of the structural field. Computed alongshore variations in transport (particularly accelerating gradients) may warrant structures to stabilize the beach fill. The downdrift limit of the structural field is established where the transport potential returns to a quasi-stable level.

2.   Shoreline Prediction

Shoreline prediction adjacent to the structures is accomplished through a combination of a simple empirical formula developed from experience, and the "log-spiral" coastline geometries tabulated by Silvester and Hsu, 1993 (or Hsu & Evans, 1989) . The latter method, including others by Yasso (1965), Pope and Dean (1986), Benenguer and Enriquez (1988), McCormick (1993), among others, are limited in their *functional* utility in that they do not indicate the *tidal elevation* of the predicted shoreline. The author's experience suggests that these previous investigators' observations appear to best apply to an elevation between mean low water (mlw) and mean tide.

For preliminary design, a simple empirical rule is that *the mean low water shoreline will be located about one-third of the structures' gap distance behind the structures' seaward face.* Specifically, in **Figure 1a**, the structures' gap distance, G, is the opening (or "control line") between adjacent structures or headlands. Here, the mlw shoreline is roughly estimated as a line parallel to the control line, located a distance G/3 behind it. The shoreline in the lee of each headland is estimated as a circular arc of radius G/3 with center at the control line's endpoints. This rough estimate is only valid where the angle between the wave crest and the structures' control line is small (say, less than about 20°). In **Figure 1b**, the structures' gap distance ("control line") is the distance G between a headland and a downdrift point of stability. Here, the mlw shoreline is a line that begins at a distance G/3 behind the headland and ends at the downdrift "stable" point. The shoreline in the headland's lee is a circular arc of radius G/3 with center at the headland.

For final design, a composite is made of this simple "one-third rule" shoreline and the predicted shoreline from Silvester & Hsu, 1993 (**Figure 2**). The stability of the beach fill is better ensured when *flanking* of the structures' heads is prevented. In this way, as shown in the figure, the heads' trunk (groin section) is extended at least as far landward as the predicted limit of nominal wave run-up at high tide, and buried within the beach fill. The elevation of the structures' heads is established so as to minimize wave overtopping during the design event of interest.

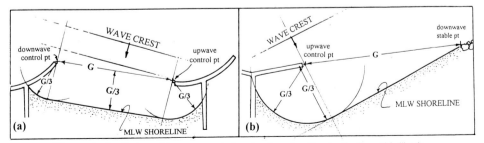

Figure 1. Prediction of the structure-induced m.l.w. shoreline by the "one-third" rule.

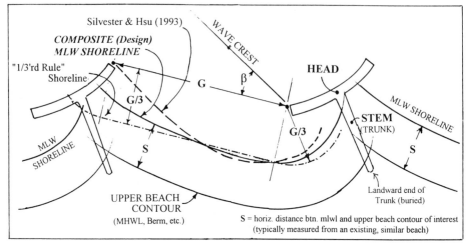

Figure 2. The "design" mlw shoreline is an average of that predicted by the "one-third rule" and Silvester & Hsu (1993) log-spiral geometry. Upper contours are drawn as a uniform offset from the design mlwl.

3.   Predicting Berm Location & Requirements

The location of the upper beach contours (i.e., the berm, the limit of storm wave run-up, etc.) is predicted by an up-slope translation of the mlw shoreline described above. This may be most reliably done by measuring the profile slope(s) of an existing, nearby beach with wave exposure and sediment type similar to the project beach fill. The *desired* ("target") location of the project's design berm must also be identified. This is the line beyond which the project's *predicted* berm should fall for incident wave angles of interest.

4.   Number and Size of Structures

From **Figure 3**, the total project shorefront length, L, is composed of n beach cells with gap-width G, and n+1 structures of head-width H; i.e., $L = n(G+H)$. As a *minimum*, the structures' head-width, H, should be large enough to ensure that the mean low water shoreline reaches the head. From the "one-third rule", this requires that $H = 2(G/3)$. *Typical* design requires that the high water or other shoreline elevation reaches the head. This requires that $H = 2(G/3 + X)$ where X is the horizontal distance between the mlw shoreline and the contour elevation of interest; i.e.,

$$H = 2G/3 + 2X, \quad \text{where } X \geq 0 \tag{7}$$

Therefore, the number of requisite beach cells is

$$n = L/(5G/3 + 2X) \tag{8}$$

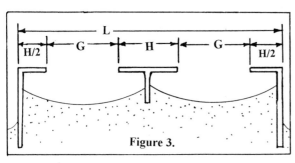

Figure 3.

This represents a family of solutions from which the number of project beach cells, n, can be selected as a function of the desired gap width, G. Of course, to maintain the project's berm at or beyond the "target" location, larger gaps (fewer cells) require larger heads located further from shore. Smaller gaps will re quire smaller structures, though more of them, built closer to shore. The ultimate decision of n, H, and G is therefore influenced by cost (i.e., many small structures vs. fewer large structures), as well as upland architectural or landscape factors.

5. Structure Orientation

The ends of the structures' heads are located so that the openings between them ("control lines") are aligned accordingly with the angle of the local wave crest. The nominal design aligns the heads' ends so that the openings are *parallel* to the principal wave angle at each opening (**Figure 4a**). In this case, the angle between the wave crest and the structures' opening is zero, and the "one-third" rule (described above) is readily employed to predict the mlw shoreline. (In contrast, the Silvester & Hsu (1993) and other predictors are not defined for angles less than about 20°.)

The stability of the beach fill is enhanced by "over-correcting" the alignment of the heads' ends so that the transport direction within the beach cell is *reversed* from its expected, open-coast sense (**Figure 4b**). This design acts to drive the fill material "updrift" so to speak. By intent, this design is less transparent to littoral drift, and may be inappropriate where downdrift erosion is of concern.

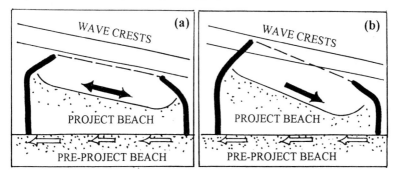

Figure 4. Relative to the expected transport direction on the pre-project beach (white arrows), aligning the opening between the structures (a) parallel with, or (b) against, the wave crests can acts to induce a null or reversal transport direction (black arrows) within the projects' beach cells.

The benefit of "tuning" the structures' head orientation to the local wave angle (relative to traditional, shore-parallel heads) is illustrated in **Figure 5**. For identically-sized structures, those with "tuned" heads yield greater shoreline stability (smaller longshore transport potential within each cell) and greater net beach area than groins with shore-parallel heads.

If the terminal structure in a field employs a head or spur on its downdrift side, it is better offset *seaward* than landward. While intuition suggests that a *landward* offset is a more natural transition from the structural field to the downdrift shoreline, it inherently induces a crenulate bay in the structure's lee that will erode into the native beach (see **Figure 1b**). Attempts to fill (nourish) this crenulate bay may be fruitless -- as the embayment shape is an irreconcilable result of the structures' proximity to the shoreline.

6. Iterative Design and Final Lay-Out

The lay-out of the structural field is usually an iterative process. For an assumed value of the heads' lengths (or the gap lengths betwixt), the number, size and spacing of the structures can be initially developed from Eqs. 7 & 8. In a first-draft layout, for a given beach cell of gap length G, the endpoint of the upwave structure's head should be located at least (G/3 + Y) seaward of the

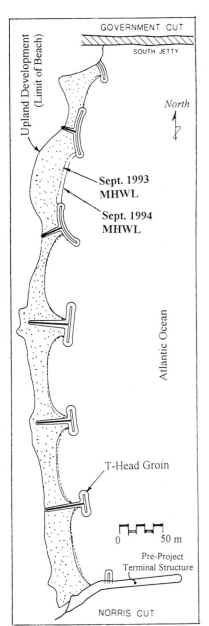

Figure 6. Fisher Island, Florida.

(Figure labels, clockwise from top) GOVERNMENT CUT; SOUTH JETTY; Upland Development (Limit of Beach); North; Sept. 1993 MHWL; Sept. 1994 MHWL; Atlantic Ocean; T-Head Groin; 0 — 50 m; Pre-Project Terminal Structure; NORRIS CUT

0.3 to 0.45. Median beach grain sizes range between 0.15 and 0.3 mm.

At Fisher Island, Florida (c. April, 1991), seven headland-rock structures were built along 650 m of shoreline immediately downdrift (south) of Miami Beach (**Figure 6**). The beach was then nourished with 20,000 m^3 of aragonite sand imported from the Bahamas. The site had been completely severed from the dominant southerly drift by the construction of the Government Cut inlet and its jetties. Structures were introduced to the project because of the site's severe erosional stress (>1 m/yr) and the presence of near-shore seagrass beds that were not to be buried by sand fill. This island site more or less represents the terminus of southeast Florida's littoral system, such that downdrift impacts were of minor concern. Four years after project construction, the in-place fill volume was within 1% of the placed volume (Raichle, 1995). The project successfully weathered Hurricane Andrew (1992) with less than 10% volume loss (subsequently recovered within the next year), and less than 1 to 2 meters of shoreline retreat. While the shoreline orientation "shifts" within the cells as a function of wave direction, the average shoreline location has changed less than 1 m. The mlw shoreline near the middle of each cell is located about 0.34 (±0.12 s.dev.) times the gap distance between adjacent structures. The orienta-tion of the two southernmost cells structures' are "over-corrected" to the local wave angle in order to impose a northerly (reversed) transport direction. The other structures' endpoints are aligned parallel with each cell's average wave angle, where the latter was estimated from grid-based wave refraction analysis using 20 years of hindcast offshore wave data. No adverse impacts (burial) were reported to the nearshore seagrass beds during 4 years of monitoring (CSA, 1995).

At Jolly Harbor, Antigua (B.W.I.), eleven rock T-head structures were built at the northern and southern ends of a 1-km long embayment and subsequently filled with dredged sand in 1994-95 (see **Figure 7**). Both sites had been previously filled with (unstabilized) dredged sand that eroded almost immediately thereafter -- presumably because of the large incident angle of the waves as they diffracted into the embayment. The structurally-stabilized design employed the protocol outlined above, except that the wave angle at each cell was estimated from examination of the nearshore bathymetric contours and visual observation from atop a nearby mountain. The net-to-gross transport ratio at these two sites is high (probably >0.8). To-date, the post-project shoreline has almost precisely matched the design predictions. Of particular note

project
under construction
(pre-beach fill)

Figure 7. Jolly Harbor, Antigua.

is the terminal structure at the south end, where the head was turned landward (as a transition to the existing beach) and where no groin trunk was constructed. The proximity of the head to the ambient beach, and the lack of a stem, led to minor erosion of the existing beach as a crenulate embayment formed in the lee of the head.

An analogous problem was noted at the terminus of a rock revetment designed (by others) along the interior of New Pass Inlet, at <u>Lighthouse Point, Florida</u> in May, 1997 (**Figure 8**). A classic crenulate embayment formed at the downdrift end of this structure within several weeks after construction. The consequent erosion of the downdrift beach (presently about 22 m) is approximately 30% of the distance between the end of the revetment and a historically stable point located further downdrift in the lee of a large shoal. The revetment was constructed to armor a shoreline that had eroded downdrift of a previously-constructed revetment. That shoreline likewise featured a crenulate shape with maximum recession of about 78 m, or about 34% of the distance between the original revetment and the previous, historical downdrift stable point.

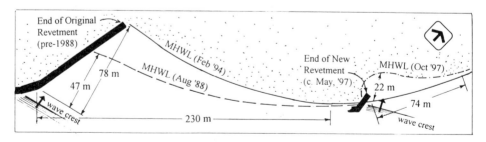

Figure 8. Shoreline recession at the terminus of rock revetments that were built in the 1980's and in 1997; Lighthouse Point (along New Pass Inlet on Florida's west coast).

At <u>Tybee Island, Georgia</u>, in 1995, three rock T-head structures were constructed downdrift of an existing rock groin, then filled with dredged sand (**Figure 9**). The site is at the southern end of the island and is adjacent to an unstable tidal channel and swift currents (1 m/s). The mean tide range is 2.1 m. The structures' heads, constructed upon rock-filled geogrid mattresses, are oriented so that the openings between gaps are aligned with the average wave direction (estimated from aerial photographs). In each of the cells, from east to west, the mlw shoreline is located behind the structures' face by distances of approximately 0.15, 0.38, and 0.57 times the cell's opening size; or, 0.37 on average. (The variations between cells are due to the effect of the long updrift groin at the east end, and a leaky groin at the west end.)

Figure 9. T-head groins at the southern end of Tybee Island, Georgia (c. 1995). Photograph: Sept., 1997.

On the north coast of <u>Lyford Cay, New Providence Island, Bahamas</u>, three different stabilized beach fill projects have been constructed since 1993, one of which is shown in **Figure 10**. Each project, built for private residences, includes about 100 to 140 m of shorefront along a once sandy coastline that has since been denuded of sand. The designs for each followed the protocol outlined above, where the average and extreme breaking wave angles at each site were estimated from examination of the local pre-project bathymetry and by refraction analysis of assumed offshore wave directions that were reckoned from limited wind data and site observations. The post-project mlw shorelines at each site, measured between 1 and 4 years after construction, were located leeward of the structures' seaward faces by a distances of 0.3 to 0.5 times the structures' gap distances at each beach cell. The measured beach slopes at each site are about 10% less (gentler) than the open-coast, natural beaches that were referenced during design. This is attributed to the lesser wave energy within the bounds of the projects' structures. By analogy, at an artificial lagoon site near these projects (Atlantis, Paradise Island), a semi-stabilized beach fill designed by others reposed to a slope almost twice as gentle as an open coast beach with similar grain size (i.e., 1:18 vs. 1:10). The lagoon site is a semi-quiescent environment subject only to tidal fluctuation (1 m range) and small long-period waves (0.1 m height and 12-15 s period).

At <u>Bonita Beach, Florida</u>, in 1995, a pair of traditional rock groins were used to stabilize the downdrift end of a 190,000 m³ beach fill updrift of a small tidal inlet and to promote a bypass bar that would naturally transfer sand to the shoreline downdrift of the inlet. After two years, net fill losses total less than 10% of the placed volume, and the bypass bar has naturally developed

(**Figure 11**). Per predictions, the locations of the shorelines updrift of the groins correspond to a profile that intersects the seaward face of the groin at about -0.8 m; or, about equal to the mean tide level minus the mean tide range. Likewise, terminal groins built at the downdrift end of a 2M m³ beach fill at <u>Amelia Island, Florida</u>, and as an interim sand-tightening measure at the south jetty of <u>Port Canaveral, Florida</u>, exhibited similar shoreline response (not shown). These groins consist of sand-filled geotextile tubes (Longard Tubes), and were placed in 1996 and 1993, respectively.

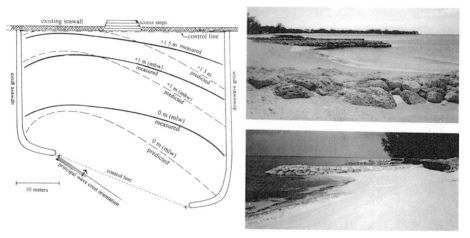

Figure 10. Surveyed beach fill contours approx. 6 months after construction of the R. Arnold stabilized beach restoration project; Lyford Cay, New Providence Is., Bahamas.

Figure 11. Groins at the downdrift end of the Bonita Beach, FL fill project (1995). Photo: August, 1997.

There are numerous other example projects designed by the author's firm and by others not mentioned herein. Recent descriptions of the latter in the U.S. include Rosati & Pope, 1989; Hanson & Kraus, 1991; Hardaway et al., 1995; Chrzastowski & Trask, 1997; among others. Other notable examples include many projects and studies in Europe and the Mediterranean (e.g., Spataru, 1990; Peña & Covarsi, 1994; Laustrup & Madsen, 1994; among others). Examination of these projects (precluded herein by space limitations) suggests that their performance is in general agreement with the design protocol and predictions described above.

SUMMARY

The stabilization of beach fill by structures may be warranted at sites where erosion stress is sufficiently severe to require otherwise impractical (frequent) renourishment intervals; or where the proximity of natural resources or marine structures preclude construction of a wide beach fill; or where the project shoreline is advanced far seaward of the adjacent shoreline or located upon a non-littoral coastline. Where the project is not located at the natural terminus of a littoral cell or upon a non-littoral coastline, adverse impacts to downdrift shorelines may be minimized by (i) advance-nourishment of the structures' impoundment field with imported beach fill, (ii) use of T-head or other headland structures that do not promote rip currents and offshore losses, and (iii) termination of the structural field in a zone of non-accelerating longshore transport potential.

Beach fill stability is enhanced when the structures' heads are oriented such that the gaps between adjacent structures are approximately aligned with (or beyond) the angle of the local, incident wave crest. The mean low water shoreline within the beach cell between structures can be roughly estimated as lying 1/3'rd of the distance of the cell's openings, behind a line drawn between the structures' seaward face. The shoreline updrift of a conventional groin (or that with a modest T-head) is approximated as being parallel to the local, average wave crest angle, where the beach profile intersects the seaward face of the groin at an elevation of 1/2 the mean tide range below mlw. Projects constructed since 1991, in 0.8 to 2 m tide ranges, with low- to moderate average wave heights (1 m), have more-or-less performed per the design protocol outlined in the paper.

REFERENCES

Berenguer, J. and Enriquez, J., 1988. "Design of Pocket Beaches, The Spanish Case", Proc. Int. Conf. on Coastal Eng., ASCE, 1411-1425.

Bodge, K., Creed, C., and Raichle, A., 1996. "Improving Input Wave Data for Use with Shoreline Change Models", J. Waterway, Port, Coastal and Ocean Eng., ASCE, 122 (5), 259-263.

Chrzastowski, M. and Trask, C. B., 1997. "Results and Lessons Learned from Coastal Monitoring at Forest Park Beach on the Illinois Shore of Lake Michigan." *Shore & Beach*, 65 (2), 27-34, April, 1997.

CSA, 1995. "Fisher Island Beach Restoration Project Biological Monitoring, Final Report", Continental Shelf Assoc., Inc., 759 Parkway St., Jupiter, FL 33477 USA.

Hanson, H. and Kraus, N., 1991. "Numerical Simulation of Shoreline Change at Lorain, Ohio," J. Waterway, Port, Coastal and Ocean Eng., ASCE, 117(1); 1-18. Jan/Feb., 1991.

Hardaway, C. S., Gunn, J. and Reynolds R. N., 1995. "Headland Breakwater Performance in Chesapeake Bay," Proc., Beach Pres. Tech., Fla. Shore & Beach Pres. Assn., Tallahassee, FL; pp. 365-382.

Hsu, J. R. and Evans, C., 1989. "Parabolic Bay Shapes & Applications", Proc. Inst. Civil Engrs. 87: 557-70.

Laustrup, C. and Madsen, H. T., 1994. "Design of Breakwaters and Beach Nourishment", Proc., 24th Int. Conf. on Coastal Eng., ASCE; 1359-72.

McCormick, M., 1993. "Equilibrium Response to Breakwaters", J. Waterway, Port, Coastal and Ocean Eng., ASCE, 119 (6), 657-670; Nov./Dec., 1993.

Peña, C. and Covarsi, M., 1994. "Project Works and Monitoring at Barcelona Olympic Beaches," Proc., 24th Int. Conf. on Coastal Eng., ASCE; 3564-78.

Pope, J. and Dean, J., 1986. "Development of Design Criteria for Segmented Breakwaters," Proc., 20th Int. Coastal Eng. Conf., ASCE, 2144-2158.

Raichle, A. W., 1995. "Fisher Island, Florida, Beach Restoration Physical Monitoring Report #4", Olsen Assoc., Inc., 4438 Herschel St., Jacksonville, FL 32210 USA; March, 1995.

Rosati, J. & Pope, J., 1989. "Colonial Beach, Virginia Detached Breakwater Project", CERC Misc. Paper 89-2, Vicksburg, MS; Jan., 1989; 34 pp.

Silvester, R. and Hsu, J. R., 1993. Coastal Stabilization. Prentice Hall, Inc., Englewood Cliffs, New Jersey; pp. 212-244.

Spataru, A., 1990. "Breakwaters for the Protection of Romanian Beaches," J. Coastal Eng., 14 (2), 129-146.

Examination of a Prefabricated Submerged Breakwater - Preliminary Results: Vero Beach, Florida, U.S.A.

J.B. SMITH[1], JOAN POPE[1] and JEFF TABAR[2]
[1]U.S. Army Corps of Engineers Waterways Experiment Station, Vicksburg, MS., USA
[2]Indian River County, Florida Department of Public Works, Vero Beach, Florida

ABSTRACT

Indian River County, Florida, USA has experienced significant shoreline erosion along portions of its coastline. In August 1996, a 915-m long prefabricated modular concrete unit submerged breakwater was deployed 70 m to 80 m offshore of the City of Vero Beach, Florida. The design of this narrow-crested submerged breakwater, installed as an erosion and wave energy reduction measure, incorporated lessons from a previous installation at Palm Beach, Florida (Dean et al., 1994a), and additional basin model tests (Dean et al., 1994b). To evaluate the effectiveness of the breakwater, a three-year monitoring program is being conducted by Indian River County and the US Army Corps of Engineers Waterways Experiment Station. The program includes quarterly hydrographic and topographic surveys, wave transmission, breakwater settlement, and scour measurements. The purpose of the program is to determine profile and areal volumetric changes, wave attenuation effects, structure stability and shoreline response relative to pre-project conditions. A unique challenge to the monitoring program includes the presence of an irregular natural limestone reef which causes variable wave transformation, and an inshore perched sand wedge which shifts onshore and offshore in response to seasonal variations and episodic events. Preliminary findings concerning shoreline response, sediment volumetric changes, wave transmission effects, and breakwater settlement relative to pre-project conditions are presented.

INTRODUCTION

Indian River County, Florida, USA is located on the Atlantic coast of Florida (Figure 1A). Shoreline erosion has occurred along portions of this coastline in the past, particularly in the vicinity of Vero Beach effectively eliminating any high tide beach in front of much of the city's seawalled and bulkheaded front. In an effort to provide a more stable, wider dry beach, the City of Vero Beach deployed a Prefabricated Erosion Prevention (P.E.P.) narrow-crested submerged breakwater (20 July through 16 August, 1996) (Figure 1B). The intent of the P.E.P. breakwater was to cause wave energy reduction landward of the breakwater both during normal and storm wave conditions, thus stabilizing the nearshore and reducing shoreline retreat without adverse impacts to the adjacent shoreline.

The breakwater is composed of 215 interlocking pre-cast reinforced concrete units, each of which weighs 25 metric tons, and measures 4.6 m (cross-shore) x 3.7 m (alongshore), x 1.8 m (height)(Figure 2). The 915-m long breakwater was placed in eleven segments (segments A-K)

Coastlines, structures and breakwaters. Thomas Telford, London, 1998

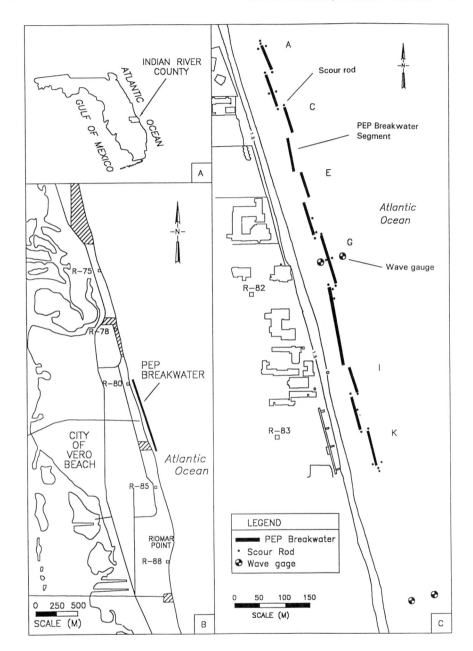

Figure 1. A) Location of Indian River County, Florida; B) Location of the Prefabricated Erosion Prevention (P.E.P.) Reef in the City of Vero Beach with some State of Florida 'R' monuments; C) Location of the breakwater segments, scour rods, and wave gauges.

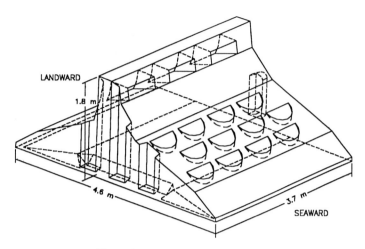

Figure 2. Cross-section of P.E.P. Reef unit.

ranging in length from 50 m to 160 m, in an alternating in an onshore/offshore configuration (Figure 1C). Distances from the seawall/dune base are 68 m and 80 m for onshore and offshore segments. Bottom elevations were -2.1 m and -2.7 m with reference to National Geodetic Vertical Datum of 1929 (NGVD, which is approximately Mean Sea Level, and is 0.58 m below Mean High Water (MHW). The design water depth above the breakwater crest alternated between 0.3 and 0.9 m for onshore and offshore segments (Figure 3).

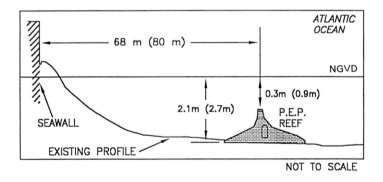

Figure 3. Schematic profile cross-section with the P.E.P. Reef. Water depths and distances from the seawall/dune base are expressed for inner and outer (in parentheses) breakwater segments.

The segmented configuration of the Vero Beach breakwater was selected after reviewing the findings of a single 1,260-m long P.E.P. breakwater installation from July 1992 to August 1995 at Palm Beach, Florida (Dean et al., 1994a). This continuous breakwater had a tendency to trap the overtopping waters, inducing strong alongshore currents landward of the structure (Browder et al., 1996). Subsequent physical model tests by Dean (1994b) suggested that a staggered or discontinuous configuration would allow more gradual offshore dissipation of the wave setup and hydraulic head.

A three-year monitoring program is being conducted by the US Army Corps of Engineers Waterways Experiment Station to provide an independent evaluation of the effectiveness of the breakwater system. This monitoring program, beginning in August 1996, includes quarterly hydrographic surveys, and wave transmission, breakwater settlement, and scour measurements, as well as an analysis of pre-project littoral conditions.

The purpose of this paper is to assess the effect of the P.E.P. Reef on coastal processes and sediment distribution patterns through the evaluation of field monitoring efforts during the initial August, 1996 to September, 1997 period.

DATA ANALYSIS AND DISCUSSION
Shoreline Change
Bathymetric surveys have been performed quarterly since June, 1996. A total of 40 profile lines extending approximately 1,500 m north and south of the breakwater terminus were established based on Florida Department of Environmental Protection 'R' Monuments R-75 to R-88, each of which are spaced approximately 300 m apart, and are part of a state-wide coastal change reference system (Figure 1B). Spacing between lines was 60 m within the breakwater limits, and 150 m outside of the breakwater limits. The June, August, December 1996, and September 1997 surveys extended 1,060 m seaward of the baseline, while the March and June 1997 surveys extended 460 m seaward of the baseline. Historical shoreline change data are based on U.S. Coast and Geodetic Survey offshore hydrographic surveys in 1881-82, 1928-30, 1946-49 and 1966-68, and National Oceanic Service (NOS) surveys in 1970, and aerial photography taken in 1986 and 1993.

During the period August 1996 (post-installation *baseline* survey) to December 1996 the entire study area shoreline (as measured at the mean high water line) retreated landward an average of 0.90 m (Figure 4). The shoreline continued to retreat landward by an additional 0.83 m through March 1997. There was some advancement of the shoreline during the summer of 1997 resulting in a net shoreline advancement of 0.25 m from August 1996 to September 1997.

Three areas were established to compare shoreline and volumetric trends in the breakwater and non-breakwater portions of the project. The breakwater area (R-80C to R-83C) addressed the area in the vicinity of the breakwater, while the north control (R-77 to R80B) and south control (R-83D to R-86A) areas extended 914m to the north and the south of the breakwater, respectively. Selection of the two control areas is based on the variable longshore sediment transport which is directed to the south in the winter, and to the north in the summer. The net longshore transport rate is approximately 56,000 m³/yr to the south, while the gross rate is 493,000 m³/yr (Walton, 1975; Stauble, 1987). Annualized rates of shoreline change over the

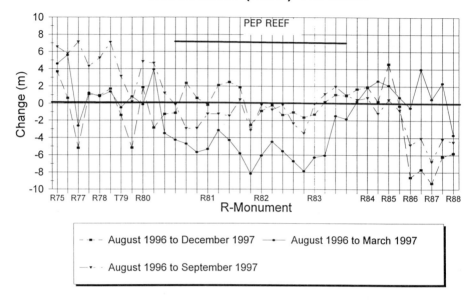

Figure 4. Shoreline change at individual R-monuments and intermediate R-monuments (R-75 to R-88) relative to the August 1996 baseline survey. Negative values indicate landward shoreline retreat; south is to the right. Note the retreat of the shoreline at the breakwater and to the south of the project, and advancement of the shoreline at northern locations over the 13-month period August 1996 to September 1997.

13-month breakwater post-installation period (August 1996 to September 1997) in the lee of the breakwater retreated landward 0.85 m, while the shoreline in the south control area also retreated landward 1.22 m. The shoreline in the north control area advanced seaward 3.87 m.

Comparison of annualized post-installation to historical shoreline changes (1880-1993) indicate that post-installation trends are similar but more exaggerated than historical trends (Table 1).

Volumetric Changes
Analysis of annualized sediment volumetric changes based on survey data indicate net erosion for the entire project length (R-75 to R-88) over the 37-month period from July 1993 to August 1996 prior to the installation of the breakwater (Table 2). Conversely, net accretion occurred over the 13-month (August 1996 to September 1997) post-installation period.

Area	Post - install	Historical
	August, 1996 to September, 1997	1880 - 1993
North	3.87	0.06
Breakwater	-0.85	-0.05
South	-1.22	-0.07
Entire Project Length (R-75 to R-88)	0.23	0.16

Table 1. Average Annual Shoreline (MHW = +0.58 m NGVD) Change at North, Breakwater, and South Areas (m/yr).

Volumetric changes are also considered with respect to breakwater, north and south areas (Table 2). Each area, which extends 914 m in alongshore length, extends in a cross-shore direction from the seawall/dune base to 76 m seaward of the breakwater axis. The breakwater area has eroded during both pre- (18,477 m³/yr) and post-(7,115 m³/yr) installation conditions suggesting that pre-installation erosion rate was 2.5 times greater than that of the post-installation period. Figure 5A illustrates post-installation incremental volumetric changes at breakwater, north, and south areas. The north and south areas eroded during the pre-installation period (9,199 m³/yr and 4,835 m³/yr, respectively), and accreted during the post-installation period (20,532 m³/yr and 3,565 m³/yr, respectively). The majority of erosion in the breakwater and south areas occurred during the first seven months following installation of the breakwater which included winter conditions (Figure 5A).

Table 2. Annualized Volumetric Changes for Pre- and Post-Installation Periods (m³/yr)

Area	Pre-installation (July 1993 - August 1996)	Post-installation (August 1996 - September 1997)
North	-9,199	20,532
Breakwater	-18,477	-7,115
South	-4,835	3,565
Total	-32,511	16,982

Much larger post-installation volumetric changes occurred landward of the breakwater axis (76 m; from the seawall/dune base to the breakwater axis) in all three areas than seaward of the breakwater axis (from the breakwater axis to 76 m seaward of the breakwater axis). Approximately 80% of the volumetric change in the north and breakwater areas occur landward of the breakwater (Figure 5B). In addition, while the south area indicates a net accretional signal, the south area landward of the breakwater has eroded 5,462 m³. Volumetric data seaward of the breakwater in all three areas indicate small changes in the north and breakwater areas, and overall accretion of 9,324 m³ in the south area. This volumetric stability of seaward cells is possibly due to the shallower subbottom elevation of hardbottom at seaward cells than at landward cells.

These data suggest that while sediment supply has been limited in historical conditions, the installation of the breakwater has accentuated erosion rates to the landward of the breakwater both in the breakwater and south areas.

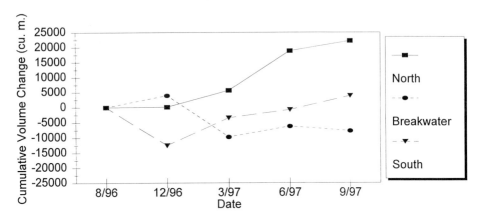

Figure 5A. Volumetric changes for the August, 1996 to September, 1997 post-installation period of the north, breakwater, and south areas (considering landward and seaward of the breakwater). During the period August 1996 to September 1997, the figure indicates volumetric accretion at northern area, erosion in the breakwater area, and stability at the southern area.

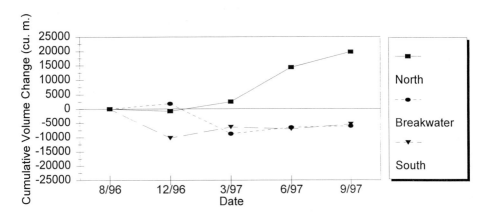

Figure 5B. Volumetric changes for the August, 1996 to September, 1997 post-installation period of the north, breakwater, and south areas (considering landward of breakwater). The accretional trend at the north area and erosional trend at the breakwater area are similar to trends presented in Figure 5A.

Scour in Vicinity of Breakwater
Scour and deposition within 3 m of the breakwater was monitored through the placement of 36 scour rods following breakwater installation at north (Segments A-C), center (segments F-H), and south (segments I-K) breakwater locations (Figure 1C).

Following breakwater installation in August, 1996, a prominent scour trench developed at the landward toe of each segment. Erosion rates for the first month following breakwater installation were -10 cm, -1 cm, and -25 cm for the north, center and south breakwater locations, respectively. The scour trench has persisted over the entire 13-month post-installation period for each of the three locations (Figure 6) apart from a period of accretion during November, 1996 to March, 1997, and June to July 1997. While it appears that an equilibrium may have been reached during these periods, the continued decrease of sand elevation suggests that the scour in the vicinity of the breakwater is still occurring.

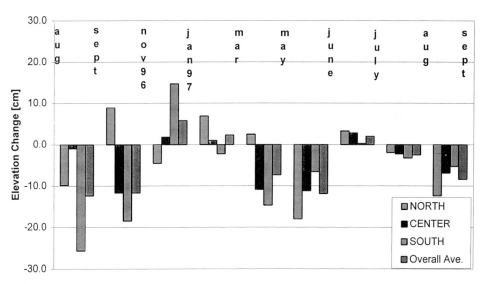

Figure 6. Average sand elevation changes for north, center, south, and overall locations over the August 1996 to September 1997 post-installation period.

An average depth of the scour trenches on the landward side of the breakwater was observed to be approximately 0.8 m, with an average width of approximately 1.8 m. A scour trench also develops on the seaward side of the breakwater during storm conditions, but is typically filled in during calmer sea conditions.

Comparison of scour data with profile survey data at the 2.1 m and 2.7 m (NGVD) contours to the north and south of the project area indicate that the erosion of the bed at breakwater locations is most likely a result of scour in the vicinity of the structures, and not due to fluctuations of the profile across the entire study area.

Settlement of Units

Breakwater elevation surveys were conducted for all quarterly surveys (including asbuilt conditions) to monitor unit settlement and alignment. Based on these data, the average settlement for all units is 0.92 m during the overall 13-month post-installation period (Figure 7). The majority of this settlement (0.62 m) occurred within 1 month of installation of the breakwater. Breakwater settlement continued until 4 months following breakwater installation when the settlement averaged 0.86 m.

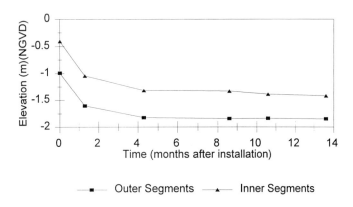

Figure 7. Average elevation change in the breakwater unit crest over the August 1996 to September 1997 post-installation period.

Breakwater settlement and the scour of sediment on the landward side of the breakwater appear to not be proportionally related. Although settlement and overall scour rates were greatest during the first four months following installation (0.86 m and 0.20 m, respectively), settlement appears to have ceased while formation of the scour trench has continued during the remainder of the monitoring period. Continued monitoring of these data will confirm the relationship between breakwater settlement and scour.

Wave Transmission Effects

Four directional wave gauges were used to measure the effectiveness of the breakwater in attenuating waves (Figure 1C). The gauges collect average pressure and bi-directional current measurements every 6 hrs. Two gauges were placed on profile line R-82 on either side of the breakwater to measure wave attenuation. The offshore gauge is located 112 m seaward of the seawall (-3.4 m NGVD)(23m seaward of the breakwater), and the nearshore gauge is located 81 m seaward of the seawall (-2.8 m NGVD)(8m landward of the breakwater)(Figure 8). Wave measurements began August 1996, and are continuing for the length of the monitoring program.

Two 'control' wave gauges were installed 265 m to the south of the breakwater for a 35-day period in January-February, 1997 (Figure 1C). The offshore gauge is located 92m seaward of the seawall (-3.1m NGVD), and the nearshore gauge is located 63m seaward of the seawall (-2.2 m

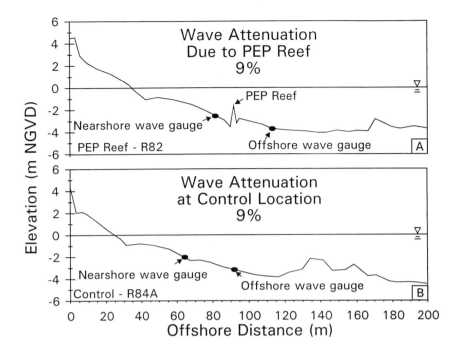

Figure 8. Schematic of profiles with wave gauges and wave attenuation information at breakwater (R-82), and control (R-84A) locations. Following settlement of the breakwater, wave attenuation averaged 9% both at P.E.P. Reef and control locations.

NGVD)(Figure 8). The purpose of these control wave gauges was to measure waves at locations unaffected by the breakwater so that wave transmission due to natural bathymetric shoaling could be isolated.

Comparison between breakwater and control wave gauges are complicated by the fact that while the offshore breakwater and control gauges are at similar depths, the nearshore breakwater gauge is approximately 60 cm deeper than the nearshore control gauge. In addition, non-breakwater influenced bathymetric changes between each pair of gauges are different. These bathymetric changes are critical because the waves are evolving through different stages of transformation at each pair of gauges which complicates wave attenuation comparisons.

Transmission coefficients have been determined from each 6 hr measurement by calculating the ratio between the measured offshore and nearshore wave heights. Comparison between the gauges located at the breakwater, and at the control site offer an indication of the attenuation owing to natural causes. Prior to settlement of the breakwater, the average significant wave height reduction between the breakwater gauges averaged 12%. Following settlement of the breakwater, the wave height reduction between the breakwater gauges averaged 9% (Figure 8)(Averaged wave height reduction values are similar for all wave heights recorded over the monitoring period). This is identical to an average wave height reduction of 9% between the control gauges during a 2-month period. This suggests that there is no reduction in wave height resulting from the breakwater following breakwater settlement.

Laboratory experiments conducted in a 3-D wave basin (1:16 scale) of the P.E.P. Reef staggered configuration as employed at Vero Beach indicated that wave height reduction for design conditions would be 10% (Dean et al, 1994b). The average wave height reduction projected for structure elevation/water depth conditions similar to the September 1997 field conditions was 0% (Dean et al, 1994b). Thus, both field-collected and laboratory experiment data indicate that wave attenuation due to the breakwater decreases as the breakwater settles.

SUMMARY/CONCLUSIONS

The Vero Beach P.E.P. Reef, designed to cause wave energy reduction in its lee and to reduce volumetric erosion and shoreline retreat landward of the installation, has altered the local coastal environment and wave conditions as determined after one year of monitoring. Historic and pre-installation shoreline and volumetric data suggest that both the breakwater and south areas have eroded, while the north area has accreted. These trends have continued following breakwater installation, particularly landward and to the south of the breakwater. Following breakwater installation, both shoreline and volumetric data suggest a net accretion in sediment over the entire project length.

Wave measurements indicate that the P.E.P. Reef reduced incident wave heights by 12% after initial installation. However, following settlement of the breakwater, wave height reduction averaged 9% at both P.E.P. Reef and control locations, suggesting that the P.E.P. Reef is no longer effective in attenuating wave energy landward of the structure.

There does not appear to be a proportional relationship between scour in the vicinity of the breakwater and breakwater settlement, although continued monitoring will help to better document this relationship. Future planned assessments include investigating current patterns to document the effect of the breakwater on inducing longshore and cross-shore rip currents. Current enhancement was predicted in the laboratory experiments (Dean et al., 1994b).

Additional analyses are being performed to compare the relative importance of the breakwater and the natural morphology (non-uniform outcropping of natural reef within the project area) on the local coastal processes. Analyses will also consider the effect of variable manmade structures (seawalls) within the project area upon local shoreline and volumetric changes.

ACKNOWLEDGMENTS

Appreciation is expressed to John Morgan, Morgan and Ekland, Inc; and Professors Lee Harris and Gary Zarillo, Florida Institute of Technology for their field operation efforts and assistance in analysis of the data. Funding was provided by Indian River County, Florida. Permission to publish this paper was granted by the Chief of Engineers.

REFERENCES

Browder, A.E., Dean, R.G., Chen, R. 1996, Performance of a Submerged Breakwater for Shore Protection, Proceedings of the 25th International Conference on Coastal Engineering, Orlando, FL., September 2-6, 1996, pp. 2312-2323.

Dean, R.G., Dombrowski, M.R., and Browder, A.E. 1994a, Preliminary Results from the P.E.P. Reef Monitoring Project, Proceedings of the 7th National Conference on Beach Preservation Technology, Tampa, FL., February 9-11, 1994, pp. 97-124.

Dean, R.G., Browder, A.G., Goodrich, M.S., and Donaldson, D.G., 1994b, Model Tests of the Proposed P.E.P. Reef Installation at Vero Beach, Florida, Report Number 94/012, University of Florida Coastal and Oceanographic Engineering Department, 28p.

Stauble, D.K., Costa, S.L., and Monroe, K.L., 1987, Sediment Dynamics of a Sand Bypass Inlet, Coastal Sediments '87, New Orleans, LA., May 11-14, 1987, pp.1624-1639.

Walton, T.L., 1976, Littoral Drift Estimates Along the Coastline of Florida, Florida Sea Grant Program, Report Number 3, 39pp.

Observations of structure induced scour adjacent to submerged narrow-crested breakwaters

THOMAS O. HERRINGTON
Research Assistant Professor, Stevens Institute of Technology, Hoboken, New Jersey, USA

MICHAEL S. BRUNO
Director, Davidson Laboratory, Stevens Institute of Technology, Hoboken, New Jersey, USA

INTRODUCTION

In July, 1993 the State of New Jersey initiated a Pilot Reef Project to determine the effectiveness of a submerged narrow-crested breakwater in reducing beach erosion. The structure, marketed as the Beachsaver Reef, was developed by Breakwaters International of Flemington, New Jersey. The reef is modular in design, composed of a number of interlocking concrete units placed in a shore-parallel orientation. Each breakwater unit is triangular in shape, weighs 21 tons and measures 3.0 m in alongshore length, 4.6 m in cross-shore length, and 1.8 m in height. The units are interlocked through mortise tendon joints located at the base of each unit and can accommodate differential settlement of up to 0.61 m. As illustrated in Figure 1, the structure has a mild sloping (3:5) ribbed seaward face and a steeply sloping (6:5) shoreward face leading up to slotted openings that run along the slightly curved crest of the structure. The design is intended to reduce the offshore loss of sand during storm events by the combined action of incident wave height reduction and the generation of a vertical current through the deflection of bottom return flow upward and through the slotted openings at the crest, as depicted in Figure 1.

Three submerged breakwater structures were placed along the New Jersey coastline between July, 1993 and August, 1994. In order to assess performance under a variety of forcing conditions, three distinctly different nearshore areas were chosen. The effectiveness and structural integrity of each submerged breakwater was assessed over a four year monitoring program funded by the State of New Jersey and conducted by Stevens Institute of Technology.

NEW JERSEY COASTAL FEATURES AND PROCESSES

The State of New Jersey is situated along the Atlantic Ocean seaboard of the United States, bordered by the State of New York to the north and the Delaware Bay to the south (Figure 2). The geologic formations along the coast are of the cretaceous and more modern ages, and are composed of flat sheets of unconsolidated strata of gravel, sand, silt and clay, which slope gently to the southeast [*Wicker, 1951*]. Large-scale coastal processes along the 201 km coastline are driven by a combination of the wind and wave climate and the shadowing effect of Long Island to the north. Superimposed on the large-scale motions are small-scale processes driven by tidal flows in the New York Harbor, Delaware Bay and by 12 smaller tidal inlets located along the coast.

Coastlines, structures and breakwaters. Thomas Telford, London, 1998

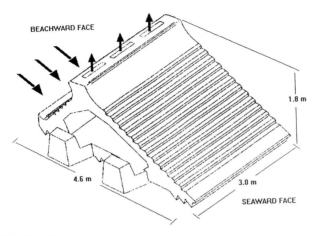

FIGURE 1: Beachsaver Reef Module. Arrows depict structure-induced flow.

FIGURE 2: Location Map, New Jersey and Vicinity.

Tides along the coast are semi-diurnal with two nearly equal high tides and two nearly equal low tides per day. The mean tidal excursion ranges from 1.22 m along the central portion of the coast to 1.42 m at the northern and southern ends [U.S. Dept. of Commerce, 1992]. The prevailing winds are from the northwest along the northern half of the coast and from the south along the southern half. Peak winds of up to 34 m/s from the northeast have been measured along the coast [USACE, 1993]. The monthly mean wave heights, based on hindcasting procedures, range from 0.67m in August to 1.34 m in December [*Hubertz, et.al., 1993*]. A maximum significant wave height of 9.3 m was measured 40 nautical miles east of the coast by NOAA buoy 44025 on December 11, 1992. The maximum storm surge on record is +2.1 m above mean sea level (MSL) at Atlantic City during the Hurricane of 1944.

BREAKWATER INSTALLATIONS

Avalon
The initial submerged breakwater installation was completed in July, 1993 and is located along the Atlantic Ocean shoreline of Avalon, New Jersey, immediately south of Townsends Inlet. Soil borings obtained prior to construction indicate that immediately offshore of the northeastern end of the island the subsurface geology is composed of a 1 m layer of sand (d_{50}=0.30 mm) overlying a 0.30 to 0.45 m layer of fine sand (d_{50}=0.15 mm). The northeastern tip of the island is exposed to wave attack from the south to northeast quadrants and is subjected to strong flood and ebb tidal currents associated with Townsends Inlet. The strong tidal flows combined with wave refraction across the ebb shoal complex of the inlet results in a localized reversal in the net southerly directed sediment transport. A consequence of this reversal is the persistent erosion of the northeastern end of the island.

In an effort to reduce the erosion rate, a 305 m long submerged breakwater was placed between 100 and 150 m seaward of the shoreline in water depths ranging from 2.2 to 3.8 m mean low water (MLW). The structure was constructed with 100 Beachsaver Reef modules, oriented in a shore parallel configuration, rigidly connected with capstone to the southern inlet jetty at the northern end and pined with a steel H pile at the southern (open) end (Figure 3). Each breakwater module was placed on top of a geotextile fabric with a mesh size of 0.25 mm. The as-built MLW elevation of the breakwater crest ranged from -0.4 m at the junction point with the jetty to -2.0 m at the southern end of the structure.

Cape May Point
The second breakwater installation was completed in May, 1994 and is located at the confluence of the Atlantic Ocean and Delaware Bay in Cape May Point, New Jersey. The Cape May Point shoreline is located on the southern headland section of Cape May and faces due south. The shoreline is stabilized by a series of timber and stone groins extending from the beach berm approximately 122 m seaward to a water depth of 2.4 to 3.0 m MLW. Each groin cell is approximately 152 m wide. Soil borings obtained within the groin cells prior to construction indicate that the subsurface geology is composed of a 0.5 m layer of fine sand (d_{50}=0.15 mm) overlying a 1.0 to 1.7 m layer of fine sand and mud (d_{50}=0.13 mm). Seaward of the groin cells the offshore slope has a 0.76 to 1.2 m surface layer of medium to fine grain sands (d_{50}= 0.15 to 0.5 mm) with varying layers of organic mud and peat. The southern tip of Cape May is exposed to wave attack from the east, south and west quadrants and is subjected to strong flood and ebb tidal currents associated with Delaware Bay. Peak ebb tidal currents can exceed 1.0 m/s in Cape May Channel immediately south of the shoreline [U.S. Dept. of

Commerce, 1994]. Nearshore sediments that are transported seaward of the groin field through wave and/or current action are then transported away from the shoreline by the strong tidal currents.

In an effort to reduce the offshore loss of beach material, the seaward end of two groin cells were closed off with two 150 m long submerged breakwaters. Each breakwater was placed 90 m seaward of the shoreline in water depths ranging from 2.1 to 2.4 m MLW. Each was constructed with 50 Beachsaver Reef modules, oriented in a shore parallel configuration. The ends were rigidly connected to the stone groins with capstone. The breakwater modules were placed on top of a geotextile fabric with a mesh size of 0.15 mm placed between two layers of geotextile with a mesh size of 0.25 mm. A 0.2 m thick, 1.3 m wide polyethylene geomattress filled with 6.25 to 10.16 cm stone was placed along the entire length of the landward and seaward edges of the structures for additional scour protection. The as-built elevation of the breakwater crest ranged from +0.15 to -0.61 m MLW.

Belmar/Spring Lake
The third and final breakwater installation was completed in August, 1994 along the Atlantic Ocean shoreline of Belmar and Spring Lake, New Jersey. The boroughs of Belmar and Spring Lake are located in the headland section of the northern New Jersey coast. The shoreline is stabilized by a series of stone groins extending from the beach berm approximately 168 m seaward to a water depth of 1.8 to 2.4 m MLW. Each groin cell is approximately 365 m wide. Soil borings obtained within the installation groin cell prior to construction indicate that a 1.0 m layer of medium grain sand (d_{50}=0.45 mm) rests on top of a 15 cm layer of hard packed clay. The safe bearing capacity of the clay layer was analyzed and determined to be 195 kPa (personnel communication, Breakwaters International). The shoreline of the northern headlands faces due east and is exposed to wave attack predominantly from the southeast and east quadrants. A steep offshore slope in this region allows larger storm waves to break close to the beach, dissipating all of their energy across only a few hundred meters of surf zone.

To determine the effectiveness of the structure in reducing incident wave energy and the offshore loss of beach material, the seaward end of one groin cell was closed off with a 305 m long submerged breakwater. The breakwater was placed 128 m seaward of the MLW shoreline in water depths ranging from 2.3 to 2.4 m MLW. The breakwater was constructed with 100 Beachsaver Reef modules, oriented in a shore parallel configuration. Both ends of the breakwater were rigidly connected to the stone groins with capstone. Scour protection again included the placement of a layered geotextile fabric and stone geomattresses along the landward and seaward edges of the structure. The as-built elevation of the breakwater crest ranged from -0.70 to -1.16 m MLW.

MONITORING PROGRAM
An extensive multi-year monitoring program was initiated in May, 1993, prior to the construction of the first submerged breakwater. The program was conducted to evaluate the structural integrity of the structures and examine the influence of the three breakwaters on nearshore dynamics and shoreline evolution. In order to assess structure interaction with the local hydrodynamics and sediment transport, the monitoring effort included high resolution beach profile surveys performed on a quarterly basis, wave and current measurements, and underwater structural inspections. Over the course of the monitoring period, the breakwaters were exposed to over 20 extratropical storms with nearshore wave heights greater than 3 m and 10 large swell events (H_{mo} > 3.6 m) generated by hurricanes moving past the coast.

Beach Profile Evolution

Methodology
High resolution topographical surveys were conducted to evaluate the impact of each submerged breakwater on the shoreline evolution. The beach surveying system consisted of a shore-based TOPCON Geodetic Total Station GTS-3B and a graduated prism pole fitted with a triple prism, adjustable to a maximum height of 4.6 m. The TOPCON total station has a range of 2,700 m with an accuracy of 5 mm in distance and can resolve horizontal and vertical angles to within 5 seconds. Repetitive topographical surveys with the total station and prism rod indicate an average vertical error of ± 2.5 cm.

At each of the three breakwater sites, a pre-construction survey was performed which included the establishment of a shore parallel baseline and a number of cross-shore profiling lines spaced between 30 and 45 m apart. Vertical control at each site was established by setting benchmarks of known elevation at a few points on each baseline. During each survey, the profiling lines were re-manned and the subaerial and nearshore portion of the beach surveyed using the prism rod and total station. The total station was set up over a point on the baseline with known elevation, and angles and distances were measured to the prism pole which was set to a constant height. Elevation measurements along each profiling line were taken at intervals sufficient to define major morphologic features (typically less than 3 m). Each profile started at the baseline and proceeded seaward to the top of the submerged breakwater. Structure elevation measurements were obtained by placing the base of the rod on the crest of the submerged breakwater.

Avalon
Prior to the completion of the submerged breakwater in July, 1993, a beach replenishment project placed approximately 146,300 m^3 of sand landward of the structure. Cross-shore profiles measured in September, 1993 indicate that the nearshore beach profile had changed very little from the post-fill template and that the structure was completely buried by the fill material. A survey conducted in November, 1993 revealed the formation of a prominent erosion zone located landward of the southern end of the structure (Figure 3). The profile lines landward of the northern portion of the reef indicated that the beach profile remained in the post-fill template in this area. The first measurements of the top elevation of the structure were obtained in November, 1993 and indicated that the center portion of the structure had settled between 0.61 and 0.73 m. Subsequent profile measurements obtained between November, 1993 and November, 1994 showed a continuing trend of increased erosion landward of the southern end of the reef. Surveys of the top elevation of the breakwater over the same time period indicate that the structure experienced settlement ranging from 0.61 m at the northern end of the site to 1.22 m along the southern 76 m of the structure. Volume changes calculated over the 14 month period from September, 1993 to November, 1994 indicated a loss of 23,700 m^3 landward of the southern 152 m of the structure and 15,300 m^3 landward of the northern 152 m.

By May, 1994, the water depth immediately landward of the structure was greater than 4.7 m, precluding direct measurements with the surveying rod. A visual inspection of the structure conducted by SCUBA divers in May, 1994 confirmed the presence of a 10 m wide, up to 1 m deep, scour hole immediately landward of the breakwater. The bottom sediment within the scour hole was observed to be cohesive black mud. In spite of the pronounced settlement, the breakwater modules along the southern 150 m of the structure were found to be interlocked. These observations led to the placement of 0.2 m thick, 1.3 m wide polyethylene geomattress filled with 6.25 to 10.16 cm stone along the landward base of the southern 76 m of the structure in an effort to reduce the observed undermining and settlement. Subsequent surveys conducted between November, 1994 and May, 1995 indicated that the structure experienced only minor additional settlement since the May, 1994 survey.

Cape May Point

Measurements of the beach profile evolution landward of the submerged breakwaters began with a pre-construction survey conducted in May, 1994 and continued on a quarterly basis until August, 1996. Figure 4 illustrates the profile changes along one of the cross-shore profiling lines and is typical of all of the profiles landward of the structure. Cumulative volume changes between May, 1994 and April, 1996 indicate that the two groin cells protected by the submerged breakwater gained between 2.5 - 13.9 m^3/m of sand. Analysis of the cross-shore profiles indicate that sediment was removed from the upper foreshore and seaward edge of the dune line and deposited between the lower foreshore and the landward toe of the submerged breakwater. A persistent feature on all of the profiles is an isolated region of scour between 0 and 0.6 m in depth located from the inshore toe of the structure and extending landward 3 to 10 m.

Measurements of the top elevation of the breakwater were obtained starting in September, 1994 and continued on a quarterly basis until August, 1996. The breakwater elevation at each of the overlapping measurement points remained relatively constant, with maximum changes of less than 15 cm observed over the 24-month period. In fact, the observed changes for the most part lie within the expected tolerance of the measurements, indicating that the structure has experienced little or no settlement since installation.

Belmar/Spring Lake

The monitoring program at Belmar/Spring Lake started with a post-construction survey in September, 1994. Subsequent surveys were conducted four times per year between November, 1994 and October, 1996. Figure 4 presents the profile evolution along one of the cross-shore profiling lines and is typical of the profiles landward of the structure. The profiles indicate a redistribution of sand from the beach berm and foreshore into a wide bar centered 45 m landward of the breakwater. By July, 1996 the net volume change within the groin cell was -3.3 m^3/m. A local scour zone 15 to 18 m wide is again evident immediately landward of the structure. The depth of the scour hole ranged from a minimum of 1.2 m in November, 1994 to a maximum of 2.1 m in July, 1996.

Measurements of the top elevation of the structure began in September, 1994 and concluded in June, 1997. Over the monitoring period the structure experienced settlement ranging from 0.12 m at the southern end of the site to 1.95 m at the center of the structure. Over the initial 6 months, the structure underwent relatively minor settlement of 0.3 to 0.7 m. A visual SCUBA inspection of the structure performed in October, 1996 indicated that the units remained interlocked. However, the geotextile mattress had settled in the areas affected by the scour hole, allowing structure undermining and increased settlement to take place.

Scour Evolution

In June of 1995, a beach renourishment project was conducted which placed an additional 400,000 yd^3 of sediment along the northern shoreline of Avalon. As a result of the

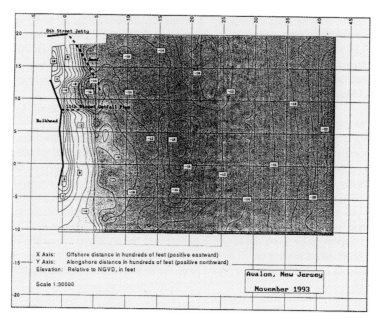

FIGURE 3: Avalon Site Plan showing elevation contours in November 1993.

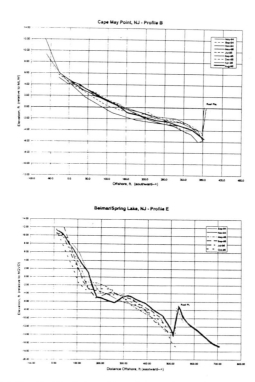

FIGURE 4: Profile Evolution, Cape May Point and Belmar/Spring Lake

renourishment project, the submerged breakwater was completely buried under a layer of new sand. The beachfill project provided the opportunity to conduct additional high resolution topographic surveys inshore of the structure in an effort to resolve the onset of the scour region observed adjacent to all three of the structures. A post fill survey was conducted in July, 1995 and two additional surveys were performed in September and December, 1995.

Presented in Figure 5 is the cross-shore profile evolution along the southern 150 m of the submerged breakwater. The post-fill profile indicates the beginning of a depression immediately landward of the crest of the structure. A visual inspection of the structure conducted in July, 1995 revealed that much of the structure was buried or only the crest of the structure was exposed. Over the two month period between the first and second surveys, the structure was exposed to three large wave events ($H_{mo} > 3.6$ m) generated by hurricanes offshore of the coast. The cross-shore profile responded by moving 30 m landward, and developing a pronounced scour zone adjacent to the breakwater. The scour zone extended 11 m landward and reached a depth of 0.76 m. By December, 1995 the scour area increased in width by 7 m and reached a depth of 1.1 m.

Near-Structure Wave and Current Measurements

Wave Transformation
Wave transformation studies were conducted over two 1 week periods at Avalon and over a 1 day period at Cape May Point. Wave and near-bottom current measurements, inshore and offshore of the submerged breakwaters, were obtained by deploying bottom mounted InterOcean Systems S4 electromagnetic current meters fitted with high resolution pressure sensors. The meters are capable of velocity measurement between 0 to 350 cm/s with an accuracy of 2% and a resolution of 0.2 cm/s, and the pressure sensor can resolve pressure measurements to within 4 mm with an accuracy of 0.25%. Each meter rested 1 m above the bottom and was programmed to record 9 minute burst samples of pressure and the two orthogonal components of velocity at 2 Hz, every hour. Figure 6 is a typical plot of the temporal variation in wave transmission coefficient and the ratio of negative freeboard to offshore significant wave height for a portion of the Avalon data set. The measurements indicate that the wave energy reduction is a strong function of both the negative freeboard and the incident wave height. The degree of wave height reduction increases for periods of low negative freeboard and periods of large incident wave height.

Vertical Current Profiles
Vertical profiles of the current at various points around the Avalon breakwater were obtained from a research vessel anchored on a two point mooring. The currents were measured by two S4 current meters attached to a weighted, winch-mounted profiling cable. Presented in Figure 7 are the locations of the vertical profiling stations. Stations 1 through 3 were sampled over a 1 hour period starting 2 hours before high water. Stations 4 and 5 were sampled over a 1 hour period starting 2 hours and 45 minutes after high water. Sixty-second average current vectors were measured over 2 minute sampling intervals at each profiling depth. Winds were directed toward the north at 2.5 to 5 m/s during the flood tide measurements and toward the southeast at 5 m/s during the ebb tide measurements. The average significant wave height over the measurement period was 0.3 m directed toward the northwest with an average peak period of 11.5 seconds. The measured vertical current profiles are presented as plots of shore-parallel (U comp) and cross-shore (V comp) velocity components for each sampling location (Figure

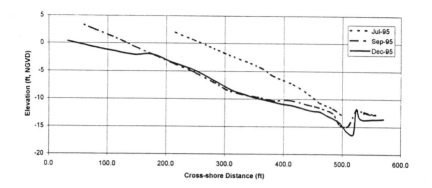

FIGURE 5: Scour Zone Evolution, Avalon, New Jersey

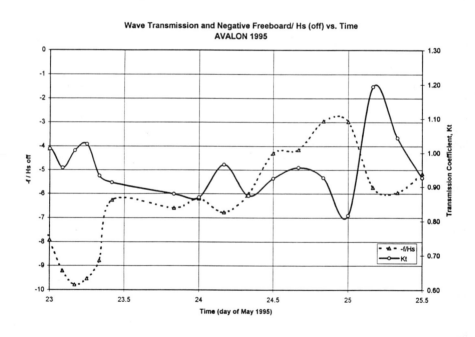

FIGURE 6: Variation of Wave Transmission and Negative Freeboard at Avalon.

7). In the plots, positive values of U and V indicate current directions toward the north and east, respectively.

Profiling points 1, 2, and 3 were located 17.6 m, 10.5 m, and 2.7 m inshore of the breakwater, respectively. During flood, all 3 vertical profiles indicate northerly directed shore-parallel currents with peak current velocities occurring 1 m below the surface. Profiles 1 and 3 indicate the presence of reduced currents at mid-depth. The cross-shore current component measured at points 2 and 3 is directed offshore in the upper half of the water column and onshore in the lower half. The cross-shore current at point 1 is directed onshore throughout the water column. Profile points 4 and 5 were located 16.9 m and 8.6 m inshore of the breakwater, respectively. During ebb, the cross-shore currents adjacent to the structure are directed offshore in the lower half of the water column and onshore in the upper half. The shore-parallel current 8.6 m from the structure is less than 5 cm/s and is directed to the north in the lower half of the water column and to the south in the upper half. The shore-parallel component is weak and variable 16.9 m from the structure.

Continuous Near-bottom Current Measurements
Continuous near-bottom current measurements were obtained 7 m inshore of the reef, 53 m north of the southern tip of the breakwater. The time history records of near-bottom and mid-depth flood currents measured over the 2 hour and 40 minute period of the flood tide are presented in Figure 8. During the observation period, winds were directed from the east at 5 m/s and the significant wave height was 0.5 m with an average peak period of 6.0 seconds.

Examining Figure 8, the shore-parallel component of velocity, 1.2 m above the bottom, was directed toward the north throughout the record. The near-bottom meter recorded currents between 2 and 5 cm/s slower than the mid-depth meter during peak flood currents, and was characterized by periods of strong currents followed in 10 minutes by slower currents. As the flood currents diminish, the near-bottom and mid-depth velocity magnitudes converge (14:50 to 15:20). The cross-shore velocity component varied between periods of onshore (-) and offshore (+) current directions and was dependent on the location in the water column. At the beginning of flood, the mid-depth meter recorded offshore directed currents between 2 and 10 cm/s. Over the same time period the near-bottom meter recorded offshore directed currents of 0.5 to 2.0 cm/s. As peak flood currents in the alongshore direction were reached, the near-bottom and mid-depth cross-shore velocity component decreased and reversed direction. After peak flood, the near-bottom cross-shore velocity component was directed offshore and varied between 0 and 2.5 cm/s. At mid-depth the currents remained directed onshore between 0 and 1.5 cm/s.

ANALYSIS
The submerged concrete breakwater is of the narrow-crested design, intended to generate a strong vertical current by deflecting wave-induced bottom return flow upwards in the water column. In theory, the structure inhibits the offshore migration of sand by deflecting the sediment-laden wave-induced bottom current vertically over the structure to be transported back onshore by the surface waves. The results of the wave transmission study indicated a dependence of wave energy dissipation on wave height and the negative freeboard of the structure. This dependency is indicative of flow interference and viscous dissipation associated with the structure-induced vertical current. Current measurements made inshore of the breakwater confirm the influence of the structure on near-bottom currents. Near-bottom currents were found to be increasingly reduced in magnitude as the distance from the structure

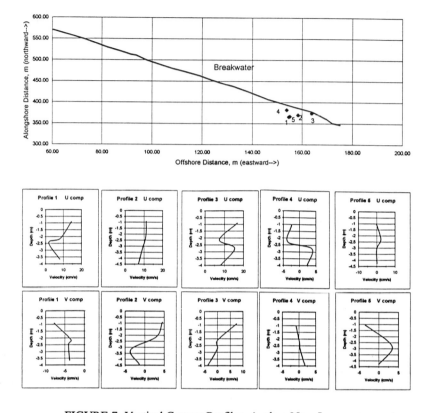

FIGURE 7: Vertical Current Profiles, Avalon, New Jersey

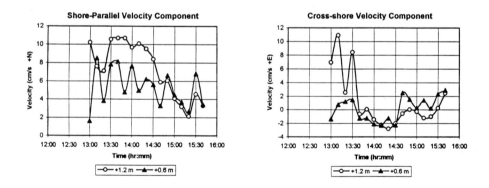

FIGURE 8: Continuous Near-Bottom Currents, Avalon, New Jersey

decreases. The current profiles suggest that the generation of the upward flowing current takes place within 10 m of the inshore face of the structure and is manifested as a reversal in the near-bottom cross-shore current direction and an offshore flow over the crest of the structure.

The beach profile evolution inshore of all three submerged breakwaters consistently indicates a pronounced scour zone within 15 m of the inshore face of the structure. This scour zone appeared regardless of erosive or accretionary conditions, energetic or calm wave climate, strong or weak tidal currents, or even structure settlement. The maximum measured depth of scour approached 2.2 m at the Belmar/Spring Lake site but averaged approximately 1.0 m. Due to the large width and depth of the scour zone, the 1.3 m wide geotextile mattresses were ineffective in providing scour protection at the three sites. Measurements of the beach profile evolution of the renourished beach at Avalon indicate that the observed scour zone will be re-established to the same breadth and depth, even when the structure is initially buried by fill material and has a large negative freeboard.

The presence of a pronounced scour zone within 10 meters of all three of the breakwaters suggests that the structure-induced vertical current is strong enough to suspend sediment immediately inshore of the structure. This structure-current interaction provides a mechanism by which sediment near the structure (0 to 15 m) is transported away from the inshore toe of the breakwater. An analysis of sediment cores taken at the Cape May Point and Belmar/Spring Lake sites reveal the presence of a layer of sand on top of cohesive sediments (mud and clay, respectively) located between 0.5 and 1 m below the seabed. At both sites, structure settlement stopped once the more resistive cohesive sediment layer was reached. The Avalon site, however, consisted of layers of coarse to fine sand and suffered the most extreme settlement. Based on the measured settlement rates, the structures are being undermined through the removal of the cohesionless sediment layer by the strong current shear observed adjacent to the structure.

CONCLUSIONS

The structural stability and performance of submerged-narrow crested breakwaters is dependent on the proper investigation of the subsurface sediment characteristics and the design of proper scour protection measures (material and dimensions). The erosion of cohesionless sediments by strong structure-induced currents undermines the structure, causing significant settlement. Structure settlement in turn causes an increase in the negative freeboard of the structure, increasing wave transmission and reducing the effectiveness of the structure. This is evident in the measured reduction in beach erosion landward of the Cape May Point breakwater installation (low negative freeboard) when compared to the performance of the Avalon breakwater (high negative freeboard).

REFERENCES

Hubertz, J.M., R.M. Brooks, W.A. Brandon, and B.A. Tracy, Hindcast Wave Information for the U.S. Atlantic Coast, WIS Rept. 30, U.S. Army Engineer Waterways Experiment Station, Vicksburg, MS, 1993.

USACE, New York District, *Atlantic Coast of New Jersey, Sandy Hook to Barnegat Inlet Beach Erosion Control Project, Section II - Asbury Park to Manasquan, New Jersey, General Design Memorandum*, Tech. Appns., Vol. II, November 1993.

U.S. Department of Commerce, NOAA/NOS, *Tide Tables 1993, High and Low Predictions,*

East Coast of North and South America including Greenland, 300pp., U.S. Government Printing Office, Washington, D.C., 1992.

U.S. Department of Commerce, NOAA/NOS, *Tidal Current Tables 1995, Atlantic Coast of North America*, 205pp., U.S. Government Printing Office, Washington, D.C., 1994.

Wicker, C.F., History of New Jersey coastline, *Proc. 1st Conf. on Coastal Engrg., Long Beach, Ca., Oct. 1950,* Council on Wave Res., The Engrg. Found., 299-319, 1951.

Happisburgh to Winterton Sea Defences : Stage Two

B A HAMER[1], S J HAYMAN[2], P A ELSDON[1], AND C A FLEMING[1]
[1]Sir William Halcrow & Partners, Swindon ; [2]Environment Agency, Anglian Region, UK

BACKGROUND

The Happisburgh to Winterton frontage, which extends for 14km of the North Norfolk coastline (Figure 1), has a long history of beach volatility, and flooding events are recorded as far back as the 13th century. Given the history of flooding, the East Suffolk and Norfolk River Board initiated the construction of a reinforced concrete seawall, which was completed in stages between 1953 and 1989. This seawall now defines the line of defences to be maintained, and a breach at any point along this defence would cause flooding of up to 6,000 hectares of hinterland.

In 1987, the National Rivers Authority (NRA), now part of the Environment Agency (the Agency), engaged British Maritime Technology (BMT) to develop a sea defence strategy for the frontage. BMT recommended a strategy based on fish-tail groynes, beach re-grading and periodic capital beach recharge. The Agency formulated and financially justified this 50-year strategy, as described in Reference 1.

Prior to final design, the Agency commissioned Halcrow to undertake a technical audit of the fish-tail groyne strategy. During the subsequent computational modelling studies, described in Reference 2, it was demonstrated that the fish-tail groyne scheme would not be as effective as an offshore reef scheme, for two major reasons : fish-tail groynes did not provide the same level of wave protection to the beach at a comparable spacing; and groynes would be severely obstructive to longshore drift. Halcrow proposed an alternative sea defence strategy in 1991, based on a combination of offshore reefs and beach management measures (Figure 1).

KEY POINTS OF 1991 SEA DEFENCE STRATEGY

The following key points of the Sea Defence Strategy should be noted :

- The Strategy was to be implemented in stages over a 20-year construction period;
- Reefs 5 to 8 were to be constructed in Stage One, where beach levels were at their lowest;
- Beach recharge would be implemented in 1995/6, to suit funding streams;
- Beaches south-east (downdrift) of Reef 8 were predicted to erode although, in 1991, these beaches were considered to be sufficiently healthy to support the anticipated level of erosion; and,
- The performance of the Strategy was to be monitored, and the Strategy was to be reviewed prior to each major construction phase.

Coastlines, structures and breakwaters. Thomas Telford, London, 1998

Figure 1

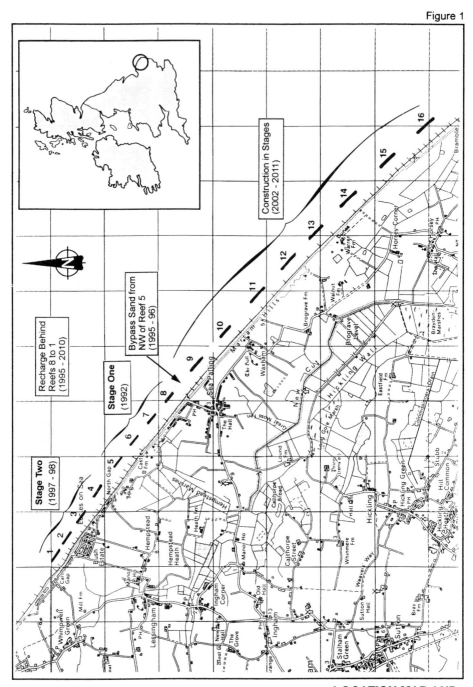

**LOCATION MAP AND
ORIGINAL STRATEGY**

EFFECTS PREDICTED IN 1991

During development of the Strategy, computational model studies were carried out, to optimise the layout of the reefs. These model studies examined the transformation of waves as they propagated inshore, and the consequential effects on the cross-shore and longshore transport of sediment.

Wave transformation modelling included the effects of wave refraction, breaking, and diffraction around the ends of the reefs. Two 2-dimensional sediment models were adopted, to make predictions of longshore transport, and to model cross-shore effects.

Calibration of the wave model was achieved during the development of the Anglian Sea Defence Management Study, by comparison with inshore wave measurements. Sediment transport models were, in turn, calibrated against the results of beach profiles, taken twice per year at 1km intervals from 1980 onwards, and more limited information on seabed levels. Longshore transport rate data are difficult to obtain, even through direct measurements made over a significant length of time. However, an indication of longshore transport rates had been estimated for the North Norfolk coastline during studies made in 1983 (Reference 3), and predicted rates were of the same order.

The predicted beach response in the vicinity of Reefs 5 to 8, after 12 months of wave action, is presented in Figure 2. These predictions demonstrate a clear tendency for the now familiar beach plan shape to form, with a series of cuspate bays. The predictions also showed that beaches between the reefs could cut back behind the original beach line, in the absence of intervention. In addition, the potential for downdrift erosion can be seen to the south-east of Reef 8.

The Strategy included management measures, to address these predicted effects. Erosion of beaches between the reefs would be managed through the artificial redistribution of sand from the reef salients back into the gaps. Whilst beach recharge was considered to be a possible requirement to address downdrift erosion, the potential accretion on the beaches updrift of the reef system was seen as a source for artificial bypassing of sand, ie removal of sand from updrift beaches for placing on the eroding downdrift beaches.

OBSERVED AND MEASURED PERFORMANCE

In order to assess the performance of Stage One, and thereby to inform the design of subsequent stages, a programme of monitoring works was developed. Monitoring comprised beach profiles twice per year, bathymetric profiles once every five years, and aerial photographs once per year. In addition to these long term measurements, a four-week campaign of physical measurements was carried out by HR Wallingford early in 1996. In the course of these studies, wave heights, currents and water levels were recorded.

It is important to note that the construction of these first four reefs was not completed until 1994, some two years later than had been envisaged. During this time, beaches along much of the frontage had suffered further erosion, with implications for the performance of the Strategy.

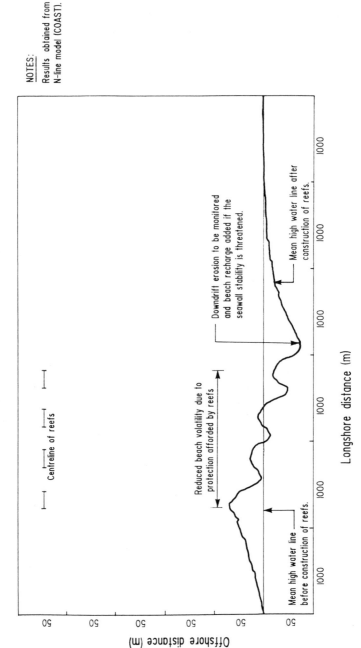

Figure 2   Predicted Longshore Beach Response (Extract from Reference 2, 1991)

Updrift Effects
Upon completion of Stage One, beaches updrift of Reef 5 were not sufficiently healthy to support the removal of material to feed eroding downdrift beaches (bypassing), as originally proposed. However, in the first twelve months following completion of Stage One, bed levels to the north-west of Reef 5 accreted significantly, especially on the nearshore sand bar located approximately 200m from the shoreline. This accretion was considered to have occurred as a result of the reduction in longshore transport rate caused by the reefs, which backed-up 100,000m³ of beach material for up to 1km updrift.

Beaches Behind Reefs
In the immediate lee of each of the reefs, a substantial quantity of material gathered under wave-driven currents. The effects of wave diffraction about the ends of the reefs drive circulatory currents within each reef bay, transporting sand away from the bay centre to settle out behind the reefs. As a consequence, the beach line between some of the reefs had cut back to the seawall within 12 months of completion of Stage One. Whilst the formation of salients had been predicted, the development of significant beaches attached directly to the lee of the reefs (ie extending landwards from the reef toe) had not been anticipated.

Design of the Stage One reefs had sought to attain a balance between the need to afford cross-shore protection to the beaches during extreme storm events, whilst minimising the impact on longshore drift under more typical wave and water level conditions. Extreme storm surges, in excess of 2m, are encountered along this coastline and, as a result, reefs had prudently been designed with a relatively high crest level, ie some longshore transport of material had been sacrificed in favour of assured cross-shore protection.

Downdrift Effects
Observations
Whilst beaches to the north-west of the completed reefs had accreted significantly, this storage of material resulted in a reduced amount of sediment feed to the beaches to the south-east of Reef 8. Indeed, the continued lowering of downdrift beaches, in conjunction with low sediment feed, resulted in the exposure of the seawall toe piles to their full depth for significant lengths of the frontage by winter 1995/6.

The quantity of material lost from these beaches was estimated to be approximately 300,000m³ in the first year, which was significantly greater than the accretion recorded on the updrift beaches. This discrepancy may be accounted for by the accelerated rates of erosion encountered on the downdrift beaches, once the vertical face of the seawall toe became exposed. The exposure of this structure resulted in high levels of wave reflection, which exacerbated erosion at the toe. These beach losses spread south-eastwards for up to 1km from Reef 8, and caused some timber groynes to be undermined, allowing erosion to continue at an even faster rate.

Remedial Works
A series of urgent works were proposed in the Autumn of 1995, comprising the construction of three rock groynes, replacing five timber and steel groynes which had been lost during storms. In addition, emergency beach recharge was carried out in the Spring of 1996, to address the immediate problem of downdrift erosion whilst a Strategy Review was completed.

STRATEGY REVIEW

Shortly after completion of Reefs 5 to 8, in early 1995, the first Strategy Review (Reference 4) was commissioned, to evaluate their performance and to recommend the way forward. In this first planned review, a range of options for developing further stages of the Strategy were evaluated, including do-nothing, in accordance with Ministry of Agriculture, Fisheries and Food guidelines (Reference 5). Whilst an existing strategy was in place, it was necessary to review all options to demonstrate that the next stage of the Strategy remained the preferred way forward.

The Strategy Review incorporated an independent review by Delft Hydraulics (Reference 6), and confirmed that offshore reefs together with beach management measures remained the preferred option. Those key issues, highlighted in the earlier description of the observed and measured performance of Reefs 5 to 8, resulted in the following recommendations :

- Due to the accretion of beaches updrift of the Stage One reefs, it was considered unlikely that Reefs 1 to 4, as originally proposed (Figure 1), would be necessary;
- Whilst lowering the crest elevation of Reefs 5 to 8 was considered, to reduce the tendency for beach accretion in their lee, the benefits of updrift accretion were considered to out-weigh the potential advantages of this measure at this stage; and,
- In developing future reefs, consideration should be given to reducing the gap between the structures, and to reducing the tendency for beach accretion in their lee.

Once it had been determined that the Strategy should continue as an offshore reef scheme, the reef design was developed in accordance with these basic principles.

STAGE TWO REEF DESIGN

Design Guidance
A review of available reef design theory was carried out, to facilitate the development of a conceptual reef design, which could then be finalised during computational model studies. References 7 and 8 were key references used in this review; they summarise a large amount of material relating to offshore reefs. Individual papers were also reviewed (References 9 to 16), although most of these are incorporated in the key references.

The main design parameters considered in the literature are defined in Figure 3. The approximate values of these parameters at the time of the Strategy Review (measured at Mean Sea Level) for Reefs 5 to 8 were :

- Offshore distance (X) = 200m;
- Structure length (Ls) = 220m;
- Gap length (Lg) = 280m;
- Salient width (Xs) = 20 to 80m (varied for Reefs 5 to 8).

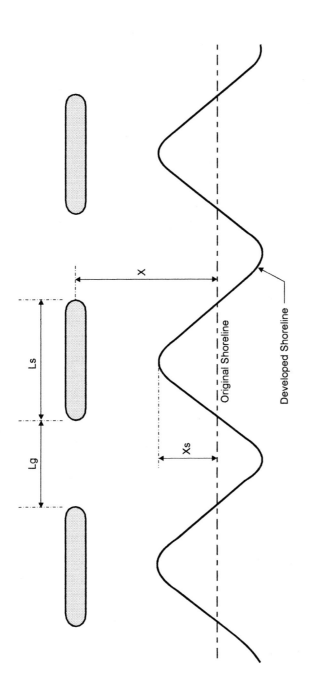

REEF DESIGN PARAMETERS
(Measured at Mean Sea Level)

Figure 3

Conceptual Reef Design

Reef design parameters were reviewed in the light of available guidance, to facilitate the development of a conceptual reef design, which was to be finalised in computational model studies :

(a)   Offshore Distance/Structure Length

Various relationships between the offshore distance of reefs and the length of structure have been derived, although References 9, 10 and 13 suggest ratios for offshore distance to structure length which are all at variance. The value adopted for Reefs 5 to 8, at 0.91, falls within the recommended range of one of the papers, but outside that of the other two.

Given knowledge of the performance of Reefs 5 to 8, together with the guidance described above, a structure placed between 1.0Ls and 2.0Ls from the original shoreline was considered to form an acceptable basis for model studies on the longshore transport regime. Under Stage One, the offshore reef distance had been optimised to coincide with the existing inshore sand bar, to minimize the required quantity of rock for construction. It was considered appropriate to continue to allow the offshore distance to be fixed by this requirement, subject to model studies demonstrating that this would not be detrimental to the cross-shore sediment regime. A study was also commissioned with the University of East Anglia, to assess the coastal morphology of the study area. The results of this literature review confirmed a process link between the beaches, nearshore and offshore banks, but the nearshore bar, at a relatively low height of 2m, was considered acceptable for the reef foundation.

With the value of X fixed at 200m, analysis of available guidance, together with observations of the Stage One reef performance, suggested that reefs should be of length 100m to 200m. Given the desire to construct reefs lower than Reefs 5 to 8, a reef length of 160m, ie towards the higher end of this range, was selected for modelling.

(b)   Gap Length

The gap length between reefs should be selected to allow some continued longshore transport, whilst ensuring that acceptable beach levels are maintained. Available guidance related gap length to either the incident wavelength, the length of the reefs, or the offshore distance. Using these relationships, an ideal gap width of 120m to 280m was determined. The erosion which had occurred on the beach opposite the gaps in Reefs 5 to 8 suggests that a relatively short gap length was appropriate.

Adopting an offshore distance of 200m and a reef length of 160m, then a gap length of 160m was considered appropriate, to avoid significant erosion of the beach and exposure of the seawall between the reefs.

(c)   Salient Width

Many of the papers reviewed suggest methods for determining whether a reef system will develop salients or tombolos on the protected beach. Observations of the growth of salients behind the completed reefs, at the time of the review, suggested that, in time, it was possible that the beach would become linked to the reefs in the absence of any intervention. Such shore links are now evident behind Reefs 5 to 8 at low water levels.

The literature review suggested that, for the adopted design of Reefs 5 to 8, either well-developed salients or tombolos were likely. By reducing the length of the structure to 160m, the probability of tombolo formation is reduced markedly.

(d)   Wave Transmission

As noted in the design guidance, salient formation is sensitive to the wave transmission through and over offshore reefs. Reefs 5 to 8 are surface-piercing at all states of the tide (crest level 1.3m above Mean High Water Springs (MHWS)), excluding extreme storm surges, and the level of wave energy transmitted in to the lee is relatively small.

Physical model tests were carried out for the design of Reefs 5 to 8 at the Danish Hydraulics Institute (Reference 17). These studies showed that, in order to achieve a target wave transmission of 60% during storms, which was considered the maximum for beach retention, a crest level of +3.0mOD would be required. Further model tests, carried out for the same reef crest level, but at a more typical water level of MHWS, indicated that 46% of wave energy was transmitted through and over the reef in breaking wave conditions.

Observation of the low level of wave penetration through and over Reefs 5 to 8 suggested that future reefs could be constructed at a lower elevation, with a reasonable degree of confidence that sand losses would be acceptable during storm events.

EFFECTS PREDICTED IN 1996

Once an outline reef design had been determined, as described in the previous section, computational model studies were carried out, to optimise the outline design. As for the original Strategy development, a wave transformation model was used to determine the nearshore wave field, and to drive two separate 2-dimensional sediment transport models. Halcrow's Beach Plan Shape Model was used to predict the effects of the proposed reefs on the longshore transport regime, whilst the COSMOS-2D model was used to study cross-shore effects. The Beach Plan Shape Model takes a sequence of wave conditions as input, at each of an array of inshore points along the coastline to be modelled. The relative transport rates along the coastline are then determined for the sequence of wave conditions, typically for periods of one year or more, and the resulting changes in beach plan shape are determined. COSMOS-2D also takes realistic sequences of wave data as input at the offshore limit of a given beach cross-section, and calculates the modification of the wave parameters as they propagate inshore. This wave field is then used to determine the development of the cross-shore profile, typically for a given storm event of several hours duration.

In order to ensure that the modelling studies were as efficient as possible, sensitivity tests were carried out, to assess the acceptable minimum range of wave periods and directions that could be used to represent the wave climate. Initial wave model runs were undertaken by building a wave transformation matrix with 18 wave directions (between north-west and south-east) and ten wave periods (from 2 to 20 seconds), meaning that for each model layout a series of 180 wave model runs were necessary. However, once these wave model runs had been performed, and the sequential inshore wave conditions had been produced, only one beach plan shape model test was necessary. By comparing the results from the beach plan shape modelling tests, based on a full

18 by 10 description of the wave climate, with similar tests based on a fewer number of wave direction and period increments, it was possible to reduce the number of wave model runs from 180 to only 15, representing 5 wave directions (the key directions for the prevailing wave conditions), and only 3 wave periods.

Wave modelling was calibrated against inshore wave measurements for March 1996, although the model had been extensively calibrated for other locations in the United Kingdom (for example, see reference 18). The wave model was modified, to consider the effects of wave transmission over relatively low-crested structures, based on Reference 19.

Beach plan shape model results were compared with the measured performance of the first four reefs, and good agreement between the measured and hindcast beach response was achieved, in general. However, actual downdrift erosion was more extensive than predicted, as the modelling takes no account of the increased inshore wave energy as the toe of the seawall becomes exposed.

Cross-shore modelling was undertaken, to determine an acceptable reef crest level which provided the optimum combination of protection against offshore losses during storms, whilst remaining as low as possible to minimise the impact on longshore drift. The results demonstrated that a reef elevation of +0.2mOD provided a reasonable level of protection to a recharged beach, even during severe storm conditions. However, there was a significant improvement in the level of protection afforded to beaches if the crest was raised to +1.2mOD, which was still 0.5m below MHWS. This higher crest level was selected, to maintain a factor of safety in the level of protection afforded to the beaches.

The wave model was then run, using a tidally-averaged transmission coefficient of approximately 30%, with a crest level of +1.2mOD, and the effects on the beach form were predicted. Various reef configurations were tested, and the results confirmed that the conceptual reef design would reduce the tendency for erosion in the gaps between reefs. Whilst the level of downdrift erosion was markedly reduced, when compared to that predicted to the south-east of Reefs 5 to 8, a significant level of erosion was still predicted (see Figure 4, which shows the predicted development of a coastline without pre-formed beach salients). Downdrift erosion was considered to be an inevitable consequence of the sea defences, and design changes would only minimise, and not remove, this tendency. Building on studies carried out in Chesapeake Bay (Reference 20), various alternatives for managing downdrift erosion were modelled. The most effective of these options was found to be the inclusion of one lower reef at the downdrift limit of the system.

It was predicted that downdrift erosion would result in losses from the beaches for approximately 1km to the south-east of the reef system. Longshore model tests were carried out for ten years of real wave data, and it was predicted that losses of up to 250,000m³ may occur in any one year, whilst the average annual loss was predicted to be 150,000m³ per year. As part of the Stage Two works, these downdrift beaches were over-filled, to accommodate the anticipated volume of sand loss in the first year. Beach recharge will continue to form an important element of the future development of the Strategy.

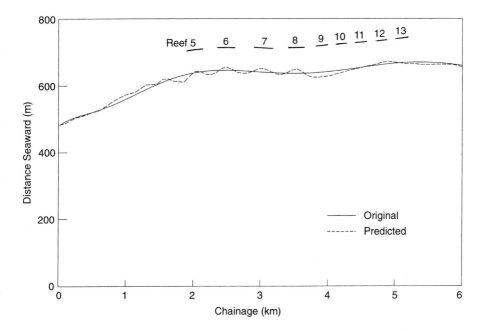

Figure 4   Happisburgh to Winterton Predicted Longshore Beach Response, 1996

The beach plan shape modelling also demonstrated that reefs may not be required over the full frontage, as the predicted effects of longshore drift did not show a significant tendency for an eroding coastline for a length of 3.5km south-east of Reef 13. Cross-shore modelling was undertaken, to determine whether these beaches would be stable during storms, in the absence of reef protection. This modelling demonstrated that rock revetment protection to the seawall would be required along this frontage, to reduce the potential for beach erosion during severe storms.

The Strategy developed as a consequence of the modelling studies described above is presented in Figure 5. A revised implementation programme was developed for the Strategy, and the most urgent of the recommended works were incorporated into the second stage. Stage Two of the Strategy comprised the construction of five offshore reefs (Reefs 9 to 13), to the south of Reef 8, and the placement of over 1 million cubic metres of sand beach recharge (Plate 1). Recharge was placed behind and between Reefs 5 to 13, and of the order of 200,000m^3 was placed to overfill downdrift beaches, such that the anticipated erosion could be accommodated.

FUTURE MONITORING AND STUDIES

During the development of the Strategy Review, a detailed programme of monitoring was prepared (Reference 21). The objectives of these monitoring proposals were as follows :

(a)   Evaluate the performance of the works.
(b)   Ensure that any remedial action after reef construction is taken in good time.
(c)   Enable works to be fine-tuned to optimise benefits.
(d)   Ensure that construction or recharge is targeted on those areas with greatest need.
(e)   Provide design data for future reef construction and obtain a greater understanding of beach and offshore seabed behaviour.
(f)   Assess the key environmental impacts and enhancements achieved by the Strategy.

In order to meet these objectives, a major campaign of monitoring has been prepared including, inter alia, beach profiles, bathymetric survey work, reef structural surveys, and environmental impact surveys.

In order that a high degree of confidence may be placed in future phases of the Strategy, based upon adequate understanding of the true effects of the stages completed to date, no further reef construction will be undertaken for a period of at least two years following completion of Stage Two. This will allow a reasonable data set to be collated, without artificial interference in the observed and measured effects. However, in the meantime, some Intermediate Works will be necessary, including beach management measures and the construction of rock toe protection along lengths of the frontage which will not be protected by reefs.

Prior to Stage Three, which is presently expected to comprise the construction of a further five offshore reefs, a second Strategy review will be undertaken. This will use the results of the monitoring studies, and compare the predicted beach response to that measured in the field.

Figure 5

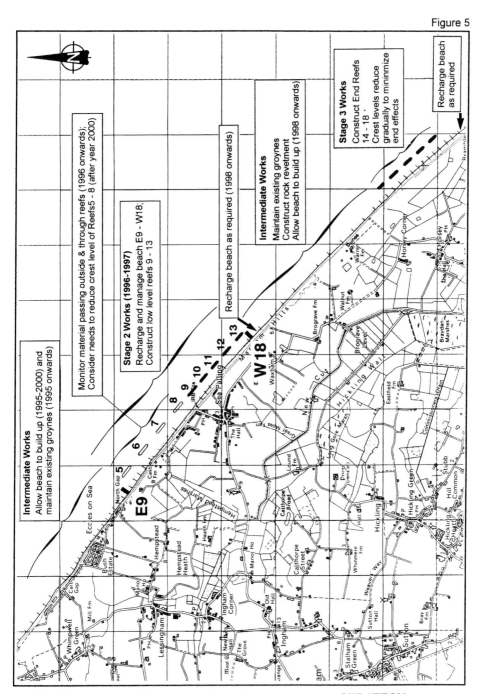

**STRATEGY,
AS UPDATED IN 1996**

Plate 1   **Aerial View of Reefs 5 (foreground) to 13**

CONCLUSIONS

The following significant conclusions may be drawn from the development and implementation of the Strategy, and the results of monitoring available to date.

- Stage One of the Strategy responded largely as predicted, although beach losses as a consequence of storm conditions prior to and during the construction period resulted in beach levels which were lower than generally expected;
- The ability of computational models, to represent the effects of offshore reefs on the wave climate and sediment regime in the vicinity of an offshore reef system, has been demonstrated;
- The importance of reef crest elevation as the dominant design parameter has been confirmed, although the over-riding priority must always be for the scheme to remain effective during storm conditions;
- The need for further understanding of the wave transmission effects within and over reefs has been highlighted, and may be addressed during forthcoming 3-dimensional physical model studies;
- Reef construction should be implemented in conjunction with beach recharge, to minimise end effects;
- Residual downdrift effects are predictable, and the use of computational models with real, sequential wave data, can facilitate the evaluation of the corresponding management commitments.

At the conference to be held in March 1998, a further description will be provided of the performance of the nine completed reefs and the beach recharge scheme over the winter period 1997/8.

REFERENCES

1   National Rivers Authority (1989). Sea Defences, Norfolk. Happisburgh to Winterton. Engineer's Report. (As revised December 1989).
2   Halcrow (1991). Sea Defences - Norfolk. Happisburgh to Winterton. Final Report on Proposed Sea Defences. Volumes 1 and 2.
3   Clayton K.M. et al. (1983). The Establishment of a Sand Budget for the East Anglian Coast and its Implications for Coastal Stability. In "Shoreline Protection", Thomas Telford Ltd, London.
4   Halcrow (1996). Happisburgh to Winterton Sea Defences : Stage Two. Strategy Review.
5   MAFF (1993). Flood and Coastal Defence: Project Appraisal Guidance Notes.
6   Delft Hydraulics (1995). Happisburgh to Winterton Sea Defences. Review of Strategy.
7   US Army Corps of Engineers (1993). Engineering Design Guidance for Detached Breakwaters as Shoreline Stabilization Structures. Technical Report CERC-93-19.
8   CIRIA (1996). Beach Management Manual. Report R153.
9   Brampton A.H. and Smallman J.V. (1985). Shore Protection by Offshore Breakwaters. HR Wallingford Report SR 8.
10   Dally W.R. and Pope J. (1986). Detached Breakwaters for Shore Protection. Technical Report CERC-86-1. US Army Corps of Engineers.

11   Seiji W.N, Uda T. and Tanaka S. (1987). Statistical Study on the Effect and Stability of Detached Breakwaters. Coastal Engineering in Japan. 30(1), pp131-141.
12   Suh K. and Dalrymple R.A. (1987). Offshore Breakwaters in Laboratory and Field. Journal, Waterway, Port, Coastal and Ocean Engineering. 113(2), pp105-121.
13   Ahrens J.P. and Cox J. (1990). Design and Performance of Reef Breakwaters. J Coast Res. pp 61 to 75.
14   Pope J. and Dean J.L. (1986). Development of design criteria for segmented breakwaters. Proceedings, 20th Int. Conf. on Coastal Engineering. Taipei, Taiwan. ASCE, pp2144-58.
15   HR Wallingford (1994). Effectiveness of Control Structures on Shingle Beaches. Report SR387.
16   University of Bristol (1997). The Design and Performance of Submerged Breakwaters.
17   Danish Hydraulic Institute (1991). Happisburgh to Winterton. Sea Defences. Hydraulic Investigations, May 1991.
18   Ilic S. and Chadwick A. (1994). "Evaluation and Validation of the Mild Slope Evolution Equation Model Using Field Data." Proc Coastal Dynamics, 1994.
19   Delft Hydraulics (1990). Data on wave transmission due to overtopping. Report H986.
20   Hardaway C.S., Gunn J.R. and Reynolds R.N. (1993). "Breakwater Design in Chesapeake Bay : Dealing with End Effects." Proc Coastal Zone 1993, Coastal Engineering Considerations in Coastal Zone Management. ASCE, New Orleans, LA, pp27-41.
21   Halcrow (1997). Sea Defences - Norfolk. Happisburgh to Winterton. Strategic Monitoring.

PROBABILISTIC OPTIMISATION
OF THE ENNORE COAL PORT

PROF.IR. DRS. J.K. VRIJLING, Delft University of Technology, Delft, the Netherlands, MR. S. GOPALAN, Ministry of Surface Transport, New Delhi, India, IR. J.H. LABOYRIE, HASKONING, Consulting Engineers and Architects, Nijmegen, the Netherlands, and IR. S.E. PLATE, Directorate-General of Public Works and Water Management, Utrecht, the Netherlands.

INTRODUCTION

As part of the national policy of extending and improving the power supply to the region around Madras (nowadays Chennai) in India, Tamil Nadu Electricity Board started the construction of a new coal-fired power station at Ennore. To operate at full capacity, it has been assumed that the New North Madras Thermal Power Station will need some 16 million tons of coal per year. This will be supplied mostly by the Talcher coal fields in the state of Orissa. The coal will be transported by train over a distance of about 200km from the Talcher fields to Paradip, a major port some 300km south of Calcutta. The coal will be shipped from Paradip to Ennore. Additional coal will be brought in from coal fields abroad.

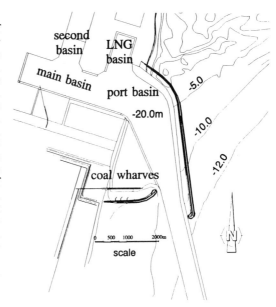

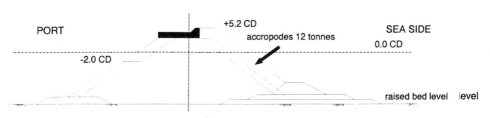

typical cross section of north breakwater
for trunk section from head to -10.40 CD (existing bed level)

Figure 1 *Lay-out harbour and cross-section breakwaters with a southern entrance at Ennore*

Coastlines, structures and breakwaters. Thomas Telford, London, 1998

A design study conducted by HASKONING in 1995/1996 led to recommendations for a new harbour for handling coal and other commodities at Ennore. The recommended harbour lay-out with a southern entrance will offer optimal conditions for these terminal imports (Figure 1). Many port-terminals are now envisaged in Ennore for reasons of modernisation, pollution relieve and capacity problems at Madras. Madras and Ennore will play complementary roles to each other.

The port of Ennore has to meet the requirements of the Tamil Nadu Electricity Board of the new North Madras Thermal Power Station (NMTPS): downtime of the power station is not permitted. The power stations in the region require a regular supply of coal for the continuous generation of power. The storage capacity of the power station is limited, so an almost uninterrupted activity in the port will occur. This sets further constraints on the tranquillity requirements of the waves in the port-area, the availability of berths for the unloading of coal and the open entrance of the channel.

The scope of this paper is to optimise the design of the breakwater, taking into account the uncertainties. In view of the optimal probability of total stoppage of port operations three classes of failure mechanisms were studied. Collapse of the breakwater, functional failure of the breakwater causing excessive wave height in the basin and obstruction of the entrance channel .
In the first class reliability calculations were carried out for the mechanisms: failure of the armour, failure of the toe, soil failure, internal erosion and settlement. In the second class the percentage of down time of the harbour caused by overtopping, transmission, diffraction and refraction was calculated using the statistics of the wave climate. Finally, the probability of a grounding ship in the entrance channel was assessed using the data of real time and fast time ship movement simulations.
The failure mechanisms are related with each other and the top event "unacceptable downtime of port operations" by means of the fault-tree given in Figure 2. With the fault-tree the probability of the top event was assessed.

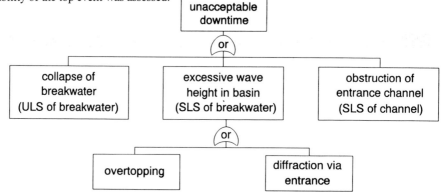

Figure 2 *Fault-tree with top event*
with ULS: Ultimate Limit State and SLS: Serviceability Limit State

As a second step the monetary damage caused by the relevant failure mechanism and subsequent downtime of port operations was calculated. Then the incremental investment in heavier armour blocks, in a flatter slope, in a higher crest, a wider entrance channel, etc. to reduce the respective probabilities of failure were calculated as a function of the decision variable. Finally the optimal failure probability of each mechanism was evaluated by minimising the total cost of investment and the present value of the risk.

BOUNDARY CONDITIONS

For the three categories of failure mechanisms, different wave climates have to be considered: the Ultimate Limit State (ULS) of the breakwater occurs under hurricane conditions, the Serviceability Limit State (SLS) is governed by the normal cycle of the north-east (NE) and south-west (SW) monsoon.

The distributions of the significant wave height H_s in m and the wave steepness s_p in percent, defined on the spectral peak period, have been determined as shown in Table 1.

Wave climate	Type of distribution	Characteristics
CYCLONE	deep water wave height: *Gumbel* distributed	$H_{s,0}$: (x, 3.31, 1.518) (*1 year cyclone*) $H_{s,0}$: (x, 9.25, 1.518) (*50 year cyclone*)
	deep water wave steepness: *Gumbel* distributed	$s_{p,0}$: (x, 2.949, 0.514)
NE MONSOON	deep water wave height: *Gumbel* distributed	$H_{s,0}$: (x, 0.861, 0.262)
	deep water wave steepness: *Normal* distributed	$s_{p,0}$: (x, 1.534, 0.656)
SW MONSOON	deep water wave height: *Normal* distributed	$H_{s,0}$: (x, 0.861, 0.223)
	deep water wave steepness: *Gumbel* distributed	$s_{p,0}$: (x, 0.949, 0.995)

Table 1 *Distributions of deep water wave height*

For the tranquillity calculations, the monsoon deep-water wave spectra have to be split into wind waves and swell. A split in the wind wave and swell has been made because they differ in peak period and direction. The wind wave follows the prevailing wind direction. The swell has a SE-direction, independent of the season.

The following values are assumed (respectively for NE and SW monsoon):

Variable	Type of distribution	Input values [m]	
		μ	σ
NE-monsoon			
H_s sea	Gumbel	0.85	0.31
H_s swell	Normal	0.45	0.35
SW-monsoon			
H_s sea	Gumbel	0.61	0.2
H_s swell	Normal	0.65	0.2

Table 2 *Input values for NE- and SW-monsoon*

The wave period of the sea is schematised to 7 s. and of the swell to 14 s. for the tranquillity study. The wave climate characteristics are transformed to the shallower conditions at the breakwaters, taking into account possible breaking of waves and bed friction.

The nearshore investigations indicate a geotechnical profile consisting of a top layer of sand overlying a layer of soft silty clay. In deeper water the sand layer diminished in thickness.

Under the breakwaters, in the deeper parts, a soil improvement is carried out, replacing the soft material by sand.

HAZARDS AND FAILURE MECHANISMS

In Figure 2 three major mechanisms that may cause the top event (excessive downtime) were distinguished.

The first major mechanism that attains the top-event is the lost of the protective function of the breakwater in the case of collapse of the breakwater. The relevant failure mechanisms that fall in this category are discussed later.

A second major mechanism is the exceedance of the wave height of 0.5m at the two coal berths. This maximum allowable value for the wave height has been derived from the design documents. This exceedance of this criterion can be described as a Serviceability Limit State: the lay-out and cross-section of the breakwater do not fulfil their functional requirements.

The third major mechanism that could cause an unacceptable downtime of the port is the event of a ship running aground in the navigation channel, thus obstructing traffic. Total stoppage of coal transport is assumed in the case of this event.

ULTIMATE LIMIT STATE OF THE BREAKWATERS

The breakwaters are composed of many components such as filter layer, toe structure, armour layer and deck. Collapse of one of these components will weaken the resistance of other components and the total structure.

In the cross-section of the breakwater the mechanisms *erosion of the Accropode armour layer*, *erosion of the toe*, *slip circle*, *excessive settlement* and *internal erosion* were considered Of these mechanisms only the first three will be treated here as they are major contributors to the probability of failure.

A first main hazard that could lead to failure is *erosion of the Accropode armour layer*. According to Van der Meer (1988), the following formula is valid:

$$\frac{H_s}{\Delta D_{n50}} = C_{acc.}$$

in which

H_s = significant wave height at the location of the breakwater [m]
Δ = density of armour material relative to the water [-]
   = $(\rho_c/\rho_w)-1$
ρ_c = mass density of concrete [kg/m³]
ρ_w = mass density of water [kg/m³]
D_{n50} = characteristic diameter of armour elements [m]
C_{acc} = constant for Accropode [-].

The following reliability function can then be derived:

$$Z = C_{acc}\left(\frac{\rho_c}{\rho_w} - 1\right) \cdot \sqrt[3]{\frac{W_{acc.}}{g \cdot \rho_c}} - H_s \quad \text{with } W_{acc.} \text{ the weight of Accropode [kN].}$$

The *erosion of the toe* is a second main hazard that may lead to failure. The following formula describes, according to Van der Meer (1995), the relation between level of damage of a toe structure, the wave height, the armour characteristics and the height of the toe structure relative to the water depth:

$$\frac{H_S}{\Delta D_{n50}} = \left(0.24 \cdot \frac{d_t}{D_{n50}} + 1.6\right) \cdot N_{od}^{0.15}$$

in which

d_t = depth of crest of the toe below water level [m]
   = $h_{max}-z_{bed}-h_t$ [m]
h_{max} = water level [CD + m]
z_{bed} = bed level [CD + m]
h_t = height of the toe [m]
N_{od} = dimensionless damage level [m].

The equation is reformulated to the following reliability function:

$$Z = \Delta \cdot \left(0.24 \cdot d_t + 1.6 \cdot D_{n50}\right) \cdot N_{od}^{0.15} - H_S.$$

The third main hazard that could lead to failure is a *slip circle failure*. The probability of slip circle failure depends on the crest level z_{crest}, cohesion of the soil c and the angle of internal friction ϕ and was calculated according to Bishop. However to reduce the computational effort, the Bishop results were approximated by the following response surface (Enevoldsen, 1994) with parameters x_i and y_i:

$$S = \left(X \cdot \cot \alpha + Y\right)\frac{4.5}{z_{crest}}$$

in which

$$X = \left(x_1 \cdot c + x_2\right) \cdot \phi + x_3 \cdot c + x_4$$
$$Y = \left(y_1 \cdot c + y_2\right) \cdot \phi + y_3 \cdot c + y_4.$$

If for the resistance, a stability factor criterion F_{sc} is taken, the reliability function can be described as:

$$Z = F_{sc} - \left(X \cdot \cot \alpha + Y\right) \cdot \frac{4.5}{z_{crest}}.$$

For each variable, a mean value, a standard deviation and the type of probability density function have been determined, based on numerical data available of the design of the breakwater structure at Ennore and expert judgement.

Six stochastic variables can be distinguished in the failure mechanism of the armour: C_{acc}, ρ_c, ρ_w, W_{acc}, H_s and f_{Hs}, an additive variable to model uncertainty of the wave climate.

For the distribution of C_{acc}, a normal distribution is assumed according to Van der Meer (1988). This standard deviation may be valid for test in a laboratory, but the uncertainty of the behaviour of Accropode in a breakwater is larger. This leads to the following set:

variable	μ	σ	type
$C_{acc.}$	4.1 [-]	1.0 [-]	Normal
ρ_c	2400 [kg/m^3]	50 [kg/m^3]	Normal
$W_{acc.}$	150 [kN]	7.5 [kN]	Normal
f_{Hs}	0 [m]	0.80 [m]	Normal

Table 3 *Input values for the failure of Accropode armour layer*

The local wave height H_s is calculated from the deep water wave statistics (Table 1), taking into account the effects of the bathymetry and the lay-out of the breakwater. The relevant wave climate for this mechanism is the cyclone. To account for the fact that the estimated distribution of the cyclonic wave heights is based on relatively small number of hindcasts, an additive uncertainty f_{Hs} has been added to the wave height. For the depth of the crest of the toe d_t, the influence of differing bed level elevation is evident. Thus, two values have to be applied for d_t. The applied input parameters and their distributions are summarised in Table 4.

Variable	μ	σ	type
h_{max}	1.57 [CD + m]	0.30 [m]	Normal
z_{bed}	-11.5 / 9.5[CD + m]	0.67 [m]	Normal
ρ_c	2650 [kg/m^3]	50 [kg/m^3]	Normal
W_{50}	3.3 [kN]	0.3 [kN]	Normal
h_t	3.0 [m]	0.5 [m]	Normal
N_{od}	3000 [-]	0.05 [-]	Normal

Table 4 *Input values for toe stability*

The angle of internal friction ϕ for Accropode is assumed to be distributed normally. The cohesion (ρ_c) is determined by the interlocking characteristics of the elements. The crest level z_{crest} is a design value. The applied input variables and their distributions are summarised in Table 5.

Variable	μ	σ	type
cot α	1.33[1] [-]	0.3[1][-]	Normal
φ	25 [°]	5.0 [°]	Normal
c_A	15 [kN/m²]	5.0 [kN/m²]	Normal
z_{crest}	5.30 [CD + m]	0.10 [m]	Normal

[1] values for Accropode

Table 5 *Input values for slip circle stability*

The probabilities of failure of the ULS mechanisms are summarised in Table 6:

mechanisms	Pf at CD - 9.5 m	Pf at CD - 11.5 m
instability for Accropode layers	$2.7 \cdot 10^{-2}$	$5.6 \cdot 10^{-2}$
instability of the toe	$2.9 \cdot 10^{-2}$	$3.2 \cdot 10^{-2}$
slip circle	$9.1 \cdot 10^{-2}$	$9.9 \cdot 10^{-2}$
internal erosion	$4.4 \cdot 10^{-2}$	$4.4 \cdot 10^{-2}$

Table 6 *Probabilities of failure in a lifetime of 100 years*

The fundamental bounds of the probability of collapse of the cross-section in a lifetime of 100 years are given by the maximum value and the sum of the probabilities of failure of the respective mechanisms:

Sea bottom at CD - 9.5 m: $\quad 9.9 \cdot 10^{-2} < P_{f,syst} < 1.9 \cdot 10^{-1}$

Sea bottom at CD - 11.5 m: $\quad 9.9 \cdot 10^{-2} < P_{f,syst} < 1.87 \cdot 10^{-1}$

Practically speaking these fundamental bounds are sufficiently narrow. An interesting point is that for most mechanisms studied here, the contribution of the resistance variables to the variance of the reliability function Z is so high, that failure events in subsequent years become dependent.

Thus the probability of collapse in the first year is of the same order of magnitude as that for 100 years. For instance, the probability of erosion of the armour layer in 1 and 100 years is $1.8 \cdot 10^{-2}$ and $5.6 \cdot 10^{-2}$ respectively. The dependence is mainly caused by the common variable C_{acc}.

SERVICEABLILTY LIMIT STATE OF BREAKWATERS

In order to establish a reliability function, the effect of the phenomena diffraction, refraction, transmission and wave generation on the basin tranquillity will be first considered. The probabilistic combination of the phenomena contributing to the wave energy in the port basin will be described.

For this, two types of uncertainty are taken into account: the variability of the wave climate and the scatter around the empirical functions of each of the phenomena.

Finally, the combined reliability function of the Serviceability Limit State of the breakwater will be presented.

In the detailed design phase the combined refraction-diffraction/reflection results of the computer computations have been taken into account. In the analysis, the two major components of the local monsoon wave climate have been considered: the component due to the year-round swell and the component caused by local wind.

It appears that different amplification factors can be distinguished for both types, due to the typical difference in wave period and direction.

Using these results the wave height inside the port basin is related to the wave height outside the port by:

$$H_d = \sqrt{\left(K_{d,sea} \cdot H_{sea}\right)^2 + \left(K_{d,swell} \cdot H_{swell}\right)^2}$$

in which

H_d	=	wave height due to diffraction inside basin [m]
K_d	=	amplification factor for sea and swell respectively
H	=	wave height outside basin of sea and swell [m].

The contribution of wave transmission and overtopping to the total wave energy within the port basin will be based on the relation for transmission and overtopping for rubble-mound breakwaters $f(H_{out}, h_{crest})$ provided by Powell and Allsop (1985). The wave height inside the port basin can be expressed in terms of the original wave height outside by use of a transmission factor. A model factor (F_m), expressing the model uncertainty, is added to the derived transmission factor:

$$H_t = \left(f\left(H_{out}, h_{crest}\right) + F_m\right) \cdot H_{out}$$

Locally generated waves within the port basin can be calculated by determining the fetch length of the basin and the prevailing wind speed.

Initial calculations have demonstrated that the effect of locally generated waves is minor.

The combined effect of wave refraction, diffraction/reflection, wave transmission and overtopping and local wave generation can be determined by adding the wave energies and neglecting H_{wind}:

$$H_{port\ basin} = \sqrt{\left(K_{d,sea} \cdot H_{sea}\right)^2 + \left(K_{d,swell} \cdot H_{swell}\right)^2 + H_t^2}$$

The reliability function follows from comparison of the allowable wave height (a design criterion) H_{all} with the actual wave height in the basin:

$$Z = H_{all} - H_{portbasin}.$$

The value for $Pr(Z<0)$ that results from the probabilistic calculations expresses the percentage of time that the requirement is not fulfilled.

The calculations were performed for three locations in the harbour. Here only the data for the East berth are presented. The distributions of the diffraction amplification factors, both for wind waves and for swell, were derived from the results of the DIFFRAC-computations for the Ennore Coal Port Project. Two cases were analysed: NE and SW monsoon.

In Table 7 the distributions applied for the reliability function are summarised:

Variable	μ	σ	type
H_{all}	0.5 [m]	0.002[m]	Normal
h_{max}	1.57 [m]	0.30 [m]	Normal
$K_{d,sea}$	0.1 [-]	0.02 [-]	Normal
K_{dswell}	0.2 [-]	0.05 [-]	Normal
z_{crest}	5.3 [CD + m]	0.1 [m]	Normal
P	0.55 [-]	0.05 [-]	Normal
cot α	3.5 [-]	0.30 [-]	Normal
F_m	0 [-]	0.025 [-]	Normal

Table 7 *Input variables for the East berth*

It should be noted that the K_d value for sea differs for the NE and the SW monsoon. The K_d value for swell for the NE and the SW monsoon, however, is the same since the swell propagates perpendicular to the depth contour lines.

Assuming a NE monsoon duration of 3 months (90 days), the number of days of wave height exceedance is for the east berth $4.2 \cdot 10^{-3}$ days per year.
With the SW monsoon being active 4 months a year (122 days), the number of days of wave height exceedance per year is $0.94 \cdot 10^{-3}$ for the east berth, bringing the total to $5.14 \cdot 10^{-3}$ days/year.
The number of days that the 0.5 m wave height at the east berths is exceeded is below the limit of 5 days per year given in the design criteria. Therefore the effect of a lowered crest on the wave heights at these locations of interest is investigated. For a crest height of 3.3m, the total number of in-operational days over both monsoon periods is 0.62 days per year.

SERVICEABILITY LIMIT STATE OF ENTRANCE CHANNEL
The top event, downtime at the coal berths, will also occur when the entrance channel is obstructed for some reason. The only failure mechanism considered is the obstruction of entrance channel by a grounding ship.

Failure in this context is described as the situation wherein the swept path exceeds the channel bounds. Apart from the physical variables, which are estimated by a fast-time ship manoeuvring simulation model, there are three other aspects which should be considered: positioning accuracy, navigation error and a safe distance from the channel banks (Marin, 1995).
The position of bow and stern can be geometrically described. As any contact between ship and bank leads to grounding, the requirements is expressed as

$$|PE + EN| + \left|\frac{L}{2}\sin\alpha\right| + \left|\frac{B}{2}\right| < \frac{CW}{2}.$$

Combining the components $\frac{L}{2}\sin\alpha$ *and* $\frac{B}{2}$ into the swept path (SP), the reliability function

reads: $Z = \dfrac{CW}{2} - \left|\dfrac{SP}{2}\right| - |PE + EN|$

in which:
CW $=$ channel width [m]
SP $=$ swept path [m]
PE $=$ position error [m]
EN $=$ error due to navigation [m]
B $=$ ship width [m]
α $=$ course angle [rad].
In channel design, a safety margin equal to the beam B (~ 35 m) is often used. Within the risk study, the latter is superfluous since it is taken into account in the probabilistic calculations by reducing the probability of grounding.

The stochastic path of bow and stern has been determined by means of real and fast-time simulations (MSCN, 1995). The division of the variance over the parameters α, PE and EN is based on an analysis of a number of simulations performed under a range of sea conditions and on expert judgement.

Variable	μ	σ	type
CW	170 [m]	15 [m]	Normal
PE	0 [m]	5 [m]	Normal
NE	0 [m]	10 [m]	Normal
α	0 [rad]	0.088[rad]	Normal
B	32.2 [m]	--	--
L	245 [m]	--	--

Table 8 *Input variables for a grounding ship*

Accounting for 266 ships passing the channel every year, an annual failure probability of $3.3 \cdot 10^{-2}$, results in a 10-years probability of 0.33 and a 100 year probability of 0.96.

SUMMARY OF FAILURE PROBABILITIES OF TOP EVENT
For the ULS and SLS involved failure probabilities have been calculated and included in the fault-tree accordingly. In Table 6 the failure probabilities of the top event defined are summarised.

Event	P_r	Days	Expected downtime d/y
Collapse op the breakwater	$1.9 \cdot 10^{-3}$	365	0.690
Excessive wave height	-	-	0.005
Obstruction entrance	$3.3 \cdot 10^{-2}$	90	2.970

Table 9 *Summary of failure probabilities of top event in 1 year*

From the table it can be observed that the entrance channel has the largest contribution to the expected downtime and functional failure leading to wave unrest in the harbour basin the smallest. The probability of collapse of the breakwater that is here averaged over the 100 year lifetime ($1.9 \cdot 10^{-1}/100$) has an intermediate contribution.

OPTIMISATION OF BREAKWATER DESIGN
Although professionally designed and well constructed, there appears to be a possibility that the structure fails. The optimal probability of failure is a question of economic reasoning. This approach equates the investment in a stronger breakwater with the reduced risk of failure. Failure entails damage to the breakwater and leads to suspended harbour operations during the period of reconstruction.

A first major failure mechanism is unacceptable damage to the breakwaters. Strengthening of the breakwaters by applying heavier blocks and by adapting the cross-sections reduce the possibility of failure of the breakwaters. In principle the cost of the breakwater increases with the applied element weight W according to:

$$I_{tot} = I_o + I_w \cdot W.$$

with I= gradient cost.

A second major failure mechanism is that the tranquillity provided by the breakwater under normal circumstances (SLS) is disappointing. Generally tranquillity can be improved by increasing the height h of the breakwater to reduce overtopping and by increasing the length L to reduce the diffracted wave entering the harbour entrance. The costs of these alterations can be added to the model of the total investment proposed above:

$$I_{tot} = I_o + I_w \cdot W + I_h \cdot h + I_L \cdot L$$

To find the optimal probability of failure the damage of the loss of the breakwater has to be estimated expressed in monetary terms. In general this will be the cost of repair and the losses incurred due to suspended harbour operation together an amount D. The risk is determined by multiplying the damage D with the probability of failure which is a function of the element weight W. As the harbour is exposed to the risk every year, the present value over the planning period has to be taken.

The same reasoning applies to the optimisation of the tranquillity. Here the percentage of non-operational days during the rough season (lasting N days) has to be multiplied with the cost per day of interrupted operation d.

The present value of the total risk over the planning period of M year:

$$[p_{failure}(W) \cdot D + p_{tranq}(h, L) \cdot N \cdot d] \cdot \left(\frac{1}{r}\right) \cdot \left(1 - \frac{1}{(1+r)^M}\right).$$

The equation of the total cost TC results from the addition of the investment and the risk component:

$$TC = I_o + I_W \cdot W + I_h \cdot h + I_L \cdot L + [p_{failure}(W) \cdot D + p_{tranq}(h, L) \cdot N \cdot d] \cdot \left(\frac{1}{r}\right) \cdot \left(1 - \frac{1}{(1+r)^M}\right).$$

The objective is to minimise the total cost by varying the block weight W, the height of the breakwater h and the length L. The minima can be found by differentiating the TC-function to the mentioned variables and equating the differential to zero.

To make the theoretical solution practical the functions relating the failure probability to the element weight and the percentage down-time to the height and the length of the breakwater have to be established.

It should however be noted that for instance an alternative W represents a complete design alternative, besides changes in primary armour, also changes in toe units an all cross-sections and changes in crest height have to be made. The probability of failure of the breakwater can be approximated by a function of armour unit size W, that reads:

$$p_{failure}(W) = e^{-\frac{W-A}{B}}.$$

The minimum total generalised cost is found when:

$$\frac{dTC}{dW} = I_W + \frac{D}{r} \cdot \left(1 - \frac{1}{(1+r)^M}\right) \cdot e^{-\frac{W-A}{B}} \cdot \left(-\frac{1}{B}\right) = 0$$

which leads to the optimum probability of failure of the breakwater with respect to the element weight:

$$p_{failure}(W_{opt}) = e^{-\frac{W_{opt}-A}{B}} = \frac{I_W \cdot r \cdot B}{\left(1 - \frac{1}{(1+r)^M}\right) \cdot D}.$$

The optimum probability of failure in 100 years will be calculated for the primary armour layer (Accropode).

Therefore upper-bound quantifications have been made for the cost of an one day suspension d of port operations and for the cost of a situation of major damage D to the breakwater.

Item	Description	US $
Cost of shipping operation	US $ 8000 per vessel / day; average 1 vessel / day; waiting 3 days extra	24,000
Loss of income MPT, direct	throughput 16 mln ton / year; port dues US $ 5.2 / ton	230,000
Loss of income MPT, indirect	bad reputation / day	140,000
Claims	TNEB, shipping lines, other parties	50,000
	SUBTOTAL	444,000
Indirect economic damage	multiplier 1.5	
	TOTAL	666,000

Table 10 *Estimated cost of one day suspension of port operation d*

In case of major damage to the breakwater, the damage cost consists of the cost of structural repair costs and of economic damage. The total estimated cost is given in Table 11.

Item	Description	US $ million
STRUCTURAL DAMAGE		
Damage to breakwater	20% of construction cost	24
Damage to other structures in port	wharf, slope protection, harbour lights	5
Mobilisation of contractor	Lump Sum	4
	SUBTOTAL	33
ECONOMIC DAMAGE		
Alternative transportation of coal to NMPTS	throughput 16 million ton/year; extra cost per tonne: US $ 6	96
Cost of shipping operation	US $ 8000 / vessel a day; average 1 vessel / day	3
Loss of MPT, direct	throughput 16 million ton/year; port dues US $ 5.2 / ton	83
Loss of income MPT, indirect	bad reputation	50
Lives lost	< 10, economic damage negligible	-
Claims	TNEB, shipping lines, other parties	100
	SUBTOTAL	332
Indirect economic damage	multiplier 1.5	504
TOTAL STRUCTURAL AND ECONOMIC DAMAGE		537

Table 11 *Estimated cost of major damage D*

In the assessment of the damage cost it has been assumed that the only activities taking place in the port are the coal handling operations. When the port expands and more terminals will come into operation, the actual damage cost will be a multiple of the cost calculated here.

The investment required to construct the breakwater at Ennore is an element of the total cost of the breakwater during its lifetime (total generalised cost). In order to determine the investment cost as a function of the probability of failure, the relation between the investment cost and the block weight has been analysed.

For the design with an Accropode armouring, the gradient of the investment cost is:
$I_w = 0.11$ M$/kN.

The crest height has a considerable influence on the investment cost of the breakwater because a small reduction of the crest level decreases the area of a breakwater cross-section considerably. The gradient cost I_h of the cost for the height of the Accropode breakwater amounts to 12 M$/m. The gradient cost I_L for the length of the breakwater amounts to 53 k$/m. The net interest rate has been chosen as 5%.

The maintenance and repair cost has been assessed by estimating the damage to the breakwater under normal wave conditions. For significant wave heights corresponding to return periods of 1, 10 an 25 years, the damage to the breakwater primary armour and toe layers has been estimated.

The expressions for maintenance cost M were used in the assessment of the optimum probability of failure, but are omitted here.

The approximating function relating the probability to the element weight W reads :

$$P_f = e^{-\frac{W-A}{B}} \quad \text{where A} = \text{-333 kN and B} = 120 \text{ s.}$$

The optimum probability of failure in 100 years has been calculated for the primary armour layer (Accropode), assuming dependence between subsequent years. The optimal failure probabilities of the armour layer is $2.5 \cdot 10^{-2}$ in the lifetime of 100 years for the Accropode alternative. Comparison of the $P_{f,opt}$ values presented in the Tables 6 and 9 with the P_f values shows that a slight decrease of the element weight might be considered to arrive at an optimised design. In view of the rather high probability of failure, an element weight of 150 kN was preferred.

In the calculation of the number of in-operational days, the NE monsoon is assumed to last 90 days and the SW-monsoon 120 days per year. Summing the in-operational days over both monsoon periods, the following result is reached for the preliminary design crest height of CD + 5.3m and a reduced crest height of CD + 3.3m

crest	days/year
CD + 5.3m	0.0042
CD + 3.3m	0.6198.

The approximating function that directly relates the crest height (h) to the number of in-operational days per year reads:

in-operational days per year $= e^{-\frac{h-A}{B}}$ where A = 3.11 and B = 0.40.

The optimal number of in-operational days equals:

$$\text{optimal number of in-operational days per year} = \frac{I_h \cdot r \cdot B}{d}.$$

Depending on the level of the real interest rate (nominal interest minus inflation) the optimal number of in-operational days varies between 0.15 and 0.35 days per year. The optimal crest height of the breakwater is around CD + 4m from this point of view. However an analysis of the construction showed that for an efficient construction-process, the core should not be overtopped. Therefore the crest level was chosen at CD + 5.4m. The length and the slope of the breakwater, and the width of the entrance were optimised following the same theoretical framework.

CONCLUSIONS

It has been demonstrated that important aspects of a harbour can be optimised, using probabilistic design methods, in the setting of a professional design project.

The armour block weight, the crest level, the outer slope and the length of the breakwater fotr the Ennore coal port were optimised by equating additional investment with teh reduction of the risk of failure.

The width of the entrance channel was optimised on the same basis.

The paper proves that the reliability theory can be applied to the various mechanisms that threaten the proper functioning of the breakwater. Additionally the economic and cost data necessary for an economic optimisation can be generated using the feasibility and cost studies that accompany any major infrastructural project.

The study supports the rather high structural failure probability of a breakwater from an economic point of view. The economically optimal probability of failure of the Ennore breakwater in the 100 year planning period lies between $0.99 \cdot 10^{-1}$ and $1.9 \cdot 10^{-1}$. In (PIANC, 1991) similar or even higher values were found for other breakwaters.

The width of the entrance channel was also optimised along probabilistic lines. Besides the classical methods of (PIANC, 1991), a new method was developed to relate the results of real and fast time simulations to the optimal channel width. The optimal probability of grounding appeared to be $0.33 \cdot 10^{-1}$ in a 10 year period for the Ennore coal port. Further study and experience is needed to refine and improve this new approach.

Studying the paper it should be borne in mind , that optimisation is an aid in the design and that the results have no absolute values. Other effects or considerations regarding the construction or the final phase may drive the final decision.

This work has be cosponsored by MAST under contract-number MAS3-CT95-0041.

REFERENCES
Delft Hydraulics, "*Tranquillity Study, Ennore Coal Port*", Delft, 1995.

HASKONING, "*Detailed Design Breakwaters, Ennore Coal Port Project*", Madras, 1996.

MSCN, "*Fast Time Simulation Study, Ennore Coal Port*", OD086.10/01, 1995.

PIANC, Working Group 12, "*Development of a partial safety coefficient system in the design of rubble mound breakwaters*", report subgroup F, PIANC, 1991.

PIANC, "*Approach Channels Preliminary Guidelines*", supplement to Bulletin no 87, April 1995.

Powell, K.A. and Allsop, N.W.H. "*Low-crest breakwaters, hydraulics performance and stability*", Report SR 57, Hydraulics Research, Wallingford, July 1985.

Van de Kreeke, J., Paape, A., "*On the optimum breakwater design*", Proc. 9th International Conference of Coastal Engineering.

Van der Meer, J.W., "*Rock slopes and gravel beaches under wave attack*", Phd Thesis, Delft University of Technology, Delft, 1988.

Van der Meer, J.W., "*Stability of Cubes, Tetrapods and Accropode*", Design of Breakwaters, Thomas Telford, London, 1988.

Von Dantzig, D. "*Economic decision problems for flood prevention*", Econometrica 24, p. 276-287, New Haven, 1956.

Vrijling, J.K. et alt. "*Computer aided evaluation of a breakwater design*", CIAD, 1985.

Vrijling, J.K. " *Probabilistic design of water retaining structures*", Engineering reliability and risk in water resources, L. Duckstein and E.J. Plate, Eds. Nijhoff, Dordrecht, 1986, p. 115-134.

Risk assessment and new risk management protocol for use in construction of coastal engineering works

J D SIMM MEng BSc(Eng) C Eng, MICE MCIWEM ACIArb, HR Wallingford, UK.
G HEALD BSc, CEng, MICE, MCIWEM, Environment Agency
I C CRUICKSHANK B Eng, C Eng, MICE, HR Wallingford, UK.
S J READ, FRICS, ACIArb, MACostE, Currie & Brown, UK

1.   INTRODUCTION

Any work in the marine environment is subject to considerable practical, technical and financial risk, which is borne by the whole industry (clients, contractors, designers, and insurers). Today's highly competitive construction market has resulted in increased attention to risk from industry, academia and government.   In the marine environment the risks associated with construction in general are compounded by variable and aggressive hydraulic conditions. Examples of disastrous failures of part-completed structures (Sines, Tripoli) and of serious time and cost overruns in coastal construction (Sea Palling, Djen Djen) are well publicised. More insidious are the time, cost and quality impacts which inadequate attention to risk can have on every coastal engineering project.   Additional risk can be inadvertently built-in during planning and design of coastal projects because of a failure to understand coastal hydraulics and the impact hydraulics has on the construction process.

Photograph 1 – Plant breakdown, West Bay, Photograph courtesy of West Dorset District Council

Coastlines, structures and breakwaters. Thomas Telford, London, 1998

Better management of hydraulically related risks (though risk identification, assessment and control) would have a dramatic impact on the out-turn cost of coastal defence, port, harbour and marine outfall construction works with potential savings of between 5 and 10% of annual construction costs. It would also be commensurate with the safety objectives enshrined within recent European directives and help to improve the recent lamentable safety record of coastal construction projects. Such improvements can only be achieved by cross-industry collaboration to improve safety and mitigate risk through dissemination of best practice.

The paper describes how, because of concerns about these issues across the whole industry, a research project has been carried out at HR Wallingford (with contributions by Currie & Brown – construction cost and risk management consultants) to establish definitive guidance on procedures to be adopted for coastal construction. The research has been funded by the UK Department of the Environment Transport Regions and supported by The Environment Agency with in-kind contributions from industry including harbour and local authority clients (Waveney District Council, Blackpool Borough Council), four consultants (Posford Duvivier, Robert West, Mouchel Management, Sir William Halcrow & Ptnrs), ten marine contractors (Alfred McAlpine, AMEC Marine, Costain, Dean & Dyball, Harbour & General, Ham Dredging, May Gurney, Stabilise, Westminster Dredging, Van Oord ACZ) and one insurance broker (Everard Insurance).

The three year research project commenced with the project definition study to define the scope of the problems and risks encountered by clients, consultants and contractors in coastal construction. Workshop sessions were held with members of the advisory committee and other clients and consultants in the second year to examine these risks in more detail assisted by in depth case study analysis. The third year focused on bringing together the findings of the previous two phases to produce a user friendly manual to help better manage these risks in the future.

The research was focussed on those hazards and uncertainties which have the greatest impact on safety , quality, time and cost. More specifically the research project examined:
- The sea in construction (wind, waves, water level & currents)
- Impacts of the sea on construction (how the uncertain sea affects construction)
- Structure specific risks (rock works, concrete seawalls, caissons, piling works, intakes and outfalls, navigation dredging and beach recharge).
- Risk identification, modelling and management techniques
- Safety, Health and the environment
- Insurance
- Procurement Strategies
- Future Protocol for coastal construction

2   THE SEA IN CONSTRUCTION

Early on in the project the sea was identified as the principal risk parameter in coastal engineering construction i.e. (wind, waves, water levels and currents). However, it was determined through the consultation process that, whilst there was a great deal of risk information available to designers, there was little information readily available for clients, contractors or insurers to help them understand and assess these construction risks. Therefore the project undertook to provide a guide to the sources of basic hydraulic and wind data that can be used by those involved in coastal construction works to help them assess the construction uncertainty related to the sea. This is broken into three sections:

- *The basic parameters.* This is aimed at providing an introduction to the basic hydraulic and wind parameters that influence construction works through an extended glossary of terms.
- *Methods of estimating site conditions.* This details the range of data and services available for estimating the site climate and extreme conditions for construction works.
- *Methods of real time forecasting and site control.* This details the range of data and services that are available for the real time forecasting during the construction works.

It is essential to grasp the importance of evaluating conditions relevant to construction and to recognise the difference between these and design conditions. With the exception of beaches, design conditions tend to be dominated by extreme events. Whilst extreme events may be important to Contractors in setting bounds on the hazards they may encounter and the likely risk of consequential damage, for temporary works design the more normal weather conditions are of much more importance. These define duration and sequencing of calmer periods in which they can work and stormier periods within which they cannot. It is therefore incumbent on designers to gather this information, as well as that required for design purposes, and to make this available to Contractors tendering for projects.

3   IMPACTS OF THE SEA ON CONSTRUCTION
The consultation workshops helped to define the risks in coastal construction and explore options for their control or removal. The following sections describe some of the more important aspects.

Coastal construction plant, availability and operability levels
The research project examined in detail how construction plant is affected by the sea. There is a significant variation in the operational limits of plant depending on the type used, local conditions and the skills of the operator. For instance, the threshold at which a barge can successfully approach a temporary berth to unload is as much dependant on the wave period, wind direction, currents, tide state and the skill of the beach master as the actual wave height.

Data on operational limits of plant is highly variable and what information is assembled remains commercially sensitive. For these reasons it was difficult to assemble information on plant operability limits. However, the critical parameters were identified and listed to provide a general guide to raise awareness across the industry.

Stability of partly completed works and temporary works
The stability of partly completed works and temporary works can be a major risk in coastal construction. Often the designer focuses on the extreme wind, wave, water level and current conditions corresponding to the permanent works and does not take into account the wave conditions that will affect the temporary works. The temporary instability of the works during the construction (e.g. before primary armour is placed) can result in catastrophic failures. It is essential that adequate consideration is given to the critical stages during the construction when the works are susceptible to damage from even mild wind, wave, water level and current conditions.

It is also important that consideration is given to the interrelation between periods when a structure is unstable above a given weather condition and the duration of that weather condition. For instance, consider a rock breakwater with only the rock core placed. Whilst a two hour storm with an $H_s=2m$ may cause some damage to the works it may be not considered to constitute a significant problem. However, if that storm were to last for two days it might well cause catastrophic damage to the core profile with significant amount of material being lost without the possibility of its retrieval

Temporary works and partially completed structures are often designed to/assessed against an arbitrary return period event (often 10 years) without due regard to the probability of its occurrence in the construction period. The return period used in the temporary works design or an assessment of the vulnerability of the structure should not be confused with the construction period. For example, if a return period of any extreme event is the same as the construction period then there is a 63% probability that this will be exceeded during the construction.

The temporary instability of circular sheet piled caissons was a fundamental risk for the contractor on the Malta Freeport Terminal 2 project. Here the contractor managed this risk by carrying out numerical modelling to establish a management system which used Met Office offshore wind and wave predictions to give local wave predictions at the site. The site team used the system to assist in making decisions as to when to commence, accelerate or terminate and make safe critical operations.

Photograph 2- Lifting barge, template and caisson on the Malta Freeport Terminal 2 project, where the sea state risk was continually monitored using a spreadsheet management system, Photograph courtesy of Costain Civil Engineering Ltd.

Seabed changes

Unlike most civil engineering works, the surface layers (sea bed and beach profile) in coastal engineering can be highly mobile, changing from day to day and season to season. These changes can be caused by:

- Long-term trends within coastal cell/subcell
- Sea-state fluctuations
- Summer/winter or storm/swell fluctuations in position of coastal bar
- Scour/accretion due to presence of plant, temporary works or partly completed permanent works.

These changes can affect the construction works in a variety of ways as it alters:

- the exposure to wave attack
- the 'dry time' available for at the works and for land access to and from the works
- draft available for marine plant at the works and in the access route to and from the works
- the nature of the surface layers affecting the works and access (e.g. sand layer removed to expose soft clay)
- the stability and design criteria used in the design of the temporary works

For instance, the contractor's tender assessment for the Happisbugh Sea Wall was based on a number of pre-construction site visits where the beach comprised of sand. However, when construction commenced on site the majority of sand (>2m depth) had eroded down to the clay bed. This change was significant because the plant had been selected to specifically operate on sand and therefore, found it difficult to operate on a clay surface, especially as it became softer. This was resolved by importing sand to make the surface stiffer. One of the methods used to keep the sand on the beach, mainly along the haulage route was the construction of a 'win row' (a win row is a line of rocks that allows sand to build up on the sea wall side by trapping sand from being carried out to sea during tides).

Timing of works

Coastal engineering tender documents issued by client usually have a contract duration specified, but rarely is an exact commencement date for the works given. The requirement for three months validity for tenders reflects a corresponding uncertainty in the commencement date. As a result, the weather statistics during the contract may reflect a more stormy or less stormy period than anticipated (especially if it is only 6 to 9 months duration).

Uncertainty about the commencement date may be controllable by the Client. Often lack of confidence in the availability and timing of funding is cited as a reason for not fixing the commencement date. However, conflicting messages have been received and as yet it is unclear to what extent this is a valid reason, or merely an excuse.

Sometimes commencement dates are vaguely expressed in the 'as soon as possible' category. The urgency of the project can arise for a number of reasons, some of which may be questionable. Typical reasons are the risk of failure of existing works, risk of loss of funds for the project (e.g. due to approach of the end of the financial year for public sector Clients) and political urgency.

Sometimes the contract is timed to run through the winter period. Whilst there may be valid reasons for this, such as concerns about damaging trade or tourism over the summer period, or more ready availability of plant and labour, fixing the timing in this way automatically increases the hazards to construction.

Variability of quantities
Excavation quantities in coastal engineering projects are subject to much greater uncertainty than excavations on land. This is because;

- the commencement surface is often a mobile beach or seabed and this may be subject to significant changes, both between issue of tender drawings and the placing of the contract and also during the course of construction.
- fill volumes for rock structures and beach nourishment may vary due to the mobility of any natural commencement surface. However, there may be further uncertainties in the commencement surface due to construction tolerances on any prior excavation and/or tolerances in the finishing surface of any previous construction.
- the uncertainty of the tonnage of material (rock or beach nourishment) required to fill that volume. These may arise from a variable degree of packing/compaction influencing as-placed density and from settlements of the underlying ground under the load of the structure being built.

Uncertain ground conditions can also affect other quantities such volumes of excavation required to achieve a foundation level of adequate quality, and the length and tonnage of steel piling.

4   STRUCTURE SPECIFIC RISKS
The consultation process identified the benefits of having pre-prepared check lists of the common risks related to the structure type. The construction forms identified were:
- rock works
- concrete armour units
- concrete seawalls
- caissons
- piling works
- intakes and outfalls
- navigation dredging
- beach nourishment

With help from the advisory committee these lists were prepared as follows:
- General risks list relating to all structure types (e.g. funding delays, errors etc)
- Risk list relating to the structure types (e.g. rock barge delays, cracking of concrete armour units)

The above are intended to act as an initial 'aide memoire' in the preparation of a risk register and to raise the awareness of those who are not familiar with the risks associated with coastal engineering. It is not intended that these risks should not be seen as exhaustive but merely assist the process. An extract from the risk check list for rock work contracts is given below:

Risk	Construction operation								
	Rock sourcing– own/contracted	Rock delivery – sea/road/rail	Temporary works –	Rock core placing	Rock underlayer	Rock armour placing	Concrete works	Finishes & Services	
Rock, block integrity									
Rock, density									
Restrictions on noise levels									
Restrictions on working hours									
Etc....									

The descriptions of the more common risks also offer suggested risk control strategies under the following categories:

- Remove
- Reduce
- Transfer
- Share
- Insure
- Accept.

An example of a risk control strategy for rock works is given below:

Possible Risk Control Strategies – Timing of the works

(i)   *Removing risk*
Whilst much can be done to reduce this risk, the inherent complex nature of project development stages means that there will always be a residual risk that projects will not be timed at the optimum time of year.

(ii)   *Reducing risk*

(a)   *Can the client optimise the planning process to ensure that funding is in place for the works to commence in the spring? Can the project be delayed to the spring of the following year if funding comes too late?*

(b)   *Can the funding body optimise the planning process to reduce increased project costs resulting from carrying out works at the wrong time of year?*

(c)   *Can the decision to avoid the tourist season be financially, commercially and environmentally justified (i.e. can the funding body implement a process to evaluate the benefits of carrying out works at certain times of the year)?*

(d)   *Can the client give the contractors a more relaxed period for completing the works? For instance, the contractor could be given a 3 month period to complete the works which will only take 1 month then the contractor can optimise the plant to partly overcome inopportune timing of the works.*

(e)   *Can the client limit the period that the contractors offer remains valid or the contractor qualify his offer so that the price tendered is based on a real evaluation of weather risks for that period?*

(f)   *Can the contractor be allowed to offer different tender prices based on different commencement dates?.............etc*

5   RISK IDENTIFICATION MODELLING AND MANAGEMENT

Once the risks were identified, the project undertook to illustrate the various approaches available for risk identification, modelling and management using practical examples from the coastal engineering sector. The project built on many of the concepts set out in CIRIA (1996) but approached the risks from the views of the client, contractor, designer and insurer at all stages of the coastal project development, construction, maintenance and demolition.

The uncertainties in coastal construction can affect the time, cost, quality, safety and environmental objectives of the project as well viability of the organisations that are involved in coastal engineering projects. Systematic risk management helps these organisations control this uncertainty by:

- Identifying and questioning the assumptions that affect the success of the project
- Concentrating the effort into controlling the risk through risk prioritisation
- Balancing the costs and benefits of the controlling measures

Risk management can be undertaken by different organisations at different stages of the project design, development, construction, maintenance and demolition. Examples are given below:

Client:
- Assessment of design options for service and constructability at feasibility stage (e.g. rock mound verses cellular sheet piled wall breakwater)
- Clear optimisation of the apportionment of risk in the contract to the organisation best able to mange it
- Assessment of bids on the basis of expected cost, time, quality, environmental and safety risks (e.g. comparing tenderers method and material risks).

Contractor:
- Basic cost model for use in cost estimation and tendering
- Risk/cost profile of alternative designs and working methods
- Cash flow model incorporating risk factors
- Identification of key risks as they affect the Contractor's exposure to risk
- Identification of the critical stages in terms of risk (e.g. by using a risk calendar)
- Identification of the interrelationship of risks
- Appropriate response to events during construction to control and minimise risk.

Designer:
- Assessment of design options for serviceability and buildability at feasibility stage
- Identify and design to reduce construction risk (e.g. incorporate a rock specification that is achievable)
- Basic cost model for use in project cost estimation including estimation of residual risk.

Insurer:
- Assessment of the project risks which are seeking insurance
- Assessment of the contractors ability to identify and control the risks
- Limit open ended liability.

- the underwriter's skills in evaluating the hazards in the construction industry
- their experience in the coastal construction market, including;
  - knowledge of the hazards related to the structure type (Part C of the manual)
  - knowledge of the hazards related to different phases of the project (e.g. vulnerability of the core prior to placement of rock armour)
  - knowledge of influence of physical conditions (e.g. surge, waves etc)
  - knowledge of probability of occurrence of the hazards during the construction period
  - data records available (e.g. wave records at the site)
  - time available for the evaluation
  - funds available for the evaluation
  - market forces present at the time.

The underwriter's relative inexperience in the somewhat unusual technical aspects of coastal engineering and lack of time and funds often results in an inadequate assessment of the risks. Inevitably this means that many coastal construction risks are not readily insurable and consequently even premiums and excesses are set at higher levels than for more 'usual' construction risks. In extreme cases insurance may not be financially viable or indeed possible. There is some basic information available (e.g. The Insurance Institute of London (1985)) but the manual will provide more comprehensive information available for use by the insurance market.

Another significant problem arises where, unlike land based insurance, vessel owners are able limit their liability under the International Limitation of Liability Act where fault or privity can not be proven. For example, this means that the contractor's vessel may accidentally damage the client's jetty neighbouring the construction works and will only be liable for say £90,000 damage (depending on the gross weight of their vessel) of the total repair cost of say £2,000,000. Many clients are not aware of this potential liability shortfall.

The manual aims to highlight these problems and provide guidance for the client (to ensure that insurance cover is adequate), for contractors (acting as a quick reference guide to the coastal insurance market) and insurers (providing background information on the risks associated with coastal construction works).

8   PROCUREMENT STRATEGIES

It was clear through the consultation process that procurement was central to how many of the risks were managed (the contract after all is supposed to allocate/apportion the risks amongst the parties concerned). What was also clear during the consultation that current procurement strategies failed to address the specific problems and risks present in the coastal engineering sector as they were formulated for use on land based projects. A review was to examine different strategies from contract clause amendments (such as that used by Blackpool Borough Council), use of different contract forms (such as the NEC), to changing the way projects are funded (including the changes to financial year spend restrictions and PFI). Some of the aspects examined are discussed below:

Provide more information in the tender

The provision of more detailed and accurate information (in particular, hydrological information) is very important in the realisation of the risk involved with any one project. As each tenderer will require this information it is more logical that the client prepares this information. Having provided the information, this will become the reference criterion in the event of claims as this is the basis on which the tender is prepared. Some clients are uneasy however with taking on the responsibility for the accuracy of this information and would prefer to transfer this element to the contractor.

Blackpool Borough Council have assisted the contractor in clarifying the risks by providing historical information from previous contracts in the specification. Where the contractor relies on such information provided by the client but in the event, the actual conditions experienced differ, then such conditions may well be deemed 'unforeseen' by the Engineer. The information given is wide ranging and includes experience on items such as with pumps, shutter design (see photograph 3) and material quantities. The following example illustrates this approach:

> *"On previous Works on the Lancashire coast, the amount of resin anchor grout actually used to anchor round mild steel bars into holes drilled into existing structures using the rotary percussion method was up to approximately 75% more than that calculated on the theoretical dimensions."*

Photograph 3 – Tidal working for the reconstruction of the North Shore Apron, Blackpool, where experience gained from working on previous projects are passed onto the contractor

Dealing with weather risk

The 1991 ICE Conditions of Contract 6th Edition, along with many other Standard forms, fails to adopt a logical approach to the allocation and management of weather risk in coastal engineering. Generally speaking individual risks are not identified as carefully defined events which, if they occur, will result in one party or another taking full responsibility in every respect for that event. There is a need to clearly state and define 'reference conditions' in respect of each risk event, and for clear identification of which of the parties is to accept responsibility in terms of time and cost should those benchmark 'reference conditions' be breached.

The 1995 ICE Engineering and Construction Contract (ECC, previously NEC) appears to offer some clarification regarding the weather risk. ECC contracts define unforeseen as the 10 year event and require that anything above this level should be compensated for by the client. There would be significant advantages to both parties in terms of realising what the actual risk element is by defining this event

This approach could be extended to define exactly what criteria (e.g. wave height, wave period, wind conditions, water levels (surge), beach levels etc) the contractor should allow for. This would refine the contractor's estimate by reducing unnecessary over-design and remove the scope for dispute with regard to "reasonably foreseen" events at a later stage.

Open Completion Date
It has been suggested that this can be left open in the tender documents for the contractor to specify, particularly if the client has no firm deadline for completion. This can reduce prices by allowing the contractor to work at a rate suited to their plant/material supply. An alternative way of achieving a similar end, where there is a firm deadline for completion is to fix the completion date, but to indicate latest dates for contract award as opposed to commencement date which can be arranged to match the contractor's programme.

Allocating risk to the party best able to manage it
Risks can be removed, reduced, transferred, shared or accepted but whatever method is used it must be actioned by means of a term in a contract. The allocation of risks is accomplished by writing terms which will control the risk situation. Such allocation therefore needs to be clear, complete and unambiguous, since uncertainty as to the definition and allocation of the risk will become a risk in its own right.

The allocation of risk is probably the most important area of consideration in the risk management process. There are no hard and fast rules on risk allocation, different parties and organisations have differing perspectives, but there is a consensus as to the type of questions that need to be asked in order to assist the process. For example:-

- which of the parties controls the events leading to the probability of that risk occurring?
- who has the best incentive for minimising and controlling the risk?
- who is in the best position to control the risk and influence its magnitude should it occur?
- will that party be motivated in dealing with the risk in the most effective way?
- is the client willing to allow complete control of that risk to be in the hands of another party? The risk may well be a significant risk to the objectives of either party.
- what will be the cost of passing that risk to another party and is it a reasonable cost?
- what are the reasons for transfer? It should be to alleviate unreasonable loss, not to generate additional profit.
- will the party be in a position to accept the consequences of the risk should it occur?
- will the allocation of this risk lead to other risks being transferred back?

Having answered the above questions with regard to risk allocation and management, the client will be in a better position to assess which of the range of procurement routes and/or standard forms of contract will be most appropriate. If risks are to be managed by a party other than the client then the risk must effectively be transferred by means of a contract or a contractual term to the contractor. Insurance is another example of risk transfer. Alternatively, risks can be shared and such arrangements are frequently found in traditional forms of contract. For example in the ICE Conditions of Contract 6th Edition, weather and ground condition risk are shared: the contractor bears the risk on both up to a point after which the client will bear the cost and time effects of poor ground conditions and the time consequences of exceptionally adverse weather. Partnering contracts extend the principle of risk sharing, often including a financial gain share/ pain share element.

The manual discusses these problems in more detail and draws conclusions as to the most appropriate procurement strategy in coastal engineering. However, the optimum solution will inevitably be different for each project.

9 FUTURE PROTOCOL

The aim of the protocol is to summarise the findings of the reviews undertaken in the research project to spell out best practice procedures and thereby improve the risk management process in coastal engineering construction. This protocol addresses the best practice procedures that can be undertaken at the various stages of the project development thereby making it easily accessible to the user at:

- Project conception
- Project development and design
- Pre-qualification
- Preparation of tender documents
- Tender period
- Award of contract
- The construction period
- Post construction.

10 CONCLUSIONS

Many detailed conclusions have been drawn from this research work some of which are too detailed to describe in this paper. It is generally agreed by those consulted during the project that better identification, assessment and control of the many risks in coastal engineering will reduce costs and provide greater price certainty in coastal engineering construction. These benefits will be felt by the funder, the client, the contractor, the designer and the insurer. Application of the recommendations/protocol in the manual on construction risk in coastal engineering will go some way towards achieving this goal.

11 ACKNOWLEDGEMENTS

This project has been undertaken by HR Wallingford in association with Currie & Brown (construction cost and risk management consultants) working closely with the Advisory Committee:

- Alfred McAlpine Construction Ltd, Andy Matthews/Steve Rowland
- AMEC Marine, Rees Lloyd
- Blackpool Borough Council, Paul Dunkerley
- Boskalis Zinkcon Ltd/Westminster Dredging, Ron Gardener/David Hough
- Costain, Mike Davison
- Currie & Brown, Steve Read, David Turner
- Department of the Environment, Peter Woodhead
- Dean & Dyball, Howard Reeves, Martin Hirst
- Environment Agency, Gordon Heald
- Everard Insurance, Richard Ellis
- Ham Dredging Ltd, Ian Fairgrieve
- Harbour and General Works Ltd, Tony Edmondson
- HR Wallingford, Ian Meadowcroft, Ian Mockett
- May Gurney & Co Ltd, Clive Orbell-Durrant, Alan Philips
- MAFF, Tony Polson
- Mouchel Management, Paul Jobling
- Posford Duvivier, John Andrews
- Robert West, Paul Coughlan
- Sir William Halcrow & Ptnrs, Patrick Godfrey
- Stabilise, David Rochford
- Waveney District Council, K Tyrell
- Van Oord ACZ, David Smart/Pieter van Oord

The following organisations provided useful information in the consultation stage:
- Health and Safety Executive, Brian Hudson
- Port of Felixstowe, George Steel

12   REFERENCES/BIBLIOGRAPHY

1.   CIRIA (1996) CIRIA:125, Control of risk: A clients guide to the systematic Management of Risk in Construction, CIRIA, London UK.
2.   Edwards, L. (1995), Practical risk management in the construction industry, Thomas Telford, London UK
3.   The Insurance Institute of London (1985), Construction and Erection Insurance, Advanced Study Group 208A, The Insurance Institute of London, London, UK
4.   Ashely, Dunlop & Parker, Impact of risk allocation and equity in construction contracts, 7th Annual Conference of Centre of Construction Law & Management, University of Texas, Austin, US
5.   Uff, J., Contract Documents and Division of Risk, 7th Annual Conference of Centre of Construction Law & Management, University of Texas, Austin, US
6.   ICE, ACE,FCEC (1991) ICE Conditions of Contract 6th Edition, Thomas Telford, London
7.   ICE (1995), Engineering & Construction Contract, 2nd Edition, Thomas Telford, London

Advances in Berm Breakwaters

S Sigurdarson[1], J Juhl[2], P Sloth[3], O B Smarason[4] and G Viggosson[1]
[1] Icelandic Maritime Administration, Kopavogur, Iceland
[2] COWI. Consulting Engineers and Planners, Lyngby, Denmark
[3] Danish Hydraulic Institute, Hørsholm, Denmark
[4] Stapi Ltd. Consulting Geologists, Reykjavik, Iceland

ABSTRACT
Berm breakwaters have been designed and constructed by the Icelandic Maritime Administration (IMA) since 1983. Over 20 berm structures have been constructed or repaired with this method so far and further 2 will be built every year for the next 2-3 years.

Berm breakwaters in Iceland are designed as statically stable structures of several stone classes with the aim to minimise stone movement, in contrast to the more commonly used dynamic design with only two stone classes. The design aims at optimising the structure with respect to wave load and possible yield from an armour stone quarry. This design process can be described as "tailor made size graded berm breakwater". The estimated yield from an armour stone quarry is used as an integrated part of the design process in an attempt to optimise the utilisation of the quarry. A thorough quarry investigation has proven to be a valuable part of the design process in preparation for successful breakwater projects.

The difference in reshaping of a berm breakwater constructed of two stone classes and a more stable Icelandic type of berm breakwater with the largest berm stones used as an armour layer covering the berm was studied by physical model tests carried out at the Danish Hydraulic Institute (DHI). A total of eight series of model tests were carried out in a wave flume covering studies of the effect of three berm breakwater solutions based on the Icelandic experience; two crest and berm freeboard elevations, and two wave steepnesses. The test results are described in the form of profile development, recession of the berm and waves generated by overtopping.

INTRODUCTION
Experience from Iceland has shown that in most cases it is advantageous to construct berm breakwaters of more than two stone classes, Sigurdarson et al (1995), Juhl et al (1995). The idea being that the largest stones are used where they will be most effective, ie as an armour layer protecting the berm. The advantage in increased stability and consequently reduced overall dimensions of the berm is far greater than the increased cost for sorting the stones.

The design process for berm breakwaters in Iceland has been developed through the years in close co-operation with all partners involved; geologists, supervisors, contractors and local governments. At the same time the designers have been directly involved in the hydraulic model studies and supervision of the construction of the breakwaters. Instead of looking at

Coastlines, structures and breakwaters. Thomas Telford, London, 1998

the berm as a mass of stones the design focuses more on each unit. No construction unit is as far from being standardised as the armour rock in the primary cover layer with regard to form, strength and durability, Viggosson (1990).

The importance of rock quality, strength and durability, was realised from the start. When the stones start to move or roll up and down the slope and hit each other, high abrasion and splitting of stones will result, regardless of the rock quality, although slower for rock of better quality. Therefore the Icelandic design aims at minimising the deformation of the berm during design conditions. In contrast to this, the usual approach to berm breakwaters has been, as stated by van der Meer (1994), that displacement of armour rocks in the first stage of its lifetime is accepted and that the critical design point was when erosion reached the upper slope above the berm.

The permeability of rubble mound breakwaters is known to have an effect on the armour layer stability, Bruun and Johannesson (1976). An armour layer placed on an impermeable core is less stable than an armour layer placed on a core of permeable stone material. This aspect is included in the stability formulae for rubble mound breakwaters established by van der Meer (1988). In some cases, the stability of rubble mound breakwaters has been increased by going from two layers of stones in the armour layer to three or four layers. One of the main features of berm breakwaters is the energy dissipation in the permeable berm.

THE TAILOR-MADE SIZE GRADED BERM BREAKWATER
The IMA has developed a variant of the original berm concept with all the advantages of the berm concept although the structure is much more stable. This variant can be described as a "tailor-made size graded berm", Sigurdarson et al (1996). The largest stones are used on top and at the front of the berm, increasing the permeability, dissipation of wave energy and thereby the stability of the structure, Figures 1 and 2. Since the berm mass is no longer homogeneous this means that even smaller stones can be used inside the berm, than in berm breakwaters of only one or two stone classes. The reinforcement has also made a reduction in berm width possible. In Iceland this design approach has been found to lead to less expensive structures than the original berm concept, although they are much more stable.

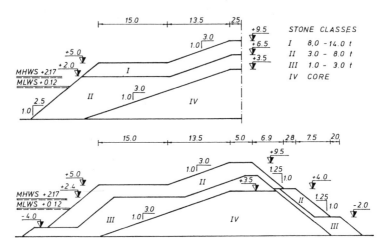

Figure 1.   The Bolungarvik breakwater, cross sections from the head and trunk section.

A thorough quarry investigation has proven to be a valuable part of the design process in preparation for successful breakwater projects in Iceland, Smarason (1994). A preliminary study of possible quarries is carried out simultaneously with the preliminary design process to establish an idea for quantities of needed and available material. Decision regarding stone classes is halted until a preliminary quarry yield prediction has been made. The final design is completed after a thorough study of a selected quarry has been undertaken. This may include detailed geological mapping, percussion and core drilling, as well as detailed studies of fractures on rock surfaces and cores. Test blasting can be avoided as quarry yield predictions have proven to be just as accurate as test quarries. This minimises any damage to the environment as the potential quarry sites remain untouched until the time of actual quarrying. An accurate quarry prediction leads to a more precise design and less problems in the execution of the construction, which in turn leads to fewer claims and thus a lower overall project cost. A quality assurance programme has been developed to guarantee that rocks intended for breakwaters are up to the required standard depending on varying wave load and climate conditions in each case.

Figure 2. *The head of the Bolungarvik breakwater*

CONSTRUCTION / CONTRACTORS

A berm breakwater can be constructed using readily available land based methods and less specialised construction equipment compared to conventional breakwaters. Usual equipment comprises a drilling rig, two or three backhoe excavators, sometimes a front loader, and some trucks. When the first berm breakwaters were built bulldozers were used to push stones to the berm. That resulted in breakage of stones and too many fines that plugged the voids. Backhoe excavators with open buckets or prong, up to 75 tonnes, are used to place stones. The number of trucks depends largely on the transport distance. Tolerances for the placement of stones are greater than for conventional breakwater design. Usually no underwater placement is necessary, as the front slope is steep. Placement of stones in a slope 1:1.3 has been achieved down to 8 -10 m water depth.

Experience from Iceland shows that small local contractors can quickly adopt the necessary technique to construct berm breakwaters successfully. The risk during construction is much lower and repairs are also much easier than for conventional breakwaters. Each breakwater project is tendered out and there is competitive bidding for the works from up to 10 contractors. The lowest bid is usually accepted.

Good interlocking by carefully placed stones is advantageous on the front and the edge of the berm. Experience from many breakwater projects has shown that working with several stone classes and placement of stones only increases the construction cost insignificantly. Until recently the maximum prescribed stone size has been 14 to 16 tonnes. The limiting factors have mainly been sizes of readily available excavators and trucks, as well as weight limits for road transportation. An attempt is being made to increase this weight in order to construct berm breakwaters in more severe wave conditions. Some quarries when carefully blasted may produce over 10% of stones over 20 tonnes. In some recent projects construction cost has been cut considerably by using dredged material, usually coarse sand and gravel, as a part of the inner core of the structure, fulfilling given requirements. The construction often extends over a two year period and experience has shown that partially completed berm breakwaters function well through winter storms, and repairs are much easier than for conventional breakwaters.

PHYSICAL MODEL TESTS
Model Set-Up
Physical model tests were carried out in a 23 m long and 0.60 m wide wave flume at the Danish Hydraulic Institute with the aim of studying profile reshaping and wave overtopping of different berm breakwater profiles. A fixed bed foreshore with a slope of 1:80 was constructed in the flume.

The profiles used in the eight test series are shown in Figure 3. The water depth in front of the berm was 0.25 m for all tests. Test series 1 to 4 were made with relatively high-crested breakwaters not allowing wave overtopping. Three alternative berm breakwaters of the Icelandic type (profiles 1, 3 and 4) were tested and compared to tests for a traditional berm breakwater consisting of two stone classes (profile 2). The subsequent four test series were made with more low-crested breakwaters with the crest elevation and berm width adjusted to the difference in wave steepness (s_{om}=0.03 and 0.05).

The berm breakwaters were constructed of two or three stone classes, ie one for the core and scour protection and one or two for the berm, crest and rear side protection. The traditional berm breakwaters (profiles 2, 5 and 7) were constructed of two stone classes, a relatively wide stone gradation for the berm, $D_{n,85}/D_{n,15}$=1.80, having a nominal diameter, D_{n50}, of 0.022 m (stone class 2) and a core with a nominal stone diameter of 0.011 m (stone class 1). A summary of the stone classes used is presented in Table 1. In testing the Icelandic type of berm breakwaters, the berm stones were separated into two classes, the lower fraction to be used for the berm (stone class 4) and the higher fraction to be used as an armour layer (stone class 5).

Test Programme
Each test series consisted of five to nine test runs each with a duration corresponding to 2000 waves. Test runs were carried out with the following deep water conditions: H_o=$H_{mo}/\Delta D_{n,50}$=

2.0, 2.5, 3.0, 3.5 and 4.0, where H_{mo} ($=4 \cdot \sqrt{m_0}$, where m_0 is the zero'th moment of the recorded surface elevations) is the wave height, Δ is the relative density and $D_{n,50}$ is the nominal stone diameter. H_0 is also called the stability parameter. In calculation of H_0, $D_{n,50}$ for the

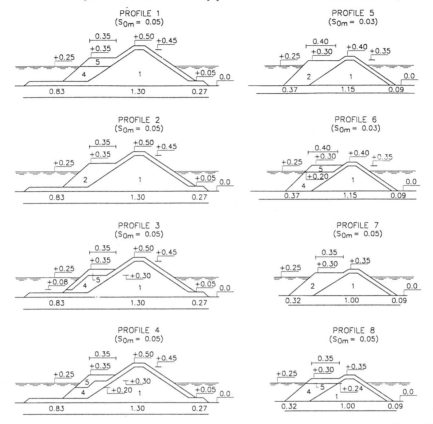

Figure 3   Tested berm breakwater profiles, stone class characteristics presented in Table 1.

Table 1   Summary of stone classes (the measured density of the stones was $\rho_s=2.68t/m^3$).

Stone class	Description	W_{50} (g)	$D_{n,50}$ (m)	$D_{n,85}/D_{n,15}$	Profiles
1	Core material	3.5	0.011	2.30	All
2	Berm material	30.2	0.022	1.80	2, 5, 7
4	Berm material	20.5	0.020	1.65	1, 3, 4, 6, 8
5	Armour layer	78.0	0.031	1.20	1, 3, 4, 6, 8

entire berm material (0.022 m) was used. Further, the long-term development was studied by continuing with another four test runs with $H_o=4.0$ (only tests with profiles 1 to 3).

The deep water wave steepness is given by the ratio between the wave height, H_{mo}, and the deep water wave length, L_{om}, calculated on basis of the mean wave period, T_{om}:

$$S_{om} = H_{mo}/L_{om} = 2\pi/g*H_{mo}/T_{om}^2$$

The tests were carried out in test series with fixed wave steepness in deep water, s_{om}=0.03 and 0.05, ie the wave steepness in front of the berm breakwater varied due to differences in wave shoaling and wave breaking on the foreshore.

Measurements

The waves were measured by a total of nine resistance type wave gauges, ie three in deep water, five in shallow water in front of the breakwater and one behind the breakwater for measuring the overtopping generated waves (only profiles 4 to 8). A multigauge technique was used for separating the incoming and reflected waves, and subsequently determining the incoming significant wave height and the reflection coefficient both in deep water and in front of the breakwater. The waves reflected from the breakwater were absorbed by the wave generator applying DHI's AWACS system (Active Wave Absorption Control System).

The breakwater profile was measured in fixed positions for every 0.10 m across the flume (five profiles) before initiation of the tests and after each test run. The profiling was made by two lasers, one laser running on a beam placed across the breakwater for measuring the vertical distance to the breakwater and another laser for measuring the horizontal position of the other laser.

Data Analysis

Analysis of the five profiles measured after each test run (for each 0.10 m across the flume) showed that the differences were very small, and thus the five profiles were averaged for the subsequent analysis. Analysis of the recorded profiles were made for determining the recession of the berm, ie erosion of the crest of the berm. The waves behind the breakwater caused by wave overtopping were analysed with respect to the maximum wave height, H_{max}, spectral wave height, H_{mo}, and mean wave height, H_{mean}.

PRESENTATION OF RESULTS

Profile developments and berm recessions for the eight tests series were compared with the aim of studying the influence of introducing an armour layer (Icelandic type), free board of berm, and wave steepness. The recession is defined as the width of the berm eroded. Further, a presentation of the results of the overtopping generated waves and of the reflection coefficients is made.

Influence of introducing an armour layer (Icelandic type)

Three alternative Icelandic type berm breakwater profiles (profiles 1, 3 and 4) were tested and compared to tests with a traditional berm breakwater profile consisting of two stone classes (profile 2). Figure 4 shows the berm recessions as function of the stability number calculated on basis of the wave height in front of the breakwater and $D_{n,50}$= 0.022 m.

All three Icelandic type breakwaters showed significant less erosion volume and berm recession compared to the traditional berm breakwater. The profile resulting in the smallest erosion volume and berm recession was profile 3 (an armour layer at the top and at the front of the berm) followed by profile 4 (armour layer placed as a hammer head), whereas profile 1 (armour at the top of the berm) showed a little less effect.

Comparisons of the test results with profiles 7 and 8 run with a wave steepness of s_{om}=0.05 also showed a significant reduction in the erosion volume and berm recession by applying the

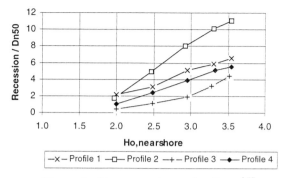

Figure 4   Berm recession as function of H_o.

largest stones for armouring the berm. The effect of the armour layer was somewhat less pronounced for profiles 5 and 6, run with a wave steepness of $s_{om}=0.03$.

Testing of profiles 1 to 3 included long duration tests consisting of 10,000 waves with $H_o=4.0$ for testing the influence of the number of waves. The results showed that an equilibrium profile was reached after about 8,000 waves, assuming no deterioration of stones.

Influence of berm free board
The combined influence of the berm free board and crest elevation was analysed by comparing results from testing with profiles 2 and 7 and results from testing with profiles 1 and 8. The berm recession was found to be smaller for the profiles with the largest berm free board and crest elevation (ie the profiles with the largest amount of berm stones and limited wave overtopping). Generally, it is expected that an increased crest elevation is resulting in an increased berm recession, and thus it can be concluded from the tests that an increased berm free board is resulting in a reduction in the berm recession. The effect of the berm free board is mainly due to the associated increased volume of berm stones.

Influence of wave steepness
The wave steepness is known to have an influence on the stability of breakwaters, and thus the berm breakwaters tested with $s_{om}=0.03$ (profiles 5 and 6) had a wider berm and larger crest elevation than the similar profiles tested with $s_{om}=0.05$ (profiles 7 and 8). As expected, the berm recession was found to be larger for the tests with $s_{om}=0.03$ than for the tests with $s_{om}=0.05$, whereas the rear side damage was found to be almost equal showing the necessity of an increased crest elevation by a decrease in the wave steepness.

Wave Overtopping Conditions
For the test series with a high crest elevation (profiles 1 to 4), the overtopping generated waves were very small. Whereas for the test series with a lower crest elevation (profiles 5 to 8), the overtopping generated waves measured 1 m behind the centreline of the breakwater were analysed. For incoming wave heights up to about 0.11 m, the waves behind the breakwater were mainly due to transmission through the breakwater, whereas for larger incoming waves the overtopping became dominant. The mean height of the overtopping waves was found to vary between 3 and 5 mm for the largest incoming waves, whereas the spectral wave height, H_{m0}, was found to vary between 5 and 9 mm (for test series 5 to 8). The maximum

wave height varied only a little for the different profiles and was about 40 mm for the largest incoming waves.

Figure 5 shows examples of the transmission coefficient, C_t, based on the spectral wave height behind the breakwater as function of the incoming stability parameter for profiles 5 to 8. The overtopping wave heights were found to be smaller for the Icelandic type of berm breakwater (profiles 6 and 8) compared to the traditional berm breakwater constructed of two stone classes (profiles 5 and 7).

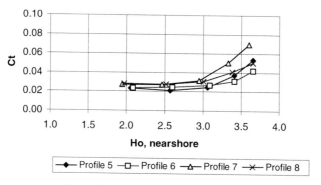

Figure 5   Overtopping generated waves.

BERM STRUCTURES IN ICELAND

The Icelandic Maritime Administration has 15 years experience in the design and construction of rubble mound berm breakwaters. Over twenty berm structures have been constructed since 1983, fourteen of those are new structures whereas the others are improvements or repairs of existing breakwaters. Berm breakwaters in Iceland have all been constructed by local contractors. Some of them have now obtained a good experience in this type of work. This section describes some examples of constructed berm breakwaters in Iceland, Figure 6. In each case only some interesting points will be highlighted.

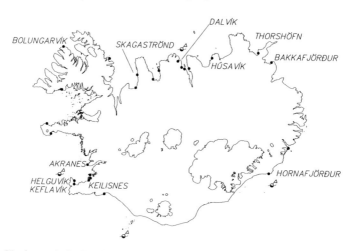

Figure 6. Harbours in Iceland referred to in the text, other berm breakw. are shown by dots.

The berm concept was introduced in Iceland through the design phase of the 900,000 m^3 Helguvik breakwater in the early 80ies by Baird et al, (1984). It is a typical two stone class berm breakwater characterised by a wide berm of homogeneous stone material, which extends down to -16 m water depth and over 20 m horizontally from the berm edge to the core. In 1996, a berm structure was built in Keflavik just 2 km from Helguvik to protect a caisson breakwater. The wave load at the site is similar to that in Helguvik and the same quarry was used. Still the IMA design used only about 40% of rock mass compared to the Helguvik design.

The berm breakwater at Bakkafjordur was built in 1983 and 1984 from stones of rather poor quality quarried at the breakwater site. Deterioration of the stones has accelerated a dynamic development of the profile. In the winter 1992/93 the breakwater is believed to have experienced waves close to the design load. The berm was eroded up to the crest and an unstable S-profile had developed. Repair took place in 1993 and in spite of the poor quality of the rock it was decided to use the local quarry again. In the fall of 1995, the structure was exposed to the design storm. Video recordings from the storm show breaking waves in front of and on the structure, resulting in heavy overtopping. Inspection of the reshaped profile showed that deterioration of the stones had caused filling and plugging of voids and the structure did not function as a berm breakwater any longer. The main conclusion that can be drawn from the Bakkafjordur breakwater is that in a dynamic structure stones will break and the voids will gradually be filled up with smaller stones. This will decrease the ability of the structure to dissipate wave energy. Inspection at the site led to the conclusion that the poor quality (highly altered basalt) of the stones in the Bakkafjordur breakwater only accelerated a development that would occur over a longer time period if it was built of better quality stones.

The Bolungarvik breakwater was built in 1992 and 1993. It is a 300 m long and the total volume is 200,000 m^3, Figures 1 and 2, Sigurdarson et al (1994). The design wave consists of swells with a significant wave height of 6.3 m and peak period 17 s. The available quarry was of good quality rock with predicted quarry yield of 34% over 1 tonne, whereas the actual yield turned out to be 38%. The design fully utilised all quarried material over 1 tonne. The breakwater has been exposed to the design wave height. Only few stones have moved from the edge of the berm in two places at the trunk where the stability parameter, H_0, is 2.8 and 3.0 and at the inner quarter of the breakwater head where the stability parameter is 2.3.

At Akranes a berm type structure was built on the ocean side of an existing pier as protection but not least to reduce wave overtopping, Viggosson (1990). The structure was investigated in 3D hydraulic model by testing 13 cross-sections of conventional and berm type. The tests resulted in lower and less voluminous cross-section for the berm type as compared to the conventional 1:2 mound, since higher permeability and lower run-up level. The crest elevation was +11.0 m compared to +11.5 and the total volume of core and rocks along the 160 m segment was 24,500 m^3 compared to 29,500 m^3. In addition a better utilisation of the quarry was obtained for the berm type. The structure can be characterised as a high structure with a narrow berm. It was built in 1991 and has succeeded several storms without any deformation.

The Keilisnes project (a proposed aluminium smelter) has a harbour where a large berm type breakwater is planned with a quay on the leeside   The total volume of the breakwater is 1,750,000 m^3. The breakwater will be constructed to a water depth of 32 m with its inner part built of dredged sand or gravel up to about 50% of the total volume. This will lower the construction cost considerably, as the cost of dredged material is less than half the price of blasted core. The largest stone class on top of the berm at the breakwater head will consist of 14 to 20 tonnes stones with stability parameter 1.6. This is possible as a special construction road will be laid for this project. On the trunk part the armour layer is of 8 to 14 tonnes stones with stability parameter 2.0.

The Dalvik breakwater, which was constructed in 1994 and 1995, is 320 m long and has a volume of 104,000 m^3. The available quarry was of good quality with predicted quarry yield of 46 to 54% over 0.3 tonne. As the wave load was moderate the design anticipated the use of dredged material in the inner part of the core, sand or gravel, up to 30% of the total volume of the structure. A 100% utilisation of all quarried material was achieved, and in spite of that the stability parameter at the top and front of the berm was as low as 1.6.

Hornafjordur is a tidal entrance on the Southeast coast of Iceland, a shore with a heavy littoral drift. An extreme storm hit the coast in January 1990. It caused large shoaling to encroach upon the entrance channel from both sides, and a breakthrough occurred between the rock headland Hvanney and the South Barrier. The inlet was closed for several weeks. A curved breakwater of the berm type was constructed during the summer 1995. Due to the severe wave action and strong current a berm structure with toe protection was chosen, Figures 7 and 8, Sigurdarson et al (1997). A rational design made it possible to construct the first phase of the jetty within 14 days to eliminate the expected tip erosion caused by current as predicted by a mathematical model. The breakwater is 330 m long and has a volume of 100,000 m^3 with several stone classes from 0.2 up to over 8 tonnes. The estimated quarry yield was 25-30% over 2 tonnes and the design aimed to utilise that completely to the advance of the structure. This was succeeded and a 100% utilisation of the quarry was achieved. The measured bulk factor from solid rock to blasted material in the structure was 1.53.

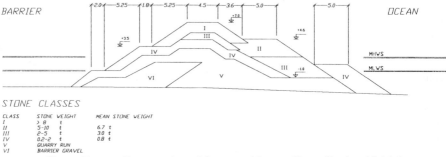

STONE CLASSES

CLASS	STONE WEIGHT	MEAN STONE WEIGHT
I	> 8 t	
II	5-10 t	6.7 t
III	2-5 t	3.0 t
IV	0.2-2 t	0.8 t
V	QUARRY RUN	
VI	BARRIER GRAVEL	

Figure 7   *Cross section of the curved jetty at Hornafjordur tidal inlet*

At Skagastrond a berm structure was built in 1997 to protect the outer part of a caisson breakwater. The caisson is a Phoenix-type concrete caisson from the Normandy landing operation in World War II, which was towed up to Iceland in 1950. The berm is only intended to secure the caisson in place and not to prevent overtopping. The berm is very narrow, only about two wave heights in width, with no crest, built around the end of the caisson. On top of the berm and at the front there is one layer of large stones 6 to 12 tonnes with stability parameter as low as 1.4 at the head and 4 to 10 tonnes with stability parameter 1.6 at the trunk. Still the critical stone size for quarry production was 1 tonne. This means that according to the quarry prediction all size grades over 1 tonne are fully utilised.

During 1997 to 1998, the breakwaters at Thorshofn and Husavik will be extended by 55 m and 100 m respectively, with the significant design wave height being 4.5 and 5.0 m. The largest stone class for both structures is 10 to 16 tonnes corresponding to stability parameters of 1.7 and 1.6, at the breakwater head. At Thorshofn where an inner breakwater is being constructed at the same time, the critical stone size for the maximum utilisation of the quarry is anticipated as low as 0.2 tonne.

Figure 8.   The berm jetty in the tidal inlet of Hornafjordur

CONCLUSIONS

Instead of a dynamic approach to berm breakwaters, as was the initial philosophy, a more stable approach has been adopted. This is based on a supply based design method rather than demand based. Therefore the Icelandic Maritime Administration has developed the "tailor-made size graded berm" which is more economical and a more stable design than the original dynamic design approach. This will minimise movement of armour stones and therefore also mechanical breaking and deterioration ensuring maximum permeability of the structure.

A thorough quarry investigation has proven to be a valuable part of the design process. Decision regarding stone classes is halted until a preliminary quarry yield prediction has been made. The final design is completed after a thorough study of a selected quarry has been undertaken. Test blasting can be avoided as quarry yield predictions have proven to be just as accurate as test quarries. This minimises any damage to the environment. An accurate quarry prediction leads to a more precise design and fewer problems in the execution of the construction and thus a lower overall project cost.

From the contractor's point of view berm breakwaters are generally easier to construct compared to conventional breakwaters. Less specialised, usually land based equipment, can be used and small local contractors can quickly adopt the necessary technique to construct berm breakwaters successfully.

A total of eight test series with berm breakwater profiles was carried out in a wave flume at the Danish Hydraulic Institute with the aim of studying the difference in reshaping of a traditional berm breakwater constructed of two stone classes and an Icelandic type berm breakwater with the largest stones armouring the berm. Wave conditions both in front of and be-hind the breakwater were measured as was the profile development. All test series consisted of five test runs (H_o=2.0, 2.5, 3.0, 3.5 and 4.0, in deep water), each with a duration corre-sponding to 2,000 waves. However, for the first three test series, another 8,000 waves with H_o=4.0 were run for studying the long-term development.

The main conclusions of the model study at DHI can be summarised as follows:

- Comparisons between traditional berm breakwaters and berm breakwaters of the Icelandic type showed a reduction in the erosion volume and recession of the berm for the latter. An armour layer protecting both the top and the front of the berm (profile 3) was found to be more effective than both the hammerhead solution (profile 4) and a thicker layer at the top of the berm (profile 1).
- Equilibrium profiles were found after exposure of about 8,000 waves with H_o=4.0.
- An increase in the berm free board is associated with an increased berm volume and was found to result in less recession of the berm.
- The berm reshaping was found to increase for decreasing wave steepness, ie increasing wave period.

The model tests have shown that a significant reduction in the berm width can be obtained by using the largest stones as an armour layer covering the berm. The effect varies with a range of parameters as for example wave steepness, stone gradation and breakwater geometry.

ACKNOWLEDGEMENTS
The model test study at Danish Hydraulic Institute was carried out as a part of the research project on Berm Breakwater Structures co-sponsored by the European Commission under contract MAS2-CT94-0087.

REFERENCES
Baird, W.F. and Hall, K.R. (1984). *The design of berm breakwaters using quarried stones.* Proc. 19th Int. Conference on Coastal Engineering Houston Texas, pp 2580-2591.

Bruun, P. and Johannesson, P. (1976). *Parameters Affecting the Stability of Rubble Mounds.* J. Waterways, Port, Coastal and Ocean Engineering, Vol 102, No2, pp 141-164.

Juhl, J; and Jensen, OJ (1995): *Features of berm breakwaters and practical experiences.* COPEDEC, Rio de Janeiro, Brazil.

Sigurdarson, S. and Viggosson, G. (1994). *Berm Breakwaters in Iceland, Practical Experi-ences.* Hydro-Port'94, Yokosuka, Japan.

Sigurdarson, S; Viggosson, G; Benediktsson, S; and Smarason, OB (1995): *Berm breakwa-ters and quarry investigations in Iceland.* COPEDEC, Rio de Janeiro, Brazil.

Sigurdarson, S., Viggosson, G., Benediktsson, S. and Smarason, O.B. (1996). *Berm Break-waters, Tailor-Made Size Graded Structures,* Proceed. of 11th Int. Harbour Congress.

Sigurdarson, S., Einarsson, S., Smarason, O.B. and Viggosson, G. (1997). *Berm Breakwater in the tidal inlet of Hornafjördur, Iceland.* MEDCOAST Qawra, Malta.

Smarason, O.B. (1994). *Quarry investigations for rubble mound structures in Iceland,* Pro-ceedings of the Hornafjordur Int. Coastal Symposium, Icelandic Harbour Authority.

Van der Meer, JW (1988): *Rock slopes and gravel beaches under wave attack.* PhD Thesis, publication No 396, Delft Hydraulics, The Netherlands.

Van der Meer, JW (1994): *Conceptual design of berm breakwaters.* Hornafjordur Interna-tional. Coastal Symposium, Icelandic Harbour Authority.

Viggosson G. (1990). *Rubble Mound Breakwaters in Iceland.* Journal of Coastal Research, SI 7, pp. 41-61, Fort Lauderdale, Florida, Spring 1990.

La Collette Reclamation Phase II

J D MORGAN
Project Manager, Edmund Nuttall Limited

INTRODUCTION

Jersey, the largest of the Channel Islands currently generates some 400,000 tns of inert waste per year. Disposal of this material has long been a problem to the States of Jersey and several reclamation projects have been carried out in the past in order to accommodate this material.

The construction of a breakwater at La Collette was undertaken for the States of Jersey by Contractor Edmund Nuttall Limited under an amended ICE 5th Edition form of Contract with Coode Blizard acting as Engineer. The purpose of the breakwater was to provide a reclamation site to receive the aforementioned inert waste. In the future the States of Jersey would have the benefit of a considerable area of land which would be suitable for development.

The project was undertaken between April 1994 and January 1996.

The tidal range in Jersey is large;

Highest Astronomical Tide (HAT)	12.3 m CD
Mean High Water Springs (MHWS)	11.1 m CD
Mean High Water Neaps (MHWN)	8.1 m CD
Mean Tide Level	6.2 m CD
Mean Low Water Neaps (MLWN)	4.1 m CD
Mean Low Water Springs (MLWS)	1.3 m CD
Lowest Astronomical Tide (LAT)	0.0 m CD

All the levels in this paper relate to chart datum.

The open sea immediately offshore St. Helier is exposed to Atlantic fetch waves between bearings 230° and 290° while the area between 230° and 80° is limited by the French coastline to a fetch of 20 to 40 miles. The offshore wave regime is considerably modified in height and period, by the complex offshore conditions and bathymetry resulting in near-structure conditions as tabulated under. These relate to a 10 year period (see page 3).

Coastlines, structures and breakwaters. Thomas Telford, London, 1998

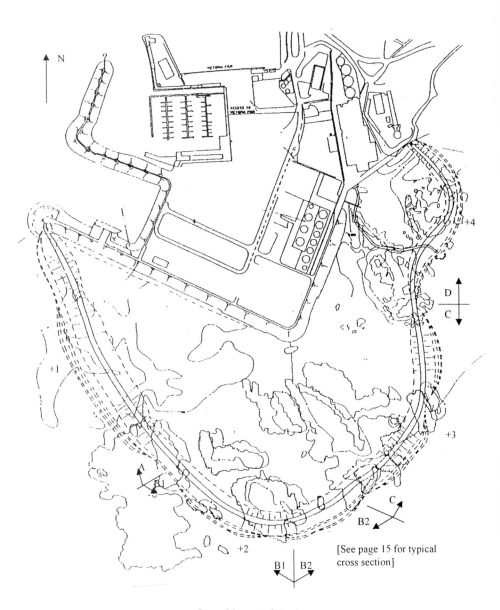

[See page 15 for typical cross section]

General Layout of Breakwater

Location	Tide State	Hs(m)	Tz (secs)
1	MHWS	3.9	7.9
1	MHWN	3.1	7.2
1	MLWN	3.0	10.5
2	MHWS	2.8	5.6
3	MHWS	2.6	5.2
4	MHWS	2.2	4.5

The breakwater, approximately 1700m long was split into sections as A, B1, B2, C and D and at the time of tender the quantities of materials were as follows;

	Approx Length m	Armour Size tns		Quantity m³	Core tns	Quantity m³
Area A	530	6-10	50% >8tn	70000	50kg-2tn	240500
Area B1	250	2-4	50%>4.5tn	14000	50kg-2tn	74000
Area B2	120	3-6	50%>3tn	9500	50kg-2tn	31800
Area C	430	1-4	50%>2.5tn	26500	10kg-1tn	108700
Area D	370	1-3	50%>2tn	18000	10kg-1tn	37500

* Cushion material		42500

* Cushion material was used in areas where the breakwater did not found on existing rock, i.e. in areas where the depth of sand was greater than 0.5m. The specification called for a layer of geotextile material to be laid over the existing sand and this was covered with a layer of cushion material. This layer was 0.5 m thick and the material was 150mm - 40mm stone.

2.SOURCING THE MATERIALS

A subcontract for the supply of all rock products was awarded by Edmund Nuttall Limited to Carrieres de l' Ouest, excluding materials supplied by Ronez (the island quarry).

2.1 Corestone

The core stone was provided from 4 main quarries, three of which were located in France at Cherbourg, Brix, Frehel, one being the local quarry on the island. A further quarry at Monteberg was used initially but because of the long haul involved was soon abandoned.

Frehel was probably the quarry best suited to supply the Contract. Frehel is situated at Cote de' Emeraude and the existing quayside was renovated. This had been used in former days for supplying materials to Paris. The only draw back with Frehel was the channel into the port which was not accessible at all tides and consequently the shipping cycle was often disrupted. During the summer months restrictions were also imposed on the quarry operators loading at night. This again had a some minor effect on the overall progress.

Frehel is a metamorphosed sand stone quarry and there were several problems experienced with the quality of the material. The material by nature has the tendency to be extremely dusty and the rock face had numerous faults contained within it which rendered the product unsuitable for inclusion in the works as armour stone greater than 4 tn. There was also a problem in achieving the top end of the range of core stone, i.e. 1-2 tn.

The quarries at **Cherbourg** and **Brix** also supplied core stone. This material was shipped from the Port of Cherbourg. At the port there was plenty of space with capacity to store up to 20,000 tns of material. The rock supplied from Cherbourg, a quartzite, was of exceptional quality, clean and well graded. The principal draw back with this material, was the extensive wear it caused to the tracks of the machines. The quarrying operation at Cherbourg would regularly produce between 750 to 1,000 tns per day and was used to supply the flat top barges and sidestone dumpers in tandem.

2.2 Armour Stone

A major source of armour stone for the contract was the old blockstone quarry at **Lanhelin**. It produced 43% of the armour required for the project. Rock supply from the quarry extended through the two seasons.

Lanhelin is situated due south and is approximately 16 miles from the port of St Malo and 43 miles from the port at Frehel. The Port of Frehel was also used in the first season for the transport of the armour stone from Lanhelin. During the later part of the second season Lanhelin armour was shipped from the Port of St.Malo.

The quarries at Lanhelin had several operators who were in the business of quarrying block stone.

Production of block stone at Lanhelin appears to have begun at the turn of the century. However as a result of the rapid development in construction equipment over the past century it was safe enough to assume that the larger 6-10tn units of armour stone would be more readily available on the perimeter of the stock pile.

Production of armour stone at Lanhelin was a simple task and involved picking ones way through the enormous stock pile and sorting the rock into the various categories. This exercise was carried out utilising gauge stones. Once the rock size had been identified it was colour coded. The 6 to 10 tn rock was split in to 2 categories 6 to 8 - 8 to 10 ton. Occasionally rock was drilled and split to achieve the correct size. This was done using hydraulic plug and feather type of equipment.

The balance of the armour stone for the project was shipped by flat top barge from **Larvik, Gotenberg, Espevik, Arklow** and various small quarries along the Brittany coast. In the case of the Scandinavian stone, cargoes were either delivered at the start of a barge charter, the start of the shipping season, or were delivered by a 20,000 tn barge, the Lapis. When using the Lapis, the cargoes were transhipped at sea onto barges Alfa and Charlie

This was necessary as it was not possible to beach the barge Lapis.

2.3 Quarry Production
The specification for the core stone was described as follows ' the core material in the sea defence shall be well graded between the limits shown';

| 50 kg - 2000 kg | Coarse core |
| 10 kg - 1000 kg | Medium core |

The materials were supplied from existing working quarries, which were predominately involved with the production of aggregate for road stone and concrete.

On the commencement of the project considerable investment was injected in to the two main quarries at Cherbourg and Frehel by Carrieres de l'Ouest. This investment was in the form of mechanical vibrating screens and plant, i.e. 360° excavators. Especially selected areas of the quarry were dedicated specifically to rock production for the project.

The screen at Cherbourg was a single deck Somerstra manufactured in Strasbourg, France by Commersa. The screen was chosen because it had the facility to separate the materials at 250mm, the undersized product then being used for cushion material and finally concrete aggregate production. The quarry at Cherbourg was the primary source of concrete supply for the nuclear power plant at Flamville.

The screen chosen for Frehel was again produced by Commersa, but because of the type of rock, a three deck screen was incorporated here.

The screens at the back up quarries, Monteberg and Brix were static 'grizzlies'. However production from these quarries was relatively small.

Each quarry usually blasted about 1000m^3 at a time and the yield at Cherbourg was as high as 80% for the 10kg - 1tn and about 50% for the 50kg - 2tn. The rock face at Cherbourg was some

20m high and is angled. Drilling patterns were tailored to the range of material required. However at Frehel there were problems because of severe faults in certain canyons, (Frehel quarry is made up of several canyons) and yields for the 10kg - 1tn was about 55% whilst the 50kg - 2tns was only 45%.

At Frehel, once the blasting exercise had been completed raw product was hauled to the screens by 35tn dump trucks. The product then passed through the 3 tiers of screens; the slower the material passed the rails, the cleaner the material generally became. For example the 50kg - 2tn material the rails were set at approximately 300mm. Rock travelling over the screens was slowed down by the use of heavy chains. A major cause of contamination (i.e. smaller materials passing over the screens) was of the speed at which the rock was fed in to the hopper.

The general output of the quarries was in the order of 750 tns/ day. This did create somewhat of an imbalance when the programme called for the delivery rate at 20,000 tns/ week. It is generally known that the shipping of the rock in cargoes of 4,500 tn/ barge is not a problem. The main problem encountered was having sufficient acceptable core stone stock piled for shipping.

Problems were encountered in supplying a material that was clean and free from dust. To over come the problem with this material it was agreed with the Engineer, that it could be placed in the centre of the bund if kept at least 2.5m away from the edge of the bund in order that the edge porosity be maintained. Being able to utilise as much of the blast product as possible was essential to the quarry operator. During the screening of the 10kg - 1tn a considerable quantity of cushion material was generated.

During the course of the project the Engineer relaxed the specification and allowed this surplus material to be incorporated into the base of the breakwater. It was also used for the construction of temporary haul roads.

Monitoring the production of the core from Frehel was a difficult task. The sandstone was covered in dust which was predominately an off white colour, making it extremely difficult to ensure that the material was suitably graded. The human eye takes a long time to adjust to a blank white screen and thus, to ensure the bottom end of the blast was being maintained, gauge rocks coloured blue were placed at random in the stock pile. This made it a lot easier to detect any inconsistencies at the bottom end of the range.

At Frehel is was generally quite easy to overcome this problem. Frehel had the capacity to store approximately 2,000 tns on the quayside and the supplier was meant to ensure there was always this amount on the quayside prior to the arrival of any barges. The haul from the screen was approximately 300m and, provided enough material had been processed, the stock pile on the quayside was kept 'topped up' during the loading cycle. In practice this was never a problem, provided enough stone had been processed. It was not possible to use the sidestone dumping vessels at this port because of space and tide limitations.

At Cherbourg it was a different matter. The quarry was about 3 miles from the quayside, on an average day a 25 tn truck could manage 15 trips. The quayside here had to feed both the sidestone dumper and the barge, which meant there had to be 6,000 tns of material in stock at any one time to accommodate these vessels.

Production through the winter months should have continued in preparation for the second season, and with the capacity of being able to move 45,000 tns in a 14 day cycle meant there needed to be approximately 80,000 tns of material in stock to keep the shipping cycle going. With this buffer of material, production of core stone could continue at the daily rate of about 750 tns and the vessels would not be stopped.

In reality this did not happen and suppliers ran very short in Mid April. As a result, he elected to take a barge out of the core stone cycle and use her to collect armour stone from Arklow (Ireland). By following this course of action, the quarry was able to keep the side stone dumping vessel running unimpeded. This problem was overcome with a few minor amendments to the site programme and had very little effect on the overall progress of the Contract.

3. PROJECT PLANNING
The contract specification called for the breakwater construction to commence in area A and progress to area D. The reason for this was that area A was the most exposed to wave action and once in place would protect the remainder of the works under construction.

The Contract called for the final alignment of the breakwater to be determined once the original site had been surveyed. A survey was undertaken working from Area D heading towards Area A, and was carried out in a conventional manner, with much of the work having to be carried out at a low spring tide. For speed the survey data was collected using a Total Station Theodolite with a data logger. The data logger was then down loaded onto the site's Personal Computer and the ground model was developed. This was done using Land Survey System (LSS) to produce a digital land model and, once the alignment had been established, the profile of the new breakwater could be superimposed on this model. It took approximately 4 months to survey the site and approximately 23,000 points were recorded. In area A, which in certain locations is permanently under water, divers were used to establish the depth and level of the sand. Two working models were then established, one for the core stone and one for the armour stone. These models were used for planning the works, especially at the low spring tides, for ordering the materials and formed the basis of the interim and final applications.

The key to the planning was the maximisation of the land based placing method and utilising the tide to the maximum advantage. For example in Area A it was decided to raise the level of the apron to a constant +1, which facilitated the placing of the armour stone and easily outweighed the additional costs incurred by the contractor for over filling this area.

The tender was based upon conforming with the specification sequence. The philosophy was the rock would be delivered and placed by sidestone dumper directly to Area A. This would be supplemented by land based placing methods using rock imported by barge. These barges would be beached and discharged at a temporary berth at 'Harve de Pas'. This berth would have an adjoining stockpile area and thus the project could have continuous operation throughout the winter. The material would be hauled by road to area A where the site was to have been accessed by a temporary ramp from the end of the existing breakwater. The method of construction would be by end tipping.

Having reviewed the situation post tender, it was decided to completely revise the tender plan. It became apparent the main haul road was used as the driving school area and in the interests of safety it was decided that it would not be prudent to have loaded Volvo dump trucks mixing with the learner drivers.

In the revised working concept it was decided to sidestone dump in Area A while simultaneously constructing the breakwater starting from Area D working towards Area A. Having reached chainage 1200 in Area C it was then proposed to construct a secondary berth which reduced the distance the rock had to be hauled and also move importation facility some 600 m from the shore line to mitigate the amount of potential noise disturbance to the public

With guidance from H.R Wallingford, who had assisted Coode Blizard with the initial design, the works were replanned. Tests were carried out in the flume at Wallingford and it was concluded that provided the breakwater was completed from the shoreline to chainage 760 by the temporary close of the works at the end of the first year the breakwater should be able to withstand the winter gales.

It was intended to ship 50% of the rock in year one and 50% in year 2. This meant having to move approximately 700,000 tns each year and not taking up the option of a third year that the contract offered.

At point 1 [see page 2], the inshore waves produce the most severe test to the stability of the armour. However in section C influenced by the offshore rock outcrops, the largest of the waves from 230° N were able to pass up a deep channel reaching the head of the breakwater end on.

It was intented to reach approximately chainage 760 by the end of year one and the tests indicated the wave attack was the most severe from 210° to 230° (the larger waves from 250° to 290° being eliminated by the existing rock outcrops) and consequently the breakwater would be liable for end on attack between Area C and B; this being exactly the area where the works would be terminating at the end of year one.

The results had indicated that the 1-4 tn armour stone, that was to be used in the permanent works would be on the small size to protect the breakwater from an end on attack. The end was therefore protected by a roundhead constructed out of 6 - 10tn armour which would have been stock piled throughout course of the year in preparation for armouring Area A the following season.

Coupled with these tests, the site staff collected weather information, in particular the wind direction and the wave patterns that were actually occurring. This information was collated over a period of 4 months. It was concluded that damage occurrence commenced at a level of +8.

The level of the haul road had to be maintained at +12 to facilitate construction. Consequently, it was decided to leave the breakwater partially constructed. This entailed completing the armour from the apron to +8. At this level a berm some 6m wide was constructed and the core profile was brought up to +12. The 4m of breakwater was then temporarily armoured. The breaking waves ran out along the berm and the haul road was protected by the temporary armour.

On the lee, a similar ledge was constructed and again the inside face was temporarily protected by armour, which was eventually retrieved and used on the crest.

Through out the winter of 1995, the breakwater in this state with stood the gales and there was very little movement to the permanent works. This method of working also allowed the works to progress during the winter months, even if on a some what reduced capacity.

To enable corestone works to progress at all states of the tide, the haul road had to be at + 12m. This in turn meant that the breakwater would be vulnerable to attack during the winter months. Having obtained the results from Wallingford it was concluded that Area A would be perfectly safe with core stone at a level of about +6 through out the winter. The end of breakwater at Area C would be best protected by a temporary roundhead.

By the end of the first season the rock which had been sidestone dumped in area A had reached a level of approximately +3. No temporary protection was carried out in this area and there was no movement during the winter months.

4. INSURANCE OF THE WORKS
Insurer's claims experience has not been good for this area and they considered the site as particularly vulnerable to the risks of heavy storm damage. Therefore at the tender stage the brokers indicated a fairly heavy rate with a substantial storm damage excess.

At award stage insurers took up the offer of a site visit and, having full details of the construction programme, were prepared to trim the rating but maintained the original excess requirements. They also were not prepared to cover any loss or damage to unprotected fill. At this point it was necessary to review the programme of construction and to examine, in conjunction with the H R Wallingford, various alternative options. The revised construction sequences arising from this detailed post tender analysis succeeded in a substantial reduction in the risk of major damage and therefore further discussions with the insurers took place.

Although not wholly convinced, they listened to the arguments and eventually relaxed their position over the exclusion relating to the unprotected fill. The contractor felt sufficiently confident in the analysis that an increased storm/ water damage excess was offered in exchange for a rating reduction. This was accepted by insurers.

Despite bad weather over the Christmas/ New Year period (1994/1995), the works did not suffer any damage and the Contract was completed without any claim being recorded against the Policy.

5. THE CONSTRUCTION TECHNIQUES

The rock was supplied by 3 means;

1]	By road from local quarries
2]	By sidestone dumping vessel
3]	By barge

The rock supplied by the local quarry was delivered at a rate of about 3,000 tns/ week and this was tipped in a stock pile adjacent to the site and was known as the rainy day stock pile.

5.1 Shipping

Side Stone Dumping

Prior to side stone dumping commencing, the site was thoroughly surveyed and all existing outcrops plotted. With this information, the dumping plan was formulated. Basically, this was a series of boxes laid out in the footprint of the breakwater about 2m short of the actual width of the breakwater to allow for over tipping.

The initial survey was done by Sounding and Conventional Land Surveying. This was then input in to L.S.S system as a Digital Ground model and tied into the National Grid. The 'skippers surveyor' then took this information and used the vessel's global positioning system (GPS), which located the vessel within the predetermined boxes.

Operationally they had the tide gauge which was also linked to GPS to give the 3rd dimension (Z). The GPS is very good in X and Y planes but it was somewhat erratic in the Z plane. The Z plane is the most important as far as vessel safety is concerned.

The vessels, Frans and Pompei, were used to carry out this exercise. The campaign began with the Frans. This is a self propelled side stone dumping vessel and has four compartments with a total carrying capacity of 1,115 tn. The length of the vessel is 65.54m and the beam is 15.08m. When fully laden, the draught is 2.75m. In reality the vessel used to carry about 900 tns. As the project progressed the Frans was replaced by the vessel Pompei, this vessel was 65.5m long and 16.03 beam. She had a deep sea carrying capacity of 1,300 tns; the moulded draft being as the Frans.

The side stone dumpers were fed from the Port of Cherbourg. At this port, which was permanently wet, the supplier had no problems in loading the vessel. Two 40tn 360° excavators were totally dedicated to loading these vessels and the duration for loading was between 3 and 4 hours. Discharge was dependant on the tidal cycle at Jersey and generally the skipper was on station about half an hour before high-water.

Having discharged at high tide, the site was surveyed by conventional means at low tide and thus the dump plan was constantly updated. The accuracy of the tipping was a function of the information fed to the computers on the vessel.

Tipping was carried out against an existing bank, i.e. the previous dump. The clearance from this bank was normally within one metre. When actually discharging the vessel, the skipper was totally dependant on the information contained on the dump plan and the vessel was simply controlled by 'joysticks'.

When the vessel was discharging from two chambers she was simultaneously ballasting her tanks. Having discharged 50% of her cargo the vessel either pulled back and turned through 180° and tipped the remaining cargo alongside the first dump or moved to the opposite side of the breakwater by using the bow thrusters to discharge her cargo.

The skipper of the vessel had the final decision as to the dump and usually insisted on 2m of clear water between the hull and rock. This criteria could often change depending on the swell running but at no time was the vessel unable to dump.

At every spring tide cycle the area where the vessel had been dumping was cleared. This involved raking the material back towards chainage 0 or chainage 500. This was done to facilitate future dumping and the platform soon built up to a level of +10, thus leaving a clear opening for the vessel to enter the main discharge area which was maintained at a level of +5m.

By Barge

The land placed rock was principally shipped by the barges, Charlie (5,000 tns), Alpha (4,500 tns) and the RSB1 (9,000 tns). The choice of the RSB1 was a bad one. The site had planned to handle cargoes of about 5,000 tns/day and the RSB1's capacity of 9,000tn meant the whole cycle was totally disrupted as it took longer than 12 hours to load and discharge this vessel.

The barges Charlie and Alpha were ideal and could be loaded in a 12hr cycle and off loaded in 12 hr cycle. Allowing a 12 hr sailing time this meant the cycle was very practical allowing the barges to be offloaded during day light hours.

The barges were towed by conventional ocean going tugs and assistance was given by an inshore tug when docking.

Two berths were constructed. These berths were built out of old containers and were in reasonably sheltered locations. The berthing Area D (known as the secondary berth) always dried out and thus there was very little problem with maintenance. Both these berths were subjected to regular inspection by the Salvage Association.

The primary berth was constructed out of an old MOD crane barge. The superstructure was again constructed out of old containers. The barge was prepared on the mainland and then towed across and scuttled in place. Once the barge was in place, with the berthing face along the seaward toe of the permanent works, backfill was placed behind the barge forming the permanent embankment. The barge was also filled with filter material to add to the weight, giving the berthing face some form of anchorage. The access ramps were concreted insitu once the berth was in the correct position. The berthing pad was located at a level of approximately +1 and thus was only on show during spring tides.

The quay was designed to accommodate the large tidal range and consequently there were three ramps; high springs, mean and high neaps. However the barge always sat on the bottom during the cycle so the mean ramp was generally used. When using the top ramp off loading had to cease for about 10 minutes whilst the barge was moved on her winches to the mean ramp.

Off loading the barges was carried out using 360° excavators loading into Volvo A25 dumptrucks. Between 4 and 8 trucks were used for this operation depending on the haul distance. The core stone was handled by buckets, the armour, depending on the size, by bucket or grab. The offloading cycle was very dependant on the haul, the progress of the works and the current state of the tide. However, it usually took about 10 hours, the quickest being 6 hours.

When handling the 6 to 10tn, armour problems were often encountered with the rock jamming in the body of the trucks, potentially causing the trucks to over turn. To overcome this problem the 'greedy boards' were cut off the trucks.

These enabled the trucks to remain multi purpose as there was still a need to be able to use the trucks for hauling core at later stage in the works.

The weather around the Channel Islands in the winter is somewhat inclement at times and the shipping operation was set to run from mid March to October. The theory was that the site would virtually close down during the winter months except for the construction of the reinforced concrete culvert. However due to the exceptional weather, shipping in year One continued until December and resumed again in mid March. By September of 1995 all the rock had been delivered to site, in total approximately 1,046,835 tonnes (in a addition 200,000 tns was delivered from the local quarry).

On completion of the shipping, the berths and pads were removed. The filter stone contained in the hold of the barge was excavated, a few minor repairs were carried out to the hull, the barge was pumped out at low tide and on the following high tide was floated away, thus enabling the final profile of the breakwater to be completed.

Breakwater Construction

The construction of the breakwater followed a set sequence. The rock was end tipped working from a level of +12, the seaward side generally being over filled. This excess material was used for the formation of the aprons. On the low spring tides the material was dragged off the overfilled batter and used for filling the apron. As this exercise continued working platforms were formed naturally in the batter. Once the apron had been filled the formation of the side slope could commence. Material was dragged down and thus formed a second berm in the breakwater.

The Site February 1995

Secondary Berth

Primary Berth

Haul road

+8m berm

Apron

D

C

B2

Temporary Winter Armour

Temporary Roundhead

Temporary Armour

Plate 10

These berms were used as platforms for the armour placing excavators to work off, the armour being delivered to the placing plant by dump truck. Generally berms were created every 4m.

Upon completion of the shipping with the balance of the material safely stockpiled, the final formation of the breakwater could return to full production. During the shipping cycle the resources had to be split; certain plant on offloading the rock and the remainder working on shaping the front face and aprons (these works being very tide dependant). However, by the time shipping was completed, the apron and toe armour construction were 90% complete and all that remained was about 90m in Area A and a large section in Area C where the berth had been. These works were completed on time and the breakwater was finally handed over to the client in January '96 some three months ahead on the Contractual completion date.

Plant
The major items of equipment used on the project was as follows;

8 No.A25 Volvo dump trucks, 4 No.40tn 360° excavators, 3 No.70tn 360° Libherer excavator c/w buckets, short and long dipper arms c/w grabs, 2 No.30tn 360° excavators, 1 No.5,000 tn barge c/w 2x 360° excavators, 1 No.4,500 tn barge c/w 2x 360° excavators, 1 No.20,000 tn barge, 3 No.Ocean going tugs, 1 No.Berthing tug, Fuel bowsers, flood lights, workboats etc. 2 No.Side dumpers - Frans and Pompei

The major items of plant were maintained on a daily basis, the largest problem being the excessive wear to the bodies of the dump trucks, the buckets and grabs. A full time fitter and two full time welders were employed to replace the wear plates that were installed in the trucks and on the grabs of the 70 tn excavators. Another major concern was the tracks on the 360° excavators. The quartzite dust caused serious damage to these components and often resulted in machines losing their tracks, which normally occurred when the machines were working at the low level. The foreman became quite proficient at repairing the machines in double quick time or at retrieving the plant and dragging the offending item above the high water level. Tyre wear was also excessive and although originally the thought had been to change all the tyres to slicks, there were reservations about the lack of grip when the trucks traversed the steel deck of Charlie and when contemplating the steel ramps. In the end it was decided to use normal earth moving tyres.

The plant on board the barges Charlie and Alfa were constantly at work and there was very little time to maintain the machines, as the plant was either loading or unloading and when not working was at sea. On these occasions when breakdowns occurred on site, i.e. when unloading, the land based plant assisted with the offloading. This was found to be the best solution because a spare machine would always be in the wrong place.

Considering the hours worked and the volume of rock moved, the down time was relatively small and credit must be given to the respective operators concerned.

SUMMARY
From 15 May 1994 to 31 August 1996, with a break between 30 November 1994 and 23 March 1995 the supplier managed to produce, and ship in excess of 1,050,700 tns of rock.

Considering this operation commenced from a cold start, this was no mean achievement.

Between the months of May 1994 and January 1996 the site managed to take delivery of and place 1,250,700 tns of rock, in the permanent works. Both of these operations were carried out with virtually no incident and should be considered a credit to all the parties concerned: Carrieres de l'Ouest for the supply, Sillanpaa Oy for the shipping by barge, Van Oord ACZ and Tideway for the side stone dumping with Edmund Nuttall Limited who were the main Contractor.

The author wishes to thank; The States of Jersey, Coode Blizard, H.R. Wallingford, Edmund Nuttall Limited, J.F. O'Hara, David Rochford, and John Placzek for their assistance in compiling this paper.

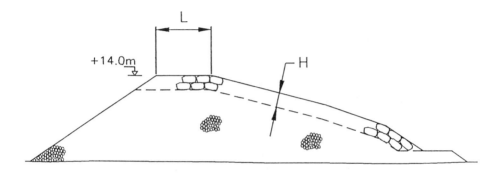

KEY

AREA	DIMENSION H (mm)	DIMENSION L (mm)
A	2900	11500
B1	2100	3500
B2	2400	3500
C	2000	3000
D	1900	3000

Typical cross section

Recovery of armour layer slopes on "Principe de Asturias" breakwater in the Port of Gijon, Spain

JOSÉ LUIS DÍAZ RATO, Ingeniero de Caminos, Port Authority of Gijón
FRANCISCO JAVIER MARTÍ UNANUE, Ingeniero de Caminos, (Constructor)

SYNOPSIS

Gijón is the leading bulk port in Spain. Located in the middle of the Cantabrian coast (Fig. 1), it discharges 10 million tonnes of iron ore and coal a year, mainly for the nearby steel plant. The "Principe de Asturias" is the main breakwater, protecting the port from the most severe storms and sheltering the bulk terminal, which is built against its final section. The cross-section is exceptional for a slope-type breakwater, with a core consisting of 90-tonne concrete blocks and outer layers made up of 120-tonne blocks, crowned with an L-shaped superstructure. From the completion the works in 1975, it was observed that blocks were being lost from the breakwater slope, changing its original shape and leaving the superstructure unprotected. This paper summarizes the works carried out to repair the slope, restoring its original cross-section.

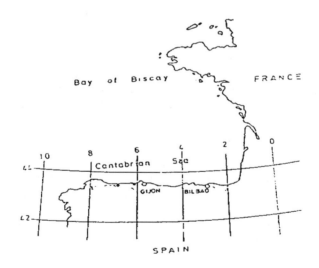

Fig. 1. Location of port of Gijón

INTRODUCTION

Located on a large bay bounded by the Torres and San Lorenzo capes, with the Santa Catalina headland in the centre, Gijón was the most romanized city on the North coast of Spain. It was on this headland that the Romans made their early settlement, and here, too, was the origin of the urban nucleus (Fig. 2). There are data from Roman times referring to the existence of a landing stage on the sandbanks to the East of the headland.

Coastlines, structures and breakwaters. Thomas Telford, London, 1998

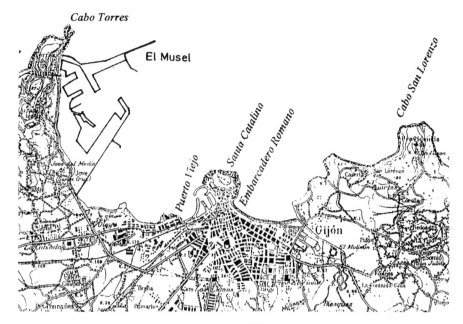

Fig. 2. Bay of Gijón

In the XVI century the construction was started on the old port, which was located to the West of the headland and served the fishing activity. This port attained its maximum development towards the end of XIX century, when it provided the main outlet for the coal, which was plentiful in the region. Owing to the lack of deep-water berths in the port, it became necessary to seek a new location and a new port was built on the Western end of the bay. Work began on the new port with the construction of a vertical, concrete-block breakwater, allowing vessels to berth against its sheltered side. At present, this breakwater is protected with an armour layer of 90-tonne blocks.

The limited supply of natural rocks with a weight of over 2 tonnes in the area near the port, combined with the difficulty of the communications in this very mountainous region, required an exceptional solution to be found for the first extension to the North Breakwater, which was undertaken in 1945. The depth in which the construction works were carried out (17 metres) together with wave heights of over 14 metres, led the designer to conceive a sloping cross-section with a core of 90-tonne blocks, perfectly safe in the face of the storms and protected by a slope of ctgα = 2.5, also constructed of concrete blocks of the same weight, crowned with an L-shaped superstructure.

The excellent performance of this solution led to its adoption for the construction of the second, 1,200-metre long extension to the breakwater, carried out between 1970 and 1975, to enable the port to accommodate the large bulk carriers bringing iron ore and coal for the steelworks (Fig. 3). The greater depth and wave heights, together with the new design criteria according to Iribarren's formula, required the armour layer to be modified to ctgα = 1.5 and to be constructed of two layers of 120-tonne blocks, forming a berm with a width of 3,75 metres at a height of +12.20.

During monitoring of the slope of this last extension to the breakwater, important movements of the blocks and a generalized descent of the upper berm were detected. This left the concrete wave screen exposed to the impact of the waves, with the result that in many cases it was acting as a mixed type breakwater, a situation for which it had not been designed. The breakwater is of fundamental strategic importance for the port of Gijón, sheltering the dry bulk terminal which is built against it. Therefore it is of prime importance to ensure its stability, and although the cross-section of the breakwater prevents its destruction, the failure or destruction of part of the wave screen could occur. For all these reasons, the repair of this last section was undertaken, with the recovery of the original armour layer slope, by placing 120-tonne blocks down to level -8, and 90-tonne blocks below this level, widening the berm so that it has a top width of 5.5 metres, and bringing it up to +13.00. Economic constraints made it advisable to adopt this solution as, due to the special design and high permeability of the breakwater, it has a greater resistance capacity than and performs differently from the typical slope-type breakwater.

Fig. 3. General view of the Port of Gijón

ENVIRONMENTAL CONDITIONS
The landward end of the Principe de Asturias breakwater abuts on the Eastern side of the Torres Cape, in water depths of 7-8 metres; with a length of 2,250 metres, it follows a broken line in a W-E direction terminating in waters 22 metres deep. The general orientation of the bathymetrics in the area is NW-SE, with some irregularities that have a considerable influence on wave propagation and, consequently, on the magnitude and direction of the waves reaching the breakwater.

The strongest storms reaching the breakwater are from the fourth quarter and, due to refraction, the largest waves arrive from N 22 W, with a maximum height limited by the water depth and by the shallows situated in front of the breakwater, of between 17 and 18 metres, with $T_p = 17$ s. Accepting a Rayleigh distribution for the wave heights, these waves can occur with a significant wave height at the foot of the breakwater of $H_s = 9.50$ m. The tidal range in the area is 4.60 metres. (Fig. 4)

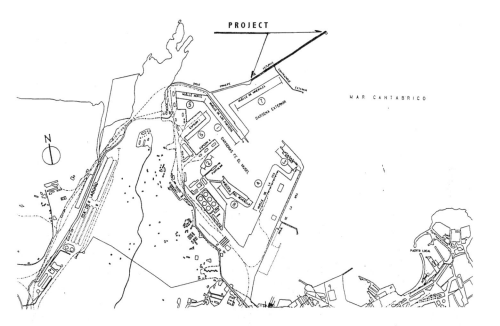

Fig. 4. Plan view of Port Layout

TYPOLOGY OF PRINCIPE DE ASTURIAS BREAKWATER

The breakwater consists of three sections: the first, which abuts on the Torres Cape, was originally a vertical, concrete-block breakwater, and is today protected by an armour layer of 90-tonne blocks; it is 600 metres long and was constructed between 1899 and 1925. The second section, with a length of 550 metres, is a slope-type breakwater, with a core of 90-tonne blocks, and an outer layer formed of the same blocks, with a slope of 2.3/1, crowned with a concrete wall. The third section, 1,200 metres long ,is called the Outer breakwater and repeats the typology of the previous section, with a core of 90-tonne blocks, but the armour layer consists of two layers of 120-tonne blocks rising to +12.20, where the berm is 3.75 metres wide. This section is crowned with a concrete superstructure reaching to +18.35. All levels are referred to low tide. The breakwater is constructed on a marl bottom, and the water depths vary from 17.00 metres at the start of the section and 22.00 metres at the end. (Fig. 5). The repair project refers to this last section.

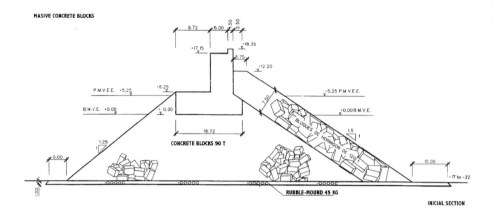

Fig. 5. Original cross-section

BEHAVIOUR OF THE BREAKWATER

Since the works of the last section of the breakwater were completed in 1975, its behaviour has been monitored mainly by means of photographs taken of the outer slope on which each of the blocks could be identified. Transverse profiles were also obtained with the aid of a 3.00 metre sphere hanging from a tower crane on rails, which was moved along the slope. In this way, data were obtained down to -10; the profile down to the foot of the breakwater was completed with a conventional probe.

From the cross profile, different kinds of failures were detected over the length of the breakwater: some sections had lost the first armour layer over a length of 6 to 8 blocks, which left them in a situation we call "Iribarren failure"; in other sections, the 90-tonne block core was exposed which, for a conventional rubble-mound breakwater, would be called "in course of destruction"; in yet other sections, the crown berm was below +8.00, showing a low-gradient slope with ctgα = 2.00, at least to level -6.00.

If the breakwater had be built in the traditional way, its situation was such as would have caused a total collapse of the structure. That this did not happen to the Gijón breakwater is due to its core of 90-tonne blocks and to the great stability, far superior to what was to be expected from the calculations, shown by its wave screen. The possibility must be considered that the breakwater was not constructed with an even slope of α = 1.50. The procedure used for its construction: a crane for placing blocks to a distance of 12 metres and the dumping of blocks from the sea, from this level to the bottom, usually produces breakwaters with concave slopes. Although there are no "as built" records, we know that the crown berm was densely constructed up to level +14.60, to compensate the settlement of the slope, and that it was, on average, more than 2 blocks wide. When the project to repair the berm was undertaken, it was in a very degraded condition over the whole length of the breakwater, with a width of only 1 block.

Lacking other information, and as the most probable fact, it must be accepted that the breakwater was correctly constructed and that it was in a state corresponding to an "Iribarren failure" progressing towards destruction, a situation in which the blocks protecting the foot of the wave screen would disappear, leaving it exposed to the action of the breaking waves. The wave height that cause an "Iribarren failure" of the breakwater are between 14 and 15 metres, which can be associated with sea conditions of $H_S = 8.0$. Data from the wave rider buoy located outside the port show that the breakwater has been subjected to such conditions several times over its life.

DESCRIPTION OF THE WORKS

The recalculation of the breakwater in view of the wave heights that actually reach it, the maximum heights being between 17 and 18 metres ($H_S = 9.5$ m) resulted in a slope of ctgα = 2 for blocks with a weight of 120 tonnes. The excessive cost of this solution made it necessary to decide on the repair of the design slope as, due to its core of 90-tonne blocks, the stability of the breakwater is greater than that of the traditional slope-type breakwaters because its core has a permeability slightly longer than 50%. Thus, although blocks might be lost from the armour layer, the breakwater will never be destroyed and so it is more economical to replace the blocks every 25 years - the time the breakwater has been in service - than to increase its section to achieve a lower gradient.

The works consisted in the recovery of the theoretical slope of the original design of the outer breakwater, crowned with a berm having a width of 5.5 metres at +13, descending with a slope of ctgα = 1.5 to the sea bed at a level of -18 to -22. 120-tonne blocks are placed from +13 to -8, and with 90-tonne blocks from -8. (Fig. 6). All these levels are referred to low water spring tide and it must be borne in mind that the tidal range in Gijón is 4.60 m.

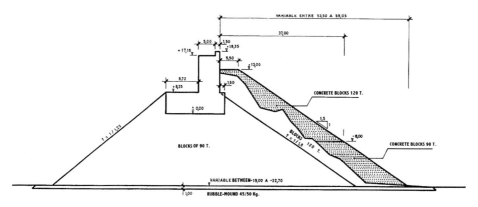

Fig. 6. Repair cross-section

FABRICATION OF CONCRETE BLOCKS

The 120-tonne blocks of the original armour layer are parallelopipedic in shape, measuring 5.5 x 2.75 x 3.43 m^3. In order to adapt to the existing ones, so that the new blocks should fit into the old ones and, on the other hand to approach a cube shape, which provides greatest stability, a compromise solution was reached, with blocks measuring a x a x 1.3a, thus obtaining, for 120 tonnes, 3.42 x 3.42 x 4.45 m³ and for 90 tonnes, 3.11 x 3.11 x 4.05 m³. 1,784 blocks of 120 tonnes and 1,242 blocks of 90 tonnes were constructed, which represents a total volume of 141,678 m³ of concrete.

The blocks were constructed inside the port, in a yard located 5 km from the breakwater, and were carried through the port on 150-tonne trailers. (Fig. 7).

Fig. 7. Transport of concrete blocks

The proportion of cement was 300 kg/m³ and cement with a 35% of fly-ash was used. Strengths of 225 kg/cm² were obtained and a water/cement ratio < 0.5 was required. The aggregate used had a maximum size of 80 mm. The minimum density obtained was 2.32 t/m³.

A "cake mould" type shuttering without openings in the side panels was used for making the blocks. The blocks remained stored for 1 month in the yard before being taken to the breakwater. The yard had a storage capacity for 800 blocks.

CONSTRUCTION METHOD

The method used for placing the blocks was entirely land based; the use of maritime means was rejected due to the great difficulty that would be encountered by the barges or dumpers to approach the intertidal area, which might lead to an insufficient armour layer being laid in said area. A DEMAG RINGLIFT CC 2000 crane, located on a 19.9 m diameter crown wheel with a 475 t counterweight, was employed to place the blocks. The length of the jib once installed was 78 metres. With this set-up, the crane can place 120-tonne blocks at a distance of 50 metres and 90-tonne blocks at a distance of 72 metres from the slewing axis. (Fig. 8).

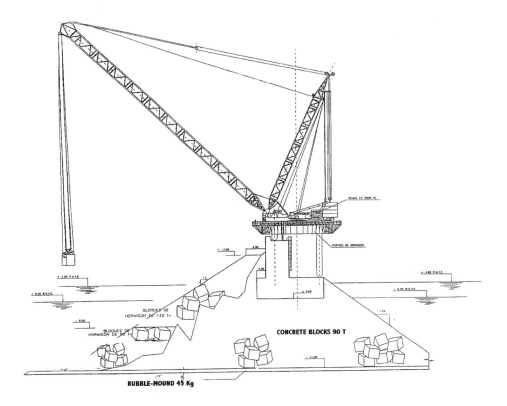

Fig. 8. Crane for placing concrete blocks

To move the crane along the breakwater and, at the same time, to raise it to the height of the wave screen, at +18.35, a reinforced concrete gantry was constructed, which supported a 20 m-diameter ring beam with a depth of 2.50 m, the top of which reached a level of +21.5, where the crane was located. A concrete structure was chosen due to the need that the structure itself should act as a counterweight for the whole assembly and the strict conditions regarding deformability to avoid the generation of significantly different seating between different points of the crown wheel. This structure also had the advantage of forming a strong monolith and great durability in the face of the severe climate and storm conditions in which it had to work. The total weight of the crane-gantry assembly was 2,400 tonnes (Fig. 9 and 10).

Fig. 9. Crane placing the blocks

Fig. 10. Friction tongs holding 120 tonne blocks.

In order to move the crane, the four gantry feet were placed on Teflon skids ensuring an adequate reduction of the friction coefficient to between 0.05 and 0.10, which slid on polished stainless steel sheets located on a steel bedplate and which were bolted to two massive longitudinal concrete beams on the upper and lower part of the wave screen. Each time the crane reached its working position, after periodical movements of 12.50 metres, it

Fig. 12. State of breakwater on completion of works

Fig. 11. State of breakwater at start of works

was locked in position, letting it rest on eight hydraulic jacks with 500 t static capacity, arranged symmetrically on both sides of the Teflon skids.

A double drum winch exerting a pull of 20 t was used for moving the crane. The winch was connected to the front bottom leg. Each drum incorporated 5 strands, bringing the total pull exerted to 200 tonnes. As an indication, at the moment of moving the crane, the load on each of the four legs was, with the jib folded back and centred, 650 tonnes. In working conditions, the maximum load per leg was around 950 tonnes.

The DEMAG crane began placing blocks in April 1994 and finished in November 1.995. The maximum number of blocks placed per day was 18.

PLACING THE BLOCKS ON THE SLOPE

The project required that the position of the blocks should be predetermined by coordinates, which required a detailed knowledge of the initial situation of the blocks on the breakwater slope. In order to make a survey of the part above water, an aerial survey was made at low tide with a scale of 1:2500, allowing an analytical detailed reconstruction to be carried out with a scale of 1:300, achieving tolerances of around 15 cm. For the submerged part, a multi-beam probe with a band-width of 90 degrees was used, providing great accuracy and covering the complete area involved in the study. With the data thus obtained and the help of a computer programme, cross profiles were drawn every 2.5 metres, the blocks required were placed on them and the coordinates obtained for each one.

The crane was equipped with three "rotating" type coding sensors for measuring its plan position on the "ringer", the inclination of the jib and the turns of the drums on which the hoisting cable was rolled up. By means of the corresponding mathematical transformation carried out by the system controller, these three data allow the coordinates of the block hanging from the crane to be determined. There was a portable computer in the crane cabin. The number of the block to be placed, together with the coordinates of its position, is shown on the screen. On another line, the coordinates of the suspended block appear in real time, so the crane driver only has to move the block until the plan orientation and the inclination of the jib coincide, when he can lower the block into its final position. If the block is within tolerance as regards height, he proceeds to deposit it, recording the coordinates of the position in the computer. Friction type tongs were used to hold the blocks, which had no kind of notch or indentation on any of their faces.

Using the data concerning block positions registered in the crane computer, a new digital model of the slope of blocks was generated, from which the corresponding transverse profiles, with the blocks already placed, was obtained. As a final check, using the same crane and positioning system, a metal sphere was passed over the breakwater slope in order to determine the final transverse profile.

As a final touch, the reinforced concrete gantry used to support and move the crane was integrated into the head of the breakwater. (Fig. 11 and 12)

Gijón, august 1.997

Decisions taken for rebuilding a breakwater under construction after a storm failure

VICENTE NEGRO-VALDECANTOS AND OVIDIO VARELA-CARNERO
Madrid Polytechnical University. Faculty of Civil Engineering. Department of Harbour and Coastal Engineering. Ciudad Universitaria, s/n. Madrid 28.040. SPAIN

INTRODUCTION

Located in the East of the Bay of Biscay, Bilbao is a maritime and river port spreading over 20 Kms. around the river Nervion estuary. Almost seven centuries of history have seen it become a modern port annually handling over 30 million tonnes, the origin and destination of traffic with 500 other ports worldwide. It is currently facing an extension into the future moving its business to new facilities in the Outer Harbour, El Abra Exterior.

The extension work was awarded on 9 October, 1991. The first phase involved an investment of 250 million dollars. The construction work actually commenced in January 1992, over a 62 month term. Completion was therefore set for Spring, 1997. The storm affecting the breakwater in the winter of 1996 pushed back work completion by more than five months.

The new port requires a West Breakwater in three alignments of 3,150 metres and a straight East Breakwater of 1,400 metres. The construction is a conventional sloping breakwater with 100 tonne blocks of concrete, d*d*1.25 d, 25 tonne toe berm at level -14.00 m, and ten metres wide, with a wave crowned at +18.00 m and concrete capping slab at +7.00 m. The main breakwater starts from the Zierbana esplanades Northwards turning Eastwards after 925 metres. It makes its first break of 80° at this point in a 1,000 metre alignment of 1,225 metres until completing the 3,150 linear metres of breakwater. The East Breakwater starts in a West 30° North direction from Santurce dock next to the lighthouse, running parallel to the coast for an overall length of 1,400 metres. The contained water (5 Km²) with very low internal agitation limits, acceptable to continuity of operation, has a 700 metre mouth opening North - Eastwards.

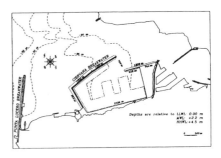

Fig. 1. Lay - out of the Port of Bilbao Extension

Coastlines, structures and breakwaters. Thomas Telford, London, 1998

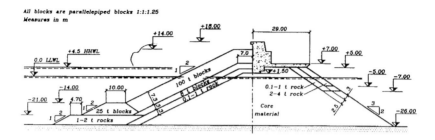

Fig. 2. Typical cross section of conventional sloping West Breakwater

The storm which arose in the early hours of 7 to 8 February, 1996 involved a significant wave height close to 8.00 metres with maximums of 12.00 m. causing great damage to the construction equipment, a crane with ringer, the provisional head and work progress in the main breakwater. This article examines the decisions and alternatives studies for repairing and rebuilding the West breakwater, after the Manitowoc 4,600 crane with ringer used up till then was put out of service and the slope was seriously damaged by the wave attack.

DESCRIPTION OF THE WAVE CLIMATE AND THE CONSTRUCTION STATUS AT TIME OF FEBRUARY 96 STORM

The storm causing the damage evolved as from 2.00 p.m. on 8 February, 1.996 with H_s close to 5.40 metres and a maximum of 8.29 m. to 7.72 m. and 12.21 m. at 0.00 hours of 8 February, with a maximum recording at the REMRO buoy in 50 metres water depth outside the estuary of 7.92 m. significant wave height and 11.66 m. maximum at 2.00 a.m. Waves of over four metres ocurred during more than 30 hours storm. Its register was NW direction rolling to NNW. The statistic of the design wave conditions and the storm's qualification related to scale and directional statistics showed a return period event close to twenty years. The wave conditions, the weather situation and buoy recording is described below.

The advance of the marine based construction process showed that the toe rubble mound and banquettes were dumped down to a level depending on the number of winters of exposure, - 5.00 m water depth for one winter of exposure, - 7.00 m for two winters of exposure and - 10.00 m for three winters of exposure, with the work being temporarily closed off with the provisional head approximately at the breakwater's 2,100 metre profile. The land based work continued with the esplanades, the fill and advance cores, the placing of rubble mound from level +7.00 m with the link in a submerged profile, the primary filter of 8.00 tonne blocks and the 100 tonne block protection layer. The layers had a maximum distance of 500 narrowing progressively as work continued towards winter. At the time of the storm the distance was 340 metres. The situation before the storm was as follows:

* Marine based core dumping. Profile 3,350
* 0.1 - 1 tonne marine based rubble mound dumping on natural ground. Profile 3,300
* 1 - 2 tonne marine based side rubble mound dumping at -21.00 m. Profile 3,220
* 8 tonne block main filter in armour layer. Profile 2,870
* 25 tonne blocks in slope toe banquette at -14.00 m. Profile 2,530
* Provisional head with 25 tonne protection blocks. Profile 2,100

* Crane situation, Profile 1,760, with last change of position on 26 January
* 100 tonne blocks placed at slope toe. Profile 1,830

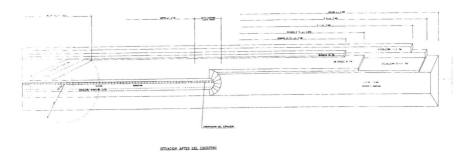

Fig. 3. Description of construction status at time February 96 storm

The advance at full construction work production could be calculated at around 200 metres/month, placing more than forty 100 tonne blocks per day working on three shifts with the night-time output slightly less.

The work was forecast to progress during the winter season, though more slowly and with less output, whilst expecting to reach the provisional head during January - April 1996 period. Precautions had been taken in weather forecasts to save the equipment and formation by stocking 100 tonne blocks as provisional protection wave walls from profile 1,800 to 2,100 on the esplanade crown, which would be arranged on the slope as the crane advanced along the running track. The working scheme is shown in the attached sketch. Likewise, the profiles approved by the Port Authorithy demonstrate the rigour and precision in forming the defence structure's protection slopes. This is shown in the "in site" survey effected although the distance between the protected and unprotected area was greater than that as set in the Construction Work's Tecnical Specifications, > 280 metres.

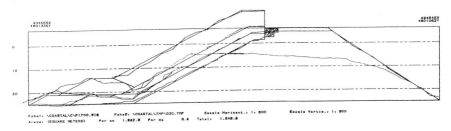

Fig. 4. Stability of partially completed breakwater cross sections. Construction Profiles P1,760

The straight lines are the theoretical required profiles
The irregular lines are "as - placed" profiles before and after the storm

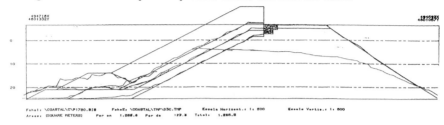

Fig. 5. Stability of partially uncompleted breakwater cross sections. Construction Profiles P2,250

The straight lines are the theoretical required profiles
The irregular lines are "as - placed" profiles before and after the storm
Internal face filter rockfill 100 to 1,000 Kg

Calculations made showed correctness of the provisional structure adjustment to all direction, 5 year return period storms. Damage evolution and progress as well as the construction process under development had been tested in significant wave height steps in the Madrid CEDEX - CEPYC multidirectional tank, together with the typical cross section of the 25 tonne block provisional head.

The presence of a North Atlantic low pressure area with its centre in the British Isles, combined with depression over the Peninsula and another approaching from the East set a shock climate situation with high winds and waves with considerable instability causing structural failure in the construction phase. It was also impossible to decide on removing the equipment since waves were passing over the fill esplanade at elevation +7.00 as from very early in the morning (7FEB) and began to open a breach which progressed at both the protected and the advance ends, washing away material and leaving the ringer crane in a notably precarious, unstable situation which caused it to collapse hours later. This situation led to the loss of the 8 tonne filters, to sliding of the 100 tonne blocks acting as a provisional wave wall to the movement of the 100 tonne block slope toewards and on the 25 tonne toe mound and to the gradual loss of the fill material in the crane running track and access between the completely built profile, P1,760 and the provisional head P2,100.

The estimated long term wave climate at the bay entrance at 50 metres depth, with the significant wave height and the return period, the wave recorders during the storm and the meteorological field is described below.

Return Period, (y)	Central estimates, all directions		10% exceedence probability estimates, significant wave height/directions		
	H_s	σ	H_s (NW)	H_s (NNW)	H_s (N)
1.00	6.40	0.50	6.70	6.00	5.00
5.00	7.40	0.60	7.70	6.90	5.80
10.00	8.30	0.60	8.60	7.70	6.40
20.00	8.90	0.70	8.90	8.00	6.70
50.00	9.50	0.90	10.10	9.00	7.50
100.00	10.00	1.00	10.70	9.60	7.90
200.00	10.50	1.20	11.40	10.70	8.40

Table n° 1: Wave Climate Bilbao Buoy, REMRO, 1.983 - 96. Zone I.[1]

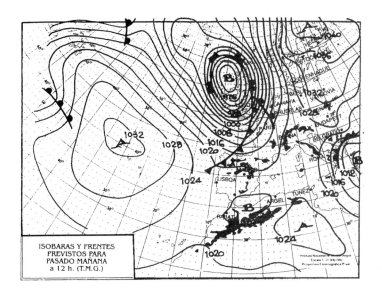

Fig. 6. Weather situation at time of February 96 storm

---

[1] REMRO: SPANISH WAVE MEASURING AND RECORDING NETWORK

WAVE RECORDING IN BILBAO BAY ENTRANCE IN 50 METRES WATER DEPTH							
DATE	HOUR	N_m	H_{mean}, m	$H_{1/3}$, m	H_{max}, m	T_z, sg	$T_{1/3}$, sg
7 Feb	14.00	0.37	3.51	5.40	8.29	7.86	9.69
7 Feb	15.00	0.37	3.33	5.32	8.80	7.74	9.75
7 Feb	16.00	0.37	3.57	5.65	10.26	7.97	10.24
7 Feb	17.00	0.37	4.03	6.39	9.59	8.45	10.34
7 Feb	18.00	0.37	4.24	6.72	10.51	8.76	10.94
7 Feb	19.00	0.38	4.38	6.93	11.54	8.93	10.94
7 Feb	20.00	0.64	4.38	6.95	12.91	9.64	13.15
7 Feb	21.00	0.42	4.39	7.13	10.12	9.44	12.64
7 Feb	22.00	0.38	4.26	6.79	10.24	9.22	12.24
7 Feb	23.00	0.40	4.75	7.34	11.45	10.51	13.88
8 Feb	0.00	0.38	4.80	7.72	12.21	10.38	14.63
8 Feb	1.00	0.38	4.61	7.55	12.22	10.09	13.71
8 Feb	2.00[2]	0.38	4.83	7.92	11.66	10.70	14.22
8 Feb	3.00	0.41	4.37	6.78	11.93	10.47	14.59
8 Feb	4.00	0.37	4.26	6.89	11.24	9.97	13.66
8 Feb	5.00	0.37	3.93	6.24	10.43	9.10	12.52
8 Feb	6.00	0.37	3.59	5.69	10.47	8.94	12.42
8 Feb	7.00	0.37	3.13	5.29	8.07	8.11	11.74
8 Feb	8.00	0.37	3.02	4.93	10.35	8.05	11.10

Table n° 2.   Wave measurements during the storm 7 to 8 February, 1.996

---

[2] MAXIMUM SIGNIFICANT WAVE HEIGHT DURING FEBRUARY STORM

REBUILDING DECISIONS. REPAIR PROCESS.
Different solutions were appraised after analyzing the design profiles, those built before the damage and afterwards, having lost the mechanical equipment in work progress:

a)   Rebuild on the transformed profile.
        a_1) Fill voids, place filter and the armour layer.
        a_2) Change the slope to a gentler one.
        a_3) Make a new 50 Tn. toe berm at -10,00 m.
        a_4) Rebuild on what is left with 100 Tn. blocks.

b)   Remove debris and return to the design solutions. This one was not considered.

The availability of equipment for marine dumping, large capacity buckets (1,000 m³) and barges with two 200 tonnes cranes, as well as the arrive of a caterpillar crane which had performed two similar construction jobs on the North Coast, La Zurriola, San Sebastian with natural 50 tonne rubble mound blocks and Orio, Guipozcoa, with 60 tonne blocks, with a long reaching jib, blocks of 100 Tn. over 68 metres distance, combined with the high costs of removing debris with doubtful reliability and low output through there being different sized interconnected pieces, recommended a reconstruction solution, by combining the different options defined in heading "a".

Finally, as a marine based operation, the toe berm was restored at -14.00 m. with 25 tonnes, recharge was carried out with a new one of 50 tonnes and the long reaching caterpillar crane was used to fill the voids found. A new slope was completed with two layers of 100 tonne blocks at 2.00 H/1 V. Debris removal was minimal.

The sequence was as follows:

By Land:
        Fill core material 10 to 25 Kg
        Filter rockfill 100 to 1,000 Kg and 1 to 2 Tonne
        Bottom and top slab concreting
        8.00 tonne filter blocks
        100 tonne blocks in two layers in 2.00/1.

By Sea:
        Core and filters up to level -4.00 m.
        50 tonne toe berm at -10.00 m.
        25 tonne toe berm at -14.00 m.
        Berm of 1 to 2 tonnes at -21.00 m. level.

Outputs achieved with both land and marine based of equipment at maximum production in the summer season, characterized by good weather, were:

Core and filters	over 200 metres per month
Bottom and top slab concreting	over 150 metres per month
8.00 tonne filter blocks	over 180 metres per month

100 tonne blocks in two layers	over 160 metres per month
	40 metres per week, 35 blocks per day on submerged slope, 55 blocks per day on surface
25 tonne toe berm at -14.00 m	35 blocks per day
50 tonne toe berm at -10.00 m	250 blocks per month
Risk distance in summertime	over 280 metres
	less than 500 metres

Reconstruction commenced with the internal fills at the beginning of March, 1996, although work on repairing the failure profile, P1760, commenced at the end of that month. An effective period of 3 months was taken from the said profile to the provisional head, and the slope was crowned at profile P2100 in August, 1996. Work continued absolutely normally during the following seasons and today the West Breakwater is completely finished except 500 metres of screen wall. The Breakwater head is also completed, using four monolithic caissons of 31.28 metres length, 17.16 metres width and 24.00 metres depth crowned at + 6.50 m. The East Breakwater is also mostly finished with the exception of 300 m of outer armour layer of rubble mound blocks of 25 tn.

Reconstruction and repair process were undertaken whilst minimizing the risk distance between the protected and unprotected areas, building in a practically complete cross section depending on the functionality and manoeuvrability of the equipment used and correcting the work schedules according to weather forecasts, wind fields and the nature of the wave action.

The total quantity of the marine construction is:

Concrete	95,000 units of 8 Tn. blocks
	40,000 units of 25 Tn. blocks
	17,500 units of 100 Tn. blocks
	Total 163,500 units
	over 2 millions of m^3 and 7 millions of Kg of steel
Core and filters	over 40 millions of Tn.
Dredging	over 6 million of m^3

Photograph illustrations before and after the 7 to 8 February storm are given hereafter.

Fig. 7. Situation of the work process. January 1996. Construction equipment profile P1,760.
Provisional Head profile P2,100

Fig. 8. Completed breakwater cross section Profile P1,700. Equipment profile P1,760. 100
Tn.blocks as provisional wave wall

Fig. 9. Situation after failure. Profile P1,760 start of damage. P2,100 Provisional Head fully damage

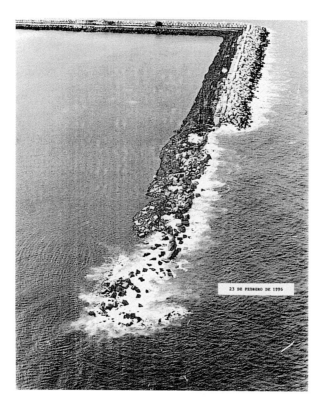

23 DE FEBRERO DE 1996

Fig. 10. Situation after failure. Photo taken on February 1996

CONCLUSION.

Marine construction calls for working with the most complete cross section possible in breakwaters, with the logical lag of machinery not greater than 200 m. between fully armoured profile and unprotected, above water, core material. A winter shutdown is recommended, closing off the site with a provisional head. If this is not done, the lag must be small and precaution and forecasting a maximum. Damage may lead to repair costs higher than the design costs. In any case, and with failure, debris removal must always be the last solution.

Failures like that described above lead to delays in work completion close to one year (an additional summer campaign) and have a very considerable repercussion on the work's budget.

REFERENCES
1. Burcharth, H.F. & Berenguer, J.M. "Design of Ciervana Breakwater" Coastal Structures and Breakwaters'95. Institution of Civil Engineers. Thomas Telford. 1996.

2. Tanimoto, K & Goda, Y. "Historical development of breakwater structures in the world" Coastal Structures and Breakwaters'91. Institution of Civil Enginners. Thomas Telford. 1991.

3. Varela, O. "Construcción de Obras de Abrigo" Curso de Proyecto y Construcción de Obras Marítimas. CEDEX - CEPYC. 1985.

4. Uzcanga, J & González, B. "Algunas consideraciones sobre el diseño de diques" I Jornadas Españolas de Costas y Puertos. Santander, 1992.

5. Negro, V & Varela, O. "H_0 parameter for preliminary design of conventional breakwater structural head. Data analysis of Spanish North Coast Harbours" 24th International Conference on Coastal Engineering. Kobe. 1994.

6. Inventario de Obras de Abrigo. Tomo I. Fachada Norte y Galicia. Ministerio de Obras Públicas y Urbanismo. Dirección General de Puertos y Costas. 1988.

7. Burcharth, H.F. "Design innovations, including recent research contributions" Coastal Structures and Breakwaters. The Institution of Civil Engineers. Thomas Telford. 1992.

8. Maritime Works Recommendations. Actions in the design of Maritime and Harbor Works. ROM 02/90. Ministry of Public Works. 1990.

9. Maritime Works Recommendations. Recommendations for the consideration of Environmental Actions. Annex I: Wave Action, Currents, Tides, and other water level variations. ROM 03/91. Ministry of Public Works. 1991.

ACKNOWLEDGEMENT
The authors like to express their sincere thanks to Mr. Ramón Ortiz and Revenga and Associates for their generous support and the discussions and valuable comments and remarks during the supervision of the reconstruction.

December, 1997

Fig. 11. Before West Breakwater failure under wave attack, 7 - 8 Feb. storm

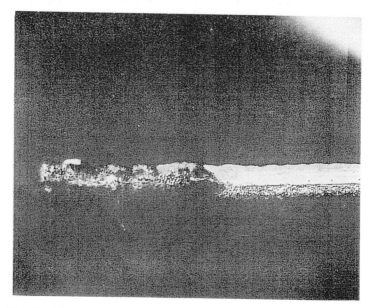

Fig. 12. After West Breakwater failure under wave attack, 7 - 8 Feb. storm

Development and Implementation of a Coastal Defence Strategy for Reculver, North Kent.

S.M. M°Farland and E.R. Edwards, Canterbury City Council, Kent, U.K.

Introduction.

On 25th January 1996 a section of seawall at Reculver in North Kent (UK) collapsed due to undermining of the toe following a prolonged period of northeasterly winds. The seawall is owned by English Heritage and protects the ruins of a Roman Fort and Medieval Church from coastal erosion. Undermining of the adjacent seawall and concrete access steps belonging to the Environment Agency had also occurred leading to partial collapse of the seawall apron.

Canterbury City Council, acting on behalf of English Heritage, carried out temporary repairs to the failed section of seawall. The repairs involved toe stabilisation works followed by treating the exposed slopes with a 75 mm skin of sprayed concrete. Repairs to the Environment Agency seawall involved filling voids with mass concrete and toe protection works using imported rock armour and local shingle recycling.

The Reculver site falls within the boundaries of management unit 5E (Reculver to Minnis Bay) as defined in the North Kent Shoreline Management Plan[1]. This paper describes the process involved in preparing a Scheme Strategy Plan for 5E and the means of progressing towards the implementation of individual schemes. Currently, both the Scheme Strategy Plan and the Engineers' reports for phase 1 works are with MAFF awaiting approval.

For the purposes of description, management unit 5E can be split into two sections, the Northern Sea Wall and Reculver, Figure 1. The Northern Sea Wall comprises the bulk of the management unit having a length of 4.4 km currently protected by an assortment of seawalls and fronted by a shingle beach. The beach is maintained by rock and timber groynes. Reculver, at the western end of the management unit comprises a melange of seawalls with a total length of about 600m. There is little or no beach present in front of the seawall at Reculver.

Description of Site.

Historical Background & Coastal Evolution.

Reculver Roman Fort and Medieval Church is sited on a low hill which delineates the western entrance to the historic Wantsum Channel. Up until the 18th century this channel separated the Thanet from the rest of Kent. Reculver Fort, together with a sister fort at Richborough, protected an important military and trade shipping route which passed through the Wantsum Channel. In 669AD a monastery was constructed within the boundaries of the abandoned Roman Fort. The

Coastlines, structures and breakwaters. Thomas Telford, London, 1998

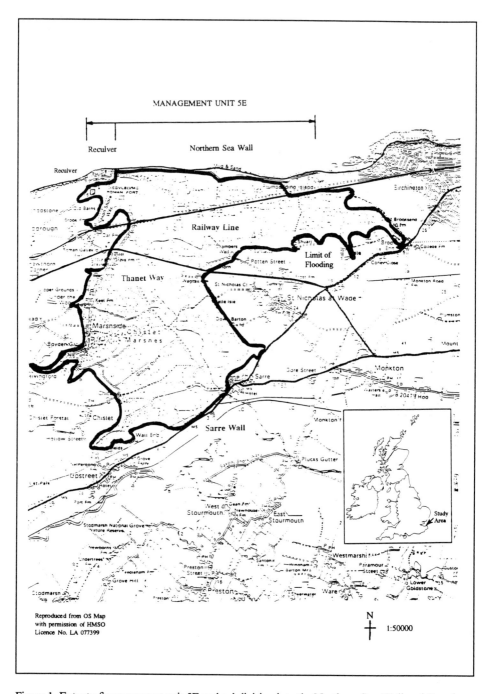

Figure 1. Extent of management unit 5E and subdivision into the Northern Sea Wall and Reculver.

church is now in ruins apart from the impressive twin towers which were added in the 13th century. These towers are a well known landmark and have been used for navigational purposes. The whole site is designated as a Scheduled Ancient Monument attracting the highest level of protection from English Heritage.

The historic evolution of the coastline is linked to the artificial reclamation and silting of the Wantsum Channel and the erosion of the cliffs at each side of the channel's northern entrance. Historic evidence suggests that the sandstone cliffs on the west side eroded at an average rate of 2 metres per year. This is consistent with rates of erosion observed at other locations on the North Kent coast. Inland the reclamation works on both banks of the tidal Wantsum Channel continued through the 8th to 18th centuries. Final closure of the Wantsum Channel occurred in the late 18th century when an embankment seawall was constructed along the line of the current defences. Coastal erosion at the site of the Roman Fort and Medieval Church continued up until 1810 when a stone revetment was constructed. By this time however the entire north eastern corner of the Roman Fort had been lost to the sea and the church had been abandoned and partly demolished.

Flooding and Erosion Hazards.

As a result of the 1953 storm, the Northern Sea Wall was breached in two places and floodwaters inundated the low lying farmland. The embankment which carried the railway line failed and trains were disrupted for over 6 months. Floodwaters continued southwards breaching the Thanet Way, finally halting at the Sarre Wall, Figure 1.

The majority of the land at risk is used for agricultural production although there are also some commercial and residential properties which would be subject to flooding. Failure of seawalls along the Northern Sea Wall would lead to immediate flooding of the low lying land however, the presence of secondary flood embankments could reduce the immediate impacts. Both the main London to East Kent rail and road links bisect the potential floodplain and could be breached.

Failure of the defences at Reculver itself would not lead to flooding straight away since the land immediately behind the seawalls is slightly higher. However, the level of the land falls away inland such that continued erosion would lead to the flooding of the area behind the Northern Sea Wall. It is estimated that 10 to 15 years of erosion would be required to bring about this situation. In the meantime, the Reculver Ancient Monument would be lost along with any buried archaeology. The gradual reduction in the height of the eroding cliffline would also increase the impact of localised flooding in the Reculver caravan parks and associated commercial properties.

Nature of Existing Defences and Coastal Defence Responsibility.

Coastal defence responsibilities in management unit 5E are split between Canterbury City Council (CCC), the Environment Agency (EA) and English Heritage (EH). CCC is the Coast Protection Authority for the largest part of Reculver however EH own and maintain some of the seawalls. The Environment Agency, as the Land Drainage Authority, maintain the bulk of the defences in the management unit including the entire length of the Northern Sea Wall and two short sections of seawall at Reculver.

Seawalls along the Northern Sea Wall were constructed in the early to mid 1950's. All are in a reasonable state of repair however, they depend on the presence of a large shingle beach to avoid undermining of the toe or damage to the seawall aprons. The land behind the seawall is low lying so that a breach in the seawall would lead to extensive flooding. A beach recharge scheme was completed along the Northern Sea Wall in late 1995 which included the construction of fourteen rock groynes to replace the timber groynes which were beyond economic repair.

Construction of the defences at Reculver dates from the early 19th century through to the early 1970's. With the exception of a short section of seawall where a rock revetment was constructed as part of the Northern Sea Wall project, all the defences are in a poor state of repair with residual lives of less than five years.

The existing defences are summarised in Table 1 where the coastline has been split into 11 sub-units, each of which has a similar character / residual life. The first 5 sub-units make up the defences at Reculver with the remainder comprising the Northern Sea Wall. In each case, the residual lives given assume that no further work, including beach recharge, is carried out.

Sub-unit	Length (m)	Description	Residual Life (yrs)
		RECULVER	
5E.1	220	Recurved concrete seawall and apron	5
5E.2	190	Full height rock revetment (+6.0 mAOD)	50
5E.3	90	Ragstone block flange apron	2
5E.4	80	Concrete wall with ragstone block backslope	1
5E.5	95	Interlocking block apron	1
		NORTHERN SEA WALL	
5E.6	1330	Seawall and apron fronted by shingle beach	20
5E.7	770	Seawall and apron fronted by shingle beach	20
5E.8	680	Saline lagoon fronted by shingle barrier	10
5E.9	680	Seawall and apron fronted by shingle beach	10
5E.10	410	Saline lagoon fronted by shingle barrier	20
5E.11	630	Seawall and apron fronted by shingle beach	5

Table 1. Nature of Existing Defences.

Requirement for a Strategic Approach to Coastal Defences.

The repairs carried out in early 1996 to the failed seawalls were intended as a temporary measure allowing investigations to be carried out to determine an appropriate long term coastal defence policy. Whilst considering a solution to the problems at Reculver, it became apparent that it would be necessary to adopt a strategic approach which examined the management unit as a whole before further works were promoted.

The reasons for pursuing a strategic approach are as follows:

- there is a process linkage throughout management unit 5E,

- there is a interconnection in the benefit areas since the same assets are put at risk by failures in defences at both the Northern Sea Wall and Reculver,
- the environmental impacts of the defence policy chosen would affect areas beyond the immediate limits of a scheme,
- the most likely solution, beach management, involved a long term policy of beach recharge and recycling,
- there was the potential for executing works at more than one location with the benefit of savings in construction costs.

It was agreed that Canterbury City Council should act as the lead Authority with responsibility for preparing a Scheme Strategy Plan for Management Unit 5E. Work on the strategy was carried out in-house commencing in January 1997. The original framework for the Scheme Strategy Plan underwent minor amendments as the study developed and as a result of the publication of MAFF's Interim Guidance for Strategic Planning[2]. Studies were carried out in two parts, the Strategy Plan and the Implementation Plan, the various stages of which are shown in Figure 2.

Strategy Plan.

The basis for commencing any strategic study is the higher level plans which in this case is the Shoreline Management Plan (SMP). The North Kent SMP, completed in September 1996, examines the wider influences on coastal processes, land use and the environment which are likely to dictate the regional coastal defence policy. The recommendation for management unit 5E was to hold the existing line.

The first stage was to define the boundaries of the study. Normally, these coincide with a management unit or group of management units which have been identified in the SMP. In this case, management unit 5E was considered to be a sufficiently discrete length of coastline to proceed with the preparation of a Scheme Strategy Plan. The adjacent management unit to the west, (5D), consists of freely eroding sandstone cliffs and has a defence policy of doing nothing. To the east, management unit 6A marks an abrupt change from shingle to sand beaches.

Recent guidelines published by MAFF[2] reinforce the view that, due to the scale at which SMP's have been produced, the strategy recommendations can be somewhat "broad brush" and it is necessary to further develop policy options over sections of the coastline. This involves additional investigations of coastal processes, environmental impacts and economic justification.

Coastal hydraulics and resulting beach mobility in North Kent have been studied by Canterbury City Council for a number of years[3]. These studies have resulted in the development of a coastal numerical model which has been calibrated using actual data on wave conditions and beach profiles collected over the last two decades. The model was extended eastwards to provide a hydraulic modelling framework for the whole of management unit 5E.

Once the preliminary studies on processes, land use and the environment were completed, the boundaries of the strategy plan were reviewed to ensure that management unit 5E was sufficiently discrete in terms of processes and benefits. It was found that whilst there were no major linkages to the other management units, there was a possibility that some strategy options could impact on neighbouring units. Where this is this case, the strategy option studies need to assess the likely

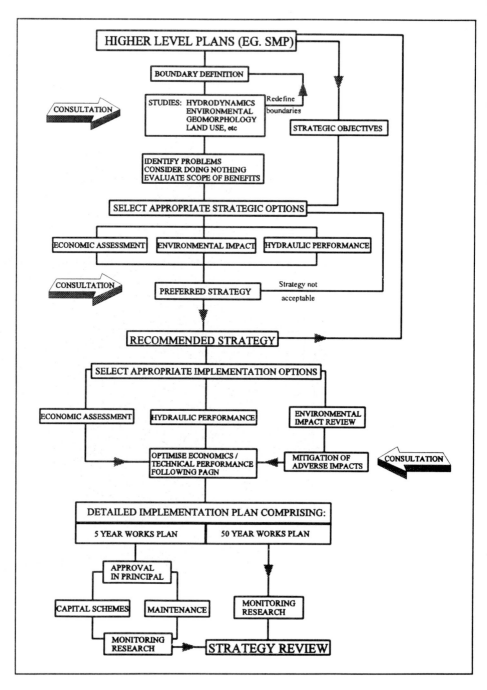

Figure 2. Flow Chart showing elements of Scheme Strategy Plan and relationship to SMP.

impacts and suggest the extent of mitigation required.

Management Unit Objectives.

Management unit objectives arise from the recommendations within the SMP, the results of the further studies detailed above and public consultation. Once collated, the objectives were split into nine broad groups with common aims. These groups, which are termed Environmental Concern Areas (ECAs), are as follows:

- geology, geomorphology and coastal processes,
- archaeological and historical,
- landscape and visual,
- ecological and ornithological,
- fisheries,
- social and economic,
- amenity and leisure,
- noise, vibration, air quality, water quality and climate,
- safety.

An environmental study was undertaken to assess the importance of each ECA and compile a list of objectives which future strategy options would aim to achieve. It should be appreciated that not all of the objectives will be achievable as it is likely that the means of delivering some objectives will be detrimental to others. Consultation with all bodies which were likely to have an interest in the future defence provision was carried out and feedback incorporated into the strategy at this stage.

The importance of the ecological designations are of particular interest. The whole of management unit 5E falls within the Thanet Coast and Sandwich Bay Special Protection Area and Ramsar Site. A pair of saline lagoons located along the Northern Sea Wall are identified as priority habitats in the UK Biodiversity Action Plan and the Thanet Coast SSSI extends throughout the site. The site is an important wintering area for migrating birds and a breeding ground for several rare species. English Nature are particularly concerned that the site should not be disturbed at sensitive times in the year.

Strategy Options.

Eight strategy options for the long term management of unit 5E were considered;

- do nothing,
- managed retreat to the Sarre Wall,
- managed retreat to the Thanet Way,
- managed retreat to the Chalk Wall / Railway Line, (4 sub-options),
- hold the line using new seawalls / repairs to the existing walls, (2 sub-options),
- hold the line using rock revetments,
- hold the line using beach management,
- advance the line by constructing new seawalls / beaches.

The aim of the strategy plan was to examine these eight options in sufficient detail to determine the broad technical requirements of any necessary engineering works, including maintenance, and to assess the environmental impacts and economic consequences of pursuing each option. This allowed decisions to be made on whether the strategy option itself was likely to be sustainable in the long term and enabled a comparison to be made between the alternative strategies.

In order to maintain consistency between the various "do something" strategy options, a minimum standard of service for overtopping was set at 20 l/m/s during the 100 year storm. This level was determined from a preliminary analysis of residual flooding.

For each option an environmental impact assessment was carried out. The environmental performance of each strategy option was graded on a scale of 1 to 5, (where 1 is a major adverse impact, 5 is a major beneficial impact and 3 is no change), for each of the nine ECAs. An overall positive environmental rating was obtained if a score of greater than 3 was achieved for most ECAs. No attempt was made to weight the ECA scores to reflect their relative importance and therefore the environmental ratings need to be treated objectively.

Costs for each option were determined on the basis of engineering works required and the value of assets lost. For the purposes of estimating, construction costs within the individual management sub-units were delayed until the year prior to anticipated seawall failure. This avoided the high up front costs associated with the adoption of a new strategy involving the replacement of existing defences before the end of their useful life. All costs were discounted to obtain the equivalent present value cost (pv) for comparison purposes. Results are summarised in Table 2.

Option	Description	P.V. Costs (£ million)	Environmental Rating
1	do nothing,	94.9	-15
2	retreat to Sarre Wall,	43.5	-13
3	retreat to Thanet Way,	33.7	-12
4A(i)	retreat to the railway line*	8.4	-7
4A(ii)	retreat to the railway line	7.3	-9
4B(i)	retreat to the railway/ Rushbourne Wall*	8.1	-5
4B(ii)	retreat to the railway/ Rushbourne Wall	7.1	-7
5A	hold the line using new seawalls	8.5	-9
5B	hold the line using emergency repairs	5.0	-12
6	hold the line using rock revetments,	5.2	-1
7	hold the line using beach management	4.9	+7
8	advance the line	33.2	-6

* existing seawall maintained with limited breaches permitted.

Table 2. Present value costs and environmental ratings for strategy options.

The do nothing option resulted in the loss of the ancient monument, inundation of farmland as far south as the Sarre Wall and the breaching of the road and rail links. It was determined that the costs of losing the transport links can be capped by constructing new links to the south of the Sarre Wall. Overall the do nothing option resulted in costs of around £95 million (pv), combined with a large negative environmental impact.

Retreating the line involves constructing new coastal defences inland of the existing structures. To minimise costs, the alternative retreated lines were chosen to coincide with existing embankment structures. In all cases the existing embankments need to be raised and have riprap placed on their seaward face. Of the retreat options considered, the most reasonable was the option to retreat the line to the Chalk Wall providing protection to road and rail links. Four sub-options were considered, the most feasible of which protected the ancient monument and allowed 250 ha of farmland to flood. Except for two discrete breaches the existing seawalls would remain in place so that the flooded area would be sufficiently protected to allow saltmarsh to develop. The present value costs of this option was £6.9 million with a small negative environmental impact. An alternative option to abandon the existing seawall completely would necessitate additional raising of the newly retreated defences and would rule out the likelihood of saltmarsh creation due to the high levels of wave energy. The present value cost of this alternative option was slightly lower at £5.8 million but it has a larger negative environmental impact.

Of the two hold the line options using seawalls, emergency repairs was the least cost at £5.0 million. Both options have a large negative environmental impact with emergency repairs being the least acceptable due to the continued need for construction works during the sensitive winter period. Construction of a rock revetment which provided protection against toe erosion and reduced overtopping was considered to be a reasonable solution having a small negative environmental impact and present value costs of £5.2 million. Maintenance requirements with this option were low. Beach management is the policy currently practised along the Northern Sea Wall and has an overall positive environmental impact. Allowing for the cost of additional rock groynes and beach recharges throughout the 50 years life of the strategy, this was the least cost option.

It was found that costs could be reduced further by adopting a combined strategy using beach management at the Northern Sea Wall and either rock revetments or emergency repairs at Reculver. The present value of this hybrid option was £3.7 million. Savings result from removing the relatively high costs involved in providing and maintaining a beach at Reculver where the foreshore is very low and there is no existing beach or beach control structures at present. Further, because of the orientation of the coastline at Reculver, beach maintenance costs were high. Additional studies indicated that the use of a combined strategy such as this would not cause conflict either within management unit 5E itself or with the adjacent units. A benefit cost ratio of 25 was obtained for this option and was demonstrated to be robust under a range of scenarios.

The preferred solution arising from the strategy study was therefore to hold the existing line using a combination of beach management along the Northern Sea Wall and rock revetments at Reculver. Results of the strategy study and environmental impact assessment were made available to consultees and the public were advised via local newspapers. At the end of this consultation period, the preferred strategy was adopted as the recommended strategy with the findings to be incorporated into the next revision of the SMP.

Implementation Plan.

Having determined the preferred strategy, several implementation options were considered with the aim of optimising the economic and technical performance of possible solutions. The end product of the implementation study being two scheme plans, detailing project requirements for both the next 5 years and for the full 50 years of the strategy. Because there are different policies for Reculver and the Northern Sea Wall, the two were treated separately in the implementation study. The options chosen were based on the strategy recommendations and included a range of performance levels from do minimum up to at least the indicative standard of protection.

For Reculver the following implementation options were considered:

- do minimum emergency repairs,
- wall repairs and toe revetment,
- wall repairs and minor beach replenishments,
- rock revetment with crest height of +5.0m AOD,
- rock revetment with crest height of +6.0m AOD.

Present value construction and residual flooding costs of these five options for each sub-unit are given in Table 3. An environmental impact review was carried out which included information obtained from the consultation process. This information was used to prepare an Environmental Impact Mitigation report, the findings of which were incorporated into the design of the five implementation options.

Implementation option.	sub-unit 5E.1 (costs in £k)	sub-unit 5E.3 (costs in £k)	sub-unit 5E.4 (costs in £k)	sub-unit 5E.5 (costs in £k)
emergency repairs (do minimum)	549.7 (52.8)	315.5 (nil)	242.1 (nil)	358.9 (68.6)
toe revetment and wall repairs	485.8 (52.8)	313.6 (nil)	145.7 (nil)	361.2 (26.8)
small beach and wall repairs	858.5 (23.6)	612.4 (nil)	321.2 (nil)	621.9 (18.9)
rock revetment (to +5.0 mAOD)	654.2 (26.8)	424.6 (nil)	216.6 (nil)	335.3 (18.9)
rock revetment (to +6.0 mAOD)	716.5 (3.9)	434.9 (nil)	233.2 (nil)	360.0 (2.6)

Table 3. Present value capital / 50 yr maintenance and residual flooding (in brackets) costs.

Carrying out emergency repairs to sections of seawall as failures occur has a high level of uncertainty since the risk of failure is difficult to assess. The cost of this option was based on the actual costs involved in the temporary repairs to the failed seawalls carried out in 1996.

There are two seawall repair and toe protection options, one using rock the other a small beach. The toe rock revetment option, Figure 3, had low maintenance requirements and was low in cost. Because of the instability of shingle beaches at Reculver, the beach option had high maintenance costs and could not guaranteed protection to the toe at all times.

The use of rock revetments reduced wave overtopping however, the additional rock costs were not justified by the reduction in localised flooding. The recommended implementation option consists of seawall repairs and toe rock revetments at each of the Reculver sub-units with the exception of the Eastern Wall. Here a rock revetment to +5.0 mAOD was considered appropriate due to the additional protection it provided to both the seawall and the land behind. Whilst the overtopping rates during the design storm are above the limits quoted in the SMP, the residual flooding costs are low and the reduced levels of protection were considered to be acceptable.

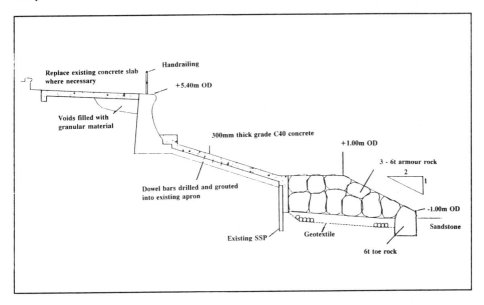

Figure 3. Typical section through seawall repairs and toe revetment.

The situation along the Northern Sea Wall is somewhat different in that the existing coastal defences are in a reasonable condition with a large shingle beach retained by rock groynes. The relative stability of the beach here is due to the orientation of the coastline which is close to equilibrium and the fact that improvements have recently been made to the defences along this frontage. There is however inadequate data on the behaviour of the new beach which has hampered a proper assessment of future implementation options.

Four beach maintenance options were considered ranging from a smaller beach than exists at present to an option involving raising the existing groynes and enlarging the beach. Each option was assessed to determine the optimum beach levels and replenishment requirements.

It was found that maintaining the beach at its 1995 design levels was the best solution.

Studies of shingle movement based on the numerical model suggest that it may be necessary to construct an additional 3 rock groynes along this frontage to improve beach retention. Due to uncertainties in how the new beach will behave, it was considered prudent to allow a period of five years of data collection before options for additional groynes or other major changes were considered. Therefore, whilst major replenishments and new groynes were programmed in the 50 year plan, the 5 year plan is mainly limited to beach recycling and monitoring.

Conclusions.

The preparation of a scheme strategy plan for management unit 5E has required high levels of cooperation between the Environment Agency, English Heritage and Canterbury City Council, all of which have coastal defence interests in the area. Such cooperation will be increasingly expected as coastal management policy continues to move away from the practice of working within administrative boundaries.

The concept of Scheme Strategy Plans is relatively new and there are few previous investigations to guide the Engineer in their preparation. Higher level plans, such as the SMP, provide a direction for the strategic studies however, the range of options considered should not be constrained by the SMP recommendations. Provided that economic and environmental issues have been adequately addressed in the Scheme Strategy Plan, the implementation of the individual projects should be more straightforward.

The format of the Reculver strategy was such that the concerns of interested parties were addressed at an early stage, reducing the potential for conflicts of interest to occur once a preferred solution had been identified. The Engineer needs to be proactive and eager to obtain and understand the views of the consultees. Clear feedback to consultees on how the project is progressing and how their views are being incorporated is vital.

Scheme Strategy Plans play an important role in the hierarchy of coastal management. Detailed studies allow for the scrutinisation and updating of Shoreline Management Plans and at the same time, provide a framework for executing individual schemes. Consultations can be carried out to resolve local problems as well as taking account of nationally or internationally designated sites. Finally the Scheme Strategy Plan can provide an effective mechanism for overcoming the difficulties associated with promoting schemes across administrative boundaries.

References.

1. Halcrow (1996), North Kent Coast, Shoreline Management Plan, (volumes 1 & 2).

2. MAFF (July 1997), Interim Guidance for the Strategic Planning and Appraisal of Flood and Coastal Defence Schemes.

3. Canterbury City Council (1994), Coastal Management Study II (3 parts).

Dinas Dinlle Coastal Works

MR. A.J. WILLIAMS BSc, CEng., MICE. Shoreline Management Partnership, Rossett, UK, and MR. M.F. DAVIES, Environment Agency, Bangor, UK.

SYNOPSIS
The coastal frontage of Dinas Dinlle lies on the west facing coast of Caernarfon Bay in North Wales and extends along a two kilometre stretch of largely sand and shingle foreshore (Figure 1).

The frontage can be split into two discrete lengths :

- A 500 m length at the southern end that provides protection to the developed village area and abuts a coastal site of Special Scientific Interest - Frontage `A'.

- A 1500 m length to the north fronting largely low quality agricultural grazing land, interspersed with a number of isolated farming and holiday properties - Frontage `B'.

Jurisdiction for coastal defence along the frontage was historically shared between the Local District Council and the National Rivers Authority.

Flooding of the area has occurred since Victorian Times and according to available records is largely attributable to two sources:

- Land Drainage   - Tidal Inundation

An eroding upper foreshore with a concomitant increase in wave energy impacting the shoreline, finally breached the defences during the severe storms of February 1990 effectively marooning a number of properties on the Morfa to the north of the village, and causing flooding damage to land and infrastructure within the village.

A scheme to provide an appropriate standard of defence along the frontage was carried out during the first half of 1994 comprising the construction of two rock promontories and associated beach nourishment to protect the village frontage(A), coupled with a policy of selective beach nourishment over the service life of the scheme, whilst allowing the coastline to revert to its natural location across the remainder of the frontage(B). In order to allow for this policy of `Managed Retreat' over frontage `B' a secondary flood embankment was constructed to provide protection to the isolated properties and the agricultural land and to allow for eventual re-location of the existing coast road, that runs immediately behind the present shoreline to a setback position on top of the embankment, at an appropriate time in the future.

Coastlines, structures and breakwaters. Thomas Telford, London, 1998

The scheme was promoted by the then National Rivers Authority (Welsh Region), under sea defence legislation, who received a contribution towards the cost of the Works and on-going management of the frontage from the Coast Protection Authority (Arfon B.C. now Gwynedd Council). Consulting Engineers for the scheme were Shoreline Management Partnership.

Following scheme completion a regime of beach monitoring and management was initiated to provide for cost effective on-going management of the complete frontage.

HISTORY AND PROBLEM DEFINITION

The village of Dinas Dinlle lies on the west facing coast of Caernarfon Bay in North Wales, to the south of the Isle of Anglesey at approximate OS grid ref. 243500, 356500, with the specific local area of interest extending over approximately 2 km of shoreline orientated NNW/SSE. Over this length there is a transition from boulder clay cliffs to the south to low lying marshland and plain to the north.

The general location of the area is shown in Fig. 1 which identifies key features on the frontage.

From the Mound just to the south of the village, the clay cliffs give way to much lower lying land the majority of which is only just above Highest Astronomical Tide level and therefore prone to flooding from overtopping of sea defences during times of storm. With the north end of the shoreline effectively forming a peninsula (the Afon Foryd outfalls through a tidal flap into Foryd Bay and thence into the Menai Straits) tidal inundation, either from overtopping or associated rising ground water levels can effectively stand with only slow discharge through a series of ditches as tide levels drop.

Foreshore conditions along the whole of this section of coastline are generally uniform consisting of sand, shingle and boulders derived from erosion of the cliffs. In front of Dinas Dinlle there is flat lower foreshore of sand, backed with a steep shingle ridge extending up to high water levels. To the north of Caernarfon Airfield the upper beach continues as a fairly narrow bank of shingle before widening out, backed by sand dunes on the approaches to the Menai Straits.

Over the first five hundred metres of frontage north of the Mound, the hinterland has been developed with a series of residential properties and hotels (many of which are used as holiday homes) and a number of shops providing services for the local population and holiday visitors. To the north of the village however there are only isolated properties surrounded by generally low grade agricultural land used largely for sheep grazing.

Historical evidence suggests that during the last century the shoreline has been in modest retreat of between 0.2 to 0.3 metres per annum which had until relatively recently been generally of little consequence, even though there are records of flooding (on extreme events) from Victorian times. With the progressive retreat of the shoreline and the concomitant diminishing protection provided by the natural defences, the frequency of overtopping increased and the need to provide man made protection resulted in the construction of a box gabion sea wall in the 1970's to effectively hold the shoreline to seaward of the road that now passed through the village and served the Airfield to the north (the only access for vehicles to this establishment). Holding the line in the form chosen however did not halt the deterioration of the natural beach protection which instead of rolling progressively to landward was now eroding downwards with a consequent increase in the wave energy impacting the shoreline. The gabion wall effectively removed the natural shingle ridge from the littoral drift and this area was utilised as a car park.

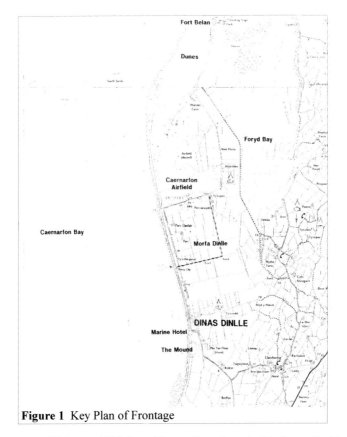

Figure 1 Key Plan of Frontage

During the storms of February 1990 the gabion wall was breached to the north side of the village with twofold consequences :

(a)   the low lying mainland was flooded effectively marooning the isolated properties for a number of days.

(b)   due to the topography of the hinterland, overtopping waters flowed back towards the village and flooded a number of properties within the developed frontage.

Littoral drift of sediment is nett longshore from south to north with wave induced effects being generally the mobiliser of shoreline sediments which are then moved longshore by the flood dominated tidal currents applying across the frontage. The foreshore across the Dinas Dinlle frontage is therefore formed by tidal and wave energies acting in concert upon the eroding cliffs to the south and thereby carrying material northwards through and on to the Morfa Dinlle frontage.

The general behaviour of sediments is shown schematically in Figure 2.

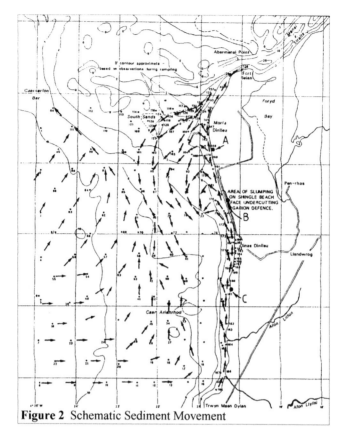

Figure 2 Schematic Sediment Movement

Holding of the coastline by the artificial defences has prevented the shoreline reaching a position of natural equilibrium to landward of its present line and future behaviour is very much a function of a combination of natural and man made influences as follows :

□   The eroding clay cliffs to the south of Dinas Dinlle.

□   The south end of the artificial defences (the Marine Hotel), that marks a change in shoreline orientation from N/S to NNW by SSE orientation along Dinas Dinlle, is a man made promontory that pushes the longshore currents away from the shoreline providing limited shelter to the developed section.

□   The north end of the village frontage, 500 metres from the Marine Hotel where the longshore currents have re-established themselves against the shoreline, causing increased longshore drift.

□   A point some 2000 metres further to the north where the shoreline changes orientation again on the approach to the Menai Straits and equilibrium conditions generally prevail.

Following the February 1990 storms a Coastal Study was carried out by Posford Duvivier on behalf of the then Coast Protection Authority (Arfon Borough Council) to pull together and examine relevant data with a view to identifying a way forward to providing improved coastal defences along the frontage. The study considered a range of solution options including :

- Offshore breakwaters;
- Shingle beach replenishment;
- Linear Armour Stone Protection.

Examination of coastal process behaviour therefore concluded that any scheme of further intervention had to address a number of key issues :

- Protection of the low lying developed and if appropriate non-developed hinterland.

- Minimal interference to existing coastal processes such that shorelines to the north were not adversely affected.

However it was clear that the economic case for carrying out large scale intervention work such as bolstering up the existing sea wall along the whole frontage would not be viable due to the low value of assets at risk particularly north of the developed frontage.

The economic case for intervention rested on the following criteria :

- Flooding and erosion losses to property and infrastructure in the village from frequent overtopping and breaches in the existing defences leading ultimately to setback of the shoreline;

- Loss of the coastal road as the only viable access to the Caernarfon Airfield and some isolated properties.

and whilst the initial solution options considered above were in isolation, either technically, economically or environmentally non-viable, they did provide the basis for development of a scheme that would be acceptable in all three categories.

SCHEME DEVELOPMENT

Natural process definition enabled the shoreline to be split into four discrete segments however before appropriate technical alternatives could be considered it was necessary for a reasonable handle to be gained on the scheme costs that could be justified set against the benefits applying.

The earlier benefit assessments had concluded that the loss of access road to the Caernarfon Airport would cause a £200,000 loss in income per annum which equated to approximately £3.0 million in nett present terms over the scheme design life. However the provision of a new access inland of the equilibrium position of the shoreline, provided a much reduced alternative to the in perpetuity loss of income the Airport would suffer.

Other benefits attributable to the scheme were evaluated under the following headings :

- <u>Business Disruption Losses</u>: Short term losses of income and stocks due to breaching and overtopping of the defences following particular storm events.

◻   Property Flooding Losses: Flood damage to properties along the developed section of frontage.

◻   Property Erosion Losses: Breaching of the defences would lead eventually to shoreline recession as the shingle ridge rolled back to an equilibrium position, with a consequent total loss of some properties along the developed frontage.

Agricultural losses were negligible due to the extremely low level usage and value associated with the land.

The total discounted present value of benefits applying for the frontage over the fifty year design life of the scheme equated to about £2.5 million (1993 prices).

The split of benefits was heavily weighted as would be expected towards the developed section of frontage with only about 20% of the total benefit set against the section to the north of the village, however this section was critical being the most vulnerable to storm damage - the 1990 breach had occurred in this section.

Even at benefit values in excess of £2.0 million it was clear that a total linear protection was not viable. Typically per metre run costs of between £1,500 and £2,000 would have produced a total capital cost for the two kilometre frontage of £3-4 million.

Furthermore 75% of that cost would be attributable to the section to the north of the village.

More importantly the longshore movement of sediment and gradual erosion of the foreshore would not have been halted by a linear construction which would in time have required further capital toe works to be constructed. It was therefore necessary to segment the frontage.

An Environmental Statement was carried out for the proposed intervention by SGS Environment.

In environmental terms there were a number of specific criteria that were identified during consultations that took place during Statement preparation :

◻   The section to the south of the village - 'The Mound' - was within the Dinas Dinlle Site of Special Scientific Interest, the northerly boundary of which was at the southern end of the gabion wall adjacent to the Marine Hotel. The specific interests associated with the site arose from the geological formation associated with the boulder clay cliffs. On top of the clay cliffs however an ancient burial site was situated which if the cliffs continued to erode would be threatened. It was important therefore for any proposals in respect of this frontage to achieve a balance between preserving the archaeological resource whilst maintaining the scientific interest associated with the eroding cliff frontage.

Any coastal defences would therefore need to avoid any significant impact on exposure conditions at the Mound.

◻   The beach consisted of glacial river shingle material and any reinforcement of the beach or coastal structures would need to be of a form or material type that was not foreign to the area and blended in with the existing materials.

□   The need to allow as far as possible for the minimum of interference to the drift regime applying across the frontage.

The Mound frontage was included in segment 1 south of the Marine Hotel where only accommodation works were proposed (Figure 3). These works were included to preserve existing conditions thereby allowing for continued erosion of the Mound frontage whilst the new regime settled down after construction of the main scheme. The works comprised a re-nourishment of the beach with natural shingle to compensate for temporary littoral changes. The frontage would be monitored at regular intervals with further nourishment as appropriate to maintain the current conditions applying at the Mound.

In segment 2 across the developed frontage it was proposed to construct a natural armour stone bastion extending approximately 60 metres offshore and shaped in plan to divert longshore drifts around its seaward extremity and provide some localised wave shelter to the north. At the northern end of this section of frontage a further shore-connected breakwater was to be constructed. These two structures to be formed from natural armour stone.

The breakwater would extend approximately 120 metres offshore and be `fishtail' shaped in plan to allow for improved beach stability to either side. This breakwater shape is derived from consideration of shore-normal and shore-parallel behaviour of structures and combines the best attributes of these two basic structure types. In between the two breakwaters the existing beach would be reinforced with nature stone of small boulder and cobble size grading - infilled and covered with shingle-sized material to facilitate access across the upper section. This material forms a pocket beach between the breakwaters and due to its increased size and improved shelter, would be much less mobile during storm activity than the indigenous material. It was not proposed to lift the crest levels of the existing beach above present sea wall levels but the berm width of the beach at crest level was extended.

The overall length of the two breakwaters was set from consideration of :

□   distance of natural shingle ridge location to landward of present shoreline.

□   potential on-shore migration of beach material during storm events.

□   relative orientation and location of breakwater extremities to determine extent of longshore drift diversion and recovery distance.

The curvature orientation and longshore extent of the breakwater arms was set from consideration of the inshore wavelength; rate of change of current direction and energy reduction requirements at the shoreline.

The works when completed would provide the necessary level of coastal protection and sea defence for the Dinas Dinlle village frontage.

In the third segment it was proposed to carry out some localised beach reinforcement immediately to the north of the shore-connected breakwater to provide a transition to the natural conditions that would develop further to the north. Any breaches of the sea wall and erosion of the hinterland would initially be reinstated on an `as-required' basis using beach reinforcement material to allow 'management' of the recession until such time that the breaches affected the coastal road, which would then be re-located inland using a macadam construction on a new embankment (constructed as part of the capital works) located to landward of the equilibrium shoreline (assuming adequate shingle material either imported or derived from natural drift). A ditch was to be constructed over the seaward length of this embankment to feed overtopping water in the short to medium term southwards to the ditch running inland across the Morfa to the Afon Foryd at the northern end of the village.

A ditch running along the boundary of the village was to be refurbished with the creation of a continuous bund along its southern flank to protect the village from inundation by overtopping water from the north. Protection to the village was to be completed by a local raising of the highway to link the ditch bund level across to the new breakwater. In this way the natural shingle ridge would be progressively relocated further inland to the north of the village at its appropriate equilibrium location following construction of the Dinas Dinlle breakwater with the coastal road relocated to landward at an appropriate time in the future.

In segment 4 it was not proposed to carry out any coastal works but this section would be monitored as part of the on-going management programme.

The proposed scheme represented a hybrid approach from the various technical options available. It separates the village frontage and provides protection by means of nourishment and promontories.

The natural location for the shingle ridge north of the village was derived from historic beach profile analysis. Where there was significant beach drawdown and consequential wave reflection off the gabion wall the beach levels were artificially low from increased wave (reflected) energy. By overlay of beach profiles from nearby more stable sections of beach the necessary uplift was derived which allowed the profile to be extended landward using compound equilibrium slopes determined from material size and level relative to tide.

Longshore momentum is diverted offshore thereby improving the shelter of the undeveloped frontage north of the village. By diverting the principal access inland it is possible to let the natural shingle ridge re-establish itself to its preferred plan location with additional artificial nourishment provided to supplement the material behind the present defences which is a mixture of sand and shingle. The scheme however depends upon a post construction system of beach management and monitoring in order that changes to the shoreline particularly to the north of the village are introduced gradually with ultimate retreat of this section being effectively managed to avoid abrupt changes to shoreline behaviour.

On-going monitoring would develop following scheme completion, as discussed later however at the time the proposals were drawn up, the following preliminary specification was defined :

Annual   Survey of the boulder clay outcrops and cliff line at the southern end of the frontage.

Biannual   Inspection of the shoreline and survey of fixed beach profiles.

The proposed scheme (shown in Figure 3) therefore provided for initial capital works, backed up by coherent monitoring to determine appropriate timing of further action to sustain satisfactory protection for the community at Dinas Dinlle.

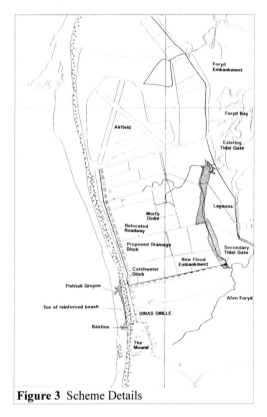

Figure 3 Scheme Details

The net present value of the proposals was approximately £1.3 million which included the on-going management of the shoreline and selected topping-up of beach levels north of the village. As such the scheme produced a comfortable benefit to cost ratio of just less than 2.0 and when considered against other potential alternatives was the most viable. Alternative schemes considered, provided a common approach for the sector north of the village but relied on different technical approaches for the village frontage.

WORKS CONSTRUCTION
The capital scheme constructed consisted of six specific elements :

- Marine Hotel Bastion
- Beach Nourishment
- E/W Flood Protection Bund
- Dinas Dinlle Fishtail Groyne
- N/S Flood embankment & associated drainage ditch
- Localised Highway Raising

Construction commenced in January 1994 and was substantially completed by the end of May that year.

Storms occurred in February (on the 4th Anniversary of the Towyn Event) which caused some localised lowering of foreshore levels against the then largely unprotected section of gabions along the frontage, however shortly after, the two rock structures were completed, followed within two months by the beach nourishment.

Construction of the works to landward of the shoreline was carried out in tandem with the beach works and required the excavation and re-use of approximately 20,000t of existing sand and shingle to form the drainage ditch and the E/W flood protection bund combined with the importation of nearly 80,000t of quarried fill to form the embankment.

Sourcing of materials for the Beach Works was relatively straightforward given the geographical position of the site. The North Wales coast is well served with quarries for armour stone.

The River Conwy forms a boundary between sedimentary carboniferous strata to the east and the largely igneous rocks to the west.

Both types of material have been used for coastal defence works along the North and Mid-Wales coasts with the latter being used primarily to provide the armour and bedstone for the breakwater structures as well as the fill material for the embankment and floodbank works.

The material used for re-charging the beach levels along the village frontage and for reinforcement of levels associated with managing the retreat of the shoreline comprised two specific types of material from two different sources :

- A washed gravel of nominal 150-40mm size from an inland pit close to the site, which derived from the same geographical source as the indigenous beach material.

- A larger quarried stone of typically 300-150mm in size from the same source(s) as the material used in the breakwater construction.

The need for two different types of material was defined from both technical and economic criteria, specifically :

- The quantity of washed gravel required was available from only one local source which therefore had an effective monopoly on supply, knowing that any other sources remote from the site were unlikely to be cost-effective. This material therefore carried a cost premium.

- The size of gravel material, in the quantities that were required was limited to 150mm maximum.

- A greater volume per metre run was required to achieve the same hydraulic performance for the gravel material than for the larger quarried stone.

- Experience of the use of quarried stone as beach nourishment material elsewhere on the North Wales coast, indicated that rounding of the material would occur over a relatively short period of time (< 10 years), thereby mitigating against the initial angular nature and texture of the material.

The scheme proposals to achieve an appropriate balance between technical performance, cost effectiveness and environmental acceptability comprised :

◻   To top up beach levels south of the Marine Hotel Bastion with the washed gravel material, where the use of other material would be alien in the vicinity of the clay cliffs.

◻   To improve levels between the two rock structures by introducing an underlayer of quarried material overlain by the gravel material. This approach provides for cost-effective construction whilst providing an indicator for the instigation of beach management actions when the quarried material becomes exposed.

◻   To use the quarried material north of the village to reinforce beach levels immediately to the north of the structure where the use of the smaller gravel material was inappropriate on this exposed length of coastline due to its more volatile behaviour under wave action.

BEACH MANAGEMENT AND MONITORING
The aims and objectives of the beach management at Dinas Dinlle are :

◻   to re-distribute and top-up with similar material (quarried sea-washed beach cobble) the imported beach to the south of the village linking into the `Mound' so that beach levels remain similar to those existing before the Works were introduced;

◻   to re-distribute and top-up with similar materials the imported beach between the structures along the village frontage ensuring that the quarried blasted rock material is generally covered with quarried sea-washed beach cobble after each beach management operation;

◻   to progressively release the shoreline to the north of the village by removal of the historic coastal defence structures and re-location of the highway so that it assumes a more natural form of shingle bank protection to the hinterland; intermediate works of `holding the line' locally using imported quarried blasted rock to be carried out until significant lengths of existing coastal defences become life-expired.

In order to monitor scheme performance and thereby define appropriate timescales for management of the shoreline along the whole of the frontage, a monitoring system has been developed that comprises the following elements :

◻   Biannual Surveys of strategic foreshore cross-sections, along the whole of the frontage including frontages to the north and south of the scheme;

◻   Annual Surveys of the areas around each of the rock structures;

◻   Annual collection of beach samples at a minimum of six locations longshore, at four tidal contours;

◻   Shoreline Inspections of the frontage, to coincide with the foreshore level survey.

In addition to the above offshore wave data from the Met. Office European Waters Wave Model and Recorded Still Water Level data is purchased to provide input data for the Analysis suite carried out, as followed :

□   Particle grading analysis of beach samples.

□   Tidal Contour Movement and Gradient analysis from beach profile data.

□   Analysis of the topographic surveys around each of the rock breakwaters using digital ground modelling techniques to establish erosion / accretion patterns around the structures.

□   Storm typicality assessment to appraise the significance of beach behaviour.

□   Longshore energy analysis to link beach behaviour to inshore wave climate.

□   Interpretation of the above data to predict likely beach behaviour and to provide input into the on-going beach management plan for the Dinas Dinlle frontage.

CURRENT POSITION
The performance of the scheme to date, some three years after it was completed, has generally been as expected with the following applying :

□   General longshore drift diversion around the village frontage with accretion of sand-sized sediments behind the Bastion structure but on-going erosion of the Mound maintained.

□   Significant lower beach accretion along the whole of the frontage indicated by a general seaward movement of the mean low water mark. This has manifested itself specifically in the formation of pocket beaches a) between the outer arms of the breakwater structures and b) on the north side of the fishtail groyne structure. These areas of beach have been well received not only from a coastal defence viewpoint but also in respect of their improved amenity value to the frontage, which has received a Blue Flag award since the scheme was constructed.

□   Seasonal movement of high water marks concomitant with impacting wave energies.

□   Landward movement of the higher water marks along the section of unreinforced shoreline north of the village.

The use of quarried material as beach reinforcement north of the village is considered (by certain parties), as being environmentally unacceptable on appearance grounds (shape and colour), however it is clear from visual observation that material imported along the frontage is rounding and blending in with the natural cobble that exists on the upper foreshore. It is not likely to be distinguishable in ten years time - the material is sourced from an updrift shoreline quarry.

During the past 18 months the existing gabion structures along the northerly section of shoreline have sustained damage and failure due to storm activity triggering their removal and beach re-profiling, in order to safeguard management objectives for the shoreline.

In the light of these events and the issues raised, including consultation with the Highway Authority, an intermediate action plan has been developed as follows :

☐   re-location of the road during 1997/98;

☐   removal of the remaining gabion defences over the northern frontage between the road to the airfield and the fishtail breakwater as they become life-expired but targeted for completion over the next five years.

☐   setback of the shoreline to win significant shingle from the hinterland area resulting in the existing car park area transferring to foreshore.

☐   monitoring of the released section of shoreline and to carry out work as required to maintain the minimum volume of shingle required between principal tidal contours.

An aerial photograph of the frontage, post-completion is shown in Figure 4.

Figure 4 Aerial Photograph of Completed Scheme

CONCLUSIONS

The Dinas Dinlle coastal defence scheme required a revised approach from previous, driven mainly by economics. The resultant works have conserved environmental value, improved amenity and provided sustainable defences for the local community. There is continual monitoring and management required to sustain the scheme to ensure that investments are limited to strict need derived from the regular measurements and inspections.

With the monitoring system largely in place annual re-appraisal of the conditions applying and their likely influence on the future behaviour of the shoreline together with fine tuning of the system, will be required to ensure that longer term performance criteria are met and the scheme is sustained as `fit for purpose'.

ACKNOWLEDGEMENTS
The authors wish to express their thanks to the Environment Agency for permission to produce this paper and to Dr. Philip Barber for his assistance in paper preparation.

REFERENCES

1. **GeoSea Consulting Ltd.**, The Sediment Transport Regime at Dinas Dinlle, Dec. 1990.

2. **Posford Duvivier**. Dinas Dinlle Report on Coastal Study, February 1991.

3. **Shoreline Management Partnership**, DINAS DINLLE Engineer's Report, July 1993.

4. **SGS Environment Ltd.**, DINAS DINLLE Environmental Statement, June 1993.

5. **Ministry of Agriculture, Fisheries & Food**, Coastal Defence and the Environment, A guide to good practice, 1993.

6. **Shoreline Management Partnership**, DINAS DINLLE COASTAL WORKS, Annual Monitoring Report, 1995

7. **Shoreline Management Partnership**, DINAS DINLLE COASTAL WORKS, Annual Monitoring Report, 1996

Monitoring of Cavallino beach (Venice - Italy)

P. DE GIROLAMO, University of Rome "La Sapienza", Rome, Italy, G. CECCONI, Consorzio Venezia Nuova, Venice, Italy, A. NOLI, University of Rome "La Sapienza", Rome, Italy, G. P. MARETTO, Consorzio Venezia Nuova, Venice, Italy, and P. CONTINI, Modimar s.r.l., Rome, Italy

SYNOPSIS
Cavallino and Pellestrina beaches, located in the North Adriatic sea along the venetian littoral, are subjected to erosion processes. To remedy the situation Consorzio Venezia Nuova decided in 1990 to undertake an artificial nourishment of the beaches (about 2×10^6 m^3 of sand for Cavallino and about 4×10^6 m^3 of sand for Pellestrina). The main function of the beaches is to protect the littoral from flooding. In order to maintain the beaches, a programme of beach monitoring has been activated. The present paper describes the programme and presents a risk analysis which will be used for the active management of the beaches.

INTRODUCTION
Venice is located in a lagoon protected from the Adriatic sea by two barrier islands, Lido and Pellestrina, and by the sand beaches of Cavallino and Sottomarina. Originally these natural islands were maintained by the regional sediment transport regime. In the last century the three lagoon inlets (called Lido, Malamocco and Chioggia) were gradually stabilised and protected by long jetties. Unfortunately, the construction of the jetties interrupted the natural longshore drift of sand to the barrier islands and as a consequence a strong erosion developed along Pellestrina and Lido beaches while Cavallino was formed to the north of the Lido inlet and Sottomarina was formed to the south of Chioggia inlet (see Fig 1). In order to reverse the erosion process, between 1750 and 1790, the Republic of Venice built rock armoured sloping sea-walls (called "murazzi") with intermittent rock groynes along Pellestrina and Lido. Nevertheless in the second part of the 20th century the erosion attacked the toe of the sea-walls, endangering their stability and the safety of the villages located in the islands. At the same time the north part of Cavallino beach was affected by a consistent erosion process.

To remedy the situation, Consorzio Venezia Nuova decided in 1990 to undertake artificial nourishment of the beaches along the littorals subjected to erosion. A new sand beach covering 10.2 km of frontage has been recently completed (April 1997) at Cavallino while at Pellestrina about 50% of the new beach has been built (at Pellestrina the completed new beach will cover 8.8 km of frontage). This works when finished will have requiring about 6×10^6 m^3 of new sand for both the littorals (about 2×10^6 m^3 for Cavallino and about 4×10^6 m^3 for Pellestrina). Both at Cavallino and at Pellestrina the new beaches are delineated longitudinally by rock groins. At Pellestrina the new beach is contained at its toe by a submerged sill. Furthermore along Cavallino some new dune areas protected by wind screens and stabilised by vegetation have been built. The beach nourishment design of Cavallino is showed by Fig. 2. More details concerning the design can be found in Silva and De Girolamo (1993), Noli et al. (1993), Cecconi and Maretto (1996) and Benassai et al. (1997).

Coastlines, structures and breakwaters. Thomas Telford, London, 1998

The adopted solution based upon soft defences requires a careful programme of beach monitoring and maintenance. During the design of the new beaches, numerical and physical test models were used in order to provide a prediction of the maintenance requirements (see HR Wallingford, 1992a and 1992b). Nevertheless the actual quantities of material required and frequencies of nourishment can only be determined by regular monitoring and by a correct analysis of the sediment dynamics. For this reason a programme of beach monitoring and maintenance has been activated. It must be mentioned that today a complete field survey performed after the completion of the works is not yet available. Therefore the real management phase has not yet begun. The aim of the present paper is to describe the monitoring programme and the experience gained so far. In the paper attention is focused on Cavallino littoral which is at a more advanced management stage.

The monitoring programme consists of three main activities:
1) field measurements (waves, wind, see levels, coastline, bottom and sediments);
2) analysis and interpretation of measured data;
3) definition of the maintenance works and of their strategy of execution.

FIELD MEASUREMENTS
Waves, wind and sea level
Offshore waves (including their direction), wind and see levels are collected at CNR tower (see fig. 1) which is located in the centre of the Venice littoral about 8 nautical miles offshore (MSL -15.5 m). Wave data are normally stored every three hours unless a threshold of 2 m significant wave height is exceeded. In this case waves are stored every hour. Continuous wave records are available since 1987.

Bottom and coast-line surveys
A periodic survey includes: beach profile surveys, coast-line surveys and sediment sample analysis. Cross-shore beach profiles are surveyed up to MSL -4 m at 50 m intervals and up to MSL -10 m at 500 m intervals. Three sediment samples are collected at MSL 0 m, -2 m and -4 m across sections spaced about 500 m. For each groin bay which has been completed, four surveys are today available:
1. one survey carried out before the works (used for the design);
2. one survey carried out after the construction of the rock groins and before the sand nourishment;
3. one survey carried out after the sand nourishment;
4. one survey carried out one year after the completion of sand nourishment.
The actual quantities of sand used for the beach nourishment have been measured by using the second and the third survey. After the completion of the works, two surveys per year will be performed (one after the summer season and one after the winter season). Fig. 3 shows the four beach profiles measured for a typical cross-section of Cavallino beach.

At Cavallino the works lasted about three years (January 1994 - April 1997) while at Pellestrina the works will last about three and half years (October 1994 - June 1998). For this reason the second, the third and the fourth survey were performed in each groin bay at different times. The first survey which will be performed simultaneously in all the groin bays after the end of the works, is planned for the autumn 1997 for Cavallino and for the autumn 1998 for Pellestrina. Therefore today it is not yet possible to evaluate the overall effect of the beach nourishment on the whole Cavallino and Pellestrina littorals.

DATA ANALYSIS
Data analysis is normally carried out after the execution of a periodic survey and includes:

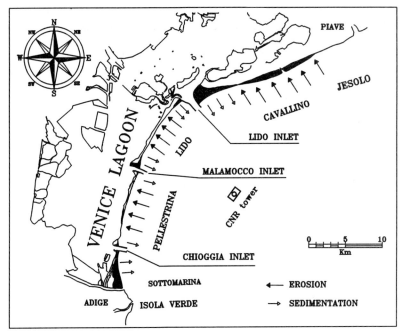

Fig. 1 — Long term beach evolution of Venecian littoral (1810–1990)

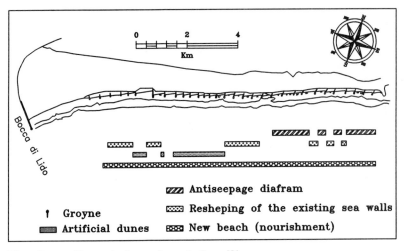

Fig. 2 — Executed works at Cavallino

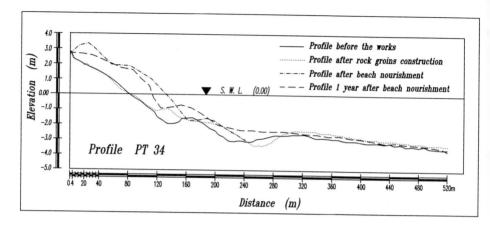

Fig. 3 - Four beach profiles measured for a cross-section al Cavallino

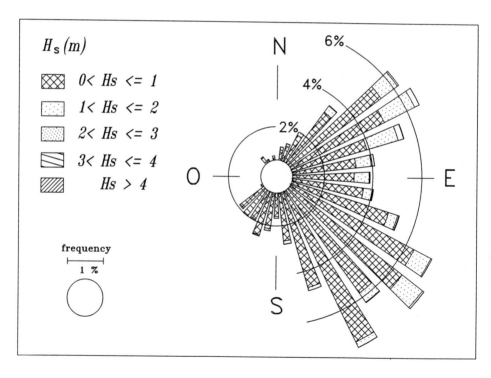

Fig. 4 - Offshore vawe climate recorded at C.N.R. tower in 1987–1997

wave analysis:
- update of the offshore wave climate (normal and extreme wave conditions) for the whole time series. This analysis includes the definition of the relationship between significant wave height and mean wave period both for normal and extreme waves;
- definition of the offshore wave climate for the time period spanning the last two surveys (this analysis includes the same items as above);
- propagation of normal and extreme wave conditions in some points located at MSL -10 m in front of Cavallino and Pellestrina beaches by means of the numerical model Merope. The model, implemented by Modimar, applies the technique developed by Abernethy and Gilbert (1975) which is based on the reverse projections of rays (Dorrestein, 1960) and on the constancy of the wave-vector spectral density along a single ray (Longuet-Higgins, 1957). This technique allows an offshore wave spectrum to be propagated inshore in one ore several selected points. The model does not include wave dissipation mechanisms. The inshore (at MSL -10 m) wave climate is worked out on the basis of the results given by Merope;
- the inshore normal wave conditions are further elaborated in order to work out some morphological mean wave conditions;
analysis of bathymetric surveys:
- the results of bathymetric surveys are represented in the form of cross-shore beach profiles and coast-line plan view;
sediment samples analysis:
- particle size distribution curves are obtained from sediment samples.

As far as wave measurements are concerned, the offshore wave climate at CNR tower over a ten year period (1987-1997) is shown by Fig. 4. The figure shows a typical bimodal distribution and the resultant of wave energy vector is directed from 101.7°N. For this reason at least two morphological wave conditions must be used for the long term evolution analysis of the beaches.

INTERPRETATION OF MEASURED DATA

In principle the actual quantities of material lost along the littoral (or inside each cell confined by a couple of groins) may be determined by comparing the changes in beach profiles and coast-lines occurred between two consecutive topographical surveys. Nevertheless this simple analysis is subjected to inevitable uncertainties (e.g., approximation in the bathymetric surveys) and limitations caused by the impossibility of separating the longshore and the cross-shore components from the total sediment budget of the littoral. This last aspect is very important for beach management because the irreversible losses of material is mainly due to the escape of sediments outside the active area in the cross-shore direction. Furthermore, such analysis does not give any information about occasional loss of material due to extreme wave conditions or about the future behaviour of the beach.

On the basis of these considerations a correct analysis of the field measurements based on the study of the sediment dynamics is always important. The main purposes of this analysis is the interpretation of morphological changes observed during the time period spanning two consecutive topographical surveys with the aim of calibrating numerical models which can be used both for the reconstruction of the sediment dynamics and to define the best strategy of maintenance work.

Starting from the common consideration that cross-shore transport influence mainly the short term evolution of the beach profile, while the long-shore sediment transport is the main cause

of the long term evolution of the coast-line, the interpretation of measured data is based on the following assumptions:
- cross-shore and long-shore sediment transport can be studied separately;
- long-shore sediment transport does not have strong influence on cross-shore dynamics;
- cross-shore dynamics may influence the coast-line evolution mainly by means of two mechanisms: reshaping the cross-shore profile (formation of bars or berms) and/or determining a definitive losses of material outside the active area of the littoral. The second mechanism is mainly due to the occurrence of extreme wave conditions (characterized by a return period greater than one year) and/or to the formation of rip currents which, for the present situation, can be facilitated by the presence of the groins used to confine each cell.

Under the above assumptions, a shore-line (one-line) model coupled with a beach profile model may be extremely useful both for the design phase and for beach management. The most important limitation of these numerical models is that they are not able to provide good results where the tridimensionality of the processes is dominant (e.g., close to structures). Nevertheless 2D (in the horizontal plane) and 3D morphological numerical models are not yet applicable in order to study very large areas and long term morphological variations. For practical purposes, the mentioned limitation of the shore-line and beach profile models may be supplied by detailed topographical surveys close to the structures. Furthermore the reliability of these models depends very much on their calibration. In the opinion of the authors this aspect is very important for the success of the work. As it is shown in the following by an example, the numerical model limitations may be supplied with the analysis of bathymetric surveys.

The interpretation of morphological changes can be divided into two phases:
1. analysis of the long-term evolution of the littoral;
2. analysis of the evolution of the littoral between two consecutive surveys.

Analysis of the long-term evolution of the littoral
The analysis of the long-term evolution of the littoral is very important in order to understand the causes which have induced the morphological changes of the beaches. This analysis is normally based on the historical data of the coast-line evolution and of the sediment supply to the beaches from rivers. Furthermore, knowledge of the cross-shore profiles before the execution of the works may be also useful for the interpretation of the sediment dynamics after beach nourishment. The main goal of this analysis is to derive:
- a basic set of parameters (closure depth, swash height, beach profiles, drift rates, groins efficiency, etc.) and boundary conditions to be used for the calibration of the shore-line numerical model in order to simulate the long term evolution of the beaches;
- a wave climate which may be considered representative of long-term evolution of the beaches.

Studies carried out during the design phase pointed out the long-term trend of the sediment drift along the Venetian littorals (see Fig. 1). For instance, historical data of Cavallino coast-line variations show that along Cavallino there is a net sediment drift going from north-east to south-west. This littoral drift caused the built up of Cavallino beach against the northern breakwater of the Lido inlet. At the same time the updrift sediment supply to the beach was decreased by the construction of structures which reduced both the longshore transport drift and the sediment input from rivers. As a consequence, the beach has tended to pivot around a point located about 3 km from the Lido inlet. To the east of this point the beach has been eroding and to the west it has accreted. During the design phase, this long term coast-line variation was used by HR Wallingford to calibrate its Beachplan numerical model (one-line model). This work has been successfully repeated with Aries, the shore-line model implemented by Modimar and ENEL, which has been used in this phase.

Various cross-shore profiles measured along the Cavallino littoral before the execution of the works are shown by Fig. 5. In the same figure, the curve through the crests of the bars of equation (Silvester, 1993):

$$h_c = 0.111 \, X_c^{0.575} \tag{1}$$

is plotted. In the previous equation X_c is the bar crest distance from the beach and h_c is the bar crest depth from the SWL. Eq. 1 is drawn in Fig. 6 together with data of bar distance X_c and crest depth h_c measured from the cross shore profiles of Fig. 5. On the basis of Fig. 5 and 6 some observations can be made. The Cavallino cross shore-profile before the works is a typical bar profile characterised by two systems of bars. Using the following expression (see Horikawa, 1988):

$$h_c = 0.59 \, H_B \tag{2}$$

the bar crest depth may be related to the breaker height H_B. Using in Eq. (2) the mean values of h_c obtained respectively from the first and the second systems of bars, it is possible to derive the significant breaking wave heights which have created the bars. In this way for the first and second bar the values $H_b = 3.0$ m and $H_b = 4.0$ m are obtained. The corresponding offshore significant waves heights coincide respectively with the return period of about 1:1 year and 1:10 years.

Analysis of evolution of the littoral between two consecutive surveys

The main purposes of this analysis is to quantify the irreversible losses of material along the littoral and inside each groin bay. These looses, which are mainly due to the offshore movement of sand outside the active area, are the most onerous from an economic point of view because their replacement is generally more expensive than the sand movement from downdrift to updrift direction. As was mentioned at the beginning of this paragraph, this analysis is carried out using the one-line numerical model.

Before the application of the numeric tool, a preliminary analysis of measured data is always important. For example, from the analysis of wave data recorded between two consecutive surveys, it is possible to ascertain whether extreme wave conditions or wave climate variations have been experienced by the littoral during the period of time under consideration. Furthermore, the analysis of cross-sore profiles may give reliable indications about the actual depth of closure of the active area and about the natural formation of bars which will protect the shore against extreme events.

In this phase, the application of the one-line numerical model has two main purposes:
1. to quantify the volume exchanged in the cross-shore direction inside each groin bays;
2. the calibration of the model intended for the verification of maintenance strategies.

The application of the one-line model must be carried out using the basic set of parameters derived from the analysis of the long term evolution of the littoral and the wave climate recorded during the period of time under consideration. If the recorded wave climate and the basic parameters are correct, the only calibration factor which must be tuned during this application of the model is the sediment transport rate in the cross-shore direction.

Here an example of application is given for four groin bays of the Cavallino littoral which were completed in April 1995. Fig. 8 illustrates the coast-line variations experienced by the four cells between April 1995 (end of the sand nourishment) and June 1996. The figure shows a shoreline receding ranging between 11 and 25 m in the four cells. Wave data analysis relating to the period 4/1/1995 - 6/30/96, shows that the maximum offshore (CNR) significant wave height on the littoral is 3.49 m (return period 1:1 year). In the same period the wave climate does not show any noticeable variation if compared to the wave climate of the last 10 years.

The cross-shore profiles measured in June 1996 point out the presence of only one bar system. Data of bar distance X_c and crest depth h_c measured from these cross-shore profiles are drawn in Fig. 7 together with Eq. 1. From the comparison of Fig. 7 and Fig. 6, and assuming that the profiles measured before the execution of the works (see Figs. 5 and 6) are representative of the quasi-equilibrium profile of the cross-shore beach, it is possible to conclude that one year after beach nourishment, the bars are still in a phase of development. In particular there is no presence of the second bar which is modelled by waves characterized by a return period of about 1:10 years, while the first bar is not yet completely developed in all the sections because the couples of X_c and h_c are not aligned along the line of Fig. 7. It should be noted that the development of the bars is important for the safety of the beach above the sea level even if it causes the receding of the shoreline. This aspect will be shown with an example in the next paragraph.

The calibration of the one line model showed that a mean drift of about 35 m^3 of sand per metre run of beach, took place in the cross-shore direction in one year. Taking into account the volume variation obtained from the beach profiles measured in April 1995 and June 1996 and the net longshore drift given by the one-line model, it was calculated that about 66% of the cross-shore drift was used by waves for the bar construction and that only 34% of it caused a definitive loss of material outside the active area. The beach line obtained with the one-line model at the end of the simulated period is shown by Fig. 8. The variation of the volume density of the nourishment material which takes place after the mixing with the pre-existing material (overfill loss) was not factored into this calculation. This volume variation (estimated for the present situation around 5%), which is more important in the first period after the beach nourishment, could reduce the computed losses of material outside the active area.

DEFINITION OF THE MAINTENANCE WORKS

As was mentioned in the introduction, the real management phase has not yet started because at Pellestrina the works will only be completed in June 1998, while at Cavallino the works were only completed last spring. This phase will enter in its full development in the spring of 1998 for Cavallino and in the spring 1999 for Pellestrina when two consecutive surveys carried out after the completion of the works will be available for both the littorals. Nevertheless, in this paragraph the general approach which will be applied in order to define the maintenance works and their strategy of execution is described.

The new sandy beaches of Cavallino and Pellestrina, have been made in order to protect the littoral from flooding caused by extreme meteorological conditions. On this matter the 1966 storm, which caused a lot of damage to structures and the flooding of the village of

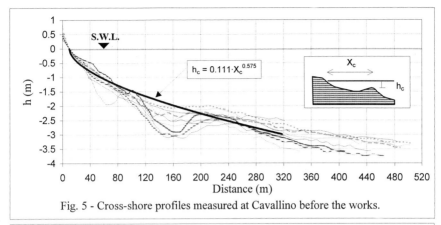

Fig. 5 - Cross-shore profiles measured at Cavallino before the works.

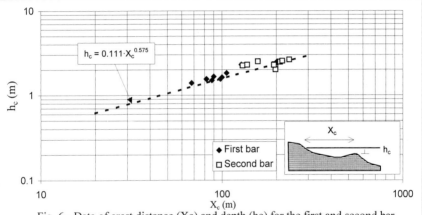

Fig. 6 - Data of crest distance (Xc) and depth (hc) for the first and second bar
measured at Cavallino

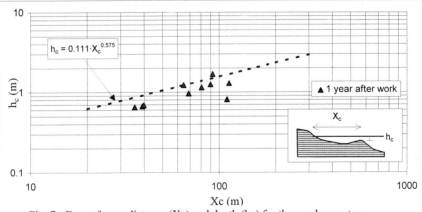

Fig. 7 - Data of crest distance (Xc) and depth (hc) for the one bar system
measured at Cavallino 1 year after the beach nourishment

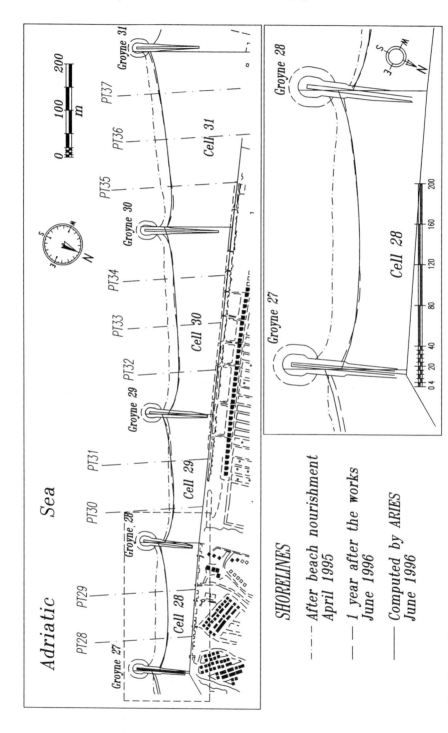

Fig. 8 Cavallino: monitored shoreline evolution and simulation carried out by the one-line model.

Pellestrina, is worth remembering. Besides their defence function, it is important to mention that the new artificial beaches offer the opportunity of developing tourism.

With reference to the defence function of the beaches, their active management must be based on maintaining the potential risk of flooding within a safe limit. The risk may be related both to the economic value and to the vulnerability of the protected properties, and to the probability of occurrence of the storms (waves+storm surge) causing the flooding. Using an approach commonly applied for rivers, the evaluation of the potential flooding risk caused by storms is expressed by the formula:

$$R_t = E V \frac{t}{T} \tag{3}$$

where:

$R_t =$ flooding risk estimated over a period of t years;
$E =$ economic value of the properties exposed to flooding;
$V =$ vulnerability of the properties; $0 \leq V \leq 1$, dimensionless;
$t =$ time horizon of the risk evaluation. This time is assumed as the time necessary to carry out a beach recharge (inclusive of the required time to let out the work on contract);
$T =$ minimum value of the storms return period (years) causing the flooding of the protected properties. This return period is function of the beach width.

Eq. 5 shows that, for constant values of E, V and t, R_t increases as the beach width decreases, because there is a decrease in the minimum value of the return period of the storms which cause the flooding. In order to apply Eq. 3 for management purposes, two aspects are important:

- it is necessary to decide the maximum acceptable value of the flooding risk (R_t);
- it is necessary to relate the flooding, which is expressed by means of a maximum acceptable value of the overtopping discharge, to a hydraulic parameter that is easier to work out: e.g., the significant wave height which impacts on the toe of the sea walls located behind the beaches.

Concerning the second point, the relation between overtopping discharges and wave heights at sea wall toe, is obtained by physical test models. Then, the definition of T is carried out by means of a beach profile numerical model. The numerical model will be run for a range of seastates (waves+storm surge) and for different cross-sections of the littoral. The model which will be applied, is called Taurus and was developed by University of Rome "La Sapienza" and ENEL. The model has been verified and calibrated against physical model tests results. A description of the model is given by Cartoni and De Girolamo (1996). The risk analysis will be carried out after each survey and the reference shoreline position, for the application of the beach profile numerical model, will be foreseen at the time t by means of the one-line model. The initial cross-shore profiles for Taurus will be derived from the last survey. The one-line model will be also used to optimise beach recharge strategies. In order to increase numerical model prediction accuracy, the one-line model will be calibrated after each survey, while the cross-shore profile model will be calibrated by physical test models.

The importance of the bars development for the safety of the emerged beach, is shown here by an example using the beach profile model. The model has been run starting from two different cross-shore profiles obtained, in the same cross-section of the littoral, from two different surveys. The first cross-shore profile, used as initial profile for the simulations, is the one measured after the beach nourishment. The second is the cross-shore profile measured one year after the end of the works. The first profile does not present any bar, while the second one shows the presence of a bar developed during the first year of life of the new beach. The

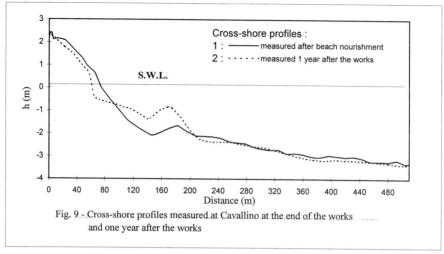

Fig. 9 - Cross-shore profiles measured at Cavallino at the end of the works and one year after the works

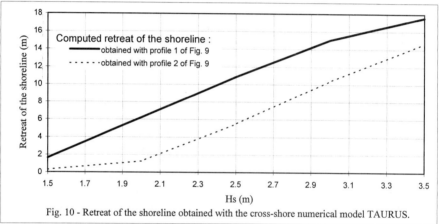

Fig. 10 - Retreat of the shoreline obtained with the cross-shore numerical model TAURUS.

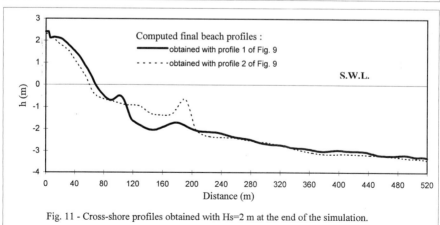

Fig. 11 - Cross-shore profiles obtained with Hs=2 m at the end of the simulation.

two profiles are represented in Fig. 9. By using these two profiles as initial bathymetry for the simulations, a range of seastates (waves+storm surge) have been simulated, measuring, after each execution, the retreat of the shore-line. The retreat, represented as function of the incoming significant wave height, is shown by Fig.10. As shown by the figure, the presence of the bar reduces the retreat of the shoreline. Fig.11 shows the cross-shore profiles obtained at the end of the simulations carried out with an incoming significant wave height of 2 m.

CONCLUDING REMARKS

Nourished beaches need careful monitoring and maintenance during their lifetime. These aspects assume an utmost importance if the main function of the new beaches is to protect littorals from flooding. In order to define maintenance works and their strategy of execution two aspects must be pointed out:

- it is necessary to carry out a periodic monitoring of the littoral based on field measurements (waves, wind, sea levels, coastline, bottom, sediment);
- it is necessary to apply numerical models which are essential both for the evaluation of sand losses and to decide the beach management strategies.

Furthermore a risk analysis may be helpful in order to decide beach recharges.

ACKNOWLEDGEMENTS

The work presented in this paper has been supported by Consorzio Venezia Nuova on behalf of the competent Italian state authority Magistrato alle Acque. The beach nourishment design was carried out by Technital. The helpful collaboration provided by D. Saltari and F. Mondini to carry out some numerical applications is very much appreciated.

REFERENCES

Abernety, C.L., Gilbert, G., (1975), Refraction of wave spectra, HR Wallingford, Report No INT 117, England.

Benassai, E., Gentilomo, M., Ragone, A., Setaro, F., Tomasicchio, U., (1997), Littoral restoration by means of protected beach nourishment. Recent Italian works (Venetian and Tyrrhenian-Calabrian coasts), AIPCN, PIC '97, Venice, Italy.

Cartoni, S., De Girolamo, P. (1996), Un recente modello numerico per lo studio dell'evoluzione del profilo trasversale di una spiaggia (in Italian). Proc. of the XXV Convegno di Idraulica e Costruzioni Idrauliche, Turin, Italy.

Cecconi, G., Maretto, G.P., (1996), La cava sottomarina per il ripascimento del litorale della Laguna di Venezia (in Italian), 4 Congresso AIOM, Padova, Italy.

Dorrestein, R., (1960), Simplified method of determining refraction coefficients for sea waves, J. Geophys. Res., V 65, No 2.

Hanson, H., Kraus, N.C., (1989), GENESIS: generalized model for simulating shore-line change, Report 1, technical reference. Tech. Rep. CERC-89-19, U.S. Army Engr. Waterways Exp. Stn., Coastal Engrg. Res. Centre, Vicksburg, MS.

Horikawa, K., (1988), Nearshore dynamics and coastal processes, University of Tokyo press, Japan.

HR Wallingford, (1992a), Venice Lagoon Study B7.2/3rd Phase: Model Tests for the Pellestrina Littoral, HR Wallingford, Report EX 2524, England.

HR Wallingford, (1992b), Venice Lagoon Study B7.2/4th Phase: Model Tests for the Cavallino Littoral, HR Wallingford, Report EX 2661, England.

Longuet-Higgins, M.S., (1957), On the transformation of a continuous spectrum by refraction, Proc. Camb. Phil. Soc., V 53, No 1.

Noli, A, Galante, F., Silva, P., (1993), Il progetto di ripascimento dei litorali veneziani eseguito dal Concessionario dello Stato sotto il controllo dell'Ufficio G.C.OO.MM. di Venezia (in Italian), Giornate Italiane di Ingegneria Costiera, Genova, Italy.

Silva, P., De Girolamo, P., (1993), Interventi di ripascimanto artificiale sul litorale di Pellestrina (VE) (in Italian), La difesa dei litorali in Italia, Edizioni delle Autonomie, Roma, Italy.

Silvester, R., Hsu, J.R.C., (1993), Coastal stabilization, Prentice-Hall, Inc., New Jersey.

Hunstanton to Heacham Beach Management

RICHARD NUNN, Environment Agency, Peterborough, UK
DR NOEL BEECH, Posford Duvivier, Peterborough, UK

ABSTRACT

The sea defences between Hunstanton, at the north-east end of the Wash, and Snettisham Scalp consist of sand/shingle ridges or hard defences, fronted by beach nourishment, and backed in most places by a secondary earth embankment. The 8.5km length of defences are extremely vulnerable to North Sea storm surge tides, having suffered severe damage during the 1953 and 1978 events.

Traditionally, hard defences had been the adopted method of maintaining the sea defences where the sand/shingle ridge was inadequate. In 1990, following extensive studies, a change in strategy was proposed which involved the importation of sea dredged sand and shingle to replenish the beach material. The longshore north to south drift deposits material at Snettisham Scalp. Each year a proportion of this material is mechanically redistributed along the frontage. The procedure for undertaking this operation is documented in a Beach Management Manual, specifically developed after implementation of the 1990 strategy.

Whilst the 1990 beach recharge scheme has had some degree of success, a recent review of the works has clearly identified weaknesses in the frontage which cannot easily be rectified by a more intense re-cycling campaign. Following detailed consideration of a large number of options, a combination of hard and soft defences is proposed in the 1997 Strategy.

The paper evaluates the beach management successes and failures of the various phases of works undertaken along the frontage.

1.0   INTRODUCTION

Prior to the construction of any built defences, flood protection of the low lying areas of Hunstanton and Heacham *(Figure 1)* relied on a natural sand-shingle ridge which fringed the beach. Further to this, a secondary landward flood embankment provided further security to more inland areas.

Up until 1953 their was little evidence of the use of hard defences along this eastern side of the Wash. This was to dramatically change following a major storm surge event that swept down the east coast of Great Britain, leaving in its wake 65 people dead in the Hunstanton-Heacham area. Repair work took the form of a variety of stepwork, seawalls, timber groynes and sleeper walls. The hard defence works were, however, substantially confined to the northern (Hunstanton) end of the frontage. In 1978, the worst ever recorded flood resulted in major breaches at Heacham and significant damage to property. Whilst more repair work was instigated, it was apparent that beach levels along the complete 8.5km frontage were

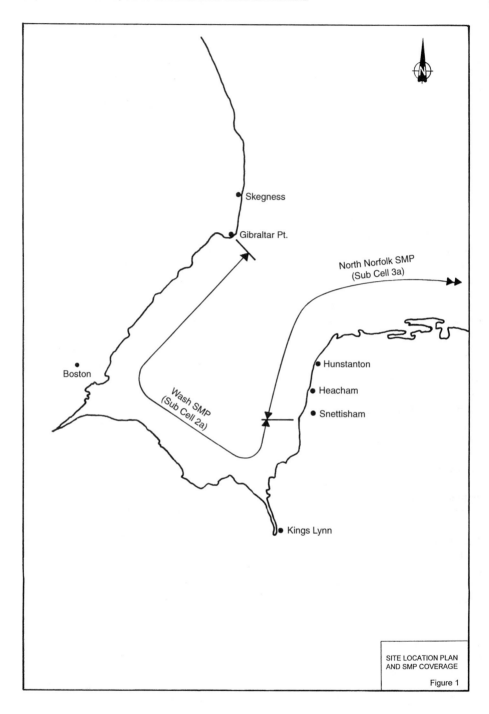

SITE LOCATION PLAN
AND SMP COVERAGE

Figure 1

falling, with increasing concern for the long term stability of the defences.

Following detailed studies, it was decided in 1990 to implement a beach recharge scheme which would restore the beach using imported material. Being one of the first major beach recharge schemes to be undertaken in the UK, it has had its difficulties and it is only through regular monitoring that we can now more fully comprehend the subtleties of the "soft" approach. This understanding has enabled the preparation of a new strategy - the 1997 Strategy.

2.0   COASTLINE APPRECIATION

Figure 2 shows the key sites along the frontage together with defences and the designation of "Areas" A to J..

2.1   The Physical Setting

For more than 6,500 years, the rate of sedimentation in the Wash has generally outpaced sea level rise resulting in the formation of the sandbanks and inter-tidal flats that are significant features of this area. The nature of the sediments forming the seabed of the Wash vary considerably, ranging from the gravels in the central deep area to mud and saltmarshes on the upper margins.

Compared with the north and south-west coastlines, the Hunstanton-Heacham coastline is not so well sheltered by offshore sandbanks. Nevertheless, the foreshore is wide and consists of a thin layer of sand over a shallow sloping (1:400) clay platform. At about +1m ODN the mobile sediments form a steeper ridge which fringes the coast. The coarser sediments, in particular, forming this upper beach are not necessarily indigenous but originate substantially from the beach nourishment campaign carried out in 1990/91. Although orientated in a generally north-east to south-west direction, the coastline is not straight but fluctuates in orientation about the various promontories, especially Snettisham Scalp, to the south of which the coastline tends towards a more north to south aspect.

The tidal range in the Wash is the largest range that occurs on the East Coast of England and Scotland (6.5m spring tidal range at Hunstanton). Due to high surges in the North Sea, extreme sea levels at Hunstanton are significantly higher than the pure astronomical tides; for example, the 1 in 100 year extreme water level at Hunstanton is +5.79m ODN.

The hydraulic characteristics of the Wash are such that slightly higher flow speeds occur on the flood than on the ebb (ref. Wash Shoreline Management Plan 1996). Imbalance in the tidal flows in the Wash give rise to a pattern of residual currents, which are directed down the central channel area returning to seawards along the banks and nearshore areas. This means that at Hunstanton and Heacham the net tidally induced currents are actually directed from south to north.

Waves within the Wash originate from two possible sources: locally generated from within the confines of the Wash, and externally generated from the North Sea. By virtue of the considerably greater fetch length, those waves originating from the latter source are potentially of much greater magnitude. The mild slope of the nearshore seabed combined with the presence of sandbanks results in an attenuation of waves propagating down the Wash (north-east to south-west). As a result, there is a significant gradient in the degree of exposure of the Hunstanton-Heacham frontage going from north to south; eg. 1 in 1 year offshore waves heights reduced from 2.7m at Hunstanton to 1.3m at Snettisham.

The attenuation of wave energy along the coast, combined with the obliquity of wave attack from the north to north east, result in a net longshore transport which is directed from Hunstanton towards Snettisham. At the upper steeper part of the beach this wave driven transport is sufficient to overcome the milder return drift set up by residual tidal currents, giving rise to a net accretion of sediment at Snettisham of between 6,000m³ and 8,000m³ per year.

2.2   The Hinterland and Infrastructure

Hunstanton town is at the northern end of the Strategy frontage. Although the land at Hunstanton rises away from the coast, there is a low lying coastal area that is principally occupied by holiday amusements and recreational facilities. The coastal strip extending, southwards between Hunstanton and Heacham contains "open space" whilst that between Heacham and Snettisham Scalp is agricultural land. The area at risk of flooding contains static caravan sites (approximately 2000 units) which are located immediately behind the sea defences between Hunstanton and Heacham. There are also numerous holiday chalets built close to the defences at Heacham and further south towards Snettisham. The area is famous for it leisure and tourism facilities. The bathing beaches comply with the Bathing Waters Directive and, although highly seasonal, Hunstanton is estimated to have one million day visitors each year.

An economic assessment of the assets at risk of flooding has demonstrated that the standard of defence for the Hunstanton-Heacham frontage should be 1 in 100 years with respect to a breach in the defences.

2.3   Conservation Designations

Below the high water mark, the area falls within the Wash Site of Special Scientific Interest being notified for ecology and habitats; sand banks, estuary mudflats and saltmarsh. It is of national importance for wintering wildfowl, waders, seals, shell fishery and fish nursery areas. The seabed is also designated as a Ramar Site and a Special Protection Area.

Landward of the defences there are a number of Country Wildlife sites. Just to the south of the area is the Snettisham Nature Reserve, a large area of mudflats and brackish pits which are of international importance for wintering and migrating wildfowl.

3.0   THE 1990 BEACH NOURISHMENT SCHEME

Historically, our predecessors have attempted to maintain beach levels by the construction of groyne fields. These have had the effect of interrupting the flow of sediment, which have led to gains in some places but losses in others. The disappearance of beach material along Hunstanton South Beach and a better understanding as to why material accumulates at Snettisham Scalp, led to the development of a beach recharge strategy. Whilst novel, and to some extent untested, it recognised that the sediment transport pathway from north to south needed a feed of beach material. In particular, it recognised the importance of being able to recycle quantities of sand/shingle from Snettisham Scalp. At the outset, it was realised that recharge alone would not provide a sustainable solution and that surplus material accumulating at the Scalp should form part of an annual replacement campaign.

3.1   Approach

In May 1989 Sir William Halcrow & Partners (Ref. 1) completed a study of the frontage which suggested the following (a) beach nourishment with sand/shingle; (b) site specific monitoring; (c) maintenance (including beach recycling).

During 1990/91 approximately 400,000 cubic metres of sand and shingle were dredged from the mouth of the River Humber and pumped ashore to the beaches of Heacham and Hunstanton. The scheme was primarily designed to reduce the quantity of overtopping in an extreme storm event and considered a combined 1 in 50 year water level with a 1 in 50 year wave height event.

The design was subsequently carried forward by consultants Babtie Dobbie, leading to construction in 1990/91.

A feature of the beach design was that it included very steep slopes in the proposed cross-sections (1 in 10 and 1 in 4 composites in the Halcrow design).   Beach nourishment proceeded on this basis but in November 1990, following a significant storm event, there was a loss of beach material which led to a flattening of the as-placed profile and severe cliffing of the upper section. This resulted in a re-appraisal of the design by Babtie Dobbie and a revised profile using a 1 in 5.5 slope (instead of 1 in 4).

4.0   BEACH MANAGEMENT 1991 TO DATE

4.1   Beach Management Plan

Upon completion of the 1990/91 scheme, the need for a Beach Management Manual was essential if the maintenance of the flood defences was to be co-ordinated properly, and in harmony with the environmental aspects of the frontage. The Manual (Ref. 2) sought to perpetuate the design philosophy of the 1990 recharge; it advised appropriate levels of monitoring both for beach level and ecological change; and, it recommended the procedures and best practice necessary to complete annual re-cycling of material.

In essence, the manual set out the criteria under which the Agency should operate for each and every re-cycling operation:-

- consult with statutory bodies and landowners
- obtain legal consent
- submit for MAFF approval
- appoint a management contractor (usually plant hire contract)
- supervise the work

4.4   Monitoring

Beach Surveys have been routinely carried out every 100m in January and July each year so as to quantify the changes in beach profiles. This has been supplemented with surveys following recycling together with a physical analysis of the in-situ beach material to determine the particle size distribution for comparison with the original recharge material. Also carried out are the bathymetric survey work every five years and annual aerial stereoscopic photographs at a scale of 1:5000.

Environmental monitoring has been undertaken periodically throughout each year to check the effects of beach recharge on flora and fauna and sediment.

4.5 Scheduled Maintenance
The greater the volume of material on the upper beach, the greater is its capacity to withstand a storm. Practise has shown that beach levels have remained relatively constant at the start of winter but the situation can quickly change from mid to late winter when action is both necessary and materials become available from Snettisham. This has resulted in February being established as the best time to undertake re-cycling from Snettisham to areas of deficit.

4.6 Investment
Since 1991, when coordinated beach management commenced, the Agency has sought to maintain an investment level which would allow, not only good beach management, but also monitoring of sediment movement (not previously carried out by our predecessors). The costs can be summarised as follows:-

- Re-cycling   £100k
- Emergency maintenance   £10k
- Beach Monitoring   £24k
- Ecological Monitoring   £20k
- Licences   £3k
- Management   £13k

     Annual Cost   £170k (September 1995 costs)

5.0 REVIEW
In 1995 Posford Duvivier were asked to review the performance and management of the Hunstanton - Heacham beaches/defences and to prepare a detailed appraisal of any specific problems. The specific problems were to include several issues which had become apparent since the beach nourishment scheme had been put in place in 1991: wind blown sand; beach cliffing (tendency for the beach to cut back at near vertical slope); local beach erosion at Hunstanton Power Boat Ramp; continued recycling from the environmentally sensitive area of Snettisham Scalp.

The following discussion makes reference to the Areas A to J shown in *Figure 2*.

5.1 Beach Recycling
The 1990 scheme employed beach recharge on a shoreline with marked longshore transport characteristics. The conditions lend themselves to recycling of material and as such the original design concept was good.

Since completion of the scheme in 1991 the Agency has re-cycled between 30,000 and 50,000 cubic metres of sand/shingle per annum, of which at least 50% has come from Snettisham Scalp. Whilst most of this is planned re-cycling and re-profiling of the beach (mainly in February of each year), there has been unscheduled emergency work eg:removal of shingle cliffs after periods of storm activity.

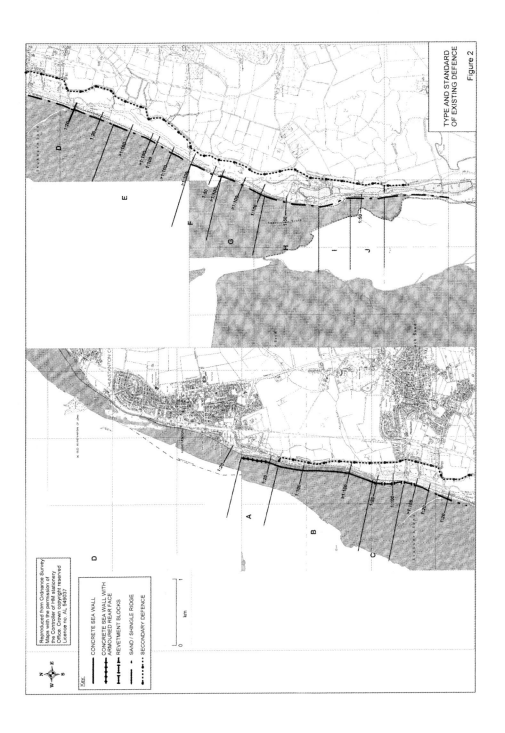

Key:

CONCRETE SEA WALL

CONCRETE SEA WALL WITH ARMOURED REAR FACE

REVETMENT BLOCKS

SAND / SHINGLE RIDGE

SECONDARY DEFENCE

TYPE AND STANDARD
OF EXISTING DEFENCE

Figure 2

An analysis of beach profile data showed that overall the upper beach volume had remained reasonably constant, ie. there were no significant gains or losses. Most areas showed reasonable stability or marginal gain, but a trend of erosion was found in areas A (Hunstanton Power Boat Ramp), C H, I and J *(see Figure 3)*. The recycling campaign was, therefore, only partially successful in maintaining beach volumes along the shore. The net loss of sediment from the borrow site, Snettisham Scalp *(Areas I and J)*, suggested that more material had been removed than was returning there by natural drift (calculated to be 6,000 to 8,000m^3 per year).

5.2   Beach Profile Behaviour

As with all beach nourishment schemes, type and sizing of the material source is critical. The material used at Heacham/Hunstanton commenced with a D_{50} of approximately 8mm, dredged from a combination of two offshore sources. Although the mixed shingle and sand that was used fell within the envelope of the design grading curve, the result of mixing two different sources to meet the required D_{50} was that of a bi-modal material ie: one which separates into two distinct bands in the grading curve.

The bi-model characteristics of the sediment made it quite difficult to predict the cross-shore behaviour of the sediment, ie. was it a sand or a shingle? The problem was studied using a range of cross-shore sediment transport models together with observed behaviour of the actual beach (ie. beach profile data). It was concluded that the beach had a natural tendency to revert to a slope (typically 1 in 12 to 1 in 15) which was much shallower than was trying to be achieved through mechanical reprofiling to the design slope (eg. 1 in 5.5 in original design). Moreover, in several areas, beach material was deficient to the extent that the hard defences became the conditioning factor in determining the standard of defence.

5.3   Defence Standards

Even now, the front line of defence is substantially reliant, in many areas, on the sand/shingle ridge that fringes the coast, whilst the present "hard" defences comprise the seawall at Hunstanton *(Areas A and B)* and a length of flexible revetment just to the south of this *(Area C)*. Some local stone has also been applied to Area J, just south of Snettisham Scalp, to try and halt erosion of the ridge there.

The hard defences were studied with respect to various failure modes: overtopping; wall failure; undermining. The results of this analysis combined with that of the beach, led to a definitive view of the standard of defence of the Hunstanton - Heacham coastline with respect to a breach and inundation. The results of this are depicted in *Figure 2*.

Although the actual standard of defence is better than the target standard (1 in 100 years) in several places, the overall standard is governed by that of the weakest sections. The weakest sections, which provide a current standard of only 1 in 20 years, are at Hunstanton South Beach (Area A), and Heacham North and South Beaches (Areas C and D).

6.0   THE 1997 STRATEGY

6.1   Development of the Strategy

The origins of the 1997 strategy date back to 1995, when two Shoreline Management Plans covering the frontage were in preparation. As mentioned above, the initial studies took the

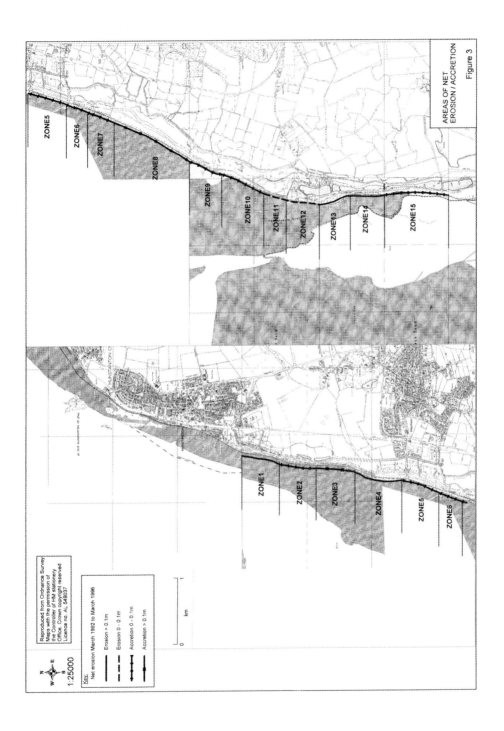

AREAS OF NET
EROSION / ACCRETION

Figure 3

form of a review of the performance of the 1990/91 scheme and its subsequent management, together with a detailed appraisal of any specific problems encountered. As the studies unfolded it became apparent that the most significant concern was a serious shortfall in the required standard of defence over much of the frontage. The study was extended through more intense analysis (eg. wave modelling) and extension of the study frontage (to the more logical closure of the secondary embankment at New Cross Bank) to produce the comprehensive 1997 Strategy (Ref. 3).

6.2   Shoreline Management Plans

The area is covered by two Shoreline Management Plans *(see Figure 1)*:

- North Norfolk SMP (Ref. 4) - Covers the strategy frontage down to Snettisham Scalp.
- Wash SMP (Ref. 5) - Covers the southernmost 1½km from Snettisham Scalp.

In both, a "hold the line" policy is recommended. The North Norfolk SMP recommends maintenance and reconstruction of the existing seawalls and groynes in these areas of existing hard defences at Hunstanton and Heacham together with beach recharge at Hunstanton and beach management elsewhere. The Wash SMP is not specific on the means of holding the line but advises periodic review to check coastal processes are maintaining foreshore stability. Thus, both SMPs reflect the importance of the beach and shoreline behaviour in sustaining the hold the line approach.

6.3   Continue Existing Practice or Sustain

Snettisham Scalp was found to have lost sediment with respect to the post-nourishment situation. Although recoverable through the action of natural drift, this loss suggested that the recycling campaign should be modified to reduce the take from Snettisham; certainly there was no case for "stepping up" the recycling campaign to mitigate the low defence standards along certain lengths of the frontage. Thus, continuing the existing practice but with a moderated beach management campaign would lead to a future lowering in the standard of defence and hence is not a satisfactory long term strategy.

Continuing existing practice would lead to a lowering from a 1 in 20 year standard. The present standard could be sustained by periodic recharge but at 1 to 20 years this standard still falls seriously short of that which is sought for the frontage (ie. 1 in 100 years).

6.4   Improvement Schemes

In considering schemes for the frontage a wide range of coastal defence tools were considered, including:

- beach recycling
- beach recharge
- seawalls (new or strengthened existing walls)
- flexible revetments
- groynes
- detached breakwaters
- beach dewatering
- counterwalls - flood embankments connecting the primary defence to the secondary defence to isolate areas with different risks and standards

■   toe structures

As discussed above, beach recycling alone cannot raise the controlling standard of defence of the frontage. Moreover, small scale recharge to maintain the present standard is not an acceptable option.

Other methods which were examined and rejected were: construction of new beach control structures (groynes and breakwaters); beach dewatering; and large toe structures (perched beach structures). The remaining options were considered in combination and in isolation in a range of five options. Considering the "extreme" cases:

Major beach nourishment: The standard of defence could be raised to 1 in 100 years by nourishing the entire frontage with 720,000m³ of sand and shingle. Despite such a large volume of material, the sustainability of the area to the south of Snettisham Scalp is still questionable. Environmentally, the scheme would attract a number of potentially adverse impacts including those which are identified with the earlier scheme (eg wind blown sand), but which would be amplified by the massive additional volume.

Hard Defences: A 1 in 100 year standard is achievable by restoring existing defences or building new ones where there are presently none, in areas of deficient standard. Such a scheme would, however, likely attract opposition due to its effect on the natural cross-shore processes, geomorphology and hence ecology.

The favoured schemes were, those using combinations of both hard and soft defences. The optimum scheme would entail the following capital works:

■   Improvement of hard defences in Areas A and C
■   Installation of flexible or light weight revetment in Areas F and J
■   Beach nourishment (total 210,000m³) in Areas D and H.

The strategy is still reliant on beach management methods to maintain the defences and sustain their standard; ie. periodic recharge, recycling, monitoring. The strategy, including beach management, provides the most economic solution with an estimated 50 year scheme life discounted cost of £14.9million.

7.0   THE 1997 BEACH MANAGEMENT PLAN
In 1996, the Construction Industry Research and Information Association (CIRIA) published in its Report 153 - "The Beach Management Manual", (Ref. 6) a comprehensive source of information relating to the guiding principles and best practice for the management of beaches. It describes beach management as a process of managing the beach by monitoring, simple intervention (eg:sand fences), recycling, renourishment or the construction of beach control structures. In essence a good Beach Management Plan should consist of two specific components. They are:-

1.   Beach Management Scheme Appraisal - in this case the 1997 Strategy.

2.   Operational Beach Management Plan - a guide for local managers and operational staff on the design features of any new scheme, standards of service, appropriate

levels of monitoring for both beach profile and ecological change and procedures and practice for the annual recycling of beach material.

The concept of a Beach Management Plan is not new to this frontage. However, since 1991 the systematic collection of data and experience of operating and managing the 1990 beach recharge has provided the Agency with valuable lessons from which to formulate an updated strategy. It is useful to consider the impact of a changing strategic stance in relation to monitoring, maintenance and cost.

7.1   Monitoring
A key concern during the operational review of this frontage has been the growth rate of Snettisham Scalp. A consideration for any new strategy was whether the continued removal of material was having any detrimental effect on the ecology of the Scalp.

The growth of the Scalp over the last fifty years has provided opportunity for the expansion of shingle vegetation and invertebrate interests. Their ability to flourish is very much dependent upon areas of stable shingle. The whole area now comes under the Habitats Directive as a Special Area of Conservation being a significant site for visiting wintering and migrating wildfowl and wading birds. By restricting access to the lower parts of the Scalp and with the full approval of the statutory environmental bodies, the Agency has been able to minimise adverse damage. The Agency also instigated baseline ecological monitoring which, to date, has demonstrated only minor impacts through continued recycling undertaken by SGS Environment.

7.2   Maintenance
A clear outcome of the 1997 Strategy is to reduce the volume of material recycled from the spit, such that the volume recovered from the Scalp is at least balanced by the volume naturally arriving through natural processes ie: maintain the status quo. In recognising a need to the limit the extent of recycling, the Agency has also improved the analysis of formal surveys and inspection surveys.

7.3   Investment
The preferred strategy provides for a continuation of recycling of beach material to maintain beach levels. Whilst other items of expenditure relating to monitoring would not decrease the reduced volume of recycled material with the new strategy will reduce the overall annual maintenance cost to approximately £95,000 (compared with £170,000 previously).

8.0   CONCLUDING COMMENTS
The paper has examined the strategic thinking which has been brought to the Hunstanton and Heacham frontage and particularly how the 1997 strategic approach will alter our future management regime. Key points arising from the learning curve of the last ten years are:-

- The original 1990 Beach Recharge was good in concept but subsequently suffered from beach cliffing due to poor mixing of the beach material. It is important that careful consideration is given to material selection at both the design and implementation stage.

■   The original beach nourishment redistributed itself along the frontage in such a way that some areas become deficient. Apart from Snettisham Scalp, it was not practical to "borrow" sediment from areas of marginal surfeit. More consideration must be given to "losses" within the system.

■   There has been a tendency to compensate for the losses mentioned above by "borrowing" more from Snettisham Scalp. This has been proved to be not sustainable indicating that future beach management cannot rely on recycling alone; periodic recharge is a prerequisite.

■   Beach nourishment has not maintained sufficient protection to several lengths of hard defences. In some cases it is quite difficult, or inefficient, to hold the beach in these places. The future strategy has, therefore, recognised this and included measures to improve the hard defences where necessary, ie. it is not so heavily reliant on the beach behaviour.

■   A well documented and continually updated Beach Management Plan or Manual is a pre-requisite for any significant strategic coastal frontage such as Hunstanton to Heacham. This will provide the operational user with a useful background to design and the procedure under which scheduled and unscheduled maintenance should be undertaken.

■   Monitoring and collection of both physical and ecological data is essential to any strategic   assessment. This requires a systematic approach to data collection with particular attention to the timing of beach surveys.

9.0   REFERENCES

1.   "Detailed Appraisal Report on Hunstanton/Heacham Beach Recharge", prepared by Sir William Halcrow and Partners for Anglian Water (1989).

2.   "Hunstanton/Heacham Flood Defence Beach Management Manual", National Rivers Authority (1994).

3.   "Hunstanton/Heacham Sea Defences - Strategy Study", by Posford Duvivier for Environment Agency (1997).

4.   "North Norfolk Shoreline Management Plan" by L. G. Mouchel Ltd for Environment Agency (1996).

5.   "Wash Shoreline Management Plan" by Posford Duvivier for Environment Agency 1996.

6.   "Beach Management Manual - Report 153" by J D Simm, A H Brampton, N W Beech and J S Brooke, CIRIA, 1996.

10.0   ACKNOWLEDGEMENTS

Thanks are extended to Sir William Halcrow & Partners, Babtie Dobbie and Posford Duvivier, consultants to the schemes at varying stages, for information provided.

Retaining Beach Sand by a Distorted Ripple Mat

ISAO IRIE[1], SATOSHI TAKEWAKA[2], NOBUYUKI ONO[1],
KEISUKE MURAKAMI[1], HIROKAZU SAKAMOTO[1], OSAHIKO SHIMADA[3]

[1] Dept. of Civil Eng.,Kyushu Univ. 6-10-1 Hakozaki Higashi-ku, Fukuoka 812 Japan
[2] Dept. of Civil Eng., Tsukuba Univ. 1-1-1 Tennoudai, Tsukuba 305 Japan
[3] Hydraulic Eng. Comp. 2-6-28 Hakataekihigashi Hakata-ku, Fukuoka 812 Japan

ABSTRACT

A method to retain beach sand by a distorted ripple mat which is made by precast concrete blocks has been examined through laboratory experiments, computer simulations
and field experiments. The strong asymmetry of ripple profile generates current near the
bottom to one direction and thus sediment movement whose concentration is high near
the bottom can be controlled. The hydraulic condition on which the distorted ripple mat
can control the sediment transport most effectively is studied experimentally and numerically and its capability to retain beach sand is tested through laboratory experiments
and field installation.

INTRODUCTION

During this half a century, various man-made changes such as river improvement, construction of dams and ports have resulted in the imbalance of annual rate of supply
and loss of sediments of the coasts and progressive change in the shoreline configuration,
mostly as the beach erosion, has taken place. The methods of beach protection have been
different depending on the state of affairs of the country. One country, for example, gave
priority on beach nourishment preserving the nature of the beach, the other country on
the construction of various shore protection structures such as groins, jetties, submerged
breakwaters as well as offshore breakwaters. The former case contributed very well for
keeping natural characteristic of the beach, however, maintenance of beach sand has
been cost consuming. The latter case, on the other hand, has well established barriers
against external attacks of storm surges, however, the existence of such bulky structures
very often caused new erosion on the neighboring and down-drift side coasts and also
they hampered keeping a beautiful view and enabling various recreational maritime activities. It is understood that the coastal area needs the development in the future due
to the lack of enough land space for development and much more shore protection will be
required. Furthermore, the expected sea level rise in the coming century would require
more devices for low cost and efficient shore protection methods. In order to cope with
the above situation, a method to retain beach sand by a distorted ripple mat composed
of precast concrete blocks has been presented in the present paper. This was originally
studied by Inman et. al. (1972) but the authors have not found the subsequent paper.
The present distorted ripple mat controls sand movement near the bottom directly and
gives very little impacts on surrounding hydraulic and ecological conditions, whereas
most of the shore protection works control waves and currents directly giving various
impacts on environments.

Coastlines, structures and breakwaters. Thomas Telford, London, 1998

BASIC FUNCTION OF 'DISTORTED RIPPLE MAT' (DRIM)

The surface profile of the distorted ripple mat (hereafter the mat made by precast concrete blocks is referred as DRIM), has the deformed shape of a sinusoidal wave profile as shown in **FIG 1**. Originally, it is modeled from a natural ripple (height $\eta = 1.0$ cm and pitch length $\lambda = 5.5$ cm) formed in a movable bed experiment with water depth $h = 35$ cm, wave period $T = 1.5$ s, wave height $H = 8$ cm and sand diameter $D = 0.16$ mm (settling velocity $W = 1.6$ cm/s at $20°C$) as shown in **FIG 2**. Two sets of fixed bed ripples are prepared for standard tests, the one is the sinusoidal wave profile with height $\eta = 1.0$ cm and wave length $\lambda = 5.5$ cm, and the other is the distorted ripple profile with the same height and length but the horizontal asymmetry is made 1:3 as shown in the figure, which is considered to be the maximum allowable deformation to keep the concrete blocks from collapsing.

First of all, those fixed bed ripples were set in 3 m length on the horizontal bed of wave channel and vertical distribution of Eulerian mean velocity under waves were measured by a magnetic type current meter. **FIG 3** shows the velocity profiles under waves of 8 cm in height and 1.5 or 2.0 s in period. It is seen that the mean velocity is onshore within the range of 0.2~0.3 time of relative water depth above the bottom (the level of ripple crest) in distorted ripples whereas it is mostly offshore in sinusoidal ripples.

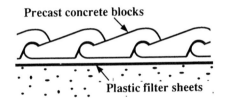

FIG 1 Distorted ripple mat (DRIM) FIG 2 Shape and scale of fixed bed ripples

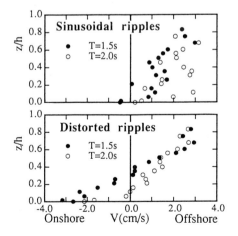

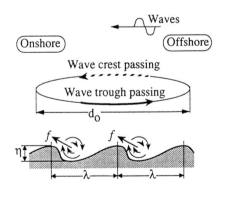

FIG 3 Vertical distribution of mean velocity in sinusoidal ripples and distorted ripples

FIG 4 Generation of controlled bottom current

Wave profile

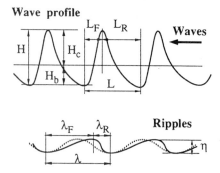

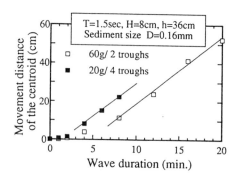

FIG 5 Definition of dimensions

FIG 6 Movement of centroid of sediment placed on the fixed bed ripples

The generation of onshore current in the case of distorted ripple mat is attributed to the relative difference of vortex formation on the both side of a ripple crest. As shown in **FIG 4**, the orbital stream of offshore phase (wave trough passing) will generate remarkable vortex in the lee of the ripple crest because of its steeper rear face and the hydrodynamic reaction between vortex and ripple surface causes the vortex to rise and subsequent reversal (onshore) flow under the wave crest sweeps the water mass of vortex onshore. On the reverse phase, formation of vortex is limited because of the milder slope of onshore face of the ripple. As the result of this difference over a wave cycle, a clear onshore current is formed near the bottom. The difference of vortex formation on the onshore/offshore side of a ripple crest, which is the major reason of stream generation near the bottom, is determined by not only the asymmetry of ripple profile but also the asymmetrical characteristic of wave profile as shown in **FIG 5**. In the figure, three factors are picked up as the dominant factors determining the relative magnitude of vortices, that is, the asymmetry of wave height $S_1 = (H_c - H_b)/H$, the tilt of wave profile $S_2 = (L_R - L_F)/L$, and the distortion of ripples $S_3 = (\lambda_R - \lambda_F)/\lambda$ (negative in the figure). In order to find out the relative contribution of those three factors to the controlling capability of sediment movement, a certain volumes of sand (same as used for ripple formation in movable bed) were placed on two to four troughs of fixed bed ripples shown in **FIG 2** and waves were acted. After the wave action, sediment of each trough of ripples was sucked up by a nozzle and weighed after drying. From the change of horizontal distribution of sediment, movement of its centroid is obtained. As shown in **FIG 6** in which sediment movement is traced in the case of sinusoidal ripples, the velocity of centroid movement becomes constant after a certain time of wave action and the more time is required as the volume of sediment per one trough of ripples increases. The steady state of centroid movement is considered to give the average sediment movement velocity, and correlation between this velocity V_g and S_1, S_2, S_3 is analyzed (Irie, et. al., 1994). The mean velocity of sediment placed on the fixed bed ripples is considered to be expressed,

$$V_g^* = \Sigma a_i S_i \qquad (i = 1, 2, 3) \qquad (1)$$

where, V_g^* is the nondimensional form of the mean velocity of the sediment movement V_g which is positive offshore, that is, $V_g^* = (V_g/U_m)(W/U_m)(h/\eta)$ in which U_m, W, h and η are the maximum orbital velocity at the bottom, the settling velocity of sediment, the water depth and the height of ripples respectively. The coefficients a_1, a_2 and a_3 are determined empirically through the experiments with fixed bed ripples by changing wave characteristics ($H = 8$cm, $T = 1.0\sim2.0$s), the bottom slope ($\tan\beta_s = 0\sim1/15$, changing the wave profile, S_1, S_2) and asymmetry of fixed ripples ($\lambda_R = \lambda/4\sim\lambda/2$) and according to the experiments, $a_1 = 0.044$, $a_2 = -0.028$, $a_3 = 0.033$, respectively.

FIG 7 shows the correlation of the mean velocity of sediment movement between hydraulic experiments and calculation using Eq.(1). The correlation coefficient was 0.91, indicating validity of the empirical equation. The criteria of onshore/offshore sediment movement when the distortion of fixed bed ripples is $\lambda_R = \lambda/4$ ($\eta = 1.0$ cm, $\lambda = 5.5$ cm) are examined by Monte Carlo Method using Eq.(1). **FIG 8** shows the results of calculation where the direction and extent of sediment movement are shown with respect to the bottom slope and relative wave height. The figure depicts that definite onshore sediment movement is expected if the relative wave height H/h is less than 0.5 (corresponding to the offshore zone).

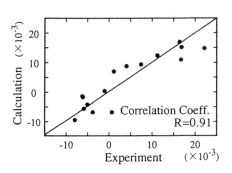

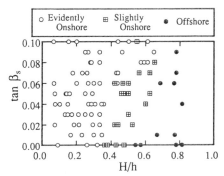

FIG 7 Comparison of V_g^* between calculation and experiments

FIG 8 Criteria of onshore movement

EFFECTIVENESS WHEN PLACED ON LABORATORY BEACH

Based on the above requirements of installing location of DRIM, its capability of controlling cross-shore sediment transport is tested in laboratory. The typical cross-section of DRIM is already shown in **FIG 1**. It is a train of precast concrete bocks and one end of a unit block is put on the other block and the plastic filter sheet is stuck on the bottom face of the blocks so that DRIM can flexibly adapts itself to the change of movable bed without damage by scour. The surface profile of DRIM is made to have the similar cross-section as distorted ripple profile shown in **FIG 2** with the distortion characteristics of $\lambda_R = \lambda/4$. Two kinds of tests are carried out to see the capability of DRIM in controlling cross-shore sediment transport;

The first case when sand is dumped intermittently

In the first case, DRIM is set in the offshore zone of an equilibrium beach profile which is formed by action of regular waves of 8cm in height and 1.6 s in period on the initial slope of 1/5 in the surf zone and 1/20 in the offshore zone. The medium diameter is 0.16 mm. Sand is dumped onshore side of DRIM intermittently to see its controlling capability of cross-shore sand movement. The rate of sediment movement under wave action is obtained by spatially integrating bottom profile change onshore from the offshore point where no significant change takes place.

The results of experiments are shown in **FIG 9**, in which the coverage area of DRIM is shown by the thick line and the volume of sand dumped during each time interval is indicated. From the figure, the direction of net sediment transport across DRIM is seen to be definitely onshore in spite of much sand supply in the onshore area. Because of the strong effect of DRIM, the bottom just offshore side of DRIM is remarkably scoured coupled with the effects of offshore sediment movement which is considered to have caused because the initial profile was not completely in equilibrium.

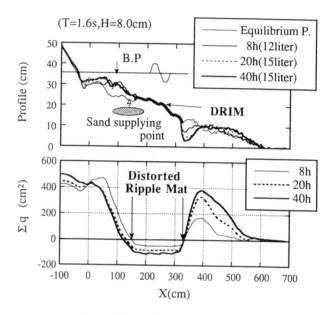

FIG 9 Beach fill by dumping

The second case when beach nourishment is carried out in a short time
The second case of laboratory study is on the checking capability of DRIM when beach nourishment is carried out in a short time as shown in **FIG 10**. In the present case, DRIM is installed in the offshore zone (this time, offshore end of DRIM is assumed to be infinite in order to find out the necessary length of DRIM). The important point is that offshore end of any nourished beach is always steeper than the original beach slope (equilibrium profile) and thereafter unlimited loss of sediment takes place under wave action. DRIM is set to check this sediment loss.
In order to reproduce this situation in the model, an equilibrium profile is made first by acting irregular waves of $H_{1/3} = 7$ cm, $T_{1/3} = 1.4$ s on the initial slope of $1/20$ in a wave channel of 35 cm in water depth. The total duration of wave action is 40 hours. The medium sediment diameter is 0.16 mm. As shown in **FIG 11**, this equilibrium profile is used as the initial profile ('Before cut' in the figure), and the offshore part of the profile is cut as shown in the figure ('After cut' in the figure). The profile just after cutting (shown in thick line in the figure) is assumed to give a slope end steeper than the equilibrium profile just like the slope end after beach nourishment. In the figure, two cases of experiments are shown, that is, 'Without DRIM and With DRIM'. In the case 'Without DRIM', eroded sediment is transported widely to the offshore.

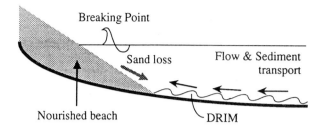

FIG 10 Beach fill in a short time

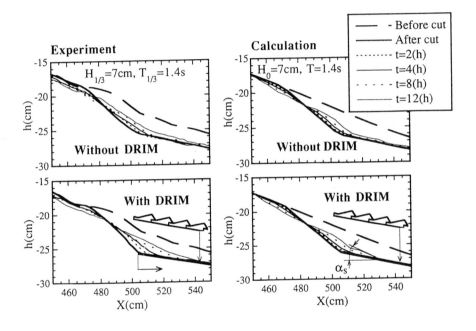

FIG 11 Checking effects of slope collapses

In the case of 'With DRIM', offshore movement of sediment is checked by DRIM and more accumulation took place within a limited area of slope end. The results of numerical calculation by Ono et. al. (1997) is also shown in the figure. One parameter which is useful to evaluate the effectiveness of checking slope collapses, will be the change of angle α_s at the toe of the slope as shown in **FIG 11**.

The results of the present experiments and calculation is shown in **FIG 12**, which shows that 'With DRIM' is keeping much steeper slope than 'Without DRIM'.The effect of DRIM in the second case in which the equilibrium profile is cut and irregular waves are used seems much inferior as compared with the first case in which DRIM is set directly on the equilibrium profile and regular waves are used.

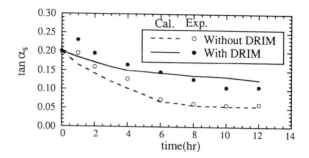

FIG 12 Comparison of toe angle α_s between 'With DRIM' and 'Without DRIM'

This reason will be attributed to the deeper water depth at which DRIM is set and also irregular waves are used in the second case. In laboratory experiments, the movement of sediment is so near to the critical movement condition in the offshore, and thus movement of sediment becomes sluggish easily with the decrease of external forces.

THE CONDITION ON WHICH 'DRIM' WORKS MOST EFFECTIVELY

The condition on which DRIM can control the cross-shore sediment transport effectively is examined in three methods; (1) By measuring the vertical distribution of horizontal mean velocity above the crest level of the distorted ripples, horizontal mass flux is obtained and the condition which will maximize the mass flux is examined (2) Sediments of various diameter and specific gravity are placed on the trough of distorted ripples and acting waves, the condition on which the sediment movement velocity is maximized is examined (3) Numerical calculation of the horizontal mass flux above the distorted ripples is carried out and the condition on which the flux is maximized is examined.

(1) Measurement of the horizontal mean velocity

The distorted ripples which have the distorted profile as shown in **FIG 2** is set in the wave channel with water depth $h = 35$cm and waves of 5~9cm in height and 0.8~2.0s in period are acted. Furthermore, distorted ripples whose scale is just twice as large as the above one, that is, with height $\eta = 2$cm and pitch length $\lambda = 11$cm is prepared and waves of similar characteristics are acted with the water depth of $h = 35$cm.

Horizontal velocity U_h above the crest of distorted ripples is measured with laser-doppler velocimeter. **FIG 13** shows an example of the measurement of mean velocity and this shoreward steady flow is observed in all cases so long as distorted ripples are used. The shoreward mass flux $Q(\text{cm}^2/\text{s})$ is obtained by integrating the onshore mean velocity and its change with d_o/λ, is examined, where d_o is water particle orbital diameter. The results are shown in **FIG 14(a)** for both pitches of distorted ripples, that is, $\eta = 1$ cm, $\lambda = 5.5$ cm and $\eta = 2$ cm, $\lambda = 11$ cm.

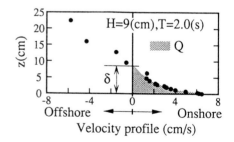

FIG 13 Onshore mass flux

Although the obtained data are scattered, the averaging curve depicts that there exists an optimum condition which makes the onshore mass flux maximum and this happens when $d_o/\lambda \simeq 1.7$.

(2) Measurement of sediment movement velocity

Sediments of various diameter and specific gravity are placed on the trough of distorted ripples and their movement velocity is measured by tracing the centroid of cross-shore sediment distribution. Three kinds of sediments are used; glass bead (diameter: 0.08 mm, specific gravity: 2.6), synthetic particle (diameter: 0.32 mm, specific gravity: 1.6), fine sand (diameter: 0.16 mm, specific gravity: 2.65). Sediments of almost 20 g were placed on the trough of distorted ripples and acting waves, movement velocity V_c of the centroid is measured.

The results of experiments are shown in **FIG 14(b)** in which the change of centroid movement velocity V_c is shown with respect to d_o/λ. In the figure, two averaging curves are drawn because the specific gravity of sediments is classified in two categories, that is, 1.6 for synthetic particles and 2.6 for fine sand and glass bead. The movement of centroid seems to be maximum when $d_o/\lambda \simeq 1.7$, which agrees well with the result of horizontal mass flux.

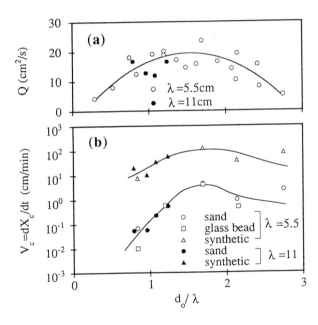

FIG 14 Results of experiments: (a) Onshoreward mass flux, and (b) sediment movement velocity, with respect to d_o/λ

(3) Numerical calculation of horizontal mass flux

The following equations for stream function ψ and vorticity ω are solved numerically introducing turbulent diffusion coefficient:

$$\frac{\partial^2 \psi}{\partial x^2} + \frac{\partial^2 \psi}{\partial y^2} = \omega \tag{2}$$

$$\frac{\partial \omega}{\partial t} + u\frac{\partial \omega}{\partial x} + v\frac{\partial \omega}{\partial y} = \nabla^2\{(\nu + \nu_t)\omega\} \tag{3}$$

where ψ is the stream function, ω is the vorticity, ν is the coefficient of kinematic viscosity and ν_t is the coefficient of eddy viscosity. The Reynold's stress is evaluated with the following Prandtl's mixing length theory;

$$\nu_t = C(\kappa l)^2 \left|\frac{\partial u}{\partial y} + \frac{\partial v}{\partial x}\right| \tag{4}$$

where κ is the Karman's constant, l is the distance from the bottom and $C = 0.35$ is used. The above equation system is transformed from rectangular coordinate (x,y) to orthogonal curvilinear coordinate (ξ,η) so that the distorted ripple profile is shown when $\eta = \eta_0$.

$$\left.\begin{array}{l} x = \xi - x_0 - \displaystyle\sum_{n=0}^{N} e^{-nk\eta} a_n \sin(nk\xi + \varphi_n) \\[2mm] y = \eta - y_0 - \displaystyle\sum_{n=0}^{N} e^{-nk\eta} a_n \cos(nk\xi + \varphi_n) \end{array}\right\} \tag{5}$$

where k is the wave number of distorted ripples and a_n, φ_n are determined so that the bottom surface reproduces the surface of the distorted ripples. **FIG 15** shows the comparison between ripple profile used for conformal mapping and actual profile used for experiments. **FIG 16** shows the results of of numerical calculation, in which the onshore mass flux Q_{cal} is shown with respect to the orbital diameter of water particle. The averaging curve is drawn taking into account the tendency obtained in **FIG 14**. The onshore horizontal mass flux is seen to take maximum value when $d_o \simeq 9$cm. From **FIG 14**, the length of distorted ripples used for calculation is $\lambda = 5.5$ cm and thus $d_o/\lambda \simeq 1.6$, which is almost identical to 1.7.

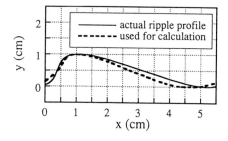
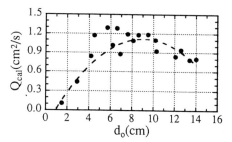

FIG 15 Ripple profile used for calculation and actual profile

FIG 16 Results of numerical calculation of onshore mass flux

The optimum condition for effective performance of DRIM

From the above three examinations, that is, (1) Measurement of horizontal mean velocity, (2) Measurement of sediment movement velocity and (3) Numerical calculation, the condition on which DRIM can control the cross-shore sediment transport is found to be $d_o/\lambda \simeq 1.7$. The physical meaning of this could be supported by the generation characteristic of natural sand ripples: **FIG 17** shows the relation between the relative ripple length λ/D and orbital diameter of water particle d_o/D, where D is the diameter of sand (Watanabe, 1989). It is well known that the ripple length steadily grows as the increase of orbital diameter, however, the growth of ripple length slows down if the orbital diameter increases beyond a certain level because it reaches to a transient state to sheet flow. From the figure, the relation between ripple length and orbital diameter is shown as $\lambda/D = 0.6 d_o/D$ during the range of steady growth of ripple length.

This relation leads to the relation $d_o/\lambda \simeq 1.7$, which is the same as the optimum condition for efficient performance of DRIM. Thus, one could say that the optimum condition for efficient performance of DRIM coincides with the condition in which the natural sand ripples grow steadily. In other words, the natural sand ripple is formed under the condition in which the energy of oscillatory flow by waves is transmitted most efficiently to the vortex formation in the lee of ripple crest, and the performance of DRIM is also highest on this condition.

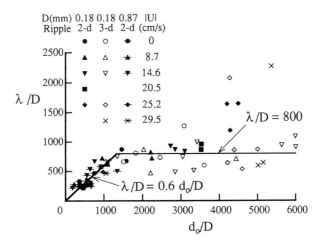

FIG 17 Relation between pitch length of sand ripples and orbital diameter of water particle (Watanabe, 1989)

THREE DIMENSIONAL CONTROL OF SEDIMENT TRANSPORT

The relative relation between DRIM and wave direction is shown in **FIG 18**. The direction of orbital velocity U will coincide with the wave direction and U will be divided into two components, U_N and U_P which are normal and parallel to the crest line of the distorted ripples respectively. α is defined as the angle between U and U_N, which represents the installation angle of DRIM relative to wave direction. Here, U_P will not contribute to any pressure gradient if the crest width of the distorted ripple mat is infinitely wide. The normal velocity component U_N, however, will contribute to the pressure gradient across the distorted ripples and the wake vortex will be formed in the same direction as shown in **FIG 18**. This suggests that the direction of the stream generated near the bottom (corresponding to β in the figure) will also be in the direction, normal to the crest line of the ripples, that is, β is possibly equal to α. This has been confirmed experimentally in a small wave basin. A set of distorted ripples of 1m square with ripple pitch length of $\lambda = 2.3$ cm is placed on the horizontal bed and acting waves of 3 cm in height and 0.5~0.7 s in period, a dye tracer which is made heavier than water is injected at the crest of the distorted ripples (near point A in **FIG 18**) and direction

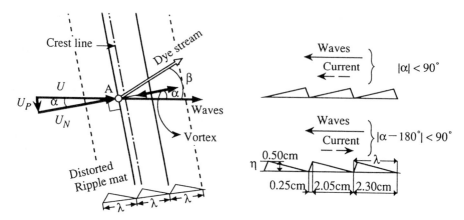

FIG 18 Direction of Wave propagation and bottom currents

FIG 19 Difference of bottom current direction

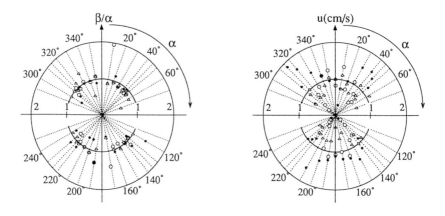

FIG 20 Results of experiments on the relation between α and β/α (left), and between α and u (cm/s), the velocity of dye centroid (right)

β of the dye centroid movement as well as its speed are observed by video tapes. The setting angle of distorted ripples is changed by 10 degrees from 0 to 360 degrees.

FIG 20 shows the results of experiments for various wave period in which setting angle α of distorted ripples is taken in clockwise along the circle and the ratio β/α is taken to radial direction. From the figure, all the data is scattered around $\beta/\alpha = 1$ so long as $|\alpha| < 50$ degrees or $|\alpha - 180$ degrees$| < 50$ degrees. This depicts that the set of distorted ripples, or DRIM is able to control bottom current so long as wave direction is within ±50 degrees from the direction normal to the crest line of the ripples. The direction of the stream is always perpendicular to the crest line of the ripples in this condition. The total coverage of the angle in which currents are controlled is 200 degrees out of 360 degrees if one includes the reverse wave direction. The data of current speed u also show the similar tendency.

FIELD INSTALLATION TO TEST THE DURABILITY AS WELL AS EF-FECTIVENESS

The prototype DRIM is installed on the artificial beach of Ehime Prefecture facing to the Seto Inland Sea. The beach is sheltered by two jetties 300 m apart each other and two offshore breakwaters of almost 80 m length as shown in **FIG 21**. On stormy season from December to March, waves of 2∼3 m in height and 6 s in period hit the coast with the inclination angle of 45 degrees from the cross-shore direction and this tilted waves generated offshore current converging at the end of offshore breakwaters. DRIM was installed focussing on this location of current convergence with the dimension of 18.5 m alongshore and 14.4 m cross-shore where the pitch length of distorted ripples was 1 m. Originally in 1993, the beach was filled with sand of 70,000 cubic meters, however, almost 10,000 cubic meters of sand was lost during one stormy season when DRIM was not installed (May, 1994). In the June of 1994 before the stormy season, DRIM was installed after refilling of sand up to the original cross-section. In the next spring of 1995, the bathymetry survey depicted that the loss was limited to 5,000 cubic meters. **FIG 22** is the cross section along the center line of DRIM. The broken line shows the cross section in May 1994 before refilling the beach, and the thin line is the cross section after refilling in June 1994 on which DRIM was installed, and the thick line shows the cross section in the spring of March 1995.

Photo.1 State of field installation

From the figure, the following points are indicated; (1) Even though the mat was installed on the refilled beach, the foreshore slope was eroded up to the sand surface naturally formed in 1994. (2) Offshore of DRIM is locally eroded and this was observed in the movable bed experiments, which is the evidence of cross-shore sediment control by DRIM. Actually, no remaining sand was observed on DRIM on calm days and also no concrete block was damaged nor lost. The growth of seaweed was remarkable as expected.

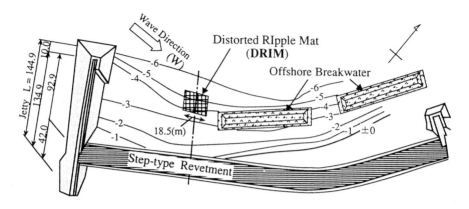

FIG 21 Layout of structures

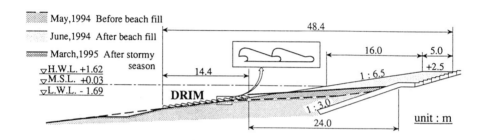

FIG 22 Beach profile change

CONCLUSIONS

(1) A distorted ripple mat which is made by precast concrete blocks (refered as DRIM) has been developed and its capability of cross-shore sediment transport is confirmed through movable bed experiments and numerical calculation.

(2) The limiting criteria of setting DRIM are as follows;

(a) The definite onshore sediment movement by the control of DRIM is expected if the relative wave height H/h is less than 0.5 (corresponding to the offshore zone), where H is the wave height and h is the water depth.

(b) The optimum condition for efficient performance of DRIM is that $d_o/\lambda \sim 1.7$, where d_o is the orbital diameter of water particle and λ is the pitch length of DRIM, and this condition coincides with the condition in which natural sand ripples grow steadily.

(c) DRIM is able to control bottom currents so long as wave direction is within ± 50 degrees from the direction normal to the crest line of ripples. By considering waves from reverse direction, $50 \times 4 = 200$ degrees out of 360 degrees is the coverage of the direction DRIM can control the bottom currents.

(d) DRIM should be set on the coast of milder wave climate because the effectiveness is confirmed so far within the condition of $d_o/\lambda < 3$.

(e) The capability of DRIM will be affected by tidal variation through such parameters as H/h, d_o/λ, etc.

(3) According to the field tests, some evidence of controlling effects of DRIM is observed in spite of small test area (18.5m×14.4m) and also unfavorable hydraulic condition of nearshore current convergence. Combination of the above functions of DRIM will yield to the utilization for various purposes, that is, for not only retaining beach sand but also protecting shoaling the navigation channel, natural sand by-passing and others.

ACKNOWLEDGEMENTS
The authors would like to express their gratitudes to Mr.Isao Kojima, former Chief of Matsuyama Branch Office of Ehime Prefectural Government, for his farseeing intelligence to understand the significance of pilot test of DRIM and affording the opportunity of field tests.

REFERENCES
[1] Inman, D.L. and E.B.Tunstall (1972): Phase dependent roughness control of sand movement, Proc. 13th ICCE, pp.1155-1171

[2] Irie, I., N.Ono, S.Hashimoto, S.Nakamura, K.Murakami (1994): Control of cross-shore sediment transport by a distorted ripple mat, Proc. 24th ICCE, pp.2070-2084

[3] Ono, N., I.Irie and S.Takewaka(1997): Prediction system of two dimensional beach profile change for evaluating alternatives of countermeasures on littoral drift (in Japanese), Proc.of 44th Japanese Conf. on Coastal Eng., JSCE, pp.501-505

[4] Watanabe, A., M.Sakinada and M.Isobe (1989): On the shape of ripples and the rate of sand transport in the field coexisted by waves and currents, Proc. of 36th Japanese Conf. on Coastal Eng.,JSCE, pp.299-303

Composite breakwaters utilizing geosystems

K. W. PILARCZYK, Manager R&D, Rykswaterstaat, Hydraulic Engineering Division, P.O. Box 5044, 2600 GA Delft, The Netherlands, Fax +31-15-2611361

INTRODUCTION

Conventional breakwaters with rock and concrete units have a long history and much experience has been gained on their design and construction (CUR/RWS, 1995). However, the increasing need for more economical designs and shortage of natural rock in certain geographical areas have stimulated in recent years the alternative designs utilizing geosystems and local materials.

Geotextile systems utilize a high-strength synthetic fabric as a form for casting large units by filling with sand or mortar. Within these geotextile systems a distinction can be made between: bags, mattresses, tubes and containers. All of which can be filled with sand or mortar. Mattresses are mainly applied as slope and bed protection. Bags are also suitable for slope protection and retaining walls or toe protection but the main application is the construction of groynes, perched beaches and offshore breakwaters. The tubes and containers are mainly applicable for construction of groynes, perched beaches and (offshore) breakwaters, and as bunds for reclamation works. They can form an individual structure in accordance with some functional requirements for the project but also they can be used complementary to the artificial beach nourishment to increase its lifetime. Especially for creating the perched beaches the sand bags and/or sand tubes can be an ideal, low-cost solution for constructing the submerged sill (with a low or moderate wave loading). Some concepts are shown in Figure 1 (Tetra Tech, 1982).

Until very recently, geosystems were mostly applied as temporary structures. The reason for that was their relatively low resistance to the hydraulic loadings (waves and currents), the lack of proper design criteria, and low durability in respect to UV-radiation and vandalism. For exposed applications, the aesthetic aspects of geosynthetics may also play a role.

In general, the sand-filled structure can be used as a permanent structure at locations with relatively low wave attack (i.e. $H < 1.5$ m, when exposed to direct wave attack), or as a submerged structure where direct wave forces are strongly reduced by submergence, or as a core of the structure. The mortar-filled units (if necessary) can be interconnected by bars or by creating a special interlocking shape, and can be used at higher wave attack (say, $H < 3$ m, when exposed). The main advantages of these systems in comparison with more traditional methods (rock, prefabricated concrete units, block mats, asphalt,

Coastlines, structures and breakwaters. Thomas Telford, London, 1998

etc.) are: a reduction in work volume, a reduction in execution time, a reduction in cost, the use of local materials, low-skilled labour and (mostly) locally available equipment. That means that in most, not too extreme cases/conditions, the work can be done by a local contractor under the supervision of the specialistic experts/company.

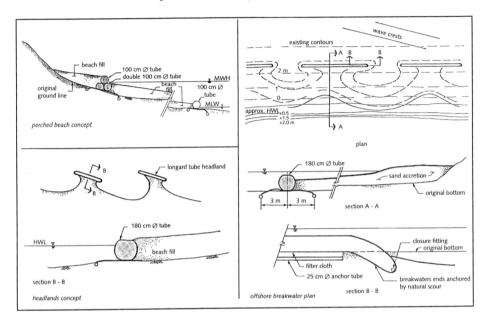

Figure 1 Some concepts of application of geosystems

In general, it can be said that all coastal protection systems and materials have some advantages and disadvantages which should be recognized before the choice is made. There is no one ideal protective system or material. Each material and system has a certain application at certain loading conditions and specific functional requirements for the specific problem and/or structural solution (Pilarczyk & Zeidler, 1996).

In the past, the design of geotextile systems for various coastal applications was based mostly on rather vague experience than on the general valid calculation methods. However, the increased demand in recent years for reliable design methods for protective structures have led to the application of new materials and systems (incl. geotextile systems) and to research concerning the design of these systems. Contrary to research on rock and concrete units, there has been no systematic research on the design and stability of geotextile systems. However, past and recent research in The Netherlands, USA and in some other countries on a number of selected geotextile products has provided some results which can be of use in preparing a set of preliminary design guidelines for the geotextile systems under current and wave attack (Den Adel, 1996, Klein Breteler, 1996, Pilarczyk, 1995, 1996, 1997, 1998, Wouters, 1995).

In the paper the large fill-containing geosystems (geotubes and geocontainers filled with sand or mortar) and their design aspects (including structural and hydraulic stability) are discussed.

DESCRIPTION OF GEOSYSTEMS APPLICABLE FOR BREAKWATERS

Large geobags, geotubes and geocontainers hydraulically and/or mechanically filled with (dredged) materials have been successfully applied in hydraulic and coastal engineering in recent years (shore protection, breakwaters, etc.) (Pilarczyk, 1995, Pilarczyk & Zeidler, 1996, Fowler et al, 1995). They can also be used to store and isolate contaminated materials from harbour dredging, and/or to use these units as bunds for reclamation works. Also, the geocurtains can be applied for construction of submerged sills and reefs.

Geobags

Geobags can be filled with sand or gravel (or cement, perhaps). The bags may have different shapes and sizes, varying from the well-known sandbags for emergency dikes to large flat shapes or elongated "sausages" (see Figure 2). The most common use for sandbags in hydraulic engineering is for temporary structures (Wouters, 1995).

Uses for sand- or cement-filled bags are, among other things:

- repair works (see Figure 2);
- revetments of relatively gentle slopes and toe constructions;
- temporary or permanent groynes and offshore breakwaters;
- temporary dikes surrounding dredged material containment areas.

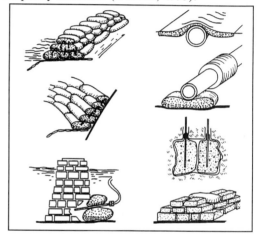

Figure 2 Application of geobags

Because this material is easy to use and cheap, it is extremely suitable for temporary structures. A training groyne is a good example. The working of a groyne is difficult to predict in advance. That is why it is a good procedure to make such a construction using a relatively cheap product first, to see how one thing and another works out, and subsequently either make improvements or, after some time, a permanent structure. Above a flow velocity of 1.5 m/s, the geosystems filled with sand cannot be used because the sand in the systems is no longer internally stable.

Sandbags can be placed as follows:

1. *As a blanket*: One or two layers of bags placed directly on the slope. An "interlocking" problem arises if the bags are filled completely. The bags are then too round. A solution is not to fill the bags completely, so that the sides flatten out somewhat, as a result of which the contact area becomes larger.
2. *As a stack*: Bags stacked up in the shape of a pyramid. The bags lie halfoverlapping with the long side parallel to the shoreline.

When installing geosystems, one should see to it that this does not take place on a rough foundation. Sharp elements may easily damage the casing of the element. Geosystems must not be filled completely. With a fill ratio of approximately 75% an optimum stability of the elements is reached. A sound soil protection is necessary if gravel (sand) sausages are used in circumstances where they are under attack of flow or waves.

Tube system

Geotube is a sand/dredged material filled geotextile tube made of permeable but soil-tight geotextile. The desired diameter and length are project specific and only limited by installation possibilities and site conditions. The tube is delivered to the site rolled up on a steel pipe. Inlets and outlets are regularly spaced along the length of the tube. The tube is filled with dredged material pumped as a water-soil mixture (commonly a slurry of 1 on 4) using a suction dredge delivery line (Figure 3). The choice of geotextile depends on characteristics of fill material. The tube will achieve its desired shape when filled up to about 80%; a higher filling grade is possible but it diminish the friction resistance between the tubes.

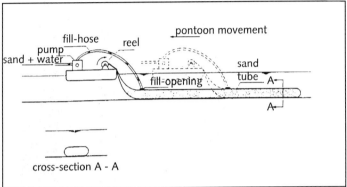

Figure 3 Filling procedure of Geotube

Tube can be filled on land (e.g. as dikes for land reclamation, bunds, toe protection or groyns) or in water (e.g. offshore breakwaters, sills of perched beaches, dikes for artificial islands or interruption of gullies caused by (tidal)currents). The tube is rolled out along the intended alignment with inlets/outlets centered on top. When a tube is to be placed in water, the effects of buoyancy on the tube geotextile prior to filling as well as on the dredged material's settling characteristics must be considered. In order to maximize inlet/outlet spacing, an outlet distant from the inlet may be used to enhance the discharge of dredged slurry and thereby encourage and regulate the flow of fill material through the tube so that sufficient fill will flow to distant points. The tube will achieve its desired shape when it is filled up to about 70 to 80% of the theoretical circular diameter or a height equal to about a half of the flat width of the tube; a higher filling grade is possible but it diminishes the frictional resistance between the tubes.

Commonly, the filter geotextile (against scour) and flat tube are fully deployed by floating and holding them in position prior to beginning the filling operation. The filter geotextile is often furnished with small tubes at the edges when filled with sand holds the filter apron at place. This apron must also extend in front and behind the unit, commonly 2 times the height of the entire structure or 2 to 3 times the local wave height.

Container system

Geocontainer is a mechanically-filled geotextile and "box" or" pillow" shaped unit made of a soil tight geotextile. The containers are partially prefabricated by sawing mill widths of the appropriate length toegether and at at the ends to form an elongated "box". The "box" is then closed in the field, after filling, using a sewing machine and specially designed seams. Barge placement of the site-fabricated containers is accomplish using a specially configured barge-mounted crane or by bottom dump hoppers scows, or split barges. The containers are filled and fabricated on the barge and placed when securely moored in the desired position. Positioning of barge for consistent placement - a critical element of constructing "stacked" underwater structures - is accomplished with the assistance of modern surveying technology. The volume of applied geocontainers was up to 1000 m³.

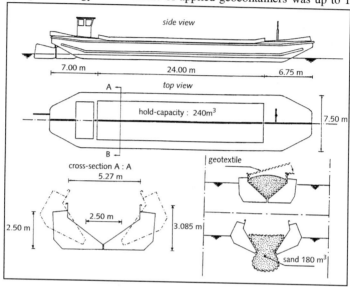

Figure 4 Filling and placing of geocontainer

The advantage of these large barge-placed geocontainers include:
*   Containers can be filled with locally available soil which may be available from simultaneous dredging activities;
*   Containers can be relatively accurately placed regardless of weather conditions, current velocities, tides, or water depths;
*   Contained material is not subject to erosion after placing;
*   Containers can provide a relatively quick system build-up;
*   Containers are very cost competitive (for larger works).

DESIGN CONSIDERATIONS
When applying geotubes and geocontainers the major design considerations/problems are related to the integrity of the units during filling, release and placement impact (impact resistance, seam strength, burst, abrasion, durability), the accuracy of placement on the bottom (especially at large depths), and the stability under current and wave attack.

The geotextile fabric used to construct the tubes is designed to:
* contain sufficient permeability to relieve excess water pressure,
* retained the fill-material,
* resist the pressures of filling and the active loads without seams or fabric rapture,
* resist erosive forces during filling operations,

* resist puncture, tearing, and ultraviolet light.

The following design aspects are particularly of importance for the design of containers:
a) Change of shape of units in function of perimeter of unit, fill-grade, and opening of split barge,
b) Fall-velocity/equilibrium velocity, velocity at bottom impact,
c) Description of dumping process and impact forces,
d) Stresses in geotextile during impact and reshaping,
e) Resulting structural and executional requirements, and
f) Hydraulic stability of structure.
Some of these aspects are briefly discussed hereafter.

Shape and mechanical strength of geotubes

For the selection of the strength of the geotextile and calculation of a required number of tubes for a given height of structure, knowledge of the real shape of the tube after filling and placing is necessary. The change of the cross-section of the tube depends on the static head of the (sand)slurry. Depending on this static head, the laying method and the behaviour of the fill-material inside the tube, it is possible that the cross-sectional shape of the filled tube (with a theoretical cross-section with a certain diameter, **D**) will vary from a very flat hump to a nearly fully circular cross-section. More recently, Liu (1978, 1981), Silvester (1985, 1990), Carroll (1994), Kazimierowicz (1994), and Leshchinsky (1995, 1996) prepared some analytical or numerical solutions and graphs allowing the determination of the shape of sand- or mortar-filled tubes based on some experiments with water. The Leshchinsky's method (PC-program) combines all the previous developments and can be treated as a design tool.

The design of the shape of the geotube is an iterative process. To obtain a proper stability of the geotube and to fulfill the functional requirements (i.e. required reduction of incoming waves/proper transmission coefficient the width and the height of the tube (= a certain crest level) must be calculated. If the obtained shape of geotube does not fulfill these requirements a new (larger) size of a geotube must be taken into account or a double-line of tubes can be used. As an example the shapes of the geotube (with the theoretical diameter of 3.25m) for the height of 1.8 m, 2.0 m and 2.1 m, based on the Leshchinsky's calculation model, is shown below (see also Figure 5). The maximum width is b = 4.15 m (d=1.8 and 2.0m) to 4.0 m (d=2.1m), and the cross-section area is A = 6.41, 6.88, and 7.06 m² respectively. The width of base of the tube (= contact width with foundation layer) is about 3.10, 2.90, and 2.60 m respectively. The required minimum pumping pressure is about 0.2 psi = 1.5 kPa = 0.15 m of a water column for d = 1.8 to 2.0m (may be it is too low for practical realization?). In case of d = 2.1 m the minimum pumping pressure is 0.4 psi = 3.0 kPa = 0.30 of a water column. The required tensile strength of geotextile is about 80 kN/m (including safety factors).

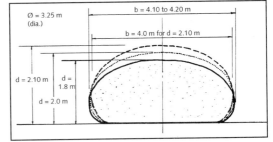

Figure 5   Shapes of geotube with 3.25m dia.

Shape and mechanical strength of geocontainers

The required perimeter of geotextile sheet must be sufficient enough to release geocontainer through the given split width b_o for a required cross-sectional area of material in the bin of barge A_f (or filling-ratio of fill-material in respect to the max. theoretical cross-section). The derivation of the required minimum length of perimeter of geotextile sheet is shown below.

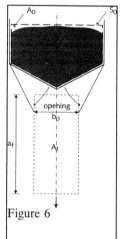

Required perimeter of geotextile sheet is $S_o = ?$
$A_o = \varphi \, S_o^2$ = total cross-sectional area (theoretical max.)
ϕ = filling-grade ratio ≤ 1
A_f = required cross-section of fill-sand (or Volume$= A_f L$)
Considering a unit passing an opening 'b_o' (Figure 6) and assuming a rectangular form of a passing unit:
$\quad A_f = b_o \, a_f \;\rightarrow\; a_f = A_f/b_o$, and the perimeter is equal to:
$S = 2 \, (a_f + b_o) = 2 \, (A_f/b_o + b_o) = S_{minimum}$
Practical requirement is $S_o > S_{min}$, therefore, it is recommended to use: $S_o = (1.25 \text{ to } 2) S_{min} = (2.5 \text{ to } 4) \, (A_f/b_o + b_o)$ (1)
The real shape on the bottom (Fig. 7) will be more close to rectangular one for low filling grade (ϕ), while more close to the semi-oval shape for a high filling grade. Therefore the max. height of geocontainer in the final position will be:
$\quad 0.25 S_o(1 - \sqrt{1 - 16 \, \varphi \, \phi}) < \; a_b \; < 0.635 S_o(1 - \sqrt{1 - 14 \, \varphi \, \phi})$ (2)
In this way an average number of required geocontainers for a given volume of design structure can be estimated.

Figure 6

The impact forces with the bottom are function of fall-velocity (dump velocity) of a geocontainer (Eq. 3) (Den Adel, 1996). The equilibrium fall-velocity is reached, when the gravitational force equals the flow resistance force. This is the maximum velocity.

$$V_{max} = \sqrt{\frac{2 \, Vol \, (\rho_s - \rho_w) \, g}{A \; \rho_w \, C_d}} \qquad (3)$$

with: V_{max} = equilibrium velocity [m/s], ρ_s = bulk density of fill material inside geocontainer [kg/m³], ρ_w = specific density water [kg/m³], Vol = volume of geocontainer [m³], A = flow catching surface area geocontainer[m²], C_d=drag coefficient[-].
During the impact on the sub soil the geocontainer is reshaped from a vertically orientated cone, through a cylinder, into a horizontally orientated ellipse (Figure 7). Just before touch down the whole geocontainer has a certain kinetic energy depending on its velocity, which must be absorbed by the strain of geotextile. The inside pressure due to impact q_o results in a tensile force of the geotextile (F).

$$F = q_0 \, R \qquad (4)$$

where

$$q_0 = K^2 \sqrt{\frac{Vol \; \rho_s \; v^2 \; E}{S \, L \, R^2}} \qquad (5)$$

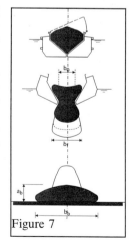

Figure 7

with: q_0 = overpressure inside geocontainer [N/m^2], Vol = fill-volume of geocontainer [m^3], ρ_s = bulk density of the fill material [kg/m^3]; ρ_s = 1600 for dry- and 2000 for saturated sand, v = velocity at the touch down [m/s], E = stiffness modulus of the geotextile [N/m], L = length of geocontainer [m], R = radius of geo container (=S/2-π)[m], S = perimeter of geocontainer [m], and K = dissipation factor [-].

It should be stated that this theoretical simulation model represents a rough schematization and be used only to give an indication.

Practical note: The prototype experience indicate that geocontainers with volume up to 200 m^3 and dumped in water depth exceeding 10 m have been frequently damaged (collapse of seams) using geotextile with tensile strength lower than 75 kN/m, while nearly no damage was observed when using the geotextile with tensile strength equal or more than 150 kN/m. This information can be of use for the first selection of geocontainers for a specific project (is an accidental damage acceptable or not).

DUMPING PROCESS OF CONTAINERS AND PRACTICAL UNCERTAINTIES

A summary of various forces during the dumping and placement process is given in Figure 8.

1. After opening of the split of a barge the geo container is pulled out by the weight of soil but at the same time the friction forces along the bin side are retarding this process. Due to these forces the tension in geotextile is developing at lower part and both sides of the geocontainer. The upper part is free of tension till the moment of complete releasing of geocontainer. The question is how far we are able to model a friction and the release process of geocontainer.

2. Geocontainer will always contain a certain amount of air in the pores of soil and between the soil and the top of (surplus) geotextile providing an additional buoyancy during sinking. The amount and location of air pockets depends on soil consistency (dry, saturated) and uniformity of dumping. The air pockets will exert certain forces on geotextile and will influence the way of sinking.

The question is how to model in a proper way the influence of soil consistency and air content on shape and stresses in geotubes/geocontainers.

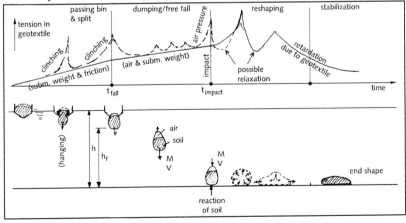

Figure 8 Development of forces during dumping process of geocontainers

3. The forces due to the impact with the bottom will be influenced by a number of factors:

* consistency of soil inside the geocontainer (dry, semi-dry, saturated, cohesie, etc.) and its physical characteristics (i.e. internal friction);
* amount of air;
* permeability/airtightness of geotextile;
* strength characteristics of geotextile (elasticity/elongation vs. stresses, etc.);
* fall-velocity (influenced by consistency of soil; saturated soil diminish amount of air but increases fall speed);
* shape and catching surface of geocontainer at impact incl. effect of not horizontal sinking (i.e. catching of bottom with one end);
* type of bottom (sand, clay, soft soil, rock, soil covered with rockfill mattress, etc.) and/or type of sublayer (i.e. layer of previous placed containers).

During the impact the cross-sectional shape of geocontainer will be undergoing a continous reshaping; from cone shape, first probably into a transitional cylindrical shape, and through a certain relaxation, into a semi-oval shape or flat triangular/rectangular shape dictated by soil type, perimeter and elongation characteristics of geotextile.
The question is how far we are able to model this impact phenomena and resulting forces/stresses in geotextile.

4. In final situation the geocontainers will perform as a core material of various protective structures or as independent structure exposed to loading by currents and waves, and other loadings (ice, debris, ship collision, vandalism, etc.). In most cases the geo containers will be filled by fine (loosely packed) soils.
The question is how these structures will behave in practice under various types of external and internal loadings.

HYDRAULIC STABILITY CRITERIA

The general calculation scheme for stability of geotubes is shown in Figure 9 where H = wave height and k = reflection coefficient (Delft Hydraulics Lab, 1973). Based on this schematisation the resistance to the horizontal displacement and to the overturning can be calculated.

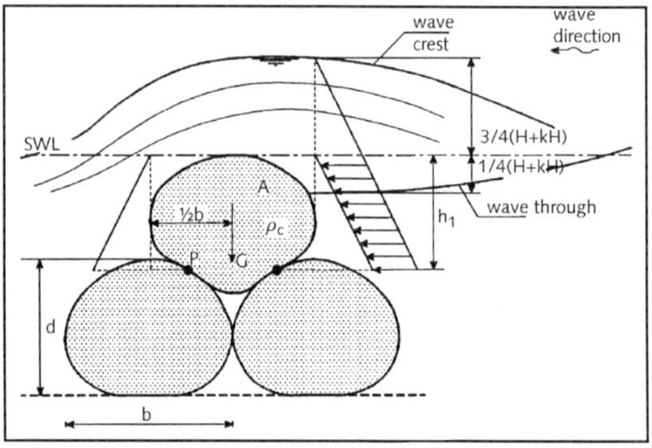

Figure 9   Calculation scheme for geotubes

During the hydraulic testing the both components of stability are implicitly included in the test results. The design method with regard to wave load based on test results can be presented as a critical relation of the load compared to strength, depending on the type of wave attack (Wouters, 1995, Klein Breteler, 1996):

$$\left(\frac{H_s}{\Delta D}\right)_{cr} = A * (\text{function of } \xi_{op}) \tag{6}$$

In which: A = revetment (stability) constant (-), H_s = significant wave height (m), Δ = relative density (-), D = thickness of the top layer (m), and ξ_{op} = breaker parameter (-). The relative density is defined as follows:

$$\Delta = \frac{\rho_s - \rho_w}{\rho_w} \tag{7}$$

with: ρ_s = density of the protection material and ρ_w = density of water (kg/m^3). For porous top layers, such as sand mattresses and gabions, the relative density of the top layer must be determined, including the water-filled pores:

$$\Delta_m = (1 - n) \cdot \Delta \tag{8}$$

In which: Δ_m = relative density including pores (-) and n = porosity of the top layer material (-). The breaker parameter is defined as follows:

$$\xi_{op} = \frac{\tan\alpha}{\sqrt{H_s/L_{op}}} \tag{9}$$

In which: $L_{op} = \frac{g}{2\pi} T_p^2$ \hfill (10)

α = slope angle (°), L_{op} = deep-water wavelength at the peak period (m), and T_p = wave period at the peak of the spectrum (s).
The advantage of this black-box design formula is its simplicity. The disadvantage, however, is that the value of A is known only very roughly for many types of structures.

The stability relation of sand, gravel or cement bags which are used as protection elements on a slope appears to deviate somewhat from the formula according to the black-box model. For regular waves the recommended formula is as follows:

$$\left(\frac{H}{\Delta D}\right)_{cr} = \frac{3.5}{\sqrt{\xi_o}} \tag{11}$$

In which Δ is the relative density if the pores are completely filled with water (Δ_m). The representative thickness D is the average thickness of the top layer, measured perpendicularly to the slope. If this stability relation is combined with the relation found between H_s and H, (significant wave height with irregular waves and the wave height with regular waves) this results in the following stability relation:

$$\left(\frac{H_s}{\Delta D}\right)_{cr} = \frac{2.5}{\sqrt{\xi_{op}}} \tag{12}$$

For concrete sausages (tubes) used as a protection element on the crest of a low or underwater breakwater, it is found that the following stability relation for regular waves can be used:

$$\left(\frac{H}{\Delta b}\right)_{cr} = 3.2 \left(\frac{H}{L_0}\right)^{1/3} \tag{13}$$

In which b is the width of the sausage. Should two sausages be connected, the widths of both sausages together can be filled in for b.
If the sausage is placed with its longitudinal direction perpendicularly to the axis of the breakwater, the following stability relation applies:

$$\left(\frac{H}{\Delta l}\right)_{cr} = 1.0 \tag{14}$$

In which l is the length of the sausage (tube).

Concerning the flow load, above a flow velocity of 1.5 m/s, the sand in the systems is no longer internally stable (as is more or less the case for all geosystems filled with fine material) and may deform. The design formulas on current attack can be found in (Pilarczyk, 1990, 1998).

Also for these systems the soil-mechanical stability should be treated according to the criteria mentioned in (Stoutjesdijk, 1996).

More information on the use of geotubes in construction of breakwaters and slope protection can be found in (Delft Hydraulics, 1973, 1975, 1983, 1994). Tanaka et al (1990) and Sawaragi (1995) provide some information on wave control by flexible underwater mound.

OTHER DESIGN CONSIDERATIONS

Durability/UV-protection. There is no problem with durability of the geosystems when they are submerged or covered by armour layers. However, in case of exposed geosystems the UV radiation and vandalism are the factors which must be considered during the design. All synthetics are vulnerable to UV. The speed of UV degradation, resulting in the loss of strength, depends on the polymer used and type of additives. Polyesters (PET) are by nature more light stable than, for example, polyamide (PA) and polypropylene (PP). As an example, the Dutch tests with geosynthetic ropes (stabilised and not stabilised) exposed to various environment have provided the following results concerning the strength of the surface yarns after 3 years (in %) in comparison with the original strength:

fabric type	land-climate	sea-climate	intertidal zone ebb-flood	50 m under the sea
PET: stabilised	63%	62%	94%	93%
PA : stabilised	33%	8%	85%	91%
PA : no	14%	6%	80%	71%
PP : stabilised	41%	46%	93%	95%
PP : no	1%	16%	92%	95%

Note: the geosynthetics under water and in the intertidal zone show very little degradation in strength in comparison with geosynthetics placed on land; in the inter-tidal zone the geosynthetics are covered very soon by algae which provide very good UV protection.

To avoid the problem with light degradation the fabrics must be properly selected (i.e. polyester) and UV stabilized (Santvoort, 1994). As the period in which the fabric is exposed is short (in terms of months), no serious problems are to be expected. In case of more or less permanent applications under exposed conditions the fabric must be protected against direct sunlight. There is a number of methods of surface protection for geosystems. To provide additional UV and abrasion protection to the exposed sections of tubes, a coating of elastomeric polyurethane is often used. This coating, however, has a tendency to peel after about a number of months and therefore, has to be reapplied.

The permanent surface protection by riprap or blockmats (Figure 10) is a rather expensive solution and it will normally be applied only when it is dictated by necessity due to a high wave loading or danger of vandalism or other mechanical damage ie. boating, anchoring, etc. In other cases it will be probably a cheaper solution to apply a temporary protection of geotextile tubes by an additional layer of a strong geotextile provided with special UV-protection layer (Figure 11).

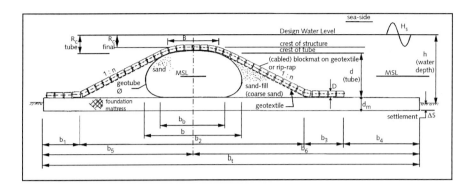

Figure 10 Geotube with a blockmat as armouring

This geotextile layer might provide a protection for at least 10 years. Every 10-years (probably more) a new geotextile surface-layer must be added, however, it can be that the life-time of this layer is much longer. There is always a possibility to pass on to a permanent protection if necessary. In case of this solution a maintenance program is necessary to quarantee the maintenance budget at a proper time. To avoid lifting up, this protective layer must be prepared by using a strong, heat-stabilized geotextile (i.e. polyester, 100kN/m), but relatively open (O_{90} = 1 to 1.5 mm).

Since a part of the tubes is exposed permanently, this geotextile layer must be provided with an extra protection against U.V.-radiation. This extra protection can be realized by adding the highly U.V.-stabilized nonwoven fleece needled onto the main fabric. The function of this felt layer is also to trap the sediment particles and algae which give again extra U.V.-protection. The experience with this system in Nigeria and in the Netherlands, under exposed conditions, was very satisfactorily (Tutuarima & van Wijk, 1984).

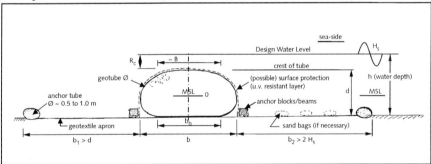

Figure 11 Geotube with a surface protection layer

This protection layer must be properly anchored by edge (concrete-) blocks/beams (about 0.5 to 1 tonne per meter of the tube). The edges of the geotextile should be wrapped up (folded over) or connected to the anchor blocks (i.e. by pins). It is also possible to anchor the edges by a heavy rock (stone class 300-1000kg, D_{50} = 0.75m) over the width of the edge of about 2m (= 3 stones). There should be an additional width of the geotextile (also about 2m) allowing the wrapping up over and under the stones.

GEOCURTAINS (BEROSIN CURTAINS)

The **BEROSIN** curtain is a flexible offshore structure made of various woven geotextiles which, after being placed near the shore and anchored to the bed, catches the sand transported by currents and waves, thus providing accretion on a shore and preventing erosion (Figure 12). The proper choice of permeability of a geotextile creates the proper conditions for the sedimentation of suspended sediment in front of or under the curtain and at the same time allows the water to flow out without creating too high forces on the curtain and, thus, on the anchors.

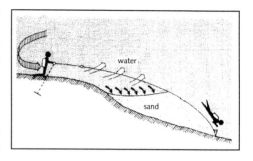

Figure 12 Principles of BEROSIN curtain

The quick sedimentation process will help to minimize the forces on the lower edges of the curtain. Special open pockets on the surface at the lower edge of a curtain are filled with sand already at the beginning of the sedimentation process and function as anchors. For the purpose of placement of the curtain, some of these pockets can initially be filled with sand, gravel, slags or other materials to provide an initial anchoring; if necessary, a small amount of additional ballast can be added. To allow the process of catching sediment, the upper edges are equipped with a floating capacity (floaters with depth compensation) adapted to the specific flow conditions and the depth (Van der Hidde, 1995, Pilarczyk & Zeidler, 1996).

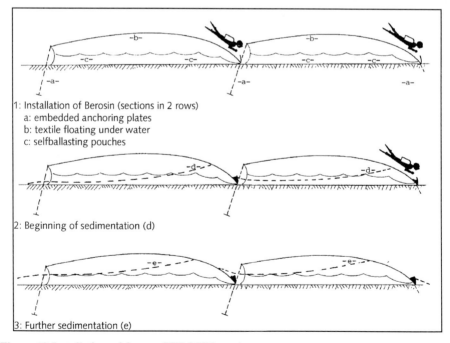

1: Installation of Berosin (sections in 2 rows)
  a: embedded anchoring plates
  b: textile floating under water
  c: selfballasting pouches

2: Beginning of sedimentation (d)

3: Further sedimentation (e)

Figure 13 Installation of 2-rows BEROSIN sections

To create the larger submerged reefs (with a sufficient wave reduction) the BEROSIN curtains can be placed in interlinked sections as shown in Figure 13.

The horizontal system can also be applied directly on the beach (in a swash zone); the sediment transported during the run-up phase (or during high tide) will be accumulated under the cover of Berosin during the run-down phase (or by tidal currents during falling tide). It will ensure a very rapid growth of the beach. In that case, however, the system can be affected by vandalism, especially in touristic areas or by ice movement.

In the case of the coast of Vlieland in the Netherlands, some of the horizontal curtains placed experimentally in the intertidal zone have provided a growth of the beach/foreshore of 0.5 to 1.0 m within a week, whereas with others it took a few weeks. It was also recognized that the sheets (curtains) can be easily damaged in the vicinity of rock, due to abrasion (one curtain was connected to the existing rock groyne). On the other hand, the heads of the existing groynes were badly damaged and the beach between the groynes was eroded during storms, whereas the area protected by the curtains remained in good condition.

It seems that this system can provide a low-cost measure for steering the morphological processes. However, more prototype experiments in various wave climates are needed before the final conclusions on the effectiveness and durability of this system in various design conditions can be drawn.

APPLICATIONS OF GEOSYSTEMS

Nicolon, BV, has copyrighted the name for GeoTubes and GeoContainers. Geotubes are commonly used to assist in dike and groin construction whereas Geoconcainers are either dumped from dump trucks or bottom dump (split) barges. Geotubes have been used extensively on the northern shores of The Netherlands and Germany for dike construction with fine-grained dredged sands pumped to form a barrier dike for subsequent hydraulic fill behind the dike and as a core for breakwaters or dikes (Figures 14 and 15).

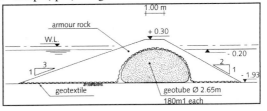

Figure 14 Marken breakwater (NL)

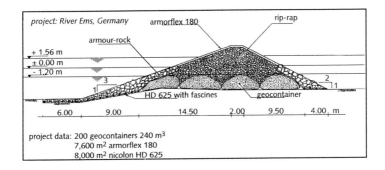

Figure 15 Geocontainers in dike construction; river Ems, Germany

Geocontainers have been used for construction of underwater berms and scour protection of banks. Dredged material filled tubes have been used as containment dikes in Brazil and France and more recently in the Netherlands for both river training structures on the rivers Waal, and Old Meuse and as shoreline protection at Leybucht on the North Sea in Germany (Spraque, 1994). Application of these systems is illustrated by a number of projects executed in the Netherlands and Germany (Figure 15). Several Geotube and Geo-container projects have recently been designed and constructed in the U.S., Taiwan, Malaysia, Philippines and Japan, and their performance is being documented so that improved design and construction methods can be recommended (Fowler et al, 1995, Pilarczyk, 1995, Van Oord-ACZ, 1995, Wouters, 1995, Leshchinsky, 1995, 1996).

CONCLUSIONS
The following conclusions can be drawn based on the actual developments and experience.
* Geotubes and geocontainers offer the advantages of simplicity in placement and constructability, cost effectiveness, and minimal impact on the environment.
* When applying this technology the manufacturer's specifications should be followed. The installation needs an experienced contractor.
* When applying geotubes and geocontainers the major design considerations/problems are related to the integrity of the units during release and impact (impact resistance, seam strength, burst, abrasion, durability etc.), the accuracy of placement on the bottom (especially at large depths), and the stability.
* The theoretical models to simulate the fall velocity and the impact of geocontainer on the subsoil have been developed and calibrated with the test results. However, the theoretical model to simulate the impact give indicative results only.
* Information presented on the stability criteria will be of help in preparing the preliminary alternative designs with geosystems.
* The geotextile systems can be a good and mostly cheaper alternative for more traditional materials/systems. These new systems deserve to be applied on a larger scale. However, there are still much uncertainties in the existing design methods. Therefore, further improvement of design methods and more practical experience under various loading conditions is still needed.

REFERENCES
Carroll, R.P., 1994, Submerged geotextile flexible forms using non-circular cylindrical shapes, *Geotechnical Fabric Report*, IFAI, St. Paul, MN, 12(8).
CUR/RWS, 1995. Manual on the use of rock in hydraulic engineering, CUR report 169, NL
Delft Hydraulics Laboratory, 1973, Breakwater of concrete fill hoses, Report1085.
Delft Hydraulics Laboratory, 1975, Artificial Islands in the Beaufot-sea: M 1271 part III, comparison of stability of shore protection with gabions and sand sausages (2-dim.); M 1271 part V, stability of shore protection with sand sausages on circular island.
Delft Hydraulics Laboratory/Delft Soil Mechanics Laboratory, 1983, Stability of ProFix sand filled mattresses under wave action, Report of model investigation, R1903.
Delft Hydraulics/Nicolon, 1994, Stability of breakwaters constructed with Geotubes or Geocontainers, 2-dimensional model tests, Report on the model investigation, H2029.
Den Adel H., 1996, Forces due to impact and deformation of geotubes (in Dutch), *Delft Geotechnics*, report CO-345040.
Den Adel, H., Hendrikse, C.H., and Pilarczyk, K.W., 1996, Design and application of geotubes and geocontainers, *Proceedings of the 1st European Geosynthetics Conference*

(EuroGeo), Maastricht, A.A. Balkema (Publisher).

Fowler, J., D. Toups, Ch. Mesa and P. Gilbert, 1995, Geotextile contained contaminated dredged material, Marina del Rey, Los Angeles and port of Oakland, California, *Proc. 14th World Dedging Congress* (WODA), Amsterdam.

Kazimierowicz, K., 1994, Simple Analysis of Deformation of Sand-Sausages, *5th Inter. Conf. on Geotextiles, Geomembranes and Related Products*, Singapore.

Klein Breteler, M., 1996, Alternatieve open taludbekledingen (Alternative open slope revetments, in Dutch), *Delft Hydraulics*, H1930.

Leshchinsky, Dov, and Leshchinsky, Ora, 1995, Geosynthetic Confined Pressurized Slurry (GeoCops): Supplement Notes for Version 1.0, May 1995 (Nicolon/US Corps).

Leshchinsky, Dov, Ora Leshchinsky, Hoe I. Ling, and Paul A. Gilbert, 1996, Geosynthetic Tubes for Confining Pressurized Slurry: Some Design Aspects, *Journal of Geotechnical Engineering*, ASCE, Vol. 122, No.8, August.

Liu, S,. Gen, 1978, Sand sausages for beach defence work, *Univ. of Western Australia.*

Liu, S., Gen, 1981, Design criteria of sand sausages for beach defences, *XIX IAHR Congress*, New Delhi, India.

Pilarczyk, K.W. (ed.), 1990. Design of seawalls and dikes - Including overview of revetments. In: *Coastal Protection*, A.A. Balkema Publisher.

Pilarczyk, K.W., 1995, Novel systems in coastal engineering; geotextile systems and other methods, *Rijkswaterstaat*, Delft.

Pilarczyk, K.W., 1996, Geosystems in hydraulic and coastal engineering - An overview, *Proceedings of the 1st European Geosynthetics Conference* (EuroGeo), Maastricht.

Pilarczyk, K.W., 1997, Application and design aspects of geocontainers, *Geosynthetics '97*, Long Beach, CA.

Pilarczyk, K.W., 1998, Stability criteria for geosystems - an overview -, *6th Inter. Geosynthetics Conference*, Atlanta, USA.

Pilarczyk, K.W. and Zeidler, R.B., 1996, Offshore breakwaters and shore evolution control, A.A. Balkema Publisher, Rotterdam.

Santvoort, G., 1994, Geotextiles and Geomembranes in Civil Engineering, A.A. Balkema

Sawaragi, T., 1995. Coastal Engineering - Waves, Beaches, Wave-Structure Interactions, Elsevier, Amsterdam - New York - Tokyo.

Silvester, R., 1986, Use of grout-filled sausages in coastal structures, ASCE, *J. Water way, Port Coastal and Ocean Engineering*, Vol. 112, No. 1, January.

Silvester, R., 1990, Flexible Membrane Units for Breakwaters, in '*Handbook of Coastal and Ocean Engineering*, John B. Herbich, ed., Vol. 1, pp. 921-938.

Sprague, C.J., 1994, Dredged material filled geotextile containers, prepared for the *US Army Corps of Engineers*, Vicksburg, MS.

Stoutjesdijk, T., 1996, Geotechnical aspects of alternative systems (in Dutch), *Delft Geotechnics*, H1930.

Tanaka, M., T. Oyama, T. Kiyokawa, T. Uda and A. Omata, 1990. Wave control by flexible underwater mound, *Proc. Offshore Tech. Conf.*, OTC 6405.

Tetra Tech, 1982, Longard Tube Applications Manual (Aldek A-S Longard), U.S.A.

Tutuarima, W.H. and W. van Wijk, 1984, ProFix mattresses - an alternative erosion control system, in *Flexible Armoured Revetments incorporating geotextiles*, T. Telford.

Van der Hidde, 1995, **BEROSIN**, product info., *Bureau van der Hidde*, Harlingen, P.O. Box 299, The Netherlands.

VAN OORD ACZ BV., 1995, Test programme of geocontainers, Van Oord ACZ/Nicolon.

Wouters, J., 1995, Stabiliteit van geosystemen (Stability of geosystems), *Delft Hydraulics*, H1930/A2.95.40 (in Dutch).

Discussion

ASSESSING SCHEME SAFETY: PAPERS 1 & 2

Dr J.E. McKenna, Babtie Group Ltd
Question to Paper 1
What prompted the introduction of the new legislation requiring the regular inspection of coastal dykes, and with whom does the responsibility lie for carrying out the inspections?

Prof. Ir. Drs J. K. Vrijling, Delft University of Technology, the Netherlands
After the 1953 flood disaster in the Netherlands it was decided and enshrined in law that all defences should be improved to Delta-standards (basic design flood frequency 1/10 000 years). These improvements were paid for by the Government.

In 1996 a new law on water defence was passed to regulate the situation after the improvement of all defences. After the improvement the responsibility of maintenance rests with the water boards, in technical as well as in financial sense. To regulate these maintenance activities a joint organization of the government, the provinces, the water boards, the laboratories and Delft University of Technology formulated design-codes, of which Paper 1 is a part. The hydraulic boundary conditions are fixed by the Government (Rijkswaterstaat).

A system of monitoring the defences is defined in the law on flood defence. Every five years the water boards have to check the safety of their defences using the hydraulic boundary conditions defined by the government and the design and monitoring codes. The results have to be reported to the provincial authorities. Consequently, the provinces have to check that the water boards have duly reported the checks and whether the defences passed the check. Finally, the provinces inform the central government.

Dr K.R. Bodge, Olsen Associates Inc, USA
Comment on Paper 1
In regard to comments regarding coastal flood insurance; in the US, flood insurance is essentially underwritten by the Federal Government through the Federal Insurance Administration (FIA), part of the Federal Emergency Management Agency (FEMA). It is the opinion of many that the ease, and reduced cost, of obtaining this subsidized insurance has historically promoted explosive (and often ill-sited) development of the US coastal zone, particularly prior to the establishment of proper state or local coastal set-back requirements for ocean-front buildings. Essentially, the National Flood Insurance Program directly contributed to the intensive ocean-front construction that it now decries and is increasingly resistant to protect through federal funding of beach nourishment.

C. Jones, GHD Macknight, Australia
Question to Paper 1
For transitional depths and flat bed slopes (<1:100), where wave breaking modifies the spectrum shape, would it be more appropriate to use $H_{1\%}$ or $H_{2\%}$ to define run-up and overtopping (acknowledging the difficulty of determining these values in practice which may require physical modelling)?

Coastlines, structures and breakwaters. Thomas Telford, London, 1998

Dr J.W. van der Meer, Paper 1

In principle it would be better to use $H_{2\%}$ instead of H_s for determining the 2% wave run-up height. Simply because in both cases for the waves as well as for the run-up the 2%-values are used. Practically it gives problems. The significant wave height is a relatively stable characteristic parameter as it is based on the average of the highest one-third of all the waves or on the whole spectrum. The 2%-value is less stable as it is based on only the highest few percent of the probability distribution of the waves. Therefore there is much more scatter in determining the $H_{2\%}$ than the H_s. Another problem is that the significant wave height in shallow water determined in the time domain (average of highest one-third) differs from the one that can be calculated from the spectral domain ($H_s = 4\sqrt{m_0}$).

Until more research has been performed on shallow water situations it is advised to use H_s in determining the wave run-up or overtopping. In some cases this may lead to a little conservative approach.

Editor's comment on discussion to paper 1

Dr van der Meer's comments on the variability of $H_{2\%}$ are important. It should be also be remembered that nearly all prediction methods for primary responses of coastal structures are described in terms of H_s. It might theoretically be desirable to move to predictions of $H_{2\%}$ and then to calculate responses using values of $H_{2\%}$, but it would probably introduce as much or more confusion than the conversion from a regular wave height to H_s. It is probably safer to simply apply corrections for shallow water conditions where those become available. In any such debate, it is also very important to identify whether the (usually small) differences between the definition of significant wave height as $H_{1/3}$, and its definition as $H_{m0} = 4\sqrt{m_0}$, have become larger. In recent research[1], there is evidence that these different measures of wave height differ strongly for low steepness waves and steep bed slopes.

Prof. Ir. Drs J.K. Vrijling, Delft University of Technology, the Netherlands

Question and comment on Paper 2

In Paper 2 you studied the risk of flooding defined as the product of the probability of flooding and the consequent damage in order to provide insurance companies with a basis to establish premiums. Did you consider the ideas that the insurance companies build flood defences in return for a part of the premium income?

The econometric model developed by Professor Van Danzig, that provided the basis for the optimal return period of 1/10 000 in the Netherlands, basically compares the present value of the insurance premium with the alternative of diking. As shown below, increasing the height of the dykes was the cheaper solution.

One of the major innovations of the committee was the statistical approach of the design storm surge levels. Wemelsfelder[2] has shown that the observed storm surge levels h followed an exponential distribution.

$$P(h) = e^{-\frac{h-A}{B}}$$

Although the question of the strengthening of the sea defences is a multi-faceted problem it is readily schematized to an economic decision problem.[3,4] The optimal return period or the optimal dyke height is found by minimizing the total cost TC consisting of the investment in the sea defences $I(h) = I_0 + I_1(h - h_0)$ and present value of the expected value of the loss in case of a flood for an infinite planning period.

$$TC(h) - I_0 + I_1 \cdot (h-h_0) + \frac{P(h) \cdot W}{r}$$

where
h = height of sea defence
$P(h)$ = probability of a flood exceeding h
W = damage by flood
r = real rate of interest.

Differentiating this model the optimal values of h and $P(h)$ are readily found.

$$P(h_{\text{opt}}) - \frac{I_1 \cdot B}{r \cdot W}$$

$$h_{\text{opt}} - A - B \cdot \ln(P(h_{\text{opt}}))$$

To take the decision it has to be checked, if the option to leave the dykes at the original height h_0 and to accept the risk, exceeds the total cost of the optimal solution

$$TC(h_{\text{opt}}) < \frac{P(h_0) \cdot W}{r}$$

It should be noted that the right-hand part of the inequality is the present value of the risk in case no action is taken. Generally speaking, the order of magnitude of a commercial insurance premium is twice the risk $P(h_0).W$. It is thus clear that improving the sea defence is cheaper than insuring the risk if it is economically advantageous to increase the dyke height from h_0 to h_{opt}.

The parameter values for Central Holland were[4]

$W = 29.2 \times 10^9$ Dfl
$r = 0.015$
$I_0 = 110.0 \times 10^6$ Dfl
$I_1 = 40.1 \times 10^6$ Dfl/m
$h_0 = 3.25$ m
$A = 1.96$ m
$B = 0.33$ m

The result of the optimization was a level of MSL +5.83 m and a return period of 125,000 years ($P_{\text{opt}} = 8.10^{-6}$ l/year). The total cost $TC(h_{\text{opt}})$ amounts to $213.5 \times 10^6 + 12.9 \times 10^6 = 226.4 \times 10^6$ Dfl.

The cost of the zero-alternative of leaving the dyke is considerably higher at 32×10^9 Dfl. The present value of an insurance premium that leaves some margin for cost and profit will exceed this value to some extent. Thus it may be concluded that the civil engineering solution of diking is more advantageous than the insurance. This result might also be valid for the English situation.

Dr R. J. Maddrell, Paper 2

As part of the Agreement between UK Government and the insurance industry, following the disastrous 1953 flood, the Government remains responsible for the flood defences and the insurance industry is obliged to insure the property potentially at risk if they do fail. The present series studies by Halcrow, carried out as a joint effort by the insurance industry and government agencies, focused not only on the risks and financial exposures of the insurance industry, but allowed the agencies to target funds in the most cost effective way, i.e. reducing risks where the financial exposure and risk to people are greatest.

We did not therefore consider the idea of insurance companies building sea defences in return for premiums (with over 350 insurance companies in the UK it would be almost impossible to organize). However, by participating in our study they have both an understanding of the risks and direct contact with those responsible for reducing the risks. I should also add that the last Government were looking into the possibility of privatizing flood defences and such a privatization could involve the insurance industry in the manner described. Such an approach might be feasible in urban areas where the amount of the premiums would be greatest, reflecting the exposure of the insurance companies.

Dr K.R. Bodge, Olsen Associates Inc, USA
Question to Paper 2
Did the analysis of different storm parameters assume equal probability of each simulated event?

Yes, at the request of the client.

I would imagine, then, that this lead to a more conservative, or at least less realistic, prediction of coastal flood risk?

Dr R. J. Maddrell, Paper 2

On the advice of the UK meteorologists, we did not attempt to put a probability on the storms used because of their many variables e.g. air pressure, storm track, wind speeds, distribution of isobars etc. However, the results of the storm, i.e. waves and surge, were compared with previously determined extreme levels, with the return period of storm conditions varying with duration, geographic location as well as between storms. Typically the peak storm conditions (wave height and total wave level) varied between 10–200 year return period when compared with the marginal extreme. It should be noted that the simultaneous occurrence of high water levels and large waves is inherently a joint probability and comparison in the marginal extreme values will not necessarily provide an accurate estimate of the time return period. However, as described, we did look at the variation in the timing of storms in order to examine more extreme, but meteorologically feasible, events.

G. Heald, Environment Agency (Anglian Region)
Comment on Paper 2
The work by Dr Maddrell for the Association of British Insurers provides a useful broad-brush picture of the risks to the insurance market. It could appear that a significant part of the UK coast is at high risk of flooding. The Environment Agency evaluates the risk of flooding against a more detailed suite of return frequencies than those required by ABI. Flood defences are justified, where possible, against these return frequencies and the risk to people and property is reduced. For these reasons, the Environment Agency assesses the area at risk to be less than the case presented by ABI.

Dr R. J. Maddrell, Paper 2

It is appreciated that Halcrow's approach, while being countrywide, is perhaps more general than the analyses adopted in each of their regions by the Environment Agency for the individual design of their defences. However, recent and ongoing studies undertaken for both the Agency and the insurance industry, have confirmed that Halcrow's analyses were in fact correct for all high risk densely populated areas, the exception being those areas where there was insufficient data. The remaining areas were analysed using newly provided data and Halcrow's methods, resulting in agreement in all cases, confirming the suitability of our approach.

D. Thomas, Posford Duvivier

Comment on Papers 1 and 2

The Chairman has already raised the issue of peak overtopping discharges as opposed to mean values. Recent work we have carried out at Chesil Beach has emphasized this issue's importance. In trying to reproduce real events which, for example, caused cars to be overturned and thrown onto other cars, our efforts using SWALLOW software based on the empirical method of Owen[6] gave low mean discharges. Not until we took note of the duration and frequency of the overtopping flow (perhaps 5 seconds every few waves – with relatively long wave periods) did we produce flows that were consistent with the resultant damage. Mean flows alone can be very misleading. This substantial difference between mean and peak was exemplified by observations at Chesil, the village just behind Chesil Beach. Houses just behind the bank suffered from severe overtopping. Those residents further down the High Street merely observed water running down the street.

My second point relates to the reliability of the overtopping figures that are predicted. The difference between 10 l/m/s and 1 l/m/s (i.e. the difference perhaps between acceptability and non-acceptability on some of the published guidance) is similar to the scatter in the experimental data, and to the errors consequent on slight changes in water level or wave height. We should be most aware of the need to approach this subject in a probabilistic, rather than a deterministic, manner. Use of the published formulae in a simple deterministic manner is dangerous indeed.

Dr R. J. Maddrell, Paper 2

Mr Thomas' comments regarding the variability in mean and peak flow overtopping quantities and scatter in experimental data are noted and was one of the reasons our overtopping damage threshold was ten times that used in the design guides.

Dr J.W. van der Meer, Paper 1

Reply to D. Thomas (and also to J.D. Simm, session 2)

There is a clear relationship between mean overtopping discharge and peak overtopping discharges. The following note will give the description in detail. In general it can be said that for small overtopping discharges the maximum overtopping of the highest wave (dimensions in l per m width) is about 1000 times higher than the mean overtopping discharge (dimensions in l/s per m width). For larger overtopping this factor is about 100. This means that a mean overtopping discharge of 1 l/s per m may give a maximum overtopping during one wave of 1 m^3 per m width!

Tests in Delft Hydraulics' large Delta flume on a prototype dyke showed that a man (attached to a life line) was swept away from the crest of the dyke for mean overtopping discharges of about 10–20 l/s per m.

Mr Thomas says that due to the large scatter in overtopping results the use of simple deterministic formulae is dangerous and that a probabilistic approach should be used. In fact this is not true. A good deterministic approach should also take into account uncertainty. In the given formulae for wave run-up as well as for wave overtopping a safety margin of one standard deviation was used. In this way it is not dangerous to use the formulae. Nevertheless, a probabilistic approach gives extra information, mainly on the influence of the various parameters, including uncertainty.

Mr Simm proposes to use the peak overtopping discharge instead of the mean overtopping. In fact the scatter for peak overtopping discharges is even larger than for the mean overtopping and further the peak overtopping depends statistically on the storm duration (or number of waves) and possibly on wave groups and/or sequences. What is important is that a designer should be aware of the difference between mean and peak discharge. Therefore, the relationship between both has been described below.

Wave overtopping volumes per wave and relationship between mean and peak overtopping

The recommended line for the mean overtopping discharge q is described in the paper. However, the mean overtopping discharge does not say much about the amount of water of a certain overtopping wave passing the crest. The overtopping volumes of individual waves deviate considerably from the mean discharge. By means of the mean overtopping discharge the probability distribution function of the overtopping discharges can be computed. This probability distribution function is a Weibull distribution with a shape factor of 0.75 and a scale factor a which is dependent on the mean overtopping discharge per wave and the overtopping probability. The probability distribution function is given by:

$$P_V = P(\underline{V} \leq V) = 1 - \exp\left\{-\left\{\frac{V}{a}\right\}^{0.75}\right\}$$

(1)

with

$$a = 0.84 \frac{T_m \, q}{P_{ow}}$$

(2)

with:

P_V = probability of the overtopping volume per unit width per wave $\underline{V}$ being less than or equal to V

V = overtopping volume per unit width per wave

T_m = average wave period ($N_w T_m$ is the storm duration or time interval considered)

q = mean overtopping discharge (in m³/s per unit width); equations 5 and 6 in the paper

P_{ow} = N_{ow}/N_w = probability of overtopping per wave

N_{ow} = number of overtopping waves

N_w = number of incoming waves during the storm duration

The probability of overtopping can be computed by

$$P_{ow} = \exp\left\{-\left\{\frac{R_c/H_s}{c}\right\}^2\right\}$$

(3)

The value of c follows from the assumption that the run-up distribution is similar to the Rayleigh distribution and that the 2% run-up is calculated with equation 2 in the paper. The relation for the coefficient c has the form of equation 2 in the paper for that reason, except for a factor $-\sqrt{\ln 0.02} = 1.98$. The value of c is found by:

$$c = 0.81 \, \gamma_b \, \gamma_f \, \gamma\beta \, \gamma_v \, \xi_{op} \text{ with a maximum of } c = 1.62 \, \gamma_f \, \gamma\beta \tag{4}$$

The reduction factors γ_b, γ_f, $\gamma\beta$ and γ_v have been defined in the paper.

Equation 6 in the paper can also be used for overtopping at vertical structures if a reduction factor of $\gamma_v = 0.6$ is used. Also equations 1 and 2 given above can be used for vertical structures if a proper formula for the probability of overtopping P_{ow} is available. This expression for vertical structures is:

$$P_{ow} = \exp\left[-\left\{\frac{R_c/H_s}{0.91}\right\}^2\right] \tag{5}$$

which is similar to equation 3 with $c = 0.91$.

As an illustration, a probability distribution function is given in Figure 1, based on equations 1–3. The presented line applies for an average overtopping discharge of $q = 1$ l/s per m, a wave period of $T_m = 5$ s and an overtopping probability of $P_{ow} = 0.10$ (10% of the incoming waves). This implies that a = 0.042 (equation 2) and that the probability distribution is given by:

$$P_V = P\left(\underline{V} \le V\right) = 1 - \exp\left[-\left\{\frac{V}{0.042}\right\}^{0.75}\right] \tag{6}$$

The volume for a certain exceedance probability $(1 - P_V)$ follows from:

$$V = a[-\ln(1 - P_V)]^{4/3} \tag{7}$$

A first estimate can be obtained for the maximum volume of one wave which can be expected in a certain period by substituting the total number of overtopping waves N_{ow}:

$$V_{max} = a[\ln(N_{ow})]^{4/3} \tag{8}$$

To give an impression of the relation between the average overtopping discharge q and the expected value of the maximum volume in the largest overtopping wave V_{max}, this relation is given for two situations in Figure 2. Conditions here are a storm duration of 1 hour, a slope gradient of 1:4 and a wave steepness of $s_{op} = 0.04$ with a T_p/T_m ratio of 1.15. Relations have been drawn for a wave height of $H_s = 1$ m and 2.5 m. For small mean overtopping discharges the ratio V_{max}/q is of the order of 1000 and for large average overtopping discharges of the order of 100, although not dimensionless but with the unity of seconds.

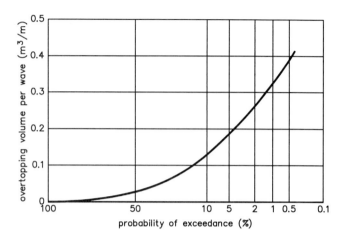

Figure 1 Probability distribution function for overtopping volumes per wave: $q = 1$ l/s per m width, $T_m = 5$ s and $P_{ov} = 0.10$.

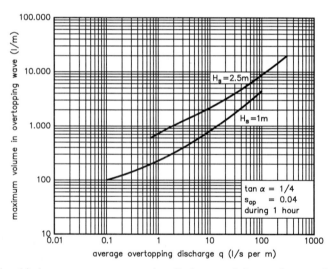

Figure 2 Relationship between mean overtopping discharge and the maximum volume during the highest wave (peak discharge).

Professor N.W.H. Allsop, University of Sheffield

Question to Papers 1 and 2

Would Dr Maddrell and Dr van der Meer comment on the interaction of assessment of sea dyke safety, frequency of inspection and routine maintenance. I have in mind a coastal river dyke in northern England which failed causing £2 million of damage. I believe that the failure, over a width of about 30 m, occurred with a still water level about 0.5–1.0 m below the crest of the embankment. There were no significant waves at this site. The strong suspicion is that failure was initiated by piping through an active or recent rabbit burrow system just below the crest of the embankment.

Investigations by Armitage[7] have identified a number of such events where animal burrows have been involved, and indeed she watched rabbits and their predators apparently living in the voids of rock armour applied to a clay/silt core embankment. This inspection suggested that the safe effective crest level for quasi-static water levels might be 0.5–1.0 m below the apparent crest level.

So given that rabbits or other animals can return to an embankment very quickly, even if eradicated, how do the presenters suggest that the safety of the dyke be assessed if inspections are only at 5-year intervals?

The suggestion for limiting overtopping discharges given by Owen[6] and included in the CIRIA/CUR rock manual[8] were originally developed by Japanese port engineers based on their assessment of safety in overtopping events at port seawalls. The discharges suggested are the mean values, probably averaged over 500 or 1000 waves. The hazard considered by the port engineers was however the effect of 1 or 2 waves, for which the instantaneous discharge would have been 100 to 1000 times greater.

The levels of tolerable overtopping were probably also influenced by the violence of the overtopping flow. This may be much increased for steep walls or other structures where impulsive breaking may occur. Some new information on this is given in this conference by Besley *et al.* Paper 4.

Dr J.W. van der Meer, Paper 1
The 5-years interval safety assessment is completely different from daily maintenance of the dykes. The safety assessment assumes that the normal maintenance by the water boards takes care of rabbits, etc. But it is indeed true that rabbit holes may create an early failure of a dyke section.

Dr R.J. Maddrell, Paper 2
In our assessment of potential failure risks we did apply a reduction factor for the crest height. However, this related to the degree of exposure (to waves and surges) and was dependent on the structure type. Had data been available on the occurrence of rabbits, then we could have included a factor for them.

Evidence from that coastal river dyke would suggest that all structures made of granular materials (clay to rock) should be treated as at risk and a factor applied. Armitage's example also reinforces the point that a defence is only as strong as its weakest link.

The only way to protect against rabbits (and there are other examples involving badgers and foxes) would be to protect below the surface of the structure with a strong, rust and rodent resistant mesh. Inspection could then be carried out after 5 years and more frequently in subsequent years.

References
1. Durand N. and Allsop N.W.H. Effects of steep bed slopes on depth-limited wave breaking. *Ocean wave measurements and analysis*, Proc Waves '97 Conference, ASCE, New York, 1997, pp1400–1413.
2. Wemelsfelder P.J. Wetmatighden in het optreden van stormvloeden. *De Ingenieur*, 1949, **9**, Den Haag.
3. Van Dantzig D. Economic decision problems for flood prevention. *Econometrica*, 1956, **24**, 276–278, New Haven.
4. Deltacommisse. *Delta rapport*. 1960, Den Haag.

5. Vrijling J.K., Beurden J. van. *Sea level rise; a probabilistic design problem.* ICCE, Delft, 1990.
6. Owen M.W. *Design of seawalls allowing for wave overtoping.* HR Report EX 924, Hydraulics Research, Wallingford, 1980.
7. Armitage J. *Initiation of breaching in flood defence embankments due to animal burrowing.* Oxford Brooks University, Oxford, PhD Thesis, 1980.
8. Simm J.D. (Ed.). *Manual on the use of rock in coastal and shoreline engineering.* CIRIA Special Publication 83, CIRIA, London, 1991.

ADVANCES IN DESIGN METHODS: PAPERS 3 & 4

Prof. Dr Techn. H.F. Burcharth, Paper 3
Supplement to Paper 3: Accropode Armour Stability
Included in my presentation, but not contained in the paper, was the following formula for the hydraulic stability of Accropode armour layer placed on a conventional filter layer and a core material with permeability similar to prototype core material $d_{50} = 0.20$ m, $d_{85}/d_{15} =$ app. 3–4, slope 1:1.33.

$$N_s = H_{mo}/\Delta D_n = A \, (D^{0.2} + 7.70) \qquad (1)$$

where

D = damage level defined as percentage of all units displaced a distance $D_n =$ (volume of unit)$^{1/3}$ or more

A = coefficient with mean value $\mu = 0.46$ and variational coefficient $\sigma = 0.02+0.05(1-D)^6$, σ being the standard deviation

H_{mo} = spectral significant wave height

Δ = $\rho_s/\rho_w -1$, ρ_s and ρ_w are mass density of armour unit and water, respectively.

The formula equation 1 is valid for the wave steepness range $0.028 \leq s_{op} \leq 0.046$ which was found to represent the lowest Accropode stability for slope 1:1.33.

The formula is based on model tests by van der Meer (1988b), Kobayashi *et al.* (1994), and Burcharth *et al.* (1998) (the last being Paper 3 in this volume, the other references are given in the paper).

J.E. Clifford, Retired
Comment on Paper 3
The tests reported in Paper 3 have the whole core of uniform material, but the provision of such a selected coarse core in practice can be costly. An example of a breakwater with core formed of three qualities of rock grading can be found in the recently completed breakwaters at the new LNG port at Ras Laffan in Qatar. Economy was achieved by using dredged rock from the new basin in the central core up to a level of about the design H_s below mean sea level. Above this level, up to the concrete cap and wave wall, the core was formed of quarry run passed over a screen to exclude small material. For the remaining core at lower levels, unscreened quarry run was used.

Due to the fine material likely to be contained in the unscreened quarry run and dredged rock, the geotechnical stability of the mound was checked under severe internal water pressures. These pressures were assessed after physical model testing, with scale adjusted rock gradings, in which pressure measurements were made.

Prof. Dr Techn. H.F. Burcharth, Paper 3
The author agrees that cores formed by more than one quality of rock grading is very often an economic solution. The fact that the model tests presented in the paper were performed with uniform core materials does of course not indicate a preference to such designs. The tests were performed in order to show the significant influence of the core porosity on Accropode armour stability. By far the largest influence comes from the core section between levels MSL ± app. H_s and extending from the seaward slope surface to the centreline of the breakwater. Theoretically, it is possible to estimate the permeability of multi-material cores and consequently also to perform correct scaling between prototypes and models.

M. Denechere, SOGREAH, France
Comment on Paper 3
We note that in Paper 3, Professor Burcharth reports that 28 rows of Accropode ® were used in his test programme. From experience, SOGREAH are currently advising that the number of rows be limited in practice to a maximum of 20. Large numbers of rows can result in gaps appearing at the top of the armour slope due to consolidation of units on the slope once in service.

SOGREAH would also like to comment on the core material used in the tests. Both core gradings used for these university tests are far too fine for any practical applications: 2 to 3 mm and 5 to 8 mm versus 4 to 30 mm in the real world. We do not know of any breakwater ever built using 1 to 25 kg core material. Again, in practice, and to facilitate the contractor's production constraints at the quarry, we actively encourage a wide core specification of, say, 1–500 kg or 1–1000 kg depending on underlayer and armouring size.

Although damage can be obtained during systematic research tests, no damage are experiences on Accropode® projects for two main reasons

- recommended safety coefficient of the order of 1.7 on the unit weight for design conditions
- transfer of SOGREAH's practical knowledge in the form of technical assistance by specialists at pertinent stages of construction.

Prof. Dr Techn. H.F. Burcharth, Paper 3
The Accropode armoured cross section tested in the model was – as said in the paper – built corresponding to recommendation laid out by SOGREAH (1991). I understand from Mr Denechere's comment that changes have been introduced with respect to number of rows. However, in the model tests we did not observe gaps appearing at the top of the armour during the consolidation of the units. That is not to say that it could not happen in prototypes where the friction between armour and underlayer is different from that between geometrically similar materials in small scale models.

Mr Denechere says that SOGREAH encourage designs with very wide graded core materials, say 1–500 kg or 1–1000 kg. However, it should be noted that although 1 kg is set as the minimum, wide graded materials can have small porosities and related small permeabilities which is not beneficial for the armour stability and the amount of overtopping water. The use of 1 kg stones as the lower limit in the upper most exposed seaward part of the core seems to me rather optimistic. I would recommend coarser material for this part of the core.

Professor H. Ligteringen, Delft Technical University and De Weger Architects and Consulting Engineers, the Netherlands
Question on Paper 3
In Paper 3, your definition of damage D makes use of the results of black and white overlay

technique. How does D relate to 'hydraulic damage' as defined traditionally, i.e. the percentage units displaced out of the layer?

Prof. Dr Techn. H.F. Burcharth, Paper 3

As specified in the paper, D is the percentage of all units displaced a distance D_n or more. D was registered by the use of colour photos. D includes both units displaced out of the layer as well as units taking part in repositioning (healing) and excessive layer slidings.

Dr P. Boswinkel, Delta Marine Consultants

Question on Paper 3

A large part of the wave dissipation by the permeable core usually takes place in the first metres. In your comparison, did you consider determining the propagation of wave energy in the core, in order to evaluate the possibilities of applying an additional coarse filter layer on top of a fine core?

Prof. Dr Techn. H.F. Burcharth, Paper 3

In the model tests we did not determine internal flow or water level fluctuations in the core (propagation of wave energy). However, as suggested by Dr Boswinkel, an additional coarse filter layer on top of a fine core will increase the armour stability.

Dr J.W. van der Meer, Infram, the Netherlands

Question on Paper 3

It is encouraging to see that you produced similar results as I did some 10 years ago. One of my reasons not to give a damage curve for Accropode is that the curve is simply too steep: after start of damage and a long storm duration the breakwater will fail. You give not only the curve, but also a standard deviation which is dependent on the damage level. As you have only a few data points it is maybe scientifically true, but has no meaning for practical engineers. With respect to the use of a safety coefficient, up to now values of around 1.5 on the stability number have been used. This gives armour weights a little lower than for Tetrapods. As you already save quite a lot of concrete by making only one layer it is my advice not to decrease the safety factor too much.

For rock slopes damage has been related to the erosion profile. For concrete armour this was changed to the number of units that were displaced out of the layer, N_{od}. You came up with a new method and definition of damage, based on the overlay technique. You recorded damage up to 100% which means that hardly any Accropode is left on the slope, certainly not around the still water level. My experience is that as soon as large holes are present in the layer, the test can be stopped as failure has been reached. This means that damages larger than 15–20% are not interesting. Can you explain why and how these high damages were measured? Is it also possible to give a relationship between your damage D and the connected number N_{od}? That would give a better comparison with earlier results.

Prof. Dr Techn. H.F. Burcharth, Paper 3

The author disagrees with Dr van der Meer that it has no meaning for practical engineers to specify a damage development curve and the related uncertainty. Such information is of course always needed in order to give insight in the type of failure. The fact that Accropode armour on steep slopes fails rather suddenly does not mean that a formula for damage development and related standard deviation should not be given. If a designer wants to design for zero-damage level, as seems to be the case for Dr van der Meer, then the formula provides the related mean value and the standard deviation of the N_s number. The standard deviation is certainly needed in order to include in a 'rational way' a safety margin.

The formula which was presented in the conference, but not included in the paper, is given above as a supplement to the paper and as a basis for this discussion. The formula makes it possible to determine the N_s-design value corresponding to any chosen failure probability and structure life time, given the long-term wave statistics for the actual location.

With respect to Dr van der Meer's question related to definition of damage, reference is given to my answer to Professor Ligteringen. Besides this, D as defined in the paper is not a new invention. Moreover, $D = 100\%$ does not necessarily mean that all units have left the slope as displacement by sliding is included. However, this is a theoretical question as nobody will use this damage level (which is inherent in the formula in order to get the upper limit correct).

For Accropode the relevant design levels when using D as damage will be $0 \le D \le 20\%$. For $D > 20\%$, the damage curve is extremely steep. $D = 10$–20% might be used only as USL (ultimate limit state) in the design.

It is possible to establish a relationship between N_{od} and D by re-analysis of the photos.

Accropodes seem to have a reasonably good self-healing ability as it has been observed that holes created by units displaced out of the layer are quite often closed by settlement of neighbouring armour units.

Dr J.W. van der Meer, Infram, the Netherlands
Question on Paper 4
Comparing overtopping results for slopes and for different spectral shapes showed very clearly that use of the peak period, instead of the mean period, brought the results together. Do you have a good reason, other than that Owen used this before, why you took the mean period?

If you did not change the spectral shape during your tests, can you then give the ratio between T_p and T_m?

Dr P. Besley, Paper 4
Our results suggest that the mean overtopping discharge and the number of waves overtopping a vertical wall are generally independent of wave period. The mean wave period T_m is only used in the equations to define whether a wave condition is 'impacting' or 'reflecting'. As the methods presented can be extended to assess the performance of existing structures, the mean period has been used as it is easily measured on site. Our model tests were carried out assuming a truncated JONSWAP spectrum, therefore the relationship between mean and peak period is given by: $T_m = 0.87 T_p$

Professor L. Franco, University of Rome 3, Italy
Comment on Paper 4
I am glad to observe an effective follow-up of my earlier work on overtopping performed at ENEL in Milan, also referred to by De Gerloni *et al.*[1] in the 1991 ICE conference on breakwaters, where the innovative method of measuring single overtopping volumes was presented. Most results and conclusions are now confirming our recommendations on tolerable discharges and our prediction equations for the number of overtopping waves and the maximum individual volume, which were derived for *deflecting waves* on deepwater vertically composite caisson breakwaters. Some divergence is noted when comparing your new data with the mean discharge prediction equation of Franco *et al.* 1994, as shown in Fig. 1 (eq.4). However, I wish to note that this equation has been already modified (with improved fit), as $Q = 0.082 \exp(-3.0\, R_c/H_s)$, after analysis of additional 230 overtopping test data from various labs under similar conditions ($h_s/H_s > 2.0$), as presented at MAST2

workshops/papers. This work[2,3] also produces new coefficients in the prediction equations to account for wave obliquity and multidirectionality. It is hoped that a new comprehensive joint paper, possibly based on further tests to cover a wider range of conditions, will soon give useful guidance to the designers of vertical seawalls and breakwaters.

Dr P. Besley, Paper 4

We note that Professor Franco's revised formula is in better agreement with our equation for reflecting or pulsating waves in relatively deep water. Of particular importance, is that the revised formula predicts significantly higher discharges at larger values of R_c/H_s, which suggests that these discharges are less likely to be underestimated. We look forward to working with Professor Franco on a joint paper in the future.

J.D. Simm, HR Wallingford

Comment on Paper 4 (and Paper 1)
I would like to pull together three points for comment.

For revetment (dyke) slopes, van der Meer's paper [Paper 1] indicates in Fig. 5 a wide scatter of results for overtopping rates for high crest deviations. These correspond to the lower overtopping rates.

The recent paper by Hedges and Reis[4] appears to argue for lower crest elevations when designing for low overtopping rates than would have previously been predicted by the Owen formulae. However, this thesis is only based on mean overtopping rates.

Putting these two points together, would the authors of Papers 1 and 4 like to comment on the proposition that at lower mean overtopping rates, when there is so much scatter between the mean and the peak overtopping rate, it would be better to design on the basis of the peak (maximum individual wave) overtopping volume and to set new allowable overtopping rates on this basis?

Dr P. Besley, Paper 4

We feel that these comments are very important, in fact the relationship between low discharges and tolerable peak overtopping has recently been addressed. In general, even if only one wave overtops in a series of 1000 waves, the mean overtopping discharge over the same period is likely to be greater than a tolerable mean discharge of 0.1 l/s/m. Mean discharges greater than this limit will be hazardous even for personnel used to working in these conditions. For vertical walls this corresponds to a limit of approximately 0.04 m^3/m for a peak volume in the largest wave. These peak volumes are associated with green water overtopping events, very aerated overtopping events (spray) are generally less important.

Analysis of the performance of a variety of structures showed that many situations in which even a small number of green water overtopping events occur are potentially hazardous. These were generally situations in which structures with high crest freeboards are attacked by large, unbroken waves. Overtopping discharge was in the form of a small number of large events. Even if the incidence of overtopping is reduced, say by increasing the crest level, the events that do occur will still be dangerous. In these cases safety can be assured only when no (green water) overtopping events take place. However, the random nature of real seas makes it difficult to specify a situation in which overtopping events are completely eliminated. A probabilistic approach is therefore required. The risk that there will be at least one overtopping event during a sequence of N_w waves is given by :

$$P(\text{overtopping}) = 1- (1-N_{ow}/N_w)N_w$$

where N_{ow}/N_w is the proportion of waves overtopping. The acceptable risk of an overtopping event occurring may depend on the use of the structure in question. It is therefore recommended that when analysis of individual overtopping volumes indicates that very small numbers of overtopping events create unsafe conditions, the structure should be optimized by limiting the risk of an overtopping event taking place to an acceptable level.

A contrasting situation occurs whenever overtopping is in the form of a larger number of small events. In this case large numbers of overtopping events can be tolerated, provided that the predicted value of peak volume, V_{max}, is below the limits discussed above. If the risk of an overtopping event occurring is unacceptably high then the maximum volume likely to overtop, V_{max}, must be estimated. It is suggested that for pedestrian and vehicle safety on structures to which the public have access, the risk of an overtopping event occurring during a sequence of 1000 waves should be less than 1%. On structures to which access is limited, less stringent criteria may apply.

References
1. De Gerloni M., Franco L. and Passoni G. The safety of breakwaters against overtopping, in *Coastal structures and breakwaters*, Thomas Telford, 1992, 335–342.
2. Franco C. *Wave overtopping and loads on caisson breakwaters under three-dimensional sea states.* MCS / PROVERBS report, Politecnico di Milano, Milan, 1996.
3. Franco C., Meer J.W. van der, and Franco L. Multi-directional wave loads on vertical breakwaters. *Proceedings of 25th International Conference on Coastal Engineering,* Orlando, ASCE, New York, 1996.
4. Hedges T.S. and Reis M.T. Random wave overtopping of simple sea walls: a new regression model. *Proceedings of the Institution of Civil Engineers*, 1998, **130** (1), 1–10.

ADVANCES IN DESIGN METHODS: PAPERS 5 & 6

Professor L. Franco, University of Rome 3, Italy
Comment on Papers 5 and 6
As Chairman of this session I wish to make a short comment to 'integrate' both papers. I just note that perforated vertical structures can also enhance marine life. As shown in my presentation at the ICE's seminar on Caissons and Breakwaters in October 1997, I enjoyed a scuba-diving inspection at the toe and inside the new multichamber perforated caissons at Porto Torres (Sardinia) and could observe a rich marine growth over the concrete walls and quite a few diverse fishes within the chambers and joints.

Fish observation during
inspection at the perforated
caisson breakwater
at Porto Torres (Italy).

With reference to Paper 5 only, I would ask the authors to provide further details on the actual features of the chamber top venting system and of the transversal walls (e.g. spacing, perforations?). The first one is quite effective in energy dissipation, while the latter ones can influence the structure's reflection response under oblique wave attack (which I believe to be relevant in this specific case given the fetches shown in Fig. 1 and the typical ship wake directions). If ad hoc three-dimensional tests were not performed, some guidance may be gained from the results of the recent MAST2-MCS-LIP research study which also investigated the reflection performance of perforated caissons under multidirectional and oblique seas.[1,2] Some results are shown in the attached figure taken from the former report: strong reductions of the reflection coefficient are achieved with very oblique waves and with the 'open deck' structure (full roof venting). The model perforated caissons were 0.9 m long, with a chamber width $B = 0.4$ m and an area porosity of 20%. In most tests the peak wave steepness was 0.04 (peak length $L_p = 3.5$ m), thus the ratio B/L_p was 0.11.

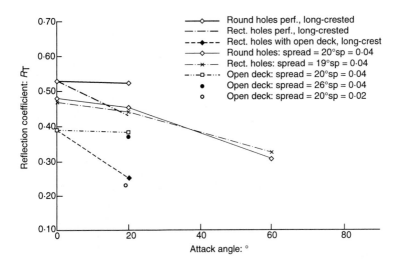

Figure 1. Reflection coefficients; three-dimensional effects on the perforated walls

Dr T. Lewis, Hydraulics and Maritime Research Centre, Ireland
Question on Paper 5
The optimization was carried out with porosity as a parameter. The configuration of the front screen was changed while maintaining the same porosity. Did you investigate the effect of the varying configurations as it is possible to achieve the same porosity with a wide variety of configurations? One large hole has the same porosity as many small ones, but obviously different hydraulic behaviour.

K. McConnell and Professor N.W.H. Allsop, Paper 5
Responses to L. Franco and T. Lewis
During the model tests on the Central seawalls, the internal configuration of the caisson was modified, based on observations of the flow processes during testing. For those tests, part of the roof had been replaced with perspex to allow the processes within the chambers to be observed, see Fig. 1. Early in the test programme, waves were occasionally seen to slam on the underside of the roof, causing concern that trapped air or direct wave impacts might cause high local pressures. To prevent air being trapped in the corner of the caisson chamber, and to reduce the risks of direct wave slam on the roof of the chamber, a curved fillet was inserted along the top of the back wall of the internal chamber, shown in Fig. 2. This recurve intercepted waves slamming against the back face of the chamber, and helped to direct the rising wave front away from direct slam against the roof, and back out through the perforated screen.

Internal walls within the chamber ran the full height of the caisson with the exception of a small opening at the recurve end to allow access from one chamber to the next. Each of the internal chambers were 5 m wide. All venting of the internal chambers were through the front screen, although in one configuration considered, a specific venting slot was included behind the outer wave wall.

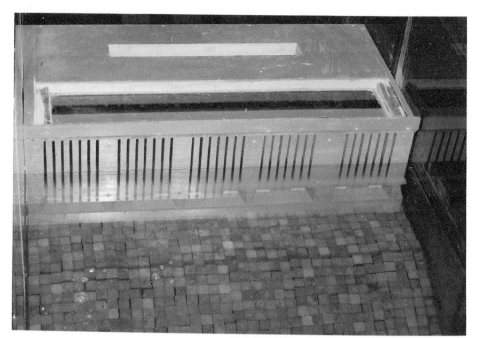

Figure 1. Central seawall model showing vertical slits, and viewing panel in the caisson roof.

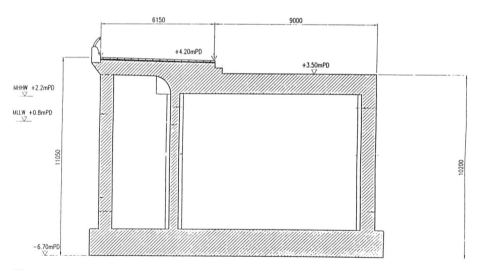

Figure 2. Section through seawall chamber showing recurve between rear wall and chamber roof.

Franco also discusses the effect of wave obliquity, and the influence of internal divide walls. In studies completed at Wallingford in 1990 and 1993, a number of alternative design for breakwaters at the Cardiff Barrage were studied in two-dimensional wave flume tests, and later under oblique waves in two-dimensional wave basin tests. Some results of physical and numerical modelling of reflections from perforated chambers/double wave screens by Allsop and McBride[3] demonstrate the effects of screen porosity, see Fig. 3.

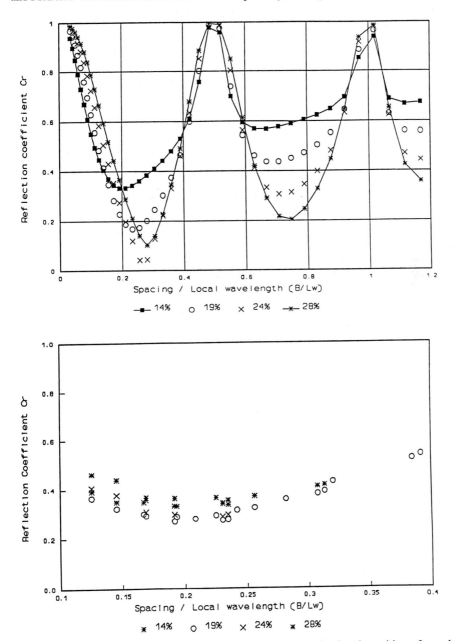

Figure 3. Reflection coefficients calculated / measured for single chamber with perforated front screen.

Results from previous tests at Wallingford for a wave screen breakwater at Plymouth discussed by Gardner *et al.*[4] were presented by Allsop and Hettiarachchi.[5] The two-dimensional random wave tests had explored whether vertical slots or horizontal slats gave any significant differences in reflection performance. From the results, it was concluded that any such effect was masked by the much stronger effects of screen porosity and relative chamber size, provided that the screen porosity was relatively even, i.e. many small apertures rather than few large holes.

At Central, the forms of the openings in the front face made by vertical members were strongly influenced by practical aspects of production, particularly considerations of formwork and rapid-casting techniques that would be needed to produce many caisson units. In the designer's view, it was preferable to minimize the number of perforations where that could be done without degrading the reflection performance. The form of the vertical members was standardized as much as possible to reduce complication, so the main change made during the optimization was in the size and spacing of these members to modify the screen porosity.

It has often also been supposed that different shapes of hole: slots or slits, circular or rectangular; would significantly alter the reflection performance of voided caissons. In general, however, where tests have been conducted to compare alternatives, the differences have usually been quite small. Certainly it has been argued that a front screen pierced by circular holes may be stronger than one pierced by rectangular holes. Contrarily, it has been argued in Italy that the rectangular holes in the Porto Torres breakwater were easier to form, see Noli *et al.*[6]

The 1993 tests for the Cardiff wave screen breakwaters[7] paid particular attention to the potential effects of internal walls on reflections. Test were conducted at 10°, 30° and 50°. It was concluded that for each of the three angles of wave incidence, reflection coefficients were generally quite similar, and relatively independent of wave spectrum or structure. As the structure was rotated (relative to the waves), the average reflection coefficients reduced from $C_r=0.36$ at $\beta=10°$, to $C_r=0.21$ at $\beta=30°$, but then increased to $C_r=0.0.26$ at $\beta=50°$. The changes are probably due to the change in effective chamber length for oblique entry, but also to increased lateral flows and attendant energy losses caused by changes to flows at the divide walls.

Dr A. Jensen, Paper 6

The important concept is that if breakwaters are to have a multifunctional role they must succeed in supplying habitat that will be used by marine life. In the case of the Sardinian perforated caissons mentioned by Professor Franco this was obviously the case. Whilst general purpose habitat is quite easy to produce, e.g. large boulder slopes with Scandinavian granite, it requires some knowledge of habitat requirements if species diversity is to be maximized or a single species targeted. This knowledge is not available from an anthropomorphic design process, it will come from detailed study of behaviour and location.

H.D. Osborn, Modernstar Ltd

Comment on Paper 6

Last year I attended a conference at the University of Strathclyde on the decommissioning of offshore structures. The diagrams attached show a proposal I put forward for a method of maintaining offshore platforms in position, and converting them to fishing stations with an extended fishing reef, thus reducing costs on decommissioning.

The artificial reef would be formed of geotextile large mesh screens, or chain-linked old car tyres, supported by HDPE flotation pipes below the effect of wave action. The screens would be anchored to the seabed by ballast filled mattresses. An arrangement is shown in Fig. 1. Figure 2 shows a plan of the platform and extended reef with long line fishing cables attached to sheaves anchored on the seabed.

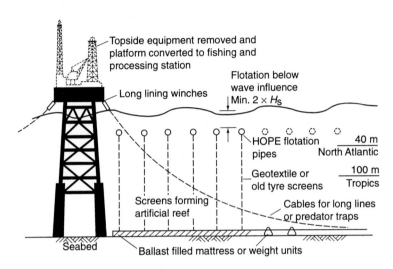

Figure 1. Artificial reef at offshore platform.

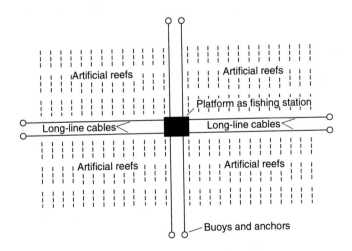

Figure 2. Plan of offshore platform and artificial reef.

The long-line fishing method employs a system of automatic baiting of snoods (hooks) and removal of fish. A new topside module would be equipped for fishing, processing, freezing, with facilities for the operating crew.

Alternatively, shorter sections of the structure could be removed and resited in shallower waters with the extended reef.

Dr A. Jensen, Paper 6

Decommissioning of offshore structures is much talked about and there are lots of imaginative ideas in circulation. Artificial reef scientists are concerned that the enthusiasm to create reefs is built upon speculation and a desire for a cost effective disposal option rather than an appreciation of what can be achieved if such large fabrications are placed as effective artificial reefs. There is a need for an assessment process in the North Sea if rigs are to be used as reefs, to determine

- how the structures are used by fish and other marine life at present, and
- how they could function as reefs if laid horizontally on the seabed.

If (and only if) a positive role as true artificial reefs (submerged structures deliberately placed to mimic some aspect of a natural reef) can be envisaged can use of the steel jackets be justified and then decisions as how best to deploy rig as reefs, e.g. either to enforce a no-trawling zone or as a means of maximizing trawl catches within the existing fisheries management regime, can be made. Until evaluation is made, the arguments for and against will continue to be based on examples from the Gulf of Mexico (not comparable environmentally or in terms of structure size) or on areas such as safety, trawling 'rights', international dumping regulations, IMO regulations and the opinion that nothing should be placed in the sea that might change its character in any manner.

Dr R.J. Maddrell, Paper 2

Question on Paper 6

I would like to answer the question of why we put signs on our rock groynes telling people they are dangerous and to keep off. The reason is that if people have accidents on them, the modern trend is to sue the owner of the structure who in turn looks to the designer. While I am in favour of making structures more eco-friendly, to do so will add another level of risk which may adversely affect the structural performance. It might be possible to offset these disbenefits against the benefits from increased biodiversity. Is it possible to put a monetary value against these benefits?

Dr A. Jensen, Paper 6

Biodiversity can be evaluated in a monetary fashion; an economist should be asked to provide such information. The point being made was that there seemed to be very little lateral thinking about the uses of breakwaters. In creating such structures there is the possibility, depending on location, to create habitat that can be used for education, recreation and possibly contribute to local fisheries. Taking this point into account at the design stage may well provide extra benefits to the local economy beyond that of protection from storms, erosion and flooding.

Professor N.W.H. Allsop, University of Sheffield

Comment on Paper 6

Concrete units have been used in some interesting experiments on coral reefs in the Maldives where Dr Alastair Edwards of Newcastle University used concrete SHED units and perforated concrete revetment blocks. These units assisted stabilizing areas of damaged coral reefs by reducing movement of loose rubble, and provided shelter to various fish species.

G. Heald, Environment Agency (Anglian Region)

Comment on Paper 6

The Environment Agency recognizes the opportunities, identified in Paper 6, of developing environmental enhancement through habitat creation in shoreline construction. The Environment Agency seeks to balance all the environmental consequences of its works.

This is progressed through environmental policies to minimize consumption of world resources, minimize waste, maximize reuse of materials, to reduce pollution and comply with the Habitats Directive. On an individual project, environmental assessment would evaluate all possible effects and opportunities. Environmental assessment may identify the opportunity to increase biodiversity, however this would require evaluation of all consequences. These could include other overriding environmental objectives, e.g. maintaining existing habitats or species, sustaining other habitats distant from the project (rainforests or landscapes), aspirations of other consultees (such as fishermen or residents).

The opportunity for biodiverse habitat creation must therefore be seen in the context of the bigger picture.

P.A. Inwood, Ministry of Agriculture, Fisheries and Food

Question on Paper 6

The paper illustrated the value of an integrated design for the prime purpose of coastal defence together with the importance of ecological enhancement. Illustrations were presented of the natural flora and fauna taking advantage of the newly created albeit foreign habitat. Could the speakers give further information on identifying the existing ecology on the site of construction and of treatments/methods of enhancing the diversity and population density of such flora and fauna other than the coastal structure construction.

This question is prompted by recognition of 'special protection areas' and the Urban Wastewater Directive together with the wide disparity of bird species and numbers in the estuaries of north-west England. The Ribble is noted as more valuable than the Lune, Duddon, Mersey and Dee. How can one influence the natural food chain? Is there value in seeding e.g. ragwort?

Dr A. Jensen, Paper 6

Scientists undertaking ecological surveys have developed a range of methods which allow the existing biodiversity to be quantified and the value of a site to be assessed in a variety of ways. Value will depend on the criteria of the evaluator, wading birds are often highly valued but the invertebrates living in the sediment on which the birds feed may often be undervalued. Biodiversity enhancement in the coastal zone may be achieved without habitat creation (building coastal structures) by minimizing negative impacts such as, for example, excessive bait-digging, destructive fishing techniques, controlling aggregate extraction, improving quality of effluent entering the sea and balancing habitat destructive coastal developments such as ports and marinas with their ecological consequences. Some aspects of mitigation may be needed to replace habitat damaged by human activities, such as the PFA dumping off Blyth which smothered rocky reefs. Seeding is only worth considering if habitat is not being exploited fully. In most cases habitat will be fully exploited as most marine life utilizes larval dispersal by water currents which is an extremely effective way of making sure that all suitable habitat is colonized. Where seeding might be of use is where an ecological pressure, such as fishing mortality, is so high that natural recruitment does not fully exploit available habitat. Experiments by MAFF (now CEFAS) have shown that hatchery reared juvenile lobsters can survive and enter the fishery.

References

1. Franco C. *Wave overtopping and loads on caisson breakwater under three-dimensional sea states.* MCS / PROVERBS report, Politechnico di Milano, Milan, 1996.
2. Frigaard P., Petersen J.H. Estimation of incident wave height. *3rd MCS project workshop*, De Voorst, 1994.
3. Allsop N.W.H. and McBride M.W. *Reflections from vertical walls: potential for improvement in vessel safety and wave disturbance.* Paper 4.3 at 2nd MCS-project Workshop, Madrid, October 1993, University of Hannover (HR published paper no. 91), 1993.
4. Gardner J.D., Fleming C.A. and Townend I.H. The design of a slotted vertical screen breakwater. *Proceedings 20th ICCE*, Taipei, November 1986, ASCE, New York, 1986.
5. Allsop N.W.H. and Hettiarachchi S.S.L. Reflections from coastal structures. *Proceedings 21st ICCE*, Malaga, June 1988, ASCE, New York, 1988.
6. Noli A., Franco L., Tomassi S., Verni R. and Mirri F. The new Porto Torres breakwater, Italy. *Proceedings of the Institution Civil Engineers*, 1985, **108**, pp 17-27.
7. Allsop N.W.H. and Beresford P.J. *Cardiff Bay Barrage Design Study - Report 10: Hydraulic modelling of caisson breakwaters.* Report EX 2783, HR Wallingford, Wallingford, 1993.

STRUCTURES TO RETAIN SHORELINES: PAPERS 7 & 8

H.R. Payne, Welsh Office
Question on Paper 7
Could the author provide an indication of the tidal ranges under which the structures were used, and what variation occurs in predominant wind directions?

Dr K.R. Bodge, Paper 7
The tide range at most of our project sites is 1.2 to 1.5 m; except at Tybee Island, Georgia, where it is about 2.5 m. We were surprised to see the design methodology, including the 'one-third' rule, hold up at the latter site. I suspect that project behaviour, however, may be different in the large (>3 m) tide ranges of the UK, but I am not sure. All of the sites are exposed to multi-directional winds and waves (±45° or more from shore normal); however, most feature a predominant direction to which the design is fundamentally developed. The project design is then considered in the light of the site's predicted wave-direction extrema in order to assess how the beach might perform when subjected to these angular extremes. Adjustments to the design are then sometimes required to ensure that the incidence of non-predominant wave angles does not unacceptably impact the project's design-shoreline objective.

The groynes' heads are not only to break-up rip currents, but (principally) to create a headland-type crenulate shoreline in the lee. We have observed no problems associated with reflection of waves from the heads. We do not recommend highly permeable structures for these works.

Dr T. Lewis, Hydraulics and Maritime Research Centre, Ireland
Question to Paper 8
My question relates to the layout of the structures with the gaps. As you already said the water piles up between the structures and the shore and so the gaps were included to allow seaward flow. We carried out some experiments on submerged breakwaters with gaps in an EU funded network involving the University of Delft, University of Liverpool, University of Barcelona

and ourselves. The three dimensional tests carried out in the wave basins in Cork and Deft showed that those return flows are strong and act like sand pumps carrying sediment offshore to the detriment of the beach.

H.R. Payne, Welsh Office
Question on Paper 8
Could the authors of Paper 8 advise what steps were taken to ensure the safety of those navigating (including small craft) in the area of the submerged breakwaters, and whether the authorities responsible for ensuring the safety of navigation were concerned about these structures?

Professor L. Franco, University of Rome 3, Italy
Question on Paper 8
It seems very surprising that anyone expected reef units of such narrow crest width to give any significant reduction of wave energy. Surely this could have been predicted from widely available literature on wave transmission of submerged breakwaters. It also seems entirely predictable that (relatively) large concrete units placed directly on sand would scour and settle.

Can the authors please describe the model tests that they refer to, and explain the basis for design assumptions on wave transmission and scour/settlement?

Finally it is surprising that such an expensive monitoring program has been proposed for a project that is unlikely to be successful.

I. Prior, University of Sheffield
Question on Paper 8
Although the structure has failed to achieve its original intention, it does however appear to have provided a habitat for sea creatures. Could the authors list any other advantages, expected or unexpected? Has the continued monitoring and the back-analysis shown why the structure failed (ignoring our pre-determined judgement of how we think it failed – I noted the comments from the audience in general that nobody could have reasonably believed it would work)? Have we learned any lessons from somebody else's mistakes? The same questions could be asked of Paper 9.

Delegate
Comment on Paper 8
The authors have presented a valuable insight into an unusual approach to shoreline protection. The use of substantial concrete units in a form and on a foundation where there is considerable settlement in service provides an excellent opportunity for new understanding to be gained on the dynamic behaviour of such constructions. The monitoring is underway as reported in the paper but the background to the whole project is only briefly referred to, yet with such an unusual scheme the background is important to place the work in its proper context. It would therefore be helpful if the authors would expand upon the background to the project – dealing with the approaches and initiatives taken by the local government, manufacture of the units, engineering designers, etc. This information will then allow the paper to serve as a baseline for future presentation of monitoring results.

J.B. Smith, J. Pope and J.T. Tabar, Paper 8
The Vero Beach P.E.P. Reef submerged breakwater was designed, manufactured and constructed by American Coastal Engineering, Inc. (ACE) of Palm Beach, Florida. ACE was also responsible for selecting the installation configuration. As stated in Mitchell[1], the intent

of the P.E.P. Reef was to provide storm protection, perch the toe of the beach, develop a habitat to marine life and be a cost-effective alternative to the use of rubble-mound structures.

The project was sponsored by Indian River County (IRC), Florida, and was approved by the State of Florida and the US Army Corps of Engineers (USACE) as an experimental prototype test. It was required to meet or exceed several specific performance criteria. The USACE Waterways Experiment Station was asked by IRC to monitor post-installation changes in the vicinity of the project in order to test the project relative to the performance criteria. The USACE had no role in developing the project design, nor in predicting anticipated performance of this commercially-developed product.

Several parties recommended against the construction and installation of the P.E.P. Reef citing that this 'alternative' form of shore protection would not stabilize the shoreline, nor stop volumetric erosion, nor attenuate wave heights as stated by the manufacturer.

The IRC government desired shore protection to mitigate historical shoreline erosion trends. The shoreline (MHW) has eroded an average of 0.71 m/yr since 1970. A county-wide vote supported the installation of the P.E.P. Reef along a 914 m length of their shoreline rather than beach nourishment. Although approximately 250,000 cubic metres of nourishment material (at US$12/m^3) could have been placed (considering the total US$3,000,000 cost of the P.E.P. Reef project), the nearshore occurrence of ecologically-sensitive hardbottom habitat precluded placement of large quantities of fill without perching the toe.

The staggered (alternating onshore / offshore segments) configuration of the Vero Beach was based upon findings of a previously-installed P.E.P. Reef at Palm Beach, Florida, described by Dean et al.,[2] and physical model studies described by Dean et al.[3] One of the major findings of the Palm Beach installation monitoring was that overtopping waves were 'ponded' behind the uninterrupted breakwater, thus locally enhancing the longshore currents. The physical model studies of a single sill and staggered configuration were conducted in a 1:16 scale laboratory three-dimensional model to evaluate the effect of the breakwater on wave height and nearshore currents in the vicinity of the breakwater.[3] Both moveable and fixed bed tests were conducted. Wave heights were measured in the model using capacitance-type wave gauges on both sides of the breakwater, and currents were measured using dye and drogues. Several breakwater arrangements were tested.

This physical model study predicted less than 10% reduction of wave heights for relative freeboard (crest elevation/water depth) ratios similar to the prototype monitoring findings of the Vero Beach P.E.P. Reef. Dean et al.[3] suggest that wave attenuation due to the P.E.P. Reef is almost negligible at freeboard ratios of –0.4 to –0.6. Current measurements in the model suggest that the staggered configuration would reduce the longshore currents and slightly increase flow through the gaps rather than around the ends of the breakwater.

Field monitoring of the Vero Beach P.E.P. Reef indicates that the staggered segments have reduced the build-up of water behind the structure and longshore losses of sediment and have allowed some cross-shore dissipation through the gaps. However, it appears that while enhanced offshore-directed flow during storms does transport sediment seaward of the breakwater, sediment is not being transported onshore during fair weather conditions. This is evidenced in part by the net volumetric loss of sediment landward of the breakwater and the accretion of sediment seaward of the breakwater particularly toward the south end of the project.

After 16 months of monitoring this narrow crested breakwater system, the results confirm that wave attenuation is a function of barrier crest width and height in the water column. In service however, this P.E.P. Reef breakwater system settled on average one-half of its total 1.8 m height (approximately 0.9 m). Average wave height reduction following settlement was 9% compared to 12% prior to settlement. It appears that a primary mechanism for this settlement was the formation of a scour trench landward of the breakwater measuring approximately 0.8 m deep and 1.8 m wide. The placement of a geotextile blanket between the breakwater and the underlying sediment might perhaps have reduced the settlement rate. Lastly, the P.E.P. Reef has successfully created a habitat for sea creatures.

The breakwater is located 25 km from the nearest marina and recreational boats rarely venture to the site. However, several navigation safety precautions were initiated. Buoys were placed at both ends of each of the 11 segments. Notices were placed at public access points in the vicinity of the breakwater and were also published in local newspapers. No accidents have occurred in the vicinity of the breakwater.

Funding for this research was provided by Indian River County, Florida.
Permission to publish this paper was granted by the Chief of Engineers, US Army Corps of Engineers.

Dr K.R. Bodge, Paper 7
Comment on Paper 8
For the record, the Vero Beach 'PEP Reef' project was opposed – or recommended against – by essentially all of the State of Florida's coastal engineering consultants, including the US Army Corps of Engineers and the State's coastal regulatory agency. It was implemented by the local municipality – having been 'sold' on the concept by the reef structures' manufacturer, despite the widely acknowledged failure of the system at another Florida location a few years earlier. As beach management and restoration projects become more prevalent in the UK, it is likely that Britain will see an ever-increasing presence of vendors soliciting so-called 'alternative technologies' for beach preservation.

References
1. Mitchell B.L. An Overview of the P.E.P. (Prefabricated Erosion Prevention) Reef Development, *Proceedings of the 7th National Conference on Beach Preservation Technology*, St Petersburg, Florida, February 9–11, 1994, pp 90–96.
2. Dean R.G., Chen R. and Browder A.E.. Full Scale Monitoring Study of a Submerged Breakwater, Palm Beach, Florida, USA. *Coastal Engineering*, 1996, **29**, pp 291–351.
3. Dean R.G., Browder A.E., Goodrich M.S. and Donaldson D.G. *Model Tests of the Proposed P.E.P. Reef Installation at Vero Beach, Florida.* University of Florida, Report UFL/COEL-94/012, 1994, 30p.
4. Browder A.E., Dean R.G. and Chen R. Performance of a Submerged Breakwater for Shore Protection, *Proceedings of the 25th International Conference on Coastal Engineering*, Orlando, FL., September 2–6, 1996, pp 2312–2323.
5. Stauble D.K. *Guidelines for Beach Restoration Projects: Part II-Engineering.* Florida Sea Grant College Report SGR-77, 1986, 100p.

STRUCTURES TO RETAIN SHORELINES: PAPERS 9 & 10

Dr T.O. Herrington, Paper 9
Note on the background to the Beachsaver Reef project
The Beachsaver Reef was designed and developed over a period of 10 years by Breakwaters International, Inc., located in Flemington, New Jersey. The first test of preproduction pilot units took place in 1984, on the Long Island Sound shore in Oakwood, New York. An emergent 100 m long breakwater was constructed 30 m offshore of the high tide line. The units were re-designed to correct a shifting tendency in the breakwater and in 1987 a set of the re-designed modules replaced the original pilot structure. The first open-ocean test occurred in 1989 at Sea Isle City, New Jersey. Two 61 m emergent Beachsaver Reefs were installed 76 m offshore. The test installation was monitored by researchers from Lehigh and Drexel Universities. The study indicated that after nine months the beach had increased by 21 m landward of the structures. Uneven settlement of individual breakwater units led to the eventual removal of the structures.

A submerged version of the Beachsaver Reef was designed by Breakwaters International in 1990. The Center for Applied Coastal Research at the University of Delaware performed 1:12 scale physical model tests of the submerged breakwater.[1] The results of the wave basin tests indicated that the submerged reef would reduce the incident wave height, increasing the deposition of sand in the lee of the structure. In 1992, the submerged Beachsaver Reef was redesigned to include slotted openings at the crest of the structure to redirect offshore bottom flowing sand vertically over the structure. In April 1992, 1:6 scale movable bed tests of the redesigned structure were conducted at Stevens Institute of Technology.[2,3] The results of the tests indicated that the submerged reef limited the movement of sandbars offshore during storm conditions when compared to the response of an unprotected beach.

Based on the modifications made to the structure by Breakwaters International and the results of the two tank tests, the State of New Jersey initiated a pilot study to examine the effectiveness of the submerged reef at three different nearshore locations in New Jersey. The results and data presented in the paper are not an endorsement of the product by either Stevens Institute of Technology or the State of New Jersey.

C. Frith, Mouchel Consulting Ltd
Question on Paper 9
Was any form of scour found on the seaward side of the breakwater?

Dr T.O. Herrington, Paper 9
No. The cross-shore beach profile at all three locations consistently showed a build-up of sand along the seaward side of the breakwaters over the 3 year monitoring period. We believe that the observed accretion on the seaward side of the structure was due to a landward and/or alongshore movement of sediment offshore of the structure. It appears that the mild slope (3:5) and the undulating ribbed surface of the seaward side of the structure aid in the retention of sand along the seaward face.

C. Frith, Mouchel Consulting Ltd
Question on Paper 9
Does the author consider that the extent and depth of scour on the landward side of the breakwater is related to the wave height and/or wave period, or to some other phenomenon?

Dr T.O. Herrington, Paper 9

Wave transformation studies conducted at the Avalon and Cape May Point breakwater installations indicate that wave transmission across the structure is a function of the depth of water above the structure (negative freeboard) and the incident wave height (Fig. 6 in Paper 9). The degree of wave height reduction increased during periods of low negative freeboard and periods of large incident wave heights. Examination of the measured wave spectra, however, indicated very little variation of energy dissipation with frequency (see Fig. 1 below).

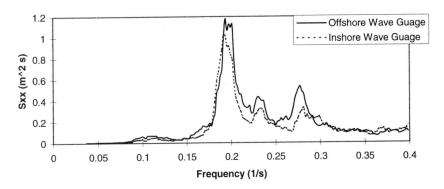

Figure 1. Wave spectrum measured on 24 May 1995.

We believe that the observed dependence of energy dissipation on wave height is indicative of the primary dissipative mechanism at work. This mechanism is the flow interference and viscous dissipation generated by the wave-induced bottom return flow being redirected upwards by the inshore face of the breakwater. The degree of attenuation is related to the strength of this vertical current. Therefore, the depth of scour on the landward side of the breakwater is considered to be related to the incident wave height, and perhaps to a lesser degree the wave period (or length). Our observation that the breadth and depth of the scour area inshore of the breakwaters remains constant after being established is indicative of the attenuation of the wave-induced bottom flow with depth.

C. Frith, Mouchel Consulting Ltd

Question on Paper 10

Can the authors elaborate on the design modifications made between the Stage 1 and Stage 2 reefs that enabled the latter to be built so much more successfully?

B. Hamer, Paper 10

Other than noting that the changes in the reef profile between Stages One and Two were made to modify the observed beach plan shape response, the authors were unable to comment on any construction implications due to current legal proceedings.

P.A. Inwood, Ministry of Agriculture, Fisheries and Food

Question on Paper 10

The photographs [presented at the conference] of the problem that the scheme is addressing showed the existence of groynes which had almost disappeared. I remember the groynes being in good condition from 1965 to 1978. The beach levels remained fairly constant over this time. In the light of Papers 7 and 8, which illustrated aspects of shore parallel and shore normal structures, would the authors be able to comment on the value of groyne maintenance and interrelationship with littoral drift and sources of same?

B. Hamer, Paper 10

The sea defence strategy, originally developed in 1991, recommended the maintenance of groynes along lengths of the frontage that were not protected by reef structures. The Environment Agency undertakes a rolling programme of groyne maintenance along the frontage.

Whilst the beaches may have appeared to be stable between 1965 and 1978, the low water line was gradually moving landward, effectively steepening the beach in front of the seawall, throughout this period. The effects of this gradual beach loss have become much more apparent in more recent years, once the high water line has eventually also begun to be noticeably affected.

Groynes were effective along this frontage when there was sufficient beach material to sustain reasonable beach levels. However, once the beach feed from the cliffs to the north reduced, as a consequence of protective works, groynes became increasingly exposed along the beach. Once groynes become significantly exposed, they can be counter-productive and cause wave focusing and accelerated erosion of the foreshore. Gradually, several groynes became undermined and failed.

The maintenance of groynes remains a strong recommendation in the strategy, in areas not protected by reefs. In these areas, the rate of longshore drift has become reduced as a consequence of the introduction of reefs further downdrift. In combination with proposed beach management measures these groynes are expected to remain effective.

Professor H. Ligteringen, Delft Technical University and De Weger Architects and Consulting Engineers, the Netherlands
Question on Paper 10
In what water depth are the breakwaters located?

B. Hamer, Paper 10
The seabed level is generally −3.0 mOD, relative to a mean high water springs level of approximately +1.7 mOD.

Professor H. Ligteringen, Delft Technical University and De Weger Architects and Consulting Engineers, the Netherlands
Question on Paper 10
Please explain the type of model applied to analyse the performance of this offshore breakwater in terms of beach response?

B. Hamer, Paper 10
Two independent two-dimensional models were used for the study. The first was a one-line model, developed by Halcrow, which considered beach plan shape response. A real time-series of offshore wave data was transformed to an array of inshore points along the frontage. The wave field was defined at each point every three hours, in terms of wave height, period and direction. The Beach Plan Shape Model takes these wave data as input, together with information on the beach slope, particle size, available volume of material (e.g. if a seawall or other structure restricts the available volume), and beach orientation. The Kamphuis equation is then used to determine the potential beach transport in each cell, which is then used to derive the beach plan shape development.

The second model was a two-dimensional cross-shore model, COSMOS-2D, which was used to consider the vulnerability of the beach to erosion under severe storm events. This model is capable of incorporating submerged reef structures, or may be driven by reducing the incident wave height using the transmission coefficients calculated as described in Reference 19. This model is not usually run for periods of more than a few days, and includes tidal water level variation with time.

Professor H. Ligteringen, Delft Technical University and De Weger Architects and Consulting Engineers, the Netherlands
Question on Paper 10
Can you give some indication of the structural performance of the breakwater, scour holes at the beach, etc?

B. Hamer, Paper 10
The structural integrity of the breakwaters is monitored on an annual basis. There is no indication of significant damage to the reefs at present, although local fishermen suggested the presence of a scour hole at the southern end of Reef 8, prior to the commencement of Stage Two (Reefs 9 to 13). The Stage Two reefs have been designed with a sacrificial toe detail, which would accommodate scour of the order of 1 to 2 m.

Professor N.W.H. Allsop, University of Sheffield
Questions on Paper 10
The speakers made reference to potential safety hazards to people at coastal structures. Would they please summarize the present state of guidance on public safety and coastal structures as developed under the recent Halcrow/EA research project? References to publicly available documents will be helpful.

B. Hamer, Paper 10
Current guidance is provided in the following references, which may be requested from the Environment Agency.
- *Public Safety of Access to Coastal Structures: Stage One Report (R&D Note).* Halcrow, 1994.
- *Public Safety of Access to Coastal Structures: Stage Two (Final Report).* Halcrow, 1997.

Professor N.W.H. Allsop, University of Sheffield
Questions on Paper 10
The comparisons between the numerical model predictions and measured shoreline positions shown by the presenters illustrated the expected position of erosion and accretion, but substantially under-predicted the extent of the shoreline movement. Would the authors please identify the relative contributions to these differences due to the simplifications inherent in the one-line beach model; differences in transmission between the real and numerical breakwaters; or other causes?

B. Hamer, Paper 10
The authors noted that the comparison was indeed between the predicted beach response, based on one typical year of wave conditions, and the actual beach response, after the first four reefs had been completed. It was noted that these reefs took longer to construct than had been anticipated, and the beach response was more marked as a consequence.

The authors considered that, rather than re-running the beach plan shape model using the actual wave data encountered over the course of the construction period (which would provide useful information on model validity itself), it would be of note to compare the raw predictions with the actual response. This latter approach provides a better feel for the validity of the overall predictive method. It is not agreed that simplifications in the one-line beach model might result in poor correlation with the actual beach responses. On the contrary, the beach model might result in poor correlation with the actual salient development in direct comparisons of this nature. Where good agreement has been reached, the models incorporated the wave transmission coefficient, derived in accordance with Reference 19, for mean sea level and the average wave height.

Dr K.R. Bodge, Olsen Associates Inc, USA
Comment on Paper 10
In noting the formation of strong salients at the northern breakwaters (which may interrupt littoral drift), our firm has abandoned some original concepts that included detached breakwaters, in favour of smaller, more closely spaced T-head groynes. When built in conjunction with requisite beach nourishment, the breakwaters appear to tend toward tombolo formation. The tombolos are resistant to 'breakage' and thus decrease, perhaps, the potential for sand bypassing to the downdrift shoreline. In contrast, the short T-head groynes appear to be better at facilitating sand bypass through or around the groyne field.

B. Hamer, Paper 10
When the strategy was last subject to a thorough review, in 1995/6, the possibility of employing groynes rather than reefs was considered along with other options. However, it was concluded that groynes with recharge would not provide adequate cross-shore protection to the frontage. In particular, short groynes would not be capable of retaining sufficient beach width to resist erosion back to the seawall in severe storm events.

References
1. Dalrymple R.A., Driscoll A.M. and Ramsey J.S. *Laboratory testing of the Beachsaver Breakwater System.* Prepared for Breakwaters International, Center for Applied Coastal Research, Dept. of Civil Engineering, University of Delaware, Newark, DE, Feb. 1991, 38.
2. Bruno M.S., McKee T.G. and Clark W.M. *Laboratory study of an artificial reef beach erosion mitigation device.* Prepared for Breakwaters International, Inc., Davidson Laboratory Technical Report SIT-DL-92-9-2676, Stevens Institute of Technology, Hoboken, NJ, 38, August 1992, 38.
3. Bruno M.S. Laboratory testing of an artificial reef erosion control device. *Proceedings, Coastal Zone '93*, ASCE , 1993, vol.2, 2147-2158.

EVALUATING PROJECT RISKS / OPTIMIZATION: PAPERS 11 & 12

Editor's comments on discussions on Paper 11
During discussions in Session 6, questions were raised with the author of Paper 11 seeking clarification on points made in the original version of the paper. These questions were generally answered in revisions made to the paper given in these proceedings. It may however be useful to summarize some points of concern, and give two additional comments made during the discussions.

Oumeraci (Leichtweiß Institute) was concerned that the initial fault tree in Figure 2 did not appear to correspond to the failure modes for which the limit-state equations had been provided. It was noted that probabilities of failure are dependent on the interaction between different 'failure modes'.

Oumeraci also questioned how the authors take account of wave heights of different periods (7 s, 14 s, 1–35 s) which are super-posed to produce an overall wave height for harbour agitation, noting that for large ships, ship motion criteria should be used instead of simple wave height criteria.

Van der Meer noted that stability of Accropode was modelled by $H_s/\Delta D_n = 4.1$ and a standard deviation of $\sigma = 1$. The paper then concluded that a cost optimum would be 15 t Accropode above 12 t, but what would be the effect if a more reasonable value of the standard deviation, say, 0.5 had been used? Would the failure probability decrease considerably and what would be the optimum weight?

Noli noted problems of sedimentation in the dredged access channel had not been considered. It had however been concluded that obstruction of the channel by a grounding ship (perhaps due to a difficult manoeuvre under beam waves and NE monsoon winds) represents the largest contribution to the functional failure of Ennore coal port. Could the design layout be optimized by introducing a less oblique (to shore) access channel route and a slightly more 'open' tip of the main breakwater (i.e. rotating seaward the deepest breakwater portion)?

Ligteringen remarked that optimization of breakwater design leads to increasing probability of damage and more frequent repairs. Has that aspect been taken into account, also from the position of the port authority, which needs to spend money from their operational budgets on such repair work?

Professor K. d'Angremond, Delft University of Technology, the Netherlands
Comment on Paper 11
When the layout of the port of Ennore and the direction of the entrance channel was discussed, very few options were open. The location of the port could not be changed. A north-east channel would lead to a fairway parallel to a shoal, with heavy breakers over a length of several miles. In spite of the known sediment transport, as is clear from the morphological development at Madras, it was still decided to opt for a south-east entrance. It was and is realized that this poses certain risks with respect to sedimentation in the channel. Eventually, therefore the long-shore transport between Madras and Ennore shall be controlled by groynes and/or offshore breakwaters. This measure goes hand in hand with the need to mitigate coastal erosion just north of Madras.

G. Rankine, Beckett Rankine Partnership
Comment on Paper 11
The port of Ennore is at an interesting location from the point of view of a port engineer, being constructed at a new 'beach' site towards the south of India's eastern coast, rather similar to the beginning of the nearby port of Madras 100 years ago. Construction at the port of Madras started in 1895 with two parallel breakwaters running out from the shore and curving symmetrically to leave an opening on the sea side (see Fig. 1a). This was not a great success with the new harbour being untenable for vessels under certain sea conditions. A few years later, in 1910, the original opening was sealed and a new opening formed on the northern side (see Fig. 1b). This was further extended in the 1920s with a new breakwater arm and roundhead (the subject of a paper presented in this building by one of my predecessors) and still further at a later stage (see Fig. 1c). Over the years there has been a considerable build up of sand resulting from longshore drift from the south, to the extent that this has fully covered the original southern breakwater giving rise to a useful area of land reclamation.

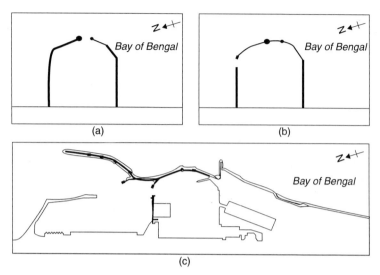

Figure 1(a) Port of Madras 1890s;(b) Port of Madras 1910;(c) Port of Chennai (Madras) 1998

This experience over 100 years represent an interesting full-scale hydraulic model study. With similar oceanographic and morphological conditions at Ennore, how helpful did the designers find this historical, yet real, information in the process of minimizing risk during planning and designing the new port?

Dr J.W. van der Meer, Infram, the Netherlands
Question to Paper 12
The author mentioned that behaviour of the structure during construction (unprotected underlayers and core) should be considered during design. This can be investigated during model testing. There is, however, a handy tool which can be used during conceptual design: the PC program BREAKWAT (Delft Hydraulics). This program gives damage profiles of underlayers and also of the core for normal wave conditions. Based on results of this program it is easy for the designer to decide what is acceptable and what is not acceptable, or for which wave conditions the underlayer will be lost.

J. Simm, Paper 12
The authors are aware of the various methods available for assessing stability of structures, including modelling. The main point to be stressed is not the merits or demerits of particular numerical models (or indeed of physical models) for the particular structural form being considered, but the need to use them in assessing the stability of part-completed structures and not just for the completed structures.

Professor K. d'Angremond, Delft University of Technology, the Netherlands
Question on Paper 12
The author of Paper 12 called on the contractor(s) to inform the client(s) in a timely manner about his doubts and of constructive ideas to limit the risks, even if there would be the risk that their ideas would be stolen. I think this is not a realistic supposition. Contractors are also human beings, who do not like to be robbed. It is a challenge for our whole industry to develop tender procedures that encourage contractors to make available their expertise, but which protect them at the same time and ensure a fair treatment and compensation.

J. Simm, Paper 12

We understand Professor d'Angremond's concerns and the importance of selecting an appropriate procurement route which encourages fair treatment of contractors. Indeed a complete chapter of the manual deals with just this subject.

However, it was the view of the nine contractors represented on the steering committee for the project that the risk of ideas being stolen was outweighed in many cases by the ability to influence the design at an early (pre-tender) stage towards one suitable for their preferred method of construction. It is in any case the duty of clients to respect the confidentiality of contractors ideas; the practice of re-tendering on an alternative tender submitted by one contractor was deprecated by the committee as being unethical.

H.R. Payne, Welsh Office and J. Horne, Ministry of Agriculture, Fisheries and Food
Comment on Paper 12

During discussion on Paper 12, Mr Heald of the Environment Agency (Anglian Region) appeared to indicate that public authorities in the UK were precluded by Treasury regulations from accepting other than the lowest tender. This is incorrect. The UK government policy is that all procurement should be on the basis of value for money and not lowest price alone. Obviously in a situation where the contractor has been shortlisted as a result of a valid selection process and has submitted a compliant tender on the basis of a detailed specification and drawings, in most cases that with the lowest price will be the most suitable tender. However, in all cases award should be on the basis of a robust selection mechanism, specific to each project and developed to evaluate quality and price (whole-life cost) of each bid in a fair, transparent and accountable manner. (*HM Treasury Procurement Guidance No. 3 – Appointment of Consultants and Contractors*).

Prof. Ir. Drs J.K. Vrijling, Delft University of Technology, the Netherlands
Comment on Paper 12

Six risk control strategies, ranging from 'remove' to 'accept' the risk, are proposed in Paper 12. In my opinion there are only two principally differing risk control strategies

- accept in some cases after reduction
- transfer to another party.

In the first case, the risk is reduced by such measures as gathering more information, installing a prediction procedure, investing in heavier plant, etc. All measures cost money, so the average cost rises but the risk is lowered.

In the second case, the risk is transferred to another partner in exchange for a certain compensation. Insurance companies are specialized in these deals, but the contractor may also be well placed to accept some additional risk in exchange for a slight increase of the contract sum.

In the case of transfer, the risk is replaced by a known and certain expenditure. This is the only way to completely remove a risk. Thus the two categories become

- accept, reduce
- transfer, share, insure, remove.

J. Simm, Paper 12

We respect Professor Vrijling's desire to simplify matters as far as possible and agree that our categories could be combined into larger ones. However, there are specific actions which can be undertaken in each of the categories which was the reason for our distinction. More details are given on this point in Part C of the Manual.

However, if one were to accept the proposed simplification, we believe that there are still four categories as two of our original categories do not fit into Vrijling's framework. The arrangement would then be as follows

- remove (by definition if a risk is removed, e.g by improved design, it is neither accepted by the client or transferred to the contractor)
- accept, in some cases after reduction
- share between the client and another party
- transfer to another party (i.e. the contractor or insurer).

On balance we prefer to retain our original classification.

Dr K.R. Bodge, Olsen Associates Inc, USA
Comment on Paper 12
In response to the questions: What is the new manual intended to do and how do we use it as practicing engineers?

Wherever practical, and especially for these projects that include complex construction requirements, our US firm increasingly favours the use of so-called 'Best Value Procurement' or 'Request for Proposal' solicitation for construction contractors. Offerors are given the plans and specifications and requested to simultaneously submit two sealed packages: a technical proposal and a cost proposal. The technical proposals must present data and answers to specific questions regarding the firm's qualifications, prior experience, capabilities and proposed method of construction. The technical proposals are opened first; and the offerors are ranked based upon a pre-determined rating scheme. The cost proposals of the highest-rated offerors are then opened and used as a 'tie-breaker' for closely-ranked qualified offers. The selection process is carefully documented (in case of protest), and all of the offerors' submittals are held in confidence of the 3 to 5 person evaluation committee. When careful thought is applied, in advance, to the solicitation's technical submittal requirements – and to the ranking (scoring) system – this method of contracting procurement has yielded great benefits to the project and owner, and in turn, is attractive to both the Engineer and Contractor.

J. Simm, Paper 12
The principal aims of the manual are to

- raise awareness of construction risks specific to coastal engineering (particularly for clients, designers, insurers and inexperienced contractors)
- set out best practice for all parties in the identification, assessment and management of these risks.

The way to use the manual is set out in the manual introduction. The practising engineer will wish to use the manual in a variety of ways depending on his own level of knowledge and experience.

- Part A of the manual provides a short summary of good practise which should be followed by all engineers.
- Part B provides background information on methods of risk assessment and management in the coastal environment and on other related issues including health safety and environment , insurance and procurement.
- Part C provides a tool kit for identifying and mitigating risks associated with particular structural forms (e.g. rock structures, caissons, beach replenishment, etc.).

We are aware of the two-envelope procedure to which Dr Bodge refers and concur that it has much to commend it. However, UK Treasury regulations preclude public authorities from such a system on the grounds that price must always be taken into account in tender assessment. Nonetheless, the Public Procurement Department also stresses the importance of considering quality.

EXPERIENCES IN BREAKWATER CONSTRUCTION: PAPERS 13 & 14

Dr T. Lewis, Hydraulics and Maritime Research Centre, Ireland
Question on Paper 13
The behaviour of the berm breakwater is dependent upon the permeability of the core material. The permeability does not scale simply by geometric scaling of the model to the prototype. The extensive tests carried out at Danish Hydraulic Institute were used to predict the performance. How do you see the scaling up of the results to the expected behaviour of the full size breakwater given these difficulties?

S. Sigurdarson, Paper 13
It is correct that the permeability of the stone material is important for the stability of breakwaters and that it is important that scaling of the permeability is considered together with the scaling of the weight/size of the stones. The methods of Jensen and Klinting[1] were used in this research together with many years of experience with physical modelling of breakwater stability to decide the scaling of the core material.

It should be noted that for berm breakwaters the permeability of the core material is of less importance compared to traditional breakwaters due to the relatively large amount of stones in the berm, where the wave energy is dissipated. This means that the permeability of the berm material is of utmost importance, which was confirmed in other model tests with berm breakwaters carried out at DHI. For traditional breakwaters, e.g. armoured with Accropodes (one layer armour blocks), the permeability of the filter layer and core material is an important parameter for the stability.

Based on the above, we do not see scaling of the results to prototype restricted by difficulties in scaling the permeability of the core material.

Dr J.-P. Latham, Queen Mary and Westfield College, University of London
Comment on Paper 13
Clearly, a great deal of information has been condensed into this stimulating and valuable paper. I would like to support the incorporation of materials considerations into the design process. In this paper, illustrating novel practice from Iceland, it was strongly recommended that the expected fragmentation curve, i.e. the block size distribution in the blast-pile, from quarries that are dedicated to the provision of construction materials for a coastal structure, should be determined prior to optimization of the final design and the setting of quantities required in each rock mass range. It is clear that the whole basis of the economic and environmental advantages of maximizing utilization of the quarry with a tailor-made design requires that the yield curves during production in the quarry are in fact close to those predicted beforehand. Perhaps greater emphasis could have therefore been given in the paper as to the reliability of such predictions and what happens if and when they are substantially inaccurate. Also, it is not clear how the true fragmentation curves were evaluated. While the types of field data needed for successful predictions are mentioned, no analysis procedures are referred to and we are left to draw our own conclusions – that an experienced geologist

can tell what will happen through previous experience of correlating field observations with the block size outputs actually obtained. If there is data to that effect, it would be of great service to share it.

It is perhaps helpful to point out that there are whole conferences addressing fragmentation and blasting science (e.g. see Mohanty[2]) because accurate prediction and control of the fragmentation is technically difficult (especially without the use of trial blasts) but is critical to cost optimization in mining and quarrying operations. Furthermore, there are references given in the CIRIA/CUR Rock Manual[3] to blast-pile yield prediction techniques and illustrations of the principles and advantages of matching yield and design curves for breakwater material requirements. A key missing reference in discussing the concept of the tailor made size graded berm breakwater is the paper on quarry-based design of rock structures by Leeuwestein *et al.*[4] A simple 'low-tech' approach to evaluating the fragmentation in blast-piles was described in Lu and Latham.[5]

Professor H. Oumeraci, Leichtweiß Institut, Germany
Question on Paper 13
The most attractive idea behind the berm breakwater concept is based on the following aspects

- the nesting effect which leads to a certain stabilized profile given certain wave conditions
- the dynamic stability given a certain large volume of unsorted rock material
- the simplicity of this structure and the optimization of yield cost carry.

The concept presented by the authors seems to have nothing in common with the initial berm breakwater concept, as it leads to a very complicated cross-section – even more complicated than a conventional rubble mound breakwater – and it assumes static instead of dynamic stability!

The most important argument of the authors is that their new concept is more economical than the original berm breakwater concept. Is this valid only for Iceland? Is it also more economical than a conventional rubble mound breakwater?

To ensure a certain acceptance of the new concept the authors should present a convincing comparative cost analysis – not only for Iceland but also for some other countries, including developing countries.

J.E. Clifford, Retired
Question on Paper 13
When we started discussing berm breakwaters some years ago, I recall they were simple mounds with a core of smaller material covered by a berm of larger rocks allowed to reshape by waves. The paper describes structures which seem to be aiming towards static stability with a large number of different rock gradings. The trend seems to be toward a conventional static layered mound. I therefore query the need to retain the berm.

S. Sigurdarson, paper 13
Reply to H.Oumeraci and J.E.Clifford
Both questions deal with the initial ideas of berm breakwaters, as wide voluminous structures built of two stone classes and with a wide gradation. The Icelandic type of berm breakwater has developed into a less voluminous, more stable structure, where large emphasis is put on maximizing the outcome of the armour stone quarry and utilizing it in the design.

First a comparative cost analysis will be presented between the Icelandic berm breakwater and the conventional two-layer rubble mound breakwater. Then the difference between the Icelandic and the dynamic approach will be discussed.

The following cost comparison is influenced by a breakwater being designed in a moderate wave climate in Iceland. The structure stands on an 11 m water depth, where the mean spring tidal difference is about 4 m. The design wave height is $H_s = 3.0$ m with mean period of $T_m = 9.2$ s. A conventional cross section is designed according to the methods of van der Meer. Armour stones are 3 to 8 t, class I. The harbour side is protected be class II, 1 to 3 t stones and class III 0.3 to 1 t stones are used as filter layer on both sides.

To ensure that the comparison is not too favourable for the berm design, the same stone size is used on top of and at front of the berm, as for the armour layer on the conventional breakwater, meaning an unusually high stability for a berm breakwater. The harbour side of the two cross sections is completely the same, as is the toe structure on the front side, the only difference being the front of the structures from crest down to toe.

The available armour stone quarry is expected to give about 10% in class I, 13% in class II and 17% in class III.

The cost estimate is very dependent upon the distance to the quarry. In general quarries for production of armour stones and core material are less than 10 to 15 km from the construction site. If the distance to a suitable armour stone quarry is more than that usually another quarry closer to the structure is used for production of the core material. In the calculated example the distance from quarry to the breakwater site is about 10 km.

It is also common to use dredged material in the inner part of the core for economical reasons. The price difference of using dredged material instead of trucking the available quarried material in the case of the conventional breakwater is about 20% per m^3 in this case.

	Conventional two-layer breakwater	Icelandic-type berm breakwater
Total volume of breakwater	801 m^3/m	846 m^3/m
Total volume of materials from quarry	398 m^3/m	414 m^3/m
Total volume of dredged sand	403 m^3/m	432 m^3/m
Total volume of rocks larger than 3 t	61 m^3/m	33 m^3/m
Total quarried material needed for production of rock	610 m^3/m	420 m^3/m
Excess quarried material	200 m^3/m	
Extra cost due to excess production	**25%**	
Extra cost due to larger total volume		**10%**
Machine needed for placing large stones	Crane 60 t	Excavator 45 t
Armour stone placing rate	30 stones/hour	60 stones/hour
Relative cost of machine per hour	2	1
Relative cost of place armour stone	4	1
Extra cost due to placing of armour stones	**10%**	
Number of capable contractors	2	10
Extra cost due to limited competition	**5–20%**	
Relative total cost	**130–150%**	**100%**

In total there is a 15% difference in cost in getting the material on site, 10% difference in placing the material and 5 to 20% difference in limited competition. This adds up to 30 to 50% higher cost for the conventional breakwater. Even in a moderate wave climate the difference is that high and with higher design wave height the difference will increase. Also a poorer quarry yield will increase the difference. Although a better quarry yield lowers the difference, the difference in placing and limited competition will remain. This should answer the question of why we retain the berm concept, even though the structure aims at static stability with a number of different rock gradings.

In the example above, a dynamic structure would need to be at least 25% more voluminous than the Icelandic berm breakwater. That cost far exceeds the cost for sorting and placing several stone classes. The largest waste in the two stone class berm breakwaters is that large stones are used in places where they are not strictly needed, at large water depth or inside the structure close to the core. Or on the other hand that the contractor is not asked to produce at least close to the maximum yield from the quarry.

In the dynamic approach we have uncontrolled movements of stones, 'rolling stones', and that can not be accepted, especially in the breakwater head.

C. Orbell-Durrant, May Gurney (Construction) Ltd
Question on Paper 14
As rock was sourced from many different quarries located in France, Jersey, Scandanavia and Ireland, why did the contractor opt for a single (French) supply subcontractor rather than arrange a number of supply contracts with a range of quarries.

J.D. Morgan, Paper 14
Post-tender negotiations with rock suppliers resulted in the selection of a single supplier, who was also responsible for managing the sea-borne delivery operations, and thus a subcontract was let on this basis. It was only during the course of the contract that the subcontractor found it necessary to go to Scandinavia and Ireland to supplement the deliveries of armourstone. This was because of the logistical problems the subcontractor was having in sorting and moving the armour to the appropriate ports.

Secondly, choosing a single supplier/subcontractor responsible for the shipping alleviated potential problems with the limited berthing facilities that were available on site.

Chairman
Comment on Paper 14
While not in a position to speak for Nuttalls regarding their motivation, I personally feel that the single subcontractor route (albeit with rock deliveries sourced from many different locations) was contractually preferable. The financial onus for coordination of supply to finite site berthing and handling facilities then rested with the chosen supply subcontractor. It avoided the claims and counterclaims that would inevitably have arisen due to competing demands on the site facilities when the inevitable variations in scheduled deliveries of rock caused by open-sea hauls of varying distances, occurred.

J.D. Morgan, Paper 14
The comments from the Chairman are correct and in line with Edmund Nuttall's thoughts.

R. Rees-Jones, Larvik Armourstone
Question on Paper 14
You chose to source the material for the armourstone layer from a dimension stone quarry. You clearly recognized the benefits, in terms of rock durability, from using stone that has not been exposed to significant explosive blasting. Did you try to predict the yield of armourstone that you expected from the dimension quarry stockpiles? You finally used armourstone from other sources, so how would you evaluate yield in the future?

J.D. Morgan, Paper 14
The stockpile from which the armourstone was selected was vast; in the opinion of Edmund Nuttall Limited there was in excess of 2 million tonnes there. Originally it was just a question

of selecting the armourstone. As with all the quarries, the yield is based on analysis of the raw product (i.e. shape, etc.) and also on the physical properties of the rock in question.

References

1. Jensen O.J. and Klinting P. Evaluation of scale effects in hydraulic models by analysis of laminar and turbulent flow. *Coastal Engineering*, 1983, **7**, 319–329.
2. Mohanty B (Ed). Rock fragmentation by blasting. *Proceedings of the fifth international symposium on rock fragmentation by blasting - Fragblast-5*, Montreal, August 1996, Balkema, 1996.
3. CIRIA/CUR. *Manual on the use of rock in coastal and shoreline engineering*, November 1991. CIRIA Special Publication 83, CUR Report 154.
4. Leeuwestein W., Frankel A., Hombergen V. and Vrijling J.K. Quarry-based design of rock structures In: River, *Coastal and shore-line protection*. Ed. Thorne C.A.R., Abt S.R., Barends F.B.J., Maynard S.T. and Pilarczky K.W. John Wiley & Sons Ltd, Chichester, 1995.
5. Lu P. and Latham J.-P. Estimation of blasted block size distribution of a blastpile combining photo-scanline technique with Ros-Ram and Schuhmann models. *Proceedings of the '96 Int. Symposium on Mining Science and Technology*, China, Eds Guo and Golosinski, Balkema, 1996, 683–688.

REPAIR / RECONSTRUCTION OF BREAKWATERS: PAPERS 15 & 16

J.E. Clifford, Retired
Question on Paper 15
The cross section of the Gijon breakwater shows a core of 90 t concrete blocks. With the long period waves some wave energy can be expected to penetrate to the lee side. Did this cause problems, particularly where the berth reclamation is along the inner length of breakwater where presumably considerable filter layers were needed?

J Díaz Rato, Paper 15
We have had some problems with the berth reclamation due to the difficulty in placing filter layers inside the Principe de Asturias breakwater. This has allowed the energy to penetrate through the core during storms, scouring the backfill. In view of the difficulty involved in installing an adequate filter system, the solution adopted was to open a large ditch all along the area where the reclamation contacts the breakwater, which serves to absorb the incoming energy. The problem is not caused by long waves but by short waves.

Professor H. Ligteringen, Delft Technical University and De Weger Architects and Consulting Engineers, the Netherlands
Question on Paper 15
I am a little puzzled by the fact that the repairs were made with 120 t blocks, restoring the same slope profile. When the performance of the breakwater is evaluated against the background of the presently available wave climate and knowledge of breakwater stability would it not have been logical to make the repairs in such a way that the structure becomes stronger?

J. Díaz Rato, Paper 15
Because its core consists of 90 t blocks, the Principe de Asturias breakwater is practically indestructible. The only problems that might arise would be that, due to the low weight of the armour layer blocks, these could be displaced during storms, leaving the wave screen

unprotected. This situation could lead to its failure. Because of its elevated permeability, the breakwater is more resistant than conventional ones, and the run-up is much less than on similar structures. For this reason, instead of undertaking a large scale repair that would entail increasing its slope to 2:1 for the same weight of blocks, it was considered advisable to reconstruct the original slope, which has behaved acceptably for 25 years, at a cost 1/3 lower than in the case of the former solution, and to repair it again when necessary in the future.

Dr R.J. Maddrell, Sir William Halcrow and Partners Ltd
Question on Paper 15
Figure 6 of Paper 15 shows the breakwater profile before the start of the repair and the proposed final profile, i.e. the repair area to be filled with some 140 000 m³ of concrete made up of their 120 t and 90 t blocks. My question is, how was the loss from the original breakwater made up, was it for example due to any of the following

- settlement of the blocks of the original breakwater, i.e. in attaining a higher degree of compaction
- settlement of the structure as a whole with the seabed
- loss of the original rectangular armour blocks out of the original profile
- loss of the original armour blocks out of the profile due to abrasion and breakage?

Can percentages in relation to the losses be put against the above or other factors?

J. Díaz Rato, Paper 15
The breakwater is constructed on marl, relatively resistant to foundation settlement, thus the loss of blocks was due, on the one hand, to the settlement of the core blocks themselves and on the other to the fact that over the life time of the breakwater, it has been exposed to wave heights similar to or even slightly greater than that of the design wave. This has meant that some blocks were carried away to the foot of the breakwater, leaving it with a steeper profile than was designed from +10.0 to –8.00.

Delegate
Question on Paper 16
What were the reasons for choosing very large rectangular concrete armour blocks, relying mainly on mass, in preference to shaped armour blocks with mass and interlock capability?

Dr V. Negro-Valdecantos, Paper 16
The main armour consists of parallellepiped unreinforced concrete blocks of side 1:1:1.25 and 100 t. That was because the wave climate and the weather conditions are quite severe, as shown in Table 1 below.

Table 1. Wave climate Bilbao Buoy, REMRO, 1.983-96. Zone 1.

Return period: year	Central estimates, all directions		10% exceedence probability estimates, significant wave height/directions		
	H_s	σ	H_s (NW)	H_s (NNW)	H_s (N)
1.00	6.40	0.50	6.70	6.00	5.00
5.00	7.40	0.60	7.70	6.90	5.80
10.00	8.30	0.60	8.60	7.70	6.40
20.00	8.90	0.70	8.90	8.00	6.70
50.00	9.50	0.90	10.10	9.00	7.50
100.00	10.00	1.00	10.70	9.60	7.90
200.00	10.50	1.20	11.40	10.70	8.40

The failure of Sines (Dolos of 42 t) and San Ciprian (Dolos of 50 and 51 t), the Spanish tradition if using blocks and cubes in the Cantabrian Sea, and the brittle response of the Accropod armour layers to waves above the design, were the main reasons for the preference for blocks instead of shaped armour blocks with interlocking capability (Table 2).

Table 2. Comparison of armour units

Armour	Interlocking macro	Size	Wave climate
Dolos	High level	No large size	$H_s < 8.00$
Tetrapod	Medium level	No large size	$H_s < 8.00$
Acropod	High level	No large size	$H_s < 9.00$
Cube and block	No interlocking	Large size	$H_s > 10.00$

It is important to notice that better interlocking contributes to stability, but normally this kind of unit increases the run-up and overtopping and causes a sudden breakdown, so these were the reasons for choosing blocks instead of shaped armour blocks.

J. Díaz Rato, Paper 15
With waves of $H_s \geq 9$ m, special concrete shapes have not proved satisfactory as armour layers on breakwaters. In Spain, the use of concrete blocks to resist such wave heights has been well tried and tested, and their behaviour is very satisfactory. Moreover, the existing slope is made up of parallelepiped-shaped blocks so the shape adopted allows the new blocks to fit in well with the existing ones.

STRATEGIC APPROACHES TO COAST DEFENCE: PAPERS 17 & 18

Dr J.-P. Latham, Queen Mary and Wesfield College, University of London
Question on Papers 17 and 18
Please would the authors of Papers 17 and 18 comment on current and future anticipated experiences of obtaining suitable coarse shingle material for beach recharge schemes.

S. McFarland, Paper 17
Traditionally shingle used on the north Kent coast for replenishment has been defined by a grading envelope aimed at replicating the naturally occurring beach. The D_{50} of these beaches varies between 10 mm and 20 mm.

Although material of the grading required exists, commercial demand is such that the (coarser) material is becoming more difficult to source economically for beach replenishment schemes. Projects such as the channel tunnel rail link are likely to place further pressures on the supply of aggregates in the south east to the possible detriment of beach management schemes requiring relatively coarse sized shingle. Concerns over the environmental impacts of dredging could further reduce the availability of suitable materials.

Canterbury City Council are approaching these uncertainties by carrying out their own research into the future provision of recharge material. Three avenues are being investigated.

(a) Increased reliance on beach recycling within the coastal management units
Ongoing research into the stability of the shingle beaches (based on a local hydraulic model and extensive monitoring of wind, waves, tides and beach profile changes) has led to successive beach management plans in which future demands for replenishment are outlined. The most recent plans involve increased beach recycling from areas which are both accreting and already above their required standard of service into areas of beach erosion. Limited

resources also exist in a number of small sediment banks located within the intertidal zone and their use may be considered in the future provided there is sufficient confidence that no significant impacts on the coastal processes regime will occur. It is however clear that recycling will not be sufficient to meet future requirements and import of material will still be required.

(b) Determination of the effects of using below specification (less coarse) material for shingle beach replenishment
Material which contains an excess of finer material is more readily available and generally less expensive to procure. The question which arises is one of whether the whole-life costs of accepting material of a lower specification is as economic. Beaches with a finer grading tend to have flatter slopes and hence are likely to require longer control structures and larger quantities of initial replenishment to perform the same function. It is also important to consider whether the use of finer material will result in an increase in beach erosion and hence future maintenance costs.

Canterbury City Council and Shepway District Council together with Posford Duvivier and the Applied Coastal Research Centre at the University of Southampton are about to engage in a pilot study on the behaviour of a newly recharged shingle beach. The work is being undertaken on behalf of the South East Coast Group with funding from Coastlink and the two Councils. The aim is to gain an improved understanding of the how newly replenished beaches behave in terms of profile changes and resorting. It is intended that one area which will be investigated is the impact of the fine and coarse beach fractions on the overall beach performance.

(c) Use of exotic beach materials in recharge
It is evident that the coarse fraction of a shingle beach plays an important role in controlling the beach gradient and may also be responsible for the improved retention of finer particles. With this in mind, the Council are cooperating with J.-P. Latham at QMW on a project to determine the impact of mixing exotic materials such as crushed stone into beach replenishment material which is otherwise generally lacking in coarser material. The aim is to determine at what point the addition of such materials would become economically viable and to identify the environmental issues associated with introducing non-native materials to the beach system. A field trial using exotic materials in one or two groyne bays could be carried out in 1999.

Sourcing beach material with a significant proportion of coarse material is likely to become increasingly problematic in many coastal areas. It is the responsibility of the coastal engineering profession to continue to address the problem of availability of material so that long term beach management strategies are supported by a knowledge that the required resources will be available.

A.J. Williams, Paper 18
There are very few suitable sources available in the UK that can provide natural, coarse grained sediments only. Offshore dredging of material can provide sand/gravel mixes of varying degrees, however the lack of suitable offshore sources for sediments in excess of 20–30 mm in grain size combined with the cost in terms of wear and tear on plant in actually retrieving such material prohibits extensive use.

Onshore sand and gravel pits are also few and far between and even then if they are not located close to the shoreline where the material is required, road transport costs can be high.

For the scheme described in the paper, natural river gravel that matched the indigenous beach material, being from effectively the same geological origin, was available within five miles of the site. Even though this material, as stated in the paper, carried a cost premium, with effectively the pit operators being able to charge whatever price they felt the market would take, there being no other suitable sources anywhere nearby, it was possible to use this material at least in part to meet scheme requirements.

However it was largely as a result of pressure from the statutory conservation body that this material was required to be used instead of more cost-effective and technically acceptable quarried stone.

Arguments against the use of quarried rock are largely confined to

- aesthetics – the material does not look natural on the foreshore
- the angular nature of blasted rock.

The first of these criteria is somewhat subjective and very much site dependent on the geology of the local area. For example coarse beach recharge has been used in three bays at Llandudno in North Wales. In two of them, quarried carboniferous limestone material was used, and in the third river gravel from the same source as used at Dinas Dinlle was used. The principal criteria governing the different materials used in these schemes was in the first two cases to match the local outcropping rock – the two rock headlands at Llandudno (the Great and Little Ormes) are formed from carboniferous limestone – the beaches having been denuded of fine and semi-coarse sediments. In the third bay the existing upper beach consisted of rounded gravel sediments and it was a planning requirement for the scheme that material used to recharge the beach matched the existing material.

In the cases of the quarried rock, visual evidence confirms its suitability in providing aesthetically acceptable and technically suitable material whilst the relative softness of the limestone has ensured that those sections of recharged beach that are within the active tidal zone have had the angular edges 'knocked-off' by movement and inter-particle abrasion.

Even in the Dinas Dinlle case where coarse quarried material was used over sections of the frontage, there has been a significant rounding of this quarried material, which is a much harder igneous rock, in the four years since the material was placed on the foreshore.

It should be noted here that the sizing of quarried material needs specific examination within recharge design considerations as rounding inevitably leads to a decrease in the effective size of material in time. The maximum size of natural gravel that is likely to be available, from my own experience, will be about 150 mm. Quarried material can be obtained using standard quarrying/crushing techniques up to twice that size and even allowing for rounding/abrasion can result in reduced recharge volumes per metre run and equivalent or improved hydraulic performance compared with rounded 'natural' material.
Although some research work has been carried out in this respect further work would clearly be useful in providing design information for use in situations where quarried material is being considered.

The key to being able to provide suitable material for future coarse graded beach recharge schemes, I believe rests on the acceptability, particularly by the environmental lobby, of the use of quarried rock where natural gravels are either unavailable or cost-prohibitive compared to cheaper blasted material.

J.D. Simm, HR Wallingford
Question on Paper 18
In Paper 7, Dr Bodge presented some rules of thumb for fishtailed/headland/T-head groyne systems. These were devised from experiences with sand beaches in micro-tidal regimes and included his 'one-third rule' approach to beach plan shape. UK experience suggests that such rules may not necessarily be applicable in macro-tidal regimes, with potentially coarser sediments, greater directional spread of wave energy and where tidal currents may also be present. Mr Williams has described in Paper 18 one such situation, at Dinas Dinlle.

Has Mr Williams developed any rules of thumb that would guide the length and spacing of such groynes in macro-tidal regimes? Would he agree that as experience around the UK coast grows there is a tendency for such groynes to become smaller and/or more closely spaced?

A.J. Williams, Paper 18
The basic philosophy behind the use of fishtail groynes developed from the need to provide beach control structures in the macro tidal regimes that exist around the coast of the UK that

- provide a wave interception/dissipation function away from the shoreline, thereby reducing wave energies impacting the shoreline specifically in the locality of the structures
- divert longshore tidal currents that would, in the absence of shore normal structures, transport sediment at the shoreline alongshore after it had been moved into suspension by wave action
- provide the means for retaining naturally or artificially enhanced foreshore levels between structures and on the immediate up and down drift sides of terminal structures.

Fishtail groynes have two offshore arms to acknowledge that in most locations incident wave directions are generally spread over a wide range of approach angles. Roundheads at the end of the arms are more gently sloped than the trunk side gradients firstly to provide a gradual transition to the foreshore and secondly to encourage wave refraction with diffraction and the natural movement of sediment into the lee of the structures.

There are no specific rules of thumb that have been developed for the spacing of structures with each particular usage governed by the site criteria applying. These would include

- specific lengths of frontage that require protection
- existing shoreline form, curvature and topography e.g. presence of existing hard spots or promontories
- foreshore topography, beach form and gradients
- range of incident wave exposure.

Notwithstanding this, experience has shown that dependent on specific site conditions applying the spacing between structures would typically be four to five times their on-offshore extent. Furthermore at the terminal structures in groups, tidal currents will generally have realigned themselves along the shoreline at some two to three times the on-offshore structure distance,

With regard to the size of structures becoming smaller as experience is gained, I would provide the following comments.

- The first fishtail groyne built in the United Kingdom on the North Wirral coast in 1980 was the smallest.
- The criteria identified above preclude such a generalization.

- Where fishtail groynes are built in a series or the shoreline plan shape dictates, it may be appropriate either to use smaller structures as intermediates between larger structures or at the extremities to provide a more gradual transition from the section of shoreline defended by fishtail groynes to the sections of shoreline at either end where such measures are not employed.
- Fishtail groynes are wave interception structures so their general geometry relates to wavelength. Inshore wavelengths along the west coast of the UK are typically between 25 and 50 m. It is necessary to size fishtail groynes on at least 2 to 3 times the wavelength for them to be effective in changing the wavefield. Smaller structures would lose wave influence and only retain their current function, similar to traditional groyne structures.

APPLICATION OF BEACH MANAGEMENT: PAPERS 19 & 20

B. Hamer, Sir William Halcrow & Partners Ltd
Question on Paper 20
With specific reference to Section 3.1 (the chronology of which seems confusing), the authors seem to have been put off beach recharge, and subsequent beach management, as an option for sea defence as a consequence of the observed performance of what appears to be the use of an inappropriate recharge material. Clearly, the performance of the 1990/91 recharge was significantly reduced by the use of a bi-modal material.

Was the decision to mix two recharge sources made on economic grounds, and how would the beach recharge design have performed if a single source had been used? Was this option considered in the recent strategy study?

R. Nunn, Paper 20
The design of a beach recharge system is complex and in 1990 did not have the benefit of codes of practice to work from. Each site is different, and the sourcing of beach material is obviously crucial to its success. The original supply source for this scheme was found to be contaminated and the alternative supply relied on a twin sited source. Obviously the mixing of two separately and differently graded materials within the marine environment must be approached with caution. It would have been preferable to base the performance of the material upon the finer of the two graded materials. It is likely that had a single source material been used, the cliffing effect subsequently experienced may have been avoided. As regards future beach performance, HR Wallingford has been commissioned to undertake numerical modelling studies so as to provide a more detailed understanding of the littoral regime between Hunstanton and Snettisham. The results of this study are awaited.

ALTERNATIVES IN COAST PROTECTION: PAPERS 21 & 22

K. McConnell, HR Wallingford
Question on Paper 21
Will the author of Paper 21 give an indication of the width in the cross-shore direction over which the ripple material should be placed? Also is there any indication of erosion at the seaside side of the installation?

Professor I. Irie, Paper 21
Although DRIM settled in the field proved its stability and indicated its effectiveness after a stormy season, the offshore side of DRIM was scoured to a considerable range. This scour also indicated that offshore sediment was transported onshore across DRIM, however this

effect will have to be avoided because, in most cases of beach nourishment, DRIM would only be required to push nourished sand back onshore and not to transport offshore sediment onshore (which results in scour). The author would like to propose the use of a special cross section for several DRIM blocks at the offshore end so that the blocks no longer have controlling capability.

DRIM is exposed to the effects of near-shore currents, mass transport due to reflected waves by coastal structures, etc., however in most cases, the bottom currents generated by DRIM will overcome the effects of those currents because the velocity of oscillatory movement by waves is very high as compared with those currents. Several examples of the use of DRIM are shown in the following figures.

Figure 1. Developing a marine farm by removing sediment and exposing bed rocks to provide a habitat for marine plants and animals.

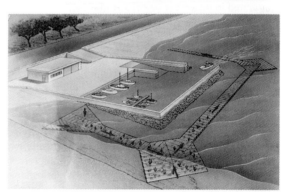

Figure 2. Sand by-passing around the port utilizing wave energy.

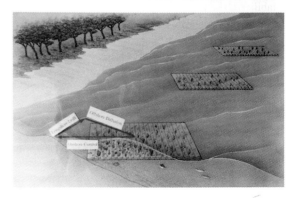

Figure 3. Beach erosion control by settling DRIM diagonal to wave direction so that the component of long-shore drift and offshore diffusion of sediment is almost balanced with onshore sediment movement caused by DRIM.

K. McConnell, HR Wallingford

Question on Paper 22

The author referred to the use of geotextile mattresses for slope protection and resulting failure due to uplift pressures. Does the author have information on the range of wave heights to which such mattresses have been exposed. Consultation with manufacturers of such mattresses has indicated that they have generally only been used for wave heights of up to 1 m in the UK.

K. Pilarczyk, Paper 22

The critical wave height for sand-filled geotextile mattresses depends on the thickness of the mattress and the criterion of internal stability of sand. Geotextile mattresses filled by sand of thickness of about 0.15 m can usually be applied under exposed wave conditions for wave height up to 1 m. When the wave height exceeds about 1.0 m the mechanisms of internal instability starts. Depending on the size and form of sand-mattresses the critical wave height can be somewhat higher with maximum of about 1.5 m (usually for temporary applications).

For concrete filled mattresses the critical wave height is determined by the thickness of the mattress and the criterion of the geotechnical stability of the subsoil. The concrete-filled mattresses are usually applied for wave heights up to 2.0 m.

These kind of design criteria have been recently developed in the Netherlands.[1,2]

I. Cooke, Posford Duvivier

Question to Paper 22

The author of Paper 22 shows instances of the use of geocontainers as a core replacement in dykes and breakwaters, and refers to projects in Japan and the USA.

We have considered the geocontainers as an alternative core material for a scheme on the east coast of the UK. However, a very real concern is the stability of the placed containers under the action of high currents and waves in excess of 4.0 m. Does the author have any information relating to the stability of the containers under such conditions?

K. Pilarczyk, Paper 22

As far as geocontainers applied as a core of a breakwater or harbour jetty, stability against wave attack is not a problem. The crest of geocontainers structure is limited by the draft of the barge dumping the geocontainers, and the thickness of the upper geocontainers. The necessary free space is of about 6 m. The effect of waves is limited and temporary. The core will be protected by an armour layer in the final construction stage. Often, the remaining free space is filled by geotubes for which stability should be calculated according to the proper stability criteria.

If necessary, the stability of the submerged geocontainers and exposed geotubes can be checked using results of model tests performed for Nicolon by Delft Hydraulics in 1994 and criteria in Pilarczyk.[2] There is also a reasonable experience gained with these systems during execution of some large coastal projects in Malaysia and Taiwan.

S. Plate, Bouwdienst Rijkswaterstaat, the Netherlands

Question on Paper 22

To which bottom depth, with which accuracy and under which conditions is it still possible to place geosystems?

How can the gaps between the geosystems (Fig. 9) be filled, once placed at great depths?

K. Pilarczyk, Paper 22

Most experience with geocontainers relate to water depths of up to 20 m, however a recent pilot project with dumping of dredge-material filled geocontainers has been carried out in the US. Relatively high placement accuracy of geocontainers have been achieved when placed under quiet conditions and using a proper mooring system. The deviation of units due to current can be calculated (and taken into account during placing) as for dumping of rock. No special criteria on placement accuracy are yet formulated.

Dr P. Boswinkel, Delta Marine Consultants

Question on Paper 22

Currently we are involved in a construction scheme in the Netherlands in which we proposed to use geotextiles as filter in a bottom protection. Unfortunately, Rijkswaterstaat did not approve the use of geotextiles. The argument was that the durability of the material was not proven. Please comment on the expected durability and knowledge about this subject in the field.

K. Pilarczyk, Paper 22

Durability of geotextiles is a frequently posed question, especially concerning the applications where a long life-span is required. Geotextile is a relatively new product – the first applications were in the 1960s. We have in the Netherlands recently tested some 30-year old geotextiles which were used as a filter in revetment structures. In general, these geotextiles were still in a good condition (still fulfilling properly the prescribed filter and strength functions). The technology of geotextiles has improved to such an extent that the durability tests under laboratory conditions indicate the life-time of geotextiles to be at least 100 years (when not exposed to UV radiation).

Some prototype tests with various geosynthetic ropes indicated that after three years under (sea)water there was no decrease in the tensile strength while very rapid deterioration was observed for ropes placed on the land.

References

1. Pilarczyk K.W. *et al.* Stability criteria for geosystems - an overview. *Sixth International Geosynthetics Conference*, Atlanta, 1998.
2. Pilarczyk, K.W. (in press). *Geosynthetics and geosystems in coastal and hydraulic engineering*. AA Balkema, Rotterdam, to be published early 1999.

Closing remarks

KEVIN R. BODGE
Senior Engineer, Vice-President; Olsen Associates, Inc., USA

Thank you for the invitation to address this Sixth conference on breakwaters; I am honoured by your consideration. I will attempt herein to briefly draw together the themes we have observed in these past two days' presentations, and to tender some ideas as to how these themes might be extended in future days.

DISSEMINATION OF FINDINGS
This conference presented a diverse sampling of extensive and recent advances that EU countries, and Iceland, have made in the design, study and construction of significant breakwater structures. The cooperative UK / Italy research efforts continue to be of particular apparent value. But the predictive design formulae that have been advanced in the EU over the past five to ten years are mostly unknown elsewhere – particularly in the USA. Probably the majority of US engineers continue to use the mostly outdated *Shore Protection Manual* (SPM). While many US engineers are vaguely aware of PIANC and other research cooperatives in Europe, there is little appreciation of the recent advances and publications created by and for these groups. Access to PIANC proceedings, for example, is very difficult in the US. I urge you to better *extend* the experience sampled at this Conference to the US and elsewhere outside the EU.

ADVANCES IN TECHNOLOGY
The fundamental technology (methods) used to create our coastal, sea and beach defences has not significantly changed since the Phoenicians built harbours in 1500 BC. We still dump a lot of big rocks, concrete, sand and gravel into the water. If you move further into beach preservation, you will encounter a lot of claims for 'alternative technologies', but in our experience, few or none have demonstrated *real* merit relative to the traditional method of beach recharge (with rock groynes or near-shore breakwaters, if appropriate), particularly in the face of elevated wave and current conditions.

Pursuant to numerous breakwater 'failures' in the early 1980s, we have concluded that risk analyses and geotechnical considerations are of added importance; and, we have improved our predictive abilities in regard to wave run-up, overtopping and impact forces. We have added one or two new armour units, studied the berm breakwater, and made some useful advances in geotextiles and geogrids. The 'stability number' has also become a more standard descriptor or armour stability. Otherwise, however, we have not found design tools of the early 1980s to be fundamentally flawed; that is, for example, the Hudson equation is still considered valid.

RISK AND PROBABILITY-BASED FORMULAE

What is needed is to extend our lately-improved predictive formulae further toward a probabilistic mode; that is, so as to better identify risk and/or probability of failure (or success) of a given project, relative to its objectives.

Our clients, as well as government agencies, often ask (as rightly they should), "Will your scheme work?" We cannot, of course, simply say "Yes" – as there are too many uncertainties and acts of nature that can undermine a coastal project. As Madrell notes in his paper, "We do not offer the *prevention* of a problem, only a reduction in risk." The difficulty lies in concisely expressing to the client the scheme's probability of success. Most fundamentally, I need to be able to say, "I give this a 50-50 chance", or "an 80-20 chance", etc. Likewise, I need to know how a project's design can be cut (in order to cut budget) before falling outside of the client's maximum desired risk.

Particularly for budget designs, we need more probabilistic design formulae. In his paper, for example, Van der Meer gave us deterministic formulae that included description of their conservatism (viz., one standard deviation above the mean of the data). This presentation allows the clever designer to then use the formulae in a probabilistic mode. It can be made even clearer if the formulae (or their empirical coefficients) are given explicitly for various confidence intervals: both low and high. Burcharth, in his paper, actually did this by giving design coefficients as an explicit function of the probability of damage. The latter is a simple and useful product for practitioners.

Vrijling, in his paper, demonstrated an application of risk calculation. Importantly, he ultimately chose not to labour over the complicated joint-probability mathematics that were required to create a singular value of the risk. Instead, he simply computed the upper and lower bounds of the potential risk. This is a very useful result. One can ask, "Is the maximum (worst-case) risk reasonable to bear?" or "Is the minimum (best-case) risk acceptably low?" or "Is the mid-range of the risk about where it should be?"

We might use our ever-increasing desktop computer power to do more Monte Carlo type analyses. This may increase the routine computation of project risk. This, in turn, would elevate the standards of practice in a useful way and would open more researchers' eyes to the need for exploring and expressing the probability (uncertainty) associated with their results and formulae.

Assigning probability to formulae requires that the phenomena being described in the formulae are clearly defined. Likewise, 'failure' or 'success' must be defined, and preferably standardized in definition. At the least, the definition should be clearly and concisely-stated in an easy-to-read, prominent section of a report – preferably in the same table as is shown the formulae and/or its coefficients, or at least in the summary.

SPACE AND TIME SCALES OF RESEARCH

The papers at this conference all dealt with macro-scale processes and semi-empirical, deterministic formulae. It is my opinion that practical engineering solutions – for both coastal sediment transport and structure design – will derive from such macro-scale studies. By the time we understand sediment transport on a grain-by-grain basis, or armour stability by virtue of a single unit's movements, we will have nearly perfected our semi-empirical design formulae. Moreover, practical application of any micro-scale research or model will always require the interpretation of a practical engineer; i.e., one who is grounded and experienced in empirical, macro-scale behaviour of coastal works.

Promoters and practitioners of *numerical models* always tell us that "they are only tools, or aides, to the engineer." The truth, however, is that many of those who immerse themselves in these models (and it almost always requires days or weeks of immersion to get the models to conclude something reasonable) forget the project's objectives – and the models' limitations – by the time they finally get an answer.

Worse, however, is that government agencies and other scientists are far more likely to 'believe' a numerical model result than a licensed engineer's opinion and intuition. These agencies' insistence and interest in numerical models falsely elevate the models' importance. In the nuisance case, the engineer spends time running a model in order to develop the result that he/she expected in the first place. In the worse case, the engineer is forced to defend her/his experience and intuition against a numerical model result that they may consider to be unrealistic. Either way, the engineer and the client both lose – in time and money, and/or by having to accept a project design that is driven by an alleged 'tool' instead of by engineering expertise.

WHEN DO REGULATORY AGENCIES OVERSTEP ENGINEERING LICENSURE?
In environmental (regulatory) permitting of a project, regulatory bodies increasingly attempt to influence or modify the project scheme. The engineer's job is to evaluate whether (warranted) modifications can be accommodated without seriously undermining the project's objectives.

But when a scheme is modified, who is responsible? Your professional licensure is on the line; after all, *you* must sign and seal the project drawings, not the government regulator. This is a *liability* issue that should be frankly discussed with your insurance carrier. It is also a *professional* issue that should be elevated and addressed by the Institution of Civil Engineers.

BEACH MANAGEMENT
Beach management strategies will likely become of increasing importance as beach recharge supplies dwindle. If it has not already been done, I recommend that an inventory of your exploitable beach recharge resources be conducted. You may need to consider increasing use of coastal structures and/or recycling that serves to increase beach fill life and to decrease renourishment frequency and cost. You may need to promote development of alternative dredging technologies to exploit new resources.

It may also be useful to begin evaluating the recreational value of your beaches. While beach visitation in the UK, for example, is less than in the USA., the economic and social value of beach-related tourism may be greater than is expected, and may ultimately influence or justify particular beach management strategies.

ACADEMIA AND PRACTICE IN COASTAL ENGINEERING
The nature, content and spirited discussions of most all of this conference's papers reflect a sound interchange between academic (research) and practising (design and construction) engineers. This is refreshing, though all too infrequent. The gap between academic and practising engineers is even wider in the USA than in most of the EU. By 'academia' I am referring here to both university and government groups that principally conduct research. By

"practice' I mean comprehensive projects design – including initial client contact, permitting, plans and specifications through construction management.

As one of the conference organizers, Dr Philip Barber, put it, "One doesn't lose academic excellence by joining with practitioners, one gains academic value." Increased interchange between researching and practising engineers can obviously improve the relevance of the research and the integrity (success) of the project. It can also improve the utility of the research by focusing its conclusions in formats more compatible with practitioners' needs.

We should determine ways to reward a practitioner's publication in refereed journals. As both a practitioner and journal editor (ASCE, *J. Waterways*), I know that this is difficult. There is little incentive for the practitioner to divert otherwise reimbursable client-time toward the lengthy and frustrating task of submitting a journal manuscript. Yet there is potential value in the practitioners' contribution. Perhaps we should identify new or separate journals that are explicitly intended to be 'practitioner-friendly.'

Conversely, we should award academic participation and interest in practitioners' problems. Currently, academic success is often correlated with the publication of papers in refereed journals that are of little or no interest to practitioners.

Particularly when embarking upon work in a mostly new area, the researcher should recall that the most effective engineering models and formulae are those that are simplest to use by the practitioner. I'm thinking here, for brief example, of the contributions of Michael Owen, Jentsje van de Meer, Robert Dean, among others.

Further, in almost all cases, the initial model need not be perfect nor even strive for perfection. From the practitioner's standpoint, it is usually sufficient to get us half or three-quarters of the way towards an answer and let us know how much uncertainty (even roughly) there is in the result. For example, are the data scattered about the model by an order of magnitude? Does the model represent the mean of the data, or seek to represent a conservative limit?, etc.

STANDARDS OF PRACTICE
Unlike other civil engineering disciplines, there is no codified standard of practice in most coastal engineering problems. In the US, the default is the *Shore Protection Manual*, though it is mostly out-of-date and incomplete. The replacement *Coastal Engineering Manual* (CEM), due in the year 2000, is not likely to fill the void. While it will include useful and considerable guidance, it is written as a lengthy textbook – not an engineering manual; and the practical (project design) chapters are authored by *research engineers* – not practitioners. In my experience, the Dutch manuals are increasingly viewed as being closer to a standards of practice. Those engineers that are not directly familiar with issues of liability, claims and expert-witness testimony, may not appreciate the importance of being able to identify – or agree upon – a standards of practice, or at least something akin thereto.

CREATIVITY
Perhaps there never will be (nor should be) a uniform, codified Standard for coastal engineering projects. After all, each site is different, project objectives vary significantly and the governing natural forces are diverse and numerous. Successful coastal engineering analysis and design is an *art* as much as a science. In the same way that one identifies an

interesting bridge as being the work of a particular architect or engineer, one can often identify the signature of a particular engineer upon a coastal project.

We should be proud of that. We should allow ourselves to be creative. Whenever possible, we should listen to biologists and architects and user-groups and attempt to accommodate their ideals or objectives in our designs. It is often not that much more expensive, and also sometimes possible to incorporate special elements integrally (not incidentally) to the work. There is some *fluidity* in coastal projects that can allow us to be creative and architectural – and to be contribute more grandly to society – at least within those fundamental physical limits that our models, formulae and practical experience have established for us.